SHAKESPEARE'S BRAIN

SHAKESPEARE'S BRAIN

READING WITH COGNITIVE THEORY

Mary Thomas Crane

PRINCETON UNIVERSITY PRESS   PRINCETON AND OXFORD

Copyright © 2001 by Princeton University Press
Published by Princeton University Press, 41 William Street,
Princeton, New Jersey 08540
In the United Kingdom: Princeton University Press,
3 Market Place, Woodstock, Oxfordshire OX20 1SY

Library of Congress Cataloging-in-Publication Data

Crane, Mary Thomas, 1956–
Shakespeare's brain : reading with cognitive theory /
Mary Thomas Crane.
   p.   cm.
Includes bibliographical references and index.
ISBN 0-691-05087-2 (alk. paper)—
ISBN 0-691-06992-1 (pbk. : alk. paper)
1. Shakespeare, William, 1564–1616—Criticism and interpretation.
2. Consciousness in literature. 3. Cognition in literature.
4. Brain—Case studies. I. Title.
PR2976.C69 2000
822.3′3—dc21   00-039143

This book has been composed in Sabon

The paper used in this publication meets the minimum
requirements of ANSI/NISO Z39.48-1992 (R1997)
(*Permanence of Paper*)

www.pup.princeton.edu

Printed in the United States of America

10 9 8 7 6 5 4 3 2 1

10 9 8 7 6 5 4 3 2 1
(Pbk.)

In Memory ————————————————————————

Contents

Acknowledgments

AN EARLIER version of chapter 2 was published as "Linguistic Change, Theatrical Practice, and the Ideologies of Status in *As You Like It*" in *English Literary Renaissance* 27 (1997): 361–92; an earlier version of chapter 5 appeared as "Male Pregnancy and Cognitive Permeability in *Measure for Measure*," *Shakespeare Quarterly* 49 (1998): 269–92. Both are reprinted here with permission.

I have benefited from the help and support of a great many people, both far and near, in writing this book. The small but growing group of scholars working on the intersections of literature and cognitive science welcomed a newcomer with warmth and generosity. Mark Turner, Ellen Spolsky, Francis Steen, and F. Elizabeth Hart all provided immensely helpful comments at different stages of this work. I am also grateful to Renaissance scholars whose range of responses to this project—excitement, skepticism, bemusement—sharpened its focus. Heather Dubrow and Barbara Kiefer Lewalski provided advice and support as always. Lars Engle, Julian Yates, Lauren Shohet, Douglas Bruster, and Katherine Rowe helped me think about this work in relation to several relevant areas of early modern studies. The interest, encouragement, and persistent questions of Judith Anderson and Gail Kern Paster helped this book find its shape. Emily Bartels, Laura Knoppers, and Naomi Miller are still the best and most dependable friends, readers, fonts of wisdom, telephone chatters, and conference mates anyone could have.

This book has grown from roots firmly planted at Boston College. First, an imperative to teach Shakespeare and more Shakespeare led me to contemplate his brain in the first place, and a sabbatical gave me the time to begin the project. Graduate students Mary Jo Kietzman, Carla Spivack, Matthew Watson, and Elizabeth Bradburn challenged and furthered my thinking in many ways. Other colleagues—James Najarian, Robert Stanton, Laura Tanner, and Elizabeth Kowaleski Wallace—contributed expertise on far-flung topics. My colleagues Amy Boesky and Dayton Haskin have made Boston College a true Renaissance Utopia. *Shakespeare's Brain* owes a great deal to Alan Richardson, who alternately goaded and encouraged my interest in cognitive science and my progress on this book; our coauthored essay "Literary Studies and Cognitive Science" was a crucial first step, and his own work has been a model of precision and thoroughness at every point. Rosemarie Bodenheimer and Andrew Von Hendy have helped me, and this book, in more ways than I can possibly enumerate here. I hope that they will accept due credit for its appearance in print and that they know how grateful I am for all they have done.

My sons, Thomas and Parker, offer amazing and alarming demonstrations of cognitive development every day. They heroically endured many hours of after-school programs and summer day camp so that I could have time to write. I thank them for their patience, and I thank Adam Travis for keeping them company.

More than anything or anyone else, Gregory Crane has influenced me: his impatience with rules of all kinds, his ability to become passionately interested in almost anything, his habit of keeping books related to those interests in piles all over the house. I first learned about cognitive science from those piles of books and owe this one to his belief that I could break rules too.

SHAKESPEARE'S BRAIN

Introduction ————————————————

Shakespeare's Brain: Embodying the Author-Function

DID SHAKESPEARE have a brain? "In proposing this slightly odd question, I am conscious of the need for an explanation." Readers may recognize my second sentence as the first sentence of Michel Foucault's "What Is an Author?" an essay that established its redefinition of an author as "a complex and variable function of discourse" so successfully that it is my question, and not Foucault's, that now seems odd.[1] Earlier critics used to assume, of course, that Shakespeare had a *mind*. G. Wilson Knight, for example, could argue that the "imaginative atmosphere" of *Timon of Athens* "seems to reflect the peculiar clarity and conscious mastery of the poet's mind."[2] Knight's sense that Shakespeare's mind was both clear and masterful represents the kind of authorial control over a text that Foucault was particularly at pains to question. Psychoanalytic critics still assume that Shakespeare possessed the Freudian apparatus of conscious and unconscious minds, but the centrality of the unconscious mind to this approach allows these critics to avoid the assumptions about clarity and control that trouble other author-centered criticisms.[3] The implications of a Shakespearean brain, however, have been almost entirely overlooked.

Shakespeare provides a particularly appropriate test case for a literary theory that purports to offer a new way of conceiving authorship, especially one that challenges the Foucauldian deconstruction of the author in several ways. Shakespeare enjoys a status in popular culture, in the Anglophone world and even beyond, as perhaps *the* archetypal author; the very nature and process of his authorship forms the subject of a recent popularly successful film. However, Foucauldian theory, along with a new emphasis on the collaborative nature of play production in early modern England, has led Shakespearean scholars to form more complex and qualified notion of Shakespearean authorship. A focus on Shakespeare's brain allows us to attend to Shakespeare as author without losing the complexity offered by contemporary theory.

Using a cognitive literary and cultural theory derived from the cognitive sciences, I want to try to reintroduce into serious critical discourse a consideration of Shakespeare's brain as one material site for the production of the dramatic works attributed to him. Current cognitive science offers the grounds for a number of theories of human subjectivity and language that are beginning to be reformulated in ways that make them readily applicable to the reading of literary and cultural texts. Virtually all branches of cognitive science are centered on investigation of the ways in which the mind (the conscious and unconscious mental experiences of perception, thought, and language) is produced by the brain and other bodily systems.[4] A literary theory derived from cognitive science, then, offers new ways to locate in texts signs of their origin in a materially embodied mind/brain. From this perspective, I argue that at least several of Shakespeare's plays experiment with different forms of polysemy and prototype effects in ways that leave traces of cognitive as well as ideological processes in the text. Further, I show how these traces of cognitive process reveal not only the possibilities but also the limits of individual agency within a biological body and a cultural matrix. I suggest that cognitive theory offers new and more sophisticated ways to conceive of authorship and therefore offers new ways to read texts as products of a thinking author engaged with a physical environment and a culture.

Cognitive theory has provided a number of approaches to literary texts, but my emphasis here is on the spatial patterns and structures, derived from early experiences of embodiment, which at least some cognitive scientists posit as the bases of human thought and language.[5] I argue that in each of the plays examined here a network of words, connected in part by spatial metaphors, functions as a structural element that reflects in its outlines some of the patterns and connections of Shakespeare's mental lexicon. I believe that Shakespeare uses these words as focal points for explorations of the spatially centered experiences of cognitive subjectivity, as it figured in the development of the "individual" in the early modern period and as those new individuals were represented by fictional characters on the space of the platform stage. In many ways the plays are as much about the coming into being of cognitive subjects in a variety of environments as they are about the construction of cultural subjects by a variety of discursive formations; the plays represent what it is like to conceive of oneself as an embodied mind, along with all of the problems and dilemmas that condition entails.

As F. Elizabeth Hart argued recently, contemporary materialist theory remains haunted by lingering and unacknowledged formalisms inherited from Saussure and Derrida.[6] A corollary of this foundational formalism, to which I will return, is the tendency of many recent materialist critics to assume that the physical reality of Shakespeare's body had little relevance to the texts of his plays. Following Foucault, they disperse the Shakespearean body into an immaterial author-function, occluding Shakespeare's material existence in time and space. As Graham Holderness, for example, suggests, "These plays were made and mediated in the interaction of certain complex material conditions, of which the author was only one." The consequence of this realization, however, has not been to consider the place of the author as one material condition among many; instead it has been to "deconstruct the Shakespeare myth" in order to discover "a collaborative cultural process" in which the role of the writer is effectively written out.[7] Examination of authorship as "a collaborative cultural process" has, in fact, proceeded along the lines suggested by Foucault, with questions about authorship shifted to such broader questions as, "What are the modes of existence of this discourse? Where does it come from; How is it circulated; Who controls it? What placements are determined for possible subjects?" (138).

Now, questions such as these have become common starting points for several approaches to Shakespearean and other early modern texts. One especially valuable kind of study has pursued the implications of the collaborative nature of textual production in the Elizabethan and Jacobean theater and in the preparation of printed texts of the plays. Margreta de Grazia and Peter Stallybrass, for example, have argued that acknowledging "the materiality of the Shakespearean text" leads to an interrogation of "the category of the single *work*," that of "the discrete *word*," "the unified *character*, who utters the word, and the autonomous *author*, who is credited with the work."[8] They quite rightly point out the many ways in which the Shakespearean text is fractured and multiple, a product of a "collaborative field" rather than a single controlling genius. Their conclusion, however, is strikingly similar to Foucault's: they end with an almost identical call to dethrone the "solitary genius immanent in the text," which is, "after all, an impoverished, ghostly thing compared to the complex social practices that shaped, and still shape, the absorbent surface of the Shakespearean text."[9]

Although Stallybrass and de Grazia break new ground in applying Foucault's insights more specifically to the processes of textual editing, the trajectory of their article essentially retraces Foucault's well-worn path and ends in the same place. It cannot get beyond this point, I would argue, because assuming a "ghostly" author involves denying the presence of a material human body as a central participant in the "complex social practices" shaping the text.[10] And if the presence of the author is denied or circumscribed in this way, then any discussion of the nature of the social practices involved must be prematurely truncated.[11] If we refuse to see the author at all, then the questions raised by Foucault can never be answered, only endlessly rediscovered and rearticulated.

Even Stephen Greenblatt finds his circulation of social energy in textual traces rather than in the processes of producing a text. He similarly begins with the concept of a total artist, "at the moment of creation complete unto himself," and makes the expected move of rejecting him.[12] He too rediscovers the "collective production of literary pleasure and interest," locating that collectivity on the even more basic level of "language itself" as "the supreme instance of a collective creation" (4). His rejection of admiration for the "total artist" in favor of the "study of the collective making of distinct cultural practices and inquiry into the relations among these practices" (5) leads to a by now familiar set of questions: "We can ask how collective beliefs and experiences were shaped, moved from one medium to another, concentrated in manageable aesthetic form, offered for consumption." (5). Greenblatt's use of the passive voice here signals his desire to avoid acknowledging the materiality of the author, for in strictly material terms it was the author's hand that physically "shaped" letters on the page, the author's eyes that scanned treatises on exorcism, the author's brain that directed the transfer of bits of them to his own texts, the author who "concentrated" these bits into an aesthetic form and received payment when they were offered for consumption.[13]

Recently there has been a salutary emphasis on the importance of the material body in the early modern period; however, the body and especially the brain of the author have been signally absent from such studies, largely because of the continuing influence of Foucault and Althusser on theories of embodiment and subject formation. In *The Tremulous Private Body*, Francis Barker offered a Foucauldian argument that the early modern period saw a process through which the body was "confined, ignored, exscribed from discourse" in the interests of the formation of a disciplined and disembodied bourgeois subject.[14] Recent work on the body has complicated and problematized Barker's account, in most cases without eschewing the Foucauldian position that the body is a product of discourse and that the early modern experience of embodiment was constructed by the dominant classed and gendered discursive formations of the period. Jonathan Sawday, for instance, has argued that the Renaissance might be described as a "culture of dissection" that "promoted the beginnings of what Michel Foucault has analyzed as the 'surveillance' of the body within regimes of judgement and punishment."[15] Gail Kern Paster has similarly traced, in remarkable detail, the influence of the prevailing early modern theories of humoral physiology on the experience of embodiment as depicted in drama of the period, especially as it supported "continuous interpellation of the subject" based on "an internal orientation of the physical self within the socially available discourses of the body," especially discourses of class and gender.[16]

Certainly, the effects of discourse in shaping perceptions of the body cannot be denied. As Paster argues, "No matter what the physical facts of any given bodily function may be, that function can be understood and experienced only in terms of culturally available discourses," so that "the interaction between bodily self-experience and its discursive realization . . . takes place in and through culture or its more politically conceptualized cognate, ideology" (4). However, this new scrutiny of bodily experience in relation to discourse has paid relatively little attention to the brain, the material place within the body where discourse is processed and therefore where discursive construction, if it occurs, must be located.[17] This may well be because the formative theories of Foucault and Althusser provide little sense of the actual processes through which discourse becomes embodied within the human brain. As Judith Butler has remarked, Foucault "does not elaborate on the specific mechanisms of how the subject is formed in submission. Not only does the entire domain of the psyche remain largely unremarked in his theory, but power in this double valence of subordinating and producing remains unexplored."[18] Butler similarly notes that Althusser's influential account of interpellation is presented, not literally (as it might occur within the subject), but as a staged "social scene" (the hailing policeman) that appears to be "exemplary and allegorical" (106).[19] And Butler herself, in attempting to use psychoanalysis to understand the mechanics of subject formation missing in the accounts of Foucault and Althusser (and reciprocally to use Foucault and Althusser to provide a critique of psychoanalysis), takes up the Marxist and psychoanalytic terms for the location of the subject and the subjectifying process—*soul, psyche, ego*—but never considers the brain as the material site where discourse enters the body, where entry into the symbolic occurs, and therefore where the subject is constructed.

Scott Manning Stevens, in an essay tracing the seventeenth-century controversy over whether the heart or the brain was to be considered the seat of the soul and thus of the self, suggests that the heart remained a central popular and religious symbol of selfhood even after medical discourse began to recognize its location in the brain because "the brain . . . seems tied to its own physicality and function, oddly separate from the more evocative term 'mind.' " Stevens argues that modern critics (like seventeenth-century writers) "may be simultaneously protective of the singularity of an individual brain while fearing that a deeper understanding of its functions will reduce mental life to a biological phenomenon (albeit wondrous) and not a spiritual mystery."[20] For Foucault and Althusser, it is perhaps power itself, and the processes through which it takes discursive form and penetrates the subject, that must remain mysterious, indeed mystified, a mystification that might be threatened by considering how discourse is materially processed inside the brain.

It is this failure to think about the brain that prevents most contemporary accounts of subject formation in the body from noting that just as surely as discourse shapes bodily experience and social interactions shape the material structures of the brain, the embodied brain shapes discourse. Terence Deacon argued recently that the human brain and language have evolved together, each exerting a formative pressure on the other. He suggests imagining "language as an independent life form that colonizes and parasitizes human brains, using them to reproduce."[21] Deacon notes that "the relationship between language and people is symbiotic" and that "modern humans need the language parasite in order to flourish and reproduce, just as much as it needs humans to reproduce. Consequently, each has evolved with respect to the other. Each has become modified in response to the peculiar constraints and requirements of the other" (112–13). Thus, although Deacon acknowledges the powerful force of culturally shared symbolic systems in shaping our sense of self, he also describes in detail the processes through which the physiological constraints of the human brain have shaped our linguistic and symbolic systems.[22]

While Deacon makes his arguments on an evolutionary scale, focusing on the long cohistory of language and the brain, critics like Elaine Scarry and N. Katherine Hayles have argued that individual subjects have a prediscursive experience of embodiment that cannot be assimilated into discourse.[23] Wilma Bucci provides a particularly useful synthesis of work by a number of cognitive scientists to summarize the position that "we can identify a prelinguistic stage in the thought development of the human child" wherein, through "perceptual analysis" of sensory experiences in the world, a child forms concepts "through image-schemas based on spatial structures."[24] Because most of our thought seems inextricably bound up with language, it may be hard to imagine that one can exist without the other. However, evidence for the existence of pre- or nonverbal mental function takes many forms; Roger Shepard and Jacqueline Metzler's work on the mental rotation of three-dimensional objects provides a particularly clear example. They found that subjects who were asked to determine whether drawings of three-dimensional objects represented different orientations of the same object used a process of mental rotation, rather than logical or verbal analysis, to solve the problem.[25] The cognitive psychologist Jean Mandler, who developed the theory of perceptual analysis, emphasizes that preconceptual image schemas are not accessible to consciousness, since "no language of thought is directly accessible," and that they are not concrete, picturelike images but "dynamic analog representations of spatial relations or movements in space" that form a kind of "architecture" of thought: "its meaning resides in its own structure," which can then be mapped onto conscious images and eventually language.[26] George Lakoff's theories of "experiential" conceptualization also suggest that our most basic concepts—up and down, inside and outside, movement toward a goal—are based on our experiences of living in our bodies, while Jean Mandler suggests a slightly different list of these schemas, including animacy, causality, agency, containment, and support. Gerald Edelman's theory of "neuronal group selection" attempts to provide a neuroscientific model for the kind of "semantic bootstrapping" described by Lakoff, in which our embodied brains create meaning out of experience of an environment.[27]

More complicated linguistic structures and rational concepts are similarly built up on these basic spatial schemas. Mandler provides as an example the basic image schemas of "containment" and "support," which, she argues, allow the early acquisition of the prepositions *in* and *on* in English-speaking infants.[28] According to Lakoff, all thought is fundamentally "imaginative, in that those concepts which are not directly grounded in experience employ metaphor, metonymy, and mental imagery—all of which go beyond the literal mirroring, or *representation*, of external reality."[29] According to such a model, metaphor becomes not an aberration from or exception to primarily logical processes of meaning but a basic component of thought and language. As Mark Turner has suggested, "Processes such as metaphor and metonymy, which most linguists deport to the alien realm of literature, are implicit and indispensable in ordinary language."[30] Similarly Antonio Damasio has offered an account of the embodied brain that stresses the implication of feelings in the most seemingly rational processes of thought.[31] Cognitive science thus provides increasingly convincing evidence that the body does shape thought and language, that the early experiences of living in the body are the armature on which consciousness and thought are formed.

The barrier to considering the brain of an author such as Shakespeare as one material source (among many) for his texts is, of course, that a long-dead author is not available to us in any living, material form. Any attempt to take into account even a living author must usually slide into talk about the immaterial "concepts" or "intentions" behind the material text that we possess. In *The Material Word: Some Theories of Language and Its Limits* the Marxist linguists David Silverman and Brian Torode clearly articulate this problem. Silverman and Torode argue against the Saussurean position that "linguistic communication consists in the transmission of immaterial ideas or concepts from one person (speaker or writer) to another (hearer [*sic*] or listener) by means of material signs such as marks on paper or vibrations of air waves." They find Saussure's belief in an extratextual "reality . . . which, he supposes, is somehow held in the brain of the communicating person," to be the source of the problem since "the brain is unavailable to the researcher. Its content, conceptual or otherwise, remains mysterious, and can only be the subject of speculation or arbitrary assumption," a "speculative mysticism" and, even worse, "*idealism*" in treating "the material sign as the mere appearance of an underlying ideal reality."[32] This "speculative mysticism" or mystification is the source of Stallybrass and de Grazia's "ghostly" genius and Greenblatt's invisible hand.

But Silverman and Torode's assumption that "the brain is unavailable to the researcher" is not quite true, although literary and cultural critics almost universally proceed as if it were. Cognitive sciences—including cognitive psychology, neuroscience, linguistics, anthropology, and studies in artificial intelligence—continue to open windows into the workings of the brain and to explore the relationship between the material brain and our immaterial concepts of mind.[33] Of course cognitive researchers are unable to understand completely even the simplest brain functions and so may seem very far indeed from explaining the processes that produced some of the most complex texts ever written. However, using computer models, studies of aphasia and other instances of brain damage, studies of language acquisition, linguistic errors, and categorization across cultures, as well as magnetic resonance imaging (MRI) and positron-emission tomography (PET) to reveal areas of activity as the brain carries out specific functions, these theorists are now beginning to chart the ways in which, to cite Stephen Kosslyn and Oliver Koenig, "the mind is what the brain does."[34]

Using this research to retheorize authorship does involve a potentially essentialist assumption that most human brains share biological and chemical components, but as we shall see, this assumption does not prevent a consideration of the ways in which material culture interacts with, shapes, and is shaped by those physical attributes. Indeed, cognitive science offers the more radical idea that social and cultural interactions have materially altered the physical shape of the brain.[35] Nor does use of concepts from bodies of knowledge commonly called "sciences" prevent us from acknowledging the role of culture in shaping their assumptions and investigations. Although I want to avoid a scientific positivism that would consider scientific insights as objective knowledge superior to the tenets of literary and cultural criticism, I do believe that theory can be derived from scientific knowledge and considered to have truth value equivalent to that of other current bodies of theoretical speculation.[36] I would only ask that we apply to cognitive theory the same tests we apply to other kinds of theory, that is, simply to consider whether it convinces or intrigues or interests us, and whether it provides us with a useful model for interpreting texts and cultures.

Cognitive scientists do not present a uniform version of the nature of "concepts" in the mind and their relation to language; however, as we have seen, they do complicate Silverman and Torode's assumption that such concepts are necessarily and completely unavailable to us. Cognitive science at present comprises, roughly speaking, two broad approaches: the approach that holds that the brain works according to logical rules in ways that are analogous to digital computers and the one that argues that mental functions are shaped by their evolution within a human body and are not essentially in accordance with formal logic or analogous to computer programs.[37] These two approaches are not mutually exclusive in every detail, and although I use material from both, I have found the second, with its focus on semantics and the cognitive bases of meaning, to be more useful for the interpretation of literary and cultural texts.[38]

Research on visual perception, memory, and category formation all suggest that concepts exist in the mind as visual models and also as discursive propositions, both developed from the preconceptual schemas described above.[39] Cognitive scientists have suggested a number of ways in which structures of language probably reflect cognitive processes. From a cognitive perspective, the relationship between concept and language is significantly different from the paradigm suggested by the Saussurean semiotics on which postmodern literary and cultural critics tend to rely.[40] John R. Taylor uses cognitive research in color terms to sketch out the differences between semiotic and cognitive theories of language. Saussure's most influential arguments posited (1) that linguistic signs are arbitrary with respect to the connections between phonetic form and meaning and between meaning and the world. The phonetic form *red* has no necessary connection with the meaning "red," nor does it have any necessary connection to any phenomenon actually existing in the world. In Taylor's words, Saussure argued that "reality is a diffuse continuum and our categorization of it is merely an artifact of culture and language."[41] Saussure also held (2) that language is a "self-contained, autonomous system": "concepts, i.e. the values associated with linguistic signs, are purely differential"; that is, they arise purely from difference from other terms in the system and not with reference to any extrasystemic reality.[42] Silverman and Torode are not alone in accepting these Saussurean concepts as the basis of their theory of language and culture. As Hart has noted, Derrida's *Of Grammatology* deconstructs Saussure's distinction between speech and writing but accepts the basic concepts of arbitrariness, self-contained systemicity, and meaning produced by difference.[43] Lacan, of course, similarly relies on Saussure for his account of the role of signification in the formation of the unconscious, as does Foucault for his argument that subjects are embedded within powerful discursive systems. In general, postmodern concepts of both the fragmented subject and its construction by an ideologically charged symbolic order can be traced to Saussure.

On the other hand, cognitive theory, in Taylor's words, "strongly emphasizes the non-arbitrary, motivated nature of language structure."[44] From a cognitive perspective, language is shaped, or "motivated," by its origins in the neural systems of a human body as they interact with other human bodies and an environment. This theoretical position has profound implications for postmodern concepts of subjectivity and cultural construction. In the first place, although the relationship between a particular phoneme *tree* and the concept that it represents is arbitrary, the meaning of the concept itself is grounded in the cognition and experience of human speakers and is structured by them. Cognitive subjects are not simply determined by the symbolic order in which they exist; instead, they shape (and are also shaped by) meanings that are determined by an interaction of the physical world, culture, and human cognitive systems. In Terence Deacon's formulation, the human brain and symbolic and linguistic systems have coevolved, and each has exercised a formative influence on the other.

Research in cross-cultural use of color terms can convey the differences between semiotic and cognitive theory more clearly. A semiotic paradigm assumes that colors "exist" in the real world as an undifferentiated spectrum; thus, distinctions among different "colors" are completely arbitrary, a product of cultural convention. According to a semiotic model, all color terms in a system would have equal value because their meanings are determined by their differences from one another; red is red because it is not blue or green. Similarly, each "red" would be equal in status to every other "red." The work of Brent Berlin and Paul Kay, however, suggests that those terms work differently. They found that although speakers of different languages tend to locate the barriers between color terms (e.g., between the terms for blue and green) quite differently, they nevertheless tend to identify the same shades of blue and green as "focal," or exemplary, colors.[45] As Taylor explains, "Although the range of colours that are designated by *red* (or its equivalent in other languages) might vary from person to person, there is a remarkable unanimity on what constitutes a good red."[46] Berlin and Kay also found that the color terms available in widely different languages tend to "progress" in a predictable way. If a language only has two color terms, they will designate focal black and white. If there is a third term, it will always designate red, and a fourth term will designate yellow or green, followed by blue, then brown, then gray, orange, pink, and purple in no particular order.

These findings correspond to research on human perception of color, which suggests that focal colors comprise wavelengths of light that affect the cone cells in the retina most strongly.[47] Color is created, in Terence Deacon's words, "by the brain as a means of maximizing distinctive experiences of photons striking the cones of the retina in blended streams of different wavelengths." Through a process called "opponent processing," the brain opposes signals from three different types of cone cell to obtain a "difference signal." Deacon argues that this process of "opponent processing" yields the structure of "color complementarity"—that is, that colors exist in relation to one another on a color wheel, green opposite red and blue opposite yellow. Deacon further argues that this complementary structuring of the spectrum causes perceptual biases that, over time, cause color names in all languages to evolve in similar ways.[48] Colors may exist in nature as an undifferentiated spectrum, then, but the human perceptual system divides them in predictable ways. The meaning of *red* is thus produced by an interaction of wavelengths of light, the human retina, a human cognitive system that can extend the concept of red to other, similar but not identical colors, cultural conditions (e.g., the range of colors available in a desert environment as opposed to those available in a rainforest), and a system of signs that arbitrarily links the phoneme *red* with a particular set of sensory and cognitive phenomena. Meaning in this sense is not entirely arbitrary, nor is it wholly produced by differences within an independent and self-contained system of signs.

Color research (as well as other work on categorization) suggests that mental models of many concepts are probably stored in human memory systems in radial categories that yield "prototype effects": when asked to make judgments about membership in a category, subjects identify certain members of the category as more typical examples of it than other members.[49] As Taylor has suggested, prototype effects shatter the Saussurean assumption that all members of a category have the same status and also the classical logical assumption that categories have firm boundaries and that membership in a category is defined by a set of common features.[50] Instead, a semantics based on the concept of prototypicality and related phenomena such as "domains," "frames," "scripts," and "mental spaces" posits meanings that have fuzzy boundaries and emerge from complex sensory and cultural experience, structured by cognitive conceptual categories.[51] Instances of multiple meaning such as polysemy, metaphor, and metonymy are, according to such an approach, not exceptions to regular rules of meaning but are instead manifestations of the ways in which structures of meaning normally work.[52] Cognitive linguists have traced a number of ways in which word meanings are based on complex domains of cultural knowledge and are extended beyond their original reference through metaphor and metonymy to form "chains" of linked meanings.[53] They have also shown how features of grammar are "motivated" by cognitive structures, for example, how tense sequence in English conditionals can be related to the structure of mental spaces that lie behind the semantic content of the sentence.[54] Like postmodern theory, these cognitive approaches recognize that human cognition and the symbolic systems through which it works are neither unified nor primarily rational. For cognitive theory, however, the preeminence of fuzzy categories in human mental functioning does not imply complete lack of agency or a triumph of irrationality. If you do not expect human cognition to be unified or logical, a way is cleared to supplement deconstruction (which essentially rediscovers its fragmentation and irrationality over and over again) with analysis of the patterns that do emerge from cognitive processes.

These cognitive theories of meaning may, in fact, accord with early modern linguistic understanding and practice more closely than does a Saussurean model, much as the cognitive concept of an embodied mind seems closer to early modern humoral physiology than the radically dualistic post-Cartesian paradigm. Ellen Spolsky suggests that early modern paintings and texts often engage the relationship between mind and body in explicitly self-conscious ways.[55] Judith Anderson has argued that early modern theories of word meaning were less "lexicalized" or restricted by an official dictionary definition than current theories and that they acknowledged a "fundamental metaphoricity" of language, which Saussurean linguistics would deny.[56] Anderson, indeed, notes the resemblance between Lakoffian theories of metaphoric extension and early modern reliance on etymological links to concrete material roots in defining abstract words.[57]

We might even revisit Foucault's influential argument in *The Order of Things* that the early modern period experienced a shift from categorization based on analogy to a more "rational" system based on difference. Foucault emphasized that this change involved "the substitution of analysis for the hierarchy of analogies," an analysis that is now able to yield (in theory) a kind of certainty and closure that was not possible before: "Complete enumeration, and the possibility of assigning at each point the necessary connection with the next, permit an absolutely certain knowledge of identities and differences."[58] Foucault is, of course, concerned to question this certainty and to suggest the ways in which the new "rational" modes of analysis are themselves the products of (and necessarily biased by) discourse. However, his critique of rationalist analysis is contaminated by his own assumption of a Saussurean theory of meaning based on difference.[59] In different ways, cognitive science has also come to question this classical rationalism and to replace it once again with a theory of meaning that is based on analogy, metaphor, and interrelationships between the mind and the world.[60] Whereas Foucault was concerned to provide a critique of assumptions about the inevitability and truth of rationalism, cognitive theory moves forward, in a sense, to explore the implications and possibilities of its a-rationality but also helps us look backward toward systems of thought that preceded the ascendancy of reason.

Portraits of Shakespeare emphasize the large dome of his forehead, accentuated by a receding hairline; he must have had a brain. And if he did, and if sixteenth-century brains functioned even approximately as modern ones do, it must have comprised occipital, temporal, parietal, and frontal lobes, as well as the gyri and sulci (bulges and creases) that neuroscientists have identified as important landmarks within the brain.[61] And if Shake-

speare's brain functioned as most normal brains do today, then the formation of a sentence—"Whether 'tis nobler in the mind to suffer / The slings
and arrows of outrageous fortune. / Or to take arms against a sea of
troubles, / And by opposing, end them," for example—probably involved
activity first in the occipital, posterior superior parietal, and posterior
inferior temporal lobes, central to the generation of mental images, and
then in the perisylvian cortex (those regions of the brain located near the
sylvian fissure, also called the lateral sulcus), where the images (slings
and arrows, arms, sea) and concepts (grounded, perhaps, in a Lakoffian
metaphoric structure, "life is a war") would be associated with appropriate words and formed into a grammatically acceptable sentence.[62] The
construction of the sentence would probably have involved the formation
and linking of several "mental spaces," or temporary areas of knowledge,
in this case, perhaps, metaphorical spaces (sea, arrows) that could be
mapped onto a more abstract conceptual space (life is difficult; should
I commit suicide?).[63] Within those regions of his brain, complex neural
networks working simultaneously (and for the most part without conscious awareness or direction) would first generate the image and then
search Shakespeare's associative memory for the appropriate lexical, cultural, syntactic, and grammatical information needed to form a meaningful sentence, and, once it was formed, send to his hand the neural mes-
sages necessary to record it on paper. The choice of individual words (my
main concern in this book) would be shaped and constrained by stored
prototypes (based on cultural knowledge), by the coordinate and collocational links within stored semantic fields, and by innate structures of syntax, sound, and lemmatization.[64] Within Shakespeare's brain, culture and
biology met to form him as a subject and to produce his texts. Within
the matrix of cultural prototype and biological structure, "Shakespeare"
would nevertheless have experienced some sense of choosing from among
various workable semantic and syntactic possibilities.

   It is worth briefly considering why the insights of cognitive neuroscience and psychology have been so neglected by literary and cultural critics, who continue to rely on Freudian (or Lacanian), Derridean, Foucauldian, and Althusserian theoretical models for constructing their views of
authorship and its relation to culture. One reason may be that these theorists and the critics who use them literally speak the same text-centered
interpretive "natural" languages. Traditional theoretical models seem
more relevant to studies of texts because they are themselves text-based.
Unlike cognitive sciences, which take the brain as their focus of study
and which often use formal languages (such as mathematics or computer
"languages") to *describe* them, the text-based theorists listed above study
the literary and cultural productions of the mind and use recognizably
literary discourses to *interpret* them.[65] Because cognitive sciences are pri-

marily descriptive of physical states and processes rather than interpretive of the verbal and textual products of those processes, they seem less obviously useful as interpretive tools.

Another reason for our neglect of cognitive sciences may lie in their relatively primitive state and in the passionate disputes and disagreements that make their findings so controversial. Since cognitive scientists do not agree on such seemingly basic concepts as the nature of intelligence, the relative roles of innate capacity and cultural forces in developing cognitive abilities, and how the brain processes information, it might seem impossible to derive even a stable *theory* of mind from their morass of conflicting assertions. Nevertheless, I believe that cognitive theory may provide some help in getting around the current critical impasse between those who assume an author with conscious control over the text he produces and those who assume that cultural construction leaves little or no room for authorial agency. While it is true that many areas of cognitive science share a similar split between innatist and cultural constructivist views of cognition, the cognitive sciences do seem to offer more theoretical orientations that assume some combination of the two. Cognitive theory also treats consciousness, intentionality, agency, and meaning in ways that both resemble and differ markedly from most postmodern literary and cultural criticisms, so it offers the possibility of seeing our own most basic assumptions from a different perspective. The current theories of cognitive psychology seem to some extent to corroborate our view of the author as fragmented, unable consciously to control language, unable to evade the mandates of his culture. But they also open a space for a more informed speculation about the role of the author within culture and the role of culture within the author's brain.

I want to begin by summarizing some of the suggestions about selfhood, consciousness, and especially language processing offered by researchers in cognitive neuroscience and psychology. Although to attempt such a summary at this point, when cognitive theorizing about these issues is provisional at best and when any such account must necessarily oversimplify complex issues, may seem foolish, I believe that it is important to provide a larger theoretical context, however tentative and piecemeal, for the linguistic concepts that are central to this book. Here again, on most of these issues it is possible to discern a split between cognitive scientists who view the brain as essentially computerlike—logical, mechanistic, processing (not creating) objective reality—and those who stress that brain function is biological, embodied, and not essentially logical.

In a sense the mind-body problem is easily resolved, as the philosopher John Searle has suggested.[66] The passage cited above from Kosslyn and Koenig, "the mind is what the brain does," sums up the dominant cognitive position. In this respect, as I have suggested, contemporary cognitive theory resembles the pre-Cartesian, Galenic materialism that shaped early modern concepts of body and mind.[67] Cognitive scientists are a long way from understanding how the brain produces the mind, however. Although computer programs and psychological testing are useful in providing models of behavior that can reveal how the mind is embodied, links between behavior and physiology are still fairly crude.

The cognitive emphasis on the embodiment of thought offers the possibility of a more radical materialism than does current Marxist theory, since it attempts to explore the literally material origins of the self.[68] Cognitive theorists do recognize the problematic nature of our perceptions of "reality," acknowledging that what seems to be our direct perception of reality is in fact "illusory: what we perceive depends on both what is in the world and what is in our heads—on what evolution has 'wired' into our nervous systems and what we know as a result of experience."[69] Nevertheless, cognitivist mental concepts seem to be "material" in three ways; (1) they emerge from and consist in the neural matter of the brain; (2) they are shaped by perceptions of physical "reality" and by the experience of living in the body; and (3) they use metaphor to extend concepts derived from material experience to immaterial abstractions.[70] F. Elizabeth Hart has suggested that a cognitive "materialist linguistics" similar to that outlined here establishes a "systematic continuity among three elements: the . . . human mind; the semiotic sign through which that mind finds expression; and the culture from/into which the mind absorbs/produces convention."[71] Mental representation, then, involves the material brain, its perceptions of material culture (from its embodied perspective), and its internal models of those perceptions. A cognitive materialism would differ sharply from Marxist theory in assuming that the subject participates in the creation of meaning as it interacts with material culture since, as Michel Pecheux describes it, the Marxist position assumes "the independence of the external world . . . with respect to the subject, *while at the same time positing* the dependence of the subject with respect to this external world."[72] In this sense it might respond to Paul Smith's call for an amendment of Marxist theory "in order to clarify the human person who is constructed at different moments as the place where agency and structure are fused."[73]

Cognitive science also offers theories of consciousness that both resemble and differ from currently dominant paradigms. Many researchers in both computer and neuroscience fields seem to agree that most mental functions are unconscious. Although literary critics are usually willing to posit a Freudian or Lacanian unconscious consisting of drives and desires that have been repressed, cognitive functions are generally treated as if they were largely conscious. However, since the brain has billions of neurons working simultaneously to perform different functions instantaneously, it is only possible for us to be conscious of a tiny fragment of these processes after they have occurred.[74] As Antonio Damasio puts it, "The present is never here. We are hopelessly late for consciousness."[75]

Wilma Bucci's recent book *Psychoanalysis and Cognitive Science* begins with the assumption, widely shared among experimental and cognitive psychologists, that the psychoanalytic "metapsychology," the theory of how the mind works, has "failed to provide a viable foundation for further theory development; a new explanatory theory is needed as a basis for clinical work and research. The physical sciences have moved far beyond the turn-of-the-century principles on which Freud's energy model was based."[76] Bucci also believes that psychoanalysis itself remains a valid method of treatment, and she offers a synthesis of current cognitive theories of the mind in order to form a basis for analysis as a clinical practice. She suggests that a concept of "the human organism as a multicode emotional information processor, with substantial but limited integration of systems," can "provide a framework for developing consistent definitions of the basic concepts and processes of psychoanalysis" (74). Bucci argues that the most important systems are the three "coding formats" of the mind: the subsymbolic, the nonverbal symbolic code, and the verbal code.[77] In Bucci's view, the attribution of consciousness is less important since all three of these coding formats have conscious and unconscious components (177–78).

From a cognitive perspective, therefore, most mental functioning is unconscious, and the unconscious mind is largely unconscious not because of repression but because mental processes are simply too complex and swift to be registered. This is not to say that the mind has no Freudian unconscious; evidence of dreams, the uncanny, and other manifestations of condensation and displacement is certainly persuasive. As Bucci notes, "The type of symbolic imagery that has been identified as having psychoanalytic meaning constitutes a subset or special case" (175) of the larger, mostly unconscious image system of the brain. The Lacanian unconscious, with its linguistic structuration, seems to some extent to include both cognitive and Freudian versions: "The presence of the unconscious in the psychological order, in other words in the relation-functions of the individual, should, however, be more precisely defined: it is not coextensive with that order, for we know that if unconscious motivation is manifest in conscious psychical effects, as well as in unconscious ones, conversely it is only elementary to recall to mind that a large number of psychical effects that are quite legitimately designated as unconscious, are nonetheless without any relation whatever to the unconscious in the Freudian sense."[78] The existence of a cognitive unconscious as well as a psychological unconscious suggests that buried links among words, for example, may represent cognitive structuration as well as (or instead of) psychological phenomena and that they might be interpreted differently as a result.[79] This broader view of unconscious mental process also means that speaking about Shakespeare's brain as one place of origin for his works does not imply complete conscious control over them. It might again be possible to write about Shakespeare as an agent, conceiving of that agency as partly conscious and partly unconscious, with an unconscious component that reflects cognitive as well as affective categories.

Cognitivism also offers views of human agency and the human subject that seem both familiar and radically different.[80] The very definitions of such terms as *subject*, *agent*, and *discourse* can be conceived differently from a cognitive perspective. For instance, while a Marxist or psychoanalytic theorist typically distinguishes *individual* ("the illusion of whole and coherent personal organization") from *subject* ("the term inaccurately used to describe what is actually the series or the conglomeration of positions, subject-positions, provisional and not necessarily indefeasible, into which a person is called momentarily by the discourses and the world that he/she inhabits"), the cognitive theorists Lakoff and Johnson identify the "system of different metaphorical conceptions of our internal structure," which is based on a distinction between *subject* ("the locus of consciousness, subjective experience, reason, will, and our 'essence' ") and *selves* ("our bodies, our social roles, our histories").[81] Although *subject* seems to mean almost the opposite in these two sets of binaries, representing multiplicity and constructedness as opposed to a unified "individual" in one case and representing that experience of unity and wholeness as opposed to multiple and constructed "selves" in the other, the most crucial difference lies in the Marxist/psychoanalytic attempt to distinguish an illusory experience of wholeness from an "actual" multiplicity of positions and the cognitive assumption that both *subject* and *self* are part of a metaphoric system through which we experience our subjectivity. For a cognitive theorist the question is not which is more accurate as a description of human selfhood but rather how we rely on both metaphors, and the difference between them, for our sense of ourselves as persons.

Agency might also be conceived quite differently in cognitive theory if we accept as a typical postmodern formulation Paul Smith's definition of *agent* as "a form of subjectivity where, by virtue of the contradictions and disturbances in and among subject positions, the possibility (indeed actuality) of resistance to ideological pressure is allowed for (even though that resistance too must be produced in an ideological context)."[82] His focus on resistance to ideology seems overly simple from a cognitive perspective, where agency is a basic and presymbolic image schema. In Mandler's words, "Perceptual analysis of causal and non-causal motion is involved not only in the formation of concepts of animacy and inanimacy but also in the development of the concept of an agent. Animate objects not only move themselves but cause other things to move; it is the latter characteristic, of course, that turns animates into agents."[83] Although a cognitive theory of agency does not disallow the idea that ideology can constrain subjects from acting as free agents, it does not define human agency solely in relation to ideology. Understanding agency as a constitutive feature of the human experience of embodied selfhood and a basic building block of thought and language extends our sense of its force in both cognitive and cultural spheres.

Although I discuss the definition of *discourse* at length in the final chapter of this book, it is worth noting here its usefulness as a term that calls attention to the role of language in the transmission and replication of culture. Although from a cognitive perspective *discourse* means simply "conversation," I use it here in a roughly Foucauldian sense that has been well articulated by Lars Engle, who describes it as "the collection of preexistent constitutive linguistic social and cultural modes, forms, or codes, themselves evolving and interacting, which surround, condition, and interpret the activity of subjects."[84] Engle's pragmatist approach resembles cognitive theory in several important ways, and I agree with his sense that it is important to rethink subjectivity and agency as "a dynamic process of mutual reflection and challenge between agents and the discursive systems in which they find themselves" (63). However, a cognitive approach differs in avoiding the assumption that discourses "preexist" the subjects that they shape, focusing instead on the very processes through which subjects produce and reproduce discursive forms of all kinds.

As we have seen, then, postmodern theory generally shares two assumptions that seriously impair the possibility of human agency: (1) that the human subject is fragmented and therefore lacking in unitary agency and (2) that subjects are formed by culture (or ideology) acting through language and therefore lack the freedom necessary to choose their actions. These assumptions work most powerfully in Freud's partitioned subject; in Saussure's system of signs, which determines meaning through difference; and, perhaps most influentially, in Lacan's application of Saussurean principles to psychoanalysis and Althusser's Lacanian theory of ideological interpellation.

Cognitive theory shares both of these assumptions to some extent. It recognizes a partitioned subject but finds it to be variously integrated; some cognitive theorists argue that its integration is illusory, while some do not. Although early psychological and computer models of mental process assumed that there was a "homunculus," or single agent in control of the mind (and thus comprising the "self"), more recent work has found such a theory to be unsatisfactory.[85] The computer scientist Marvin Minsky has argued that the brain contains a "society of mind" made up of multiple agents that are not *controlled* by any single entity. Minsky believes that models of a controlling self are common because "so much of what our minds do is hidden from the parts of us that are involved with verbal consciousness."[86] Cognitive neuroscientists now sketch out complex neural networks that regulate themselves according to identifiable principles but are not controlled by any central entity or mechanism within the brain.[87] Damasio describes a self that, while it does not possess "a single central knower and owner," nevertheless experiences most phenomena from "a consistent perspective, as if there were indeed an owner and knower for most, though not all, contents." Damasio locates this perspective in "a relatively stable, endlessly repeated biological state" based on "the predominantly invariant structure and operation of the organism, and the slowly evolving elements of autobiographical data."[88] George Lakoff has recently surveyed the "system of metaphors" that "allows us to conceptualize the experience of consciousness," concluding that "there is not just one single, monolithic, self-consistent, correct cultural narrative of what a person is"; instead "there are many partially overlapping and partially inconsistent conventional conceptions of the Self in our culture."[89] A completely integrated "individual" self, then, may, strictly speaking, indeed be a myth, as both psychoanalytic and Marxist theory suggest; however, the concepts of a tripartite self (id, ego, superego) or of "subject position" may be themselves too schematic to describe the multiplicity of competing processes going on within a given brain at any moment or to explain the effective integration of those processes.

Cognitive theory similarly recognizes the powerful role of culture in forming the subject but insists that there is an interaction between the biological subject and its culture. Meaning is not just the product of an exterior system of signs but is fundamentally structured by human cognitive processes. Fredric Jameson perhaps most clearly articulates (from a Marxist perspective) the Lacanian and Althusserian assumption that language enters the subject from outside and in the process both alienates and subjects the self. Jameson describes Lacan's theory of the "production of the Unconscious by way of a primary repression which is none other than the acquisition of language." As Jameson characterizes it, "The Law, represented by the parents, and in particular by the father, passes over into the very nature of language itself, which the child receives from outside and which speaks him just as surely as he learns to speak it."[90] Many cognitive linguists (Noam Chomsky, Steven Pinker, Ray Jackendoff) posit innate linguistic capacities, and almost all cognitive scientists see language acquisition as involving both biological and cultural factors. Studies of language acquisition and creolization provide compelling evidence that children are able, to some extent, to "create" as well as "learn" language. If children are exposed to a pidgin language (lacking in such grammatical resources as word order, tense, clear distinctions between subject and object), they will independently and without exposure to any other language convert it to a creole form "with standardized word orders and grammatical markers that are lacking in the pidgin" spoken by their parents.[91] If language comes from inside as well as outside the subject, it is unlikely to be as profoundly alienating as Lacan has suggested.

If, as Lakoff, Edelman, and Damasio have argued, thought and language emerge from our perception of a self within a body as it interacts with an environment, then some form of agency is fundamental to language. Indeed, as Mandler, Ronald Langacker, and others suggest, agency is reflected in our grammar at the most basic levels—in the Silverstein hierarchy, for example, which identifies a gradient of "concrete, agentive, egocentric qualities" and can predict such grammatical phenomena as nominative-accusative patterning in split-ergative languages or the use of *of* or -'s genitive forms in English.[92] Additionally, Edelman's theory of "value" and Damasio's theory of "somatic markers" suggest that cultural constraints (ideology), acting in concert with biological predispositions and constraints, can shape the subject prior to the acquisition of language. Thus, language itself is not so essentially implicated in ideology or cultural constraint. Certainly the difficulty of talking about anything other than simple intentional agency reflects the strength of the concept. Transcripts of conversations with aphasics suggest that people feel immense frustration if their ability to choose appropriate words is impaired. For example, in answer to an interviewer's question, "What happened to make you lose your speech?" one patient responded, "Head, fall, Jesus Christ, me no good, str, str . . . oh Jesus . . . stroke."[93] This patient evinced anger and frustration at his inability to control his speech, to use language to express his intended meaning. Even if such control is illusory, it is still clearly a powerful expectation. However, if conscious agency (defined as actual control over such mental processes as decision making, language production, etc.) is, finally, a meaningless concept, then issues of whether or not ideology controls subjects within a given culture may be both limited and limiting as constitutive questions for criticism. Instead, we might need to consider ways in which mental processes are both facilitated and constrained by the interaction of biological structures and cultural forces.

The relative roles of innate biological structures and culture in determining human thought and behavior are, of course, vehemently debated within almost every branch of cognitive science.[94] Most people are familiar with the debates about the factors determining human intelligence and, perhaps to a lesser extent, debates about the Chomskian proposition that language is essentially an innate, rather than learned, ability.[95] Most cognitive sciences, however, posit some form of interaction between culture and organism, although they differ, of course, on the relative importance of each factor. Certainly the extreme cultural constructivist views of Benjamin Whorf and Edward Sapir, who argued that the cultural constraints of language determined what could be thought or even perceived, have been generally rejected. On the other hand, cognitive linguists such as Lakoff, Langacker, and Taylor argue that the meanings of words are always ultimately based on complex, "encyclopedic" knowledge of the culture in which they are produced.[96] The research on perception of color described earlier, for example, indicates that even if a given culture lacks certain color words, its members are nevertheless able to perceive focal colors that they lack the vocabulary to name, although they are less able to *remember* differences between nameless colors.[97] Such research, as we have seen, also indicates that color terms are acquired by cultures according to an almost universal pattern.

Cognitive science suggests that the power of culture to shape individual selves must be filtered through the material, biological constructs of the brain, which are common, though in different forms, to all (normally functioning) people across cultures. It argues that there is a material basis for a limited sense of "essential" human attributes as well as space for individual arrangements of neurons. The political implications of accepting biological as well as cultural determinants of selfhood are complex and have by no means been worked out fully. Certainly arguments asserting that intelligence, for example, is biologically rather than culturally determined have been associated with racist politics. Steven Pinker, who argues that there is a separate and innate "language instinct," suggests that racist interpretations of biological determinism are based on a false claim that the supposition of innate commonalties among all people also means "that differences between individuals, sexes, and races are innate."[98] Instead, Pinker cites the studies of Walter Bodmer and Luca Cavalli-Sforza suggesting that genetic variations within "racial" groups are much greater than differences between them. Recent studies suggest some ways in which gender affects cognitive functioning, but they also suggest that both structures and constraints common to all brains, regardless of gender, as well as individual differences in neuronal groupings, are more salient in determining the nature of brain function.[99]

As I suggested above, cognitive theory accords with most poststructuralist theory in questioning the very concept of rationalism. Failures in the development of artificial intelligence, on the one hand, and the development of prototype theory, on the other, suggest that older theories of mind placed too much emphasis on rationality. Many cognitive theorists now stress the role of fuzzy boundaries, encyclopedic cultural knowledge, metaphoric extension, and emotion in constituting even the most seemingly rational mental operations. As Gerald Edelman notes, "Whatever the skill employed in thought—that of logic, mathematics, language, spatial or musical symbols—we must not forget that it . . . undergoes flights and perchings, is susceptible to great variations in attention, and in general, is fueled by metaphorical and metonymic processes. It is only when the results of many parallel, fluctuating, temporal processes of perception, concept formation, memory and attentional states are 'stored' in a symbolic object— a sequence of logical propositions, a book, a work of art, a musical work—that we have the *impression* that thought is pure."[100] Damasio similarly charts the large role of emotion in rational decision making.

Derrida's critique of Western rationalism might thus be reconceived in cognitive terms: the metaphors that in a deconstructive reading seem to disrupt the surface logic of the text could also be interpreted as traces of basic cognitive structures.[101] These seemingly contradictory metaphors are present in a text because thought, from a cognitive perspective, is able to accommodate contradiction and recursivity. A Derridean reading focuses on contradiction because it *expects* the mind to work rationally and because it assumes (in order to deconstruct) the rigid binary categories of classical logic. Derridean "play" or difference could be reinterpreted as a trace of the prototype effect and the radial structure of meaning. Meaning does (to use Lacan's term) "slide," but not without moorings since despite its fuzzy and inexact correspondences, it is motivated (and constrained) by physical experience. Of course the Derridean "there is no outside the text," based as it is on Saussurean formalism, clearly does not fit a cognitive theory. Indeed, from a cognitive perspective, meaning is anchored (although ambiguously and insecurely) by a three-way tether: brain, culture, discourse.

In this book I look at a series of plays in which Shakespeare seems, in a sense, to have been doing cognitive research on his own mental lexicon. Critics have long recognized that Shakespeare had an unusually large mental lexicon that was perhaps organized around particularly strong image-based mental models.[102] He was also particularly adept at coining "new" words that came to be accepted as additions to the larger cultural lexicon and was fascinated by the forms of homonymy that yield puns.[103] He seems to have been intrigued by polysemy, more "aware" (consciously or unconsciously) than most people of prototype effects, semantic webs, and meaning chains, and interested in exploring the multiple meanings of single words (famously, *nothing* and *honest*) as well as the nature of cultural metaphors of various kinds (e.g., clothing as representing a person's role in life and the multiple associations of children, both in *Macbeth*).[104] By "exploring" I do not necessarily mean a fully conscious phenomenon but simply that the mental connections and associations of semantic webs and prototypes seem especially evident in Shakespeare's work. It seems possible that the process of creating fictional characters to exist in a three-dimensional stage space brought out the spatial structures of language to an unusual degree. Perhaps it is enough to say that these effects "emerge" through Shakespeare's almost uniquely rich use of language. Shakespeare (i.e., Shakespeare's language-processing functions) causes us to notice these connections—which in turn reveal information about his culture and also about the organizational tendencies of the brain.

Cognitive theory makes it possible to identify patterns of language use that extend throughout Shakespeare's writing career and that can, I think, help us to arrive at a fuller sense of the complex interactions between author and culture that produced these texts. Many of Shakespeare's plays contain striking repetitions of words and images; these have previously been studied to yield either thematic or psychoanalytic insights.[105] I am interested here in what seems to be a special focus on polysemic words of various kinds, especially those that were taking on new meanings in this period in concert with significant institutional and cultural changes. In a given play or group of plays Shakespeare typically hovers around one of these words (or a group of related words), repeating it, worrying it, using it in all of its different senses, punning on it, in ways that reveal its embeddedness in semantic webs and its implication in ongoing social process. Eve Sweetser has argued that the linked phenomena of polysemy and meaning change are areas of linguistics that particularly challenge the Saussurean assumption of "the arbitrariness of the sign" since "if all uses of signs are taken as arbitrary, then multiple uses of the same sign must also be seen as arbitrary, and so the relationships between them might be assumed to be uninteresting."[106]

Shakespeare's repetition of words undergoing changes in meaning insists on the intermediate stage of polysemy that Sweetser argues must always accompany diachronic change: "If a word once meant A and now means B, we can be fairly certain that speakers did not just wake up and switch meanings on June 14, 1066. Rather, there was a stage when the word meant both A and B" (9). In *As You Like It*, for example, the polysemic words *villain* and *clown* are repeated in ways that reveal (and question) the role of semantic change in the negotiation of changing possibilities for social mobility in the period. It seems almost silly to say that Shakespeare was fascinated by words and the ways his mind associated them and by the ways in which cultural structures could shape and change their meanings (and that words themselves could mediate ideological change), but I think it is important to reassert this assumption. These plays are introspective in the sense that they consist, among other things, in explorations of the cognitive and cultural forces that determine the meanings of words and the shape of subjectivity. They are public introspections written for commercial consumption, but these facts simply ensure that their plays on meaning are constrained by the necessity to make them readily understandable within the cultural framework of the Eliza-bethan and Jacobean stage.

In the chapters that follow I focus on a series of such words that, I argue, delineate Shakespeare's changing conception of the material conditions, both cultural and biological, under which subjects were formed through language in early modern England. I focus on *house* and *home* in *The Comedy of Errors*, *villain* and *clown* in *As You Like It*, *suit* in *Twelfth Night*, *act* in *Hamlet*, *pregnant* in *Measure for Measure*, and *pinch* in *The Tempest* because these instances provide particularly rich examples of both cultural and cognitive patterns. Clearly, other words and plays could easily have been chosen. Each of the words that I focus on here is embedded in the discursive formations of larger cultural institutions and also, strikingly, has special reference to material conditions of theatrical composition or production. Shakespeare's mental lexicon shares general structural principles with other human language-processing systems but also exhibits particular patterns shaped by his own personal experiences and history. Thus, each of these words can be associated with basic spatial concepts emerging from the embodiment of cognitive process, but the fact that theatrical domains of meaning have such central roles suggests that Shakespeare's mental lexicon was, understandably, shaped by his professional as well as his personal life.

We can trace a progression in the course of these plays from an interest in the origins of the self within changing versions of both nation and household, to the placement of that self within a shifting grid of status, to the expression of the self between constraint and desire. I believe that we can discern a movement about 1600 from depicting the body as it is contained within a cultural space to representing the ways in which the self inhabits the body; the word *act* in *Hamlet* serves as a kind of fulcrum, shifting from legal to physical connotations. At the same time, Shakespeare's exploration of stage space shifts from experiments in using the stage to represent a cultural environment to suggestions that it functions as a larger reflection of the body, as, for example, in *Hamlet*, when the fortified walls of Elsinore mirror on a larger scale the central image of ears that are fortified against unwelcome or dangerous language. *Measure for Measure* and *The Tempest* evince a new interest in the physical nature of creativity, including an awareness of the brain as a physical organ within the material body just as the body is located within material culture. The physical and mental implications of *pregnancy* and *pinching* are the means through which these issues are explored. At all points, ideas about the self are thought through using theatrical as well as more generally cultural frames of meaning.

This pattern of development may seem implausibly self-serving in that it makes Shakespeare anticipate my own movement from focusing on the self within culture to the self within its body. I do not mean to suggest that Shakespeare discovered modern neuroscience in the seventeenth century. Certainly his imagined representations of brain function are shaped by the theories of faculty psychology and humoral physiology that were dominant at that time, theories that resemble cognitivism only in their (uneasy) emphasis on the materiality of the mind. Nancy Siraisi has emphasized the extent to which "humoral theory is probably the single most striking example of the habitual preference in ancient, medieval, and Renaissance medicine for materialist explanations of mental and emotional states."[107] Paster notes that our sense of our bodies as "containing" our emotions may stem from humoral physiology; Lakoff, of course, has argued for the universality of this sense based on our kinesthetic experiences of embodiment, and theories of the humors may have been formulated in part to explain the physical sensations that Lakoff describes. However, in most other ways the humoral body (and the mind described by faculty psychology) seems very different from the cognitive brain. Certainly its permeability, the fungibility of its fluids, and the close parallel between thought and sexual reproduction that results from these beliefs differ in varying degrees, as we will see, from the properties of mind posited by cognitive science. Shakespeare, then, certainly experienced his embodied mind in ways that were shaped by his understanding that both body and mind were controlled by the humors. As we look for signs of "cognitive" patterns in the plays, it will be important to keep in mind Shakespeare's culturally determined sense of how the mind was embodied.

A reader might wonder how this "cognitive" approach to the Shakespearean lexicon differs from such previous philological or New Critical studies as C. S. Lewis's *Studies in Words*, William Empson's *The Structure of Complex Words*, Raymond Williams's Marxist *Keywords*, or, more recently, Patricia Parker's *Shakespeare from the Margins*.[108] Although the readings that I produce here may at various points seem very similar to those generated by these other word-based approaches, they are based in a different theory of meaning and emphasize different patterns and structures. Studies of the human mental lexicon have produced a great deal of information about how words are stored in the brain and how their meanings are shaped by basic conceptual structures. Our mental lexicon is evidently organized in ways that facilitate both production and comprehension of language, and Shakespeare's texts seem marked by patterns of word use and syntax that make the organizational features of his mental lexicon especially evident. Studies of word association indicate that, as Jean Aitchison puts it, "word lemmas (meaning and word class) seem to be organized in semantic fields, and within these fields there are strong bonds between coordinates which share the same word class, such as *lion, tiger,* or *knife, fork, spoon*."[109] Tests also reveal strong bonds between words with collocational links (words usually connected in speech, e.g., *salt water*), superordinates (the word *color* and examples of colors, e.g., *red*), and synonyms. Shakespeare's strikingly frequent use of doublets or lexical sets" such as "complotted and contrived" (*Richard II* 1.1.96), "exsufflicate and blown" (*Othello* 3.3.180), "weary, stale, flat, and unprofitable" (*Hamlet* 1.2.133), and "His companies unlettered, rude, and shallow, / His hours filled up with riots, banquets, sports" (*Henry V* 1.1.55–56), seem to reflect these aspects of lexical storage as well as the Elizabethan practice of copious expression.[110] On the other hand, as Aitchison notes, "word forms (sound structure) . . . are organized with similar sounding words closely linked, such as *referee* for 'refugee,' *reciprocal* for 'rhetorical' " (223).[111] Comic malapropisms such as those made famous by Dogberry, Verges, and Elbow (*odorous* for *odious*, *respected* for *suspected*, etc.) reflect this feature, as, perhaps, does Shakespeare's notorious fondness for puns. These structures of lexical organization are, of course, virtually universal in humans with normal linguistic capacities; however, verbal habits especially associated with Shakespeare's style seem to reflect these structures more directly than do the works of many writers. Shakespeare's tendency to play on and with the mental links between words (which most writers efface) means that his texts are marked by particularly evident traces of cognitive process.

A similar playfulness in Shakespeare's texts also seems to emphasize the complex links that structure the meanings of polysemic words. According to cognitive linguists such as George Lakoff or Ronald Langacker, the meanings of words are determined not by a collection of features or by a system of differences within a semiotic system but by "encyclopedic" cultural knowledge that provides domains, frames, and scripts within which words have meaning.[112] A monosemic word thus comprises a category organized around a single prototype, with knowledge of the prototype based on complex cultural knowledge. The polysemic words that seem to have been particularly interesting to Shakespeare belong to categories of meaning that are structured by several linked prototypes.

Of course, as John Taylor points out, prototype theory suggests that monosemy and polysemy cannot be definitively separated—like all categories, these also have fuzzy boundaries.[113] The words that interest me here illustrate a variety of types of polysemy, ranging from prototype shifts within an essentially monosemic category to polysemy that includes instances of what might be considered homonymy. In *The Comedy of Errors*, for instance, *house* and *home* are essentially monosemous words with basic definitions that remain virtually the same but over time and in relation to cultural change experience shifting prototypes, so that, in Taylor's words, "a non-central member of a monosemous category increases in salience to the point where it constitutes a secondary conceptual centre of the category" (103). In this case, an earlier sense of the prototypical *home* as village shifts to designate either "nationality" or "private domestic space." In concert with these prototype shifts, cognate and related words like *homely* and *housewife* undergo change to true polysemy. In other cases, such as the case of *villain* in *As You Like It*, a word both takes on a new meaning in relation to cultural change and actually works to mediate the change, illustrating an instance in which a polysemic web is implicated in ideology in complex ways. The multiple kinds of suits in *Twelfth Night*, including lawsuits, romantic suits, suits of clothes, and suitable behaviors, illustrate polysemy that verges on homonymy, since some of these senses of the word (*suit* of clothes and law*suit*) have a separate dictionary entry, but according to cognitive theory can be seen to be linked by complex chains and extensions of meaning *that* are structured by spatial concepts of following and pursuit. Each of these instances of multiple and changing meaning illustrates a different kind of interaction between cognitive and cultural structures. In these plays Shakespeare seems to insist on the full range of possible meanings and to explore the ways in which they are linked, thus revealing the underlying semantic paradigms. Again, we need not imagine that Shakespeare does this consciously, but simply that he writes in a way that reveals the underpinnings of the mental lexicon (and thus the conceptual structures of the brain) in various complex ways.

A cognitive approach to Shakespeare's lexicon will therefore differ from previous studies of words on several accounts. I differ from Raymond Williams in focusing on a single author's multiple uses of words that do not necessarily have the status of culturally central "keywords." Like Williams, I am interested in correlating changes in meaning with changes in material culture; however, I am more concerned to identify synchronic polysemous structures that have emerged from historical change. Williams is concerned to see a particular (Marxist) narrative movement of history behind changing keywords, but Shakespeare's plays sometimes problematize the relationship between historical change and the polysemy that it produces. C. S. Lewis, of course, was mainly concerned to warn readers away from anachronistic misinterpretations; he argued (against Empsonian ambiguity) that "in ordinary language the sense of a word is governed by the context and this sense normally excludes all others from the mind."[114] The purpose of *Studies in Words* is to aid the reader in weeding out irrelevant meanings, whereas I accord with cognitive theorists who suggest that any given "sense" of a word is motivated by its place within a radial category of related meanings, which, because of this connection, are never, finally and absolutely, irrelevant.

William Empson's ideas about polysemy are closer to those suggested by cognitive theory and for that reason deserve more lengthy treatment. Empson was largely concerned in his study to refute assertions by linguists that poetic language was purely emotive and to demonstrate the complex cognitive content of poetic language by tracing the fine distinctions elicited by its polysemy. A cognitive approach, on the other hand, might follow Damasio in insisting that cognitive and emotional content cannot be separated. Empson argues that complex words have a "head sense" or "typical" meaning that in some ways seems similar to a prototype effect. Empson's "head sense," however, seems to have very firm boundaries, unlike the fuzzy distinctions recognized by cognitive theorists today. He is concerned to identify "equations" of meaning whereby the complex attitudes and implications conveyed by words could be brought under control and correctly interpreted. Meanings for Empson are complex and multiple, but the intelligent reader is able to sort them out.

Empson's treatment of the development of the word *fool* in the sixteenth century and Shakespeare's use of the word in *King Lear* reveals some of the assumptions behind his treatment of meaning and also suggests some of its shortcomings. He seems to argue that "complex words" are the medium through which authors lead readers to make fine moral and ethical distinctions; words posit complex "equations" of meaning that the reader must solve. Before Shakespeare could use the word *fool* in *King Lear* to convey the folly of incomplete renunciation, it first needed to accumulate several "Implications" and "Emotions" (ranging from Erasmian innocence to imbecility, to madness, to witty mockery, to affectionate regard for a dependent). Empson comments that *fool* became an affectionate term in 1530 and came to mean "pure imbecile" in 1540; "now the introduction of these two further meanings into the word was necessary to complete it as an instrument; given these extra two, the whole group of ideas could be imposed on the hearer by mere word play; to a far greater extent than at any other time, the very subtle thought of *Lear* was inherent in the language."[115] A reader's appreciation of this subtlety is based on an awareness of the full range of relevant meanings as well as an ability to exclude irrelevant implications or emotions. After considering the "shocking" and "embarrassing" racist implications taken on by the word *native*, for example, Empson concludes that "the ordinary user . . . had not intended" for the word to take on such an embarrassing implication. Empson argues that *native* marks an exception: "As a rule, in a successful literary use [of a complex word], the equation does just what the writer and his audience wanted; and this is even more true of the equations carrying the stock ideas of a period, where as a rule there is no tension between individuals or groups" (79). Empson views words as "instruments" that an author can use to convey subtle and complex ideas.

In his history of the changing implications of the word *fool* from the Erasmian "innocent simpleton" to Shakespeare's nexus of clown, imbecile, lunatic, and affectionate dependent, Empson overlooks many of the ways in which social institutions (medicine, law) and the material conditions of theater influence the concept of fool. Although he briefly glances at the legal procedure for assuming the wardship of "idiots and fools natural" (115), he does not consider the socially charged implications of *clown*, which in precisely this period took over from the shifting word *villain* the expression of a special connection between rusticity, low social status, and boorish behavior (see chapter 2 below). This is the kind of "embarrassing" implication that Empson associates with *native* and views as an exception. But the repeated inflections of *fool*, *clown*, and *villain* in *As You Like It* reveal that, unlike Empson, Shakespeare did not underestimate the cultural work done by words. Empson also neglects the material conditions of theatrical production and thus misses the most likely reason why *fool* came to be used more frequently than *clown* as Shakespeare's term for a comic performer after about 1600; in that year the notorious clown Will Kemp left the Chamberlain's Men and was replaced by the more refined "fool" Robert Armin (see also below).

It probably is not surprising that a New Critic such as Empson neglects cultural forces in order to focus on the importance of a close reading of words that convey finely controlled ethical distinctions. New Historicism and other forms of materialist criticism have already attacked and sought to correct this failing of formalism. But cognitive theory offers more than a materialist or historicist supplement to formalism, providing in addition a way of tracing in the text the interactions between culture, language, and cognition. The focus of a cognitivist approach to Shakespeare's use of repeated words includes the ways in which those words reflect the patterns of association and rules of combination within the mind as well as within the culture. In a cognitive approach, words are not strictly separated from images but will sometimes create their meanings in combination with models and images (or as a reflection of an unarticulated model).

In a cognitive approach to Shakespeare's plays the point is not to cause readers to make fine distinctions but to explore linkages and connections between words and, thus, between cultural concepts and between brain, language, and environment. Sometimes Shakespeare seems to push against the socially constructed meanings of words and to explore the extent to which an individual can bend their cultural mandate. In other cases the linkages and connections seem to be less consciously explored and to represent the lineations and filiations of the mind at work. Empson is disturbed by "doctrines" covertly conveyed by words and has as his goal to teach readers to recognize and disarm them. Shakespeare seems to have been interested in the many kinds of work that words and images could do. On a verbal level, the plays trace in and through language the complex and reciprocal processes by which culture and body form the self.

In its insistence on attention to the complex networks of words that link text and culture, this study perhaps most closely resembles Patricia Parker's *Shakespeare from the Margins*. Parker's readings of rich and historically dense polysemic structures are similar in many ways to the kinds of readings that I offer here. Taking issue with early New Historicist assumptions about the ideologically constrained nature of all discourse, Parker identifies her critical stance in this way: "The methodological presupposition in the chapters that follow is that Shakespearean wordplay—far from the inconsequentiality to which it has been reduced not only by the influence of neoclassicism but by continuing critical assumptions about the transparency (or unimportance) of the language of the plays—involves a network whose linkages expose (even as the plays themselves may appear simply to iterate or rehearse) the orthodoxies and ideologies of the texts they evoke."[116] Parker does not, however, offer a theoretical account (in either early modern or contemporary terms) of why wordplay might sometimes work to expose ideological formations in this way. Cognitive theory can, however, offer a clearer account of what these "linkages" are and why puns and other kinds of wordplay can sometimes seem to have a subversive effect. Although I agree with Parker that Shakespeare's play on polysemic words can "expose" something crucial about the workings of language, I argue that it exposes not just the hegemonic discursive formations of his culture but also the patterns that emerge as the human brain thinks through those formations. I want to be more precise about the agency *behind* this exposure—I think it emerges as language reflects the clash of physiological and cultural constraints—and also *indicated by* this exposure—I think it suggests that some common conceptions of human agency are problematized by the structures of cognition as they are reflected in language.

From a cognitive perspective, the "linkages" that Parker traces reflect the outlines of the mental lexicon, which is organized around linked modules, some, as Jean Aitchison has argued, containing "semantic-syntactic" or meaning-related information, some storing "phonetic phonological" or sound-based information: "Each module is to be a complex network, with relatively tight links to other items within the module and somewhat looser links to items outside of the module. Within each module there should be clusters of dense, multiplex mini-networks."[117] As the brain attempts to retrieve and understand or produce a stored word, "numerous links must be activated simultaneously" involving "links for many more words than will eventually be required" (230). Wordplay, for example, play on the literal (spatial) sense of *preposterous*, which Parker argues exposes the constructedness of Tudor and Stuart discourses of hierarchy, might have this effect because the network of linkages attaching that word to related words would not comprise a neatly ordered lineal succession of meanings but complex and multiple links involving a surplus of meaning, "links for many more words than eventually will be required." Parker notes both semantic links, such as concepts of right order in class and gender hierarchies and ideas of "sequence, succession, sequitur" (28), and sound links to *posterior* and thence to *ass* and the *arsie-versy*. It is in this surplus of cognitive linkage that simple, hierarchical relations of meaning become inadequate, at least in the writing of an author who tends to highlight, rather than suppress, such links. Wordplay of this kind is not necessarily subversive, but it can often have subversive effects if it exposes buried links and structures that complicate ideological formations that tend to take simpler and more rational forms.

It is no accident that so many of the linked word networks that Parker traces have a spatial structure: the sense of "back for front" suggested by *preposterous*, the mechanics of rhetorical "joining" and linking, the sense of dislocation and movement implied by *translation*, the ways in which *dilation* forms an interface between inside and outside. As Lakoff and others have argued, the spatial structuration of so many cognitive concepts reflects the shaping influence that the experience of embodiment has on cognition and discourse. The wordplay that Parker traces often involves a kind of spatial dislocation—back before front, inside revealed outside—a sense that her title, with its emphasis on bringing the marginal to the center, also reflects. The fact that play on the spatial patterns that inflect discursive ideological structures such as hierarchy and succession might be subversive may represent a bodily surplus of meaning that cannot be completely contained within the limited spaces of official discursive or generic structures.

Certainly some Lakoffian spatial constructs (e.g., "up is better than down") are easily assimilable to concepts of social hierarchy; however, Shakespearean wordplay, in exploring the spatial structurations of polysemic words, can sometimes also expose the ways in which spatial relationships work to create meaning. The body and the embodied brain structure meaning through complex linkages and networks that have a subterranean multiplicity from which simpler ideological structures emerge. I want, then, to offer cognitive theory as a possible background for Parker's methodological assumptions and to look more directly at Shakespeare's play on words that seem to explore the processes of subject formation involving both the body and culture. I do not believe that Shakespearean wordplay is always subversive; rather, it registers complexities of meaning and ambivalences of feeling that sometimes disrupt simple ideological structures.

An objection to my attempt to read cognitive structures behind the
Shakespearean lexicon might center on the fact that these plays were
products not of a single author's brain but of a complicated and multiply
collaborative process. Certainly the texts of Shakespeare's plays as we
have them reflect the collaborative conditions of Elizabethan and Jacobean theater. And contemporary emphasis on the multiplicity of texts and
dispersion of authorship in the period provides a salutary corrective to
the fetishization of the nonexistent uncontaminated Shakespearean "original." But at the risk of resembling Samuel Johnson in his truculent kick-
ing of the stone, I want to point out that even though the whole text might
be the product of a number of hands, every single word of each version
of a text was physically put there by one person wielding a pen or a compositor's stick. And if, in the multiple texts of a play attributed to Shakespeare, the same word appears in every instance of a particular line, there
is a good chance that there was some sort of material connection between
Shakespeare's brain and that word.

Certainly Shakespeare was constrained by the tastes of his audience,
the availability of actors and costumes, the shape of the stage, and the
social and collaborative nature of language itself. But, however cognizant
of the many hands though which most theatrical texts passed on their
way to publication, we must also remain aware of the material fact of
their authorship by William Shakespeare, a fact that has left several kinds
of historical trace: Shakespeare's name among the shareholders of the
company, contemporary references to him as an envied or esteemed author, the use of his name as a selling point to attract paying customers to
the theater and readers to purchase quarto volumes. Stephen Orgel, while
acknowledging the extent to which all theatrical texts from the period
exist as the products of collaboration, has suggested that Shakespeare
had more control over the process of producing a play text than most
playwrights because of his status as a shareholder of the company.[118]

Jeffrey Masten has extended the concept of collaboration to include
any use of language: "If we accept that language is a socially-produced
(and producing) system, then collaboration is more the condition of discourse than its exception."[119] The cognitive scientist Leslie Brothers has
recently argued that "the mind" is not "something packed inside a solitary skull" but "a dynamic entity defined by its transactions with the rest
of the world."[120] Cognitive theory, then, suggests that language, and even
the mind itself, is produced through the interaction of human brains in
social contexts; from this perspective, the most meaningful collaboration
would have taken place within Shakespeare's brain.

It is also true, as Masten, Arthur Marotti, Joseph Loewenstein, and
others (including myself) have demonstrated, that in the early modern
period authorship and intellectual property were conceived quite differ-

ently than they had come to be by the nineteenth century, with less emphasis on the originality and proprietary rights of the author.[121] However, to
insist on Shakespeare's material role in the production of these texts is not
to deny the different constructions of authorship in the period; instead, it
can provide a slightly different perspective from which to examine Shakespeare's representation of both the cognitive and the cultural structures
that shaped this act of authorship. Indeed, some of the words examined
here (e.g., *clown* and *pregnant*) include concepts of collaboration and
authorial agency within their polysemic web and reflect complex and ambivalent feelings about them. If every act of authorship is collaborative,
then the patterns of word usage that I examine here point to the heart of
this collaborative process.

It may seem as if the point of a cognitive approach is the impossible
goal of reading Shakespeare's mind rather than his plays. My purpose is
simply to look for traces of a mind at work in the text. But if our purpose
must now be to ask, for example, in Jean Howard's words, "how gender,
class, race, and social marginality or centrality impinge on the way characters are depicted as bearers of theatrical power," or if it is, in Stephen
Greenblatt's words, "the study of the collective making of distinct cultural
practices and inquiry into the relations among those practices," then we
need to be able to read signs of cognitive, as well as cultural, practice in
texts.[122] The word *how* in the first instance and *relations* in the second
bring us face to face with the agency of the author, however partial, collaborative, or constructed. In this book I want to show that texts bear evidence of formation by cognitive process as well as ideology. The signs of
cognitive and cultural fashioning cannot always be discerned or separated, but I believe that some of Shakespeare's plays offer interesting
points of collocation between them. I do not wish to return to the masterful, omniscient, transcendent Shakespeare; but neither can I offer a Shakespeare who was just a conduit or space within which rival cultural structures collided. I argue here that the brain constitutes the material site
where biology engages culture to produce the mind and its manifestation,
the text; these Shakespearean texts reveal traces of a particularly fertile
collaboration between the two.

No Space Like Home: *The Comedy of Errors*

A RELATIVELY old-fashioned critical commonplace about *The Comedy of Errors* is that it begins to transform the flat characters of Roman comedy and farce into three-dimensional individuals. Anne Barton, for example, contrasts ancient comedy, where "identity . . . is principally a matter of establishing parentage and social class," and Shakespeare's new focus in this play on "the inner life" and feelings of psychological incompleteness.[1] Critics have, however, traditionally seen Shakespeare's representation of the individual in this play as incomplete either because it was written early in his career, before he had learned to represent such characters in their full depth and complexity, or, according to a more recent view, because of a historicist argument that the concept of "inwardness" was only beginning to be developed when this play was written.[2] In an influential article written in the early 1960s Harold Brooks notes that although the Antipholi and Adriana "do not develop in the sense of being felt to change in character as a result of the action, their attitudes of mind develop, so that each is felt to have an inner self. That is, they are not wholly flat characters, such as might be fitting protagonists of pure farce. They are simple, but have just enough depth for the play."[3] By 1991 Barbara Freedman could argue that the characters lack fully rounded depth and individuality because the play as a whole represents an almost postmodern sense of "the impossibility of self-presence."[4] It would be more accurate to say that in the course of this play Shakespeare "thinks through" some of the issues at stake in fashioning such a self-present individual, in society and on the stage, and that in doing so he explores how characters are fashioned by the words they speak and also how, within the shifting semantic fields of those words, there can be space to imagine different versions of subjectivity.

Critics' persistent references to "depth" in their discussions of these characters reflect a commonplace metaphorical concept—that the relative resemblance of fictional characters to real people can be described as a progression from "flat" one-dimensionality, like a drawing or photograph in a text, to "round" three-dimensionality, with an interior space capable of containing a complicated inner self. Cognitive theorists such as George Lakoff or Jean Mandler would derive a cultural metaphor of this kind from a preconceptual image schema based on the developmentally crucial human experiences of embodiment. We should recall Mandler's argument that these image schemas "are more abstract than images," consisting of "dynamic spatial patterns that underlie the spatial relations and movements found in actual concrete images."[5] In this case, early kinesthetic experience of our bodies as containers and as themselves contained within spaces of various kinds, as well as observations of other containers in the surrounding environment, are metaphorically extended (or "projected") to structure more abstract notions of containment. In the case of literary critical discussion of characterization, a foundational sense of the self as contained within the body is easily extended to describe fictional characters that more directly represent this kind of containment than do other abstract versions of containment.[6]

The fact that depth of character has been so frequently adduced in discussions of this particular play is not an accident since *The Comedy of Errors* is especially concerned with imagining characters as they inhabit changing cultural spaces; in this play Shakespeare traces linkages and analogies among homes, bodies, and the theater as containers for different forms of subjective interiority. The play is centered on its characters' varying senses that some sort of containing home is necessary in order to possess a "rounded" interior life and their simultaneous sense that a private home and an individual self can be stifling and confining. This central organizing metaphor of containment is manifested in the play in several ways, most obviously through interlinked polysemic webs of words— *house, home, mart*—that represent powerful but changing discursive formations in this period and also through experiments with new ways of staging domestic scenes on the open space of the platform stage. I hope to show that the spatially charged words at the center of this play provided Shakespeare with a medium for working out the intersections and conflicts of embodied experience and cultural forms.

A cognitive reading of the role of spatial perception in subject formation resembles but also differs in several ways from more familiar psychoanalytic accounts. Both Freud and Lacan emphasize the importance of an *image* of the body in the formation of the ego: Freud suggests that the ego is a projection of the body's surface, and Lacan elaborates that idea in his theory of the mirror stage, which involves the infant's specular identification with an image of the whole body.[7] The cognitive theorists Gerald Edelman, Antonio Damasio, and George Lakoff also offer versions of the basic role of spatial orientation in the development of consciousness, selfhood, and language. Damasio bases his account of a neural theory of selfhood and consciousness on "primordial representations of the body proper" within the brain "whenever an interaction between organism and environment takes place."[8] This representation includes "states of biochemical regulation in structures of the brain stem and hypothalamus," "the viscera, including not only the organs in the head, chest and abdomen, but also the muscular mass and the skin," and "the musculoskeletal frame and its potential movement" (23). It is spatially organized because "the brain's somatosensory complex, especially that of the right hemisphere in humans, represents our body structure by reference to a body schema where there are midline parts (trunk, head), appendicular parts (limbs), and a body boundary. A representation of the skin might be the natural means to signify the body boundary because it is an interface turned both to the organism's interior and to the environment with which the organism interacts" (231). George Lakoff, Jean Mandler, and others have argued that we form preconceptual image schemas based on these early kinesthetic experiences of embodiment and that these schemas structure our cognitive processes and ultimately language itself; the schema that grows most directly out of the sensations described by Damasio is, of course, that of containment, the schema that is also most directly relevant to this play.

Although cognitive theory shares with psychoanalysis a recognition that the spatiality we experience living in our bodies plays an important role in subject formation, it differs in its sense of the processes involved and the kind of self formed in this way.[9] Psychoanalytic theories of subject formation tend to emphasize the fragmentation of body and mind and to posit a more thoroughgoing and pervasive role for language and the symbolic in the process of forming a conscious and speaking human subject. For Lacan in particular, the mirror stage involves alienation and fragmentation of the self (even before the accession of language and the symbolic) because of the inescapable gap between the subject and the image that it perceives: "This form situates the agency of the ego, before its social determination, in a fictional direction, which will always remain irreducible for the individual alone, or rather, which will only rejoin the coming-into-being of the subject asymptotically, whatever the success of the dialectical syntheses by which he must resolve as his discordance with his own reality."[10]

Most contemporary Lacanians continue to emphasize the subject's lack of access to the real and the imaginary except through symbols and therefore conceive of the subject as alienated and fragmented by its exposure to language. Bruce Fink, for instance, holds that the Lacanian "Other as language is assimilated by most children" is "an insidious, uninvited intruder that unceremoniously and unpropitiously transforms our wishes."[11] Joan Copjec similarly argues that "the body is written, it is constructed by language and not pregiven; all the work on the 'technologies of the body' have repeated this often enough. Lacan would not deny this—in fact, it is largely his theory that enables this position to be taken."[12] Copjec reinforces the link between language and bodily fragmentation when she notes that "when Lacan tells us that language carves up the body . . . he is speaking of a more unkind cut than that which merely carves *out* (or defines)," indicating instead a cut that "carves *up* (divides) the body image" (50).

A cognitive version of the spatial formation of subjectivity involves not just an image of the embodied self, however, but a tangible experience of it based on somatosensory signals from both inside and outside the body that are combined into a coherent body image. On the one hand, this body image may be essentially fragmentary since it does not actually *exist* in any single location in the brain. as Damasio notes, "Nowhere can we find a single area toward which all of those separate products would be projected in exact registration."[13] On the other hand, our perceptions of embodiment *are* integrated—Damasio speculates that "our strong sense of mind integration is created from the concerted action of large-scale systems by synchronizing sets of neural activity in separate brain regions, in effect a trick of timing" (95). Evidence supplied by such neural disorders as *anosognosia*, in which the patient loses any sense of his body as his own, suggests what true disintegration of body image might entail. The anosognosiac's inability to recognize, for example, that the entire left side of his body is paralyzed differs markedly from most people's experience of inhabiting their own bodies.[14] According to Damasio, anosognosiacs have experienced damage in "the insula, the parietal lobe, and the white matter containing connections among them and, in addition, connections to and from thalamus, to and from frontal cortex and to basal ganglia," resulting in "disruption of cross-talk among regions involved in body-state mapping" (153–54). Interestingly, anosognosiacs retain the sense of self based in language; they remember "who they are, where they live and worked, who the people close to them are" (155). Thus, our basic spatial sense of ourselves as living in our bodies seems to exist apart from language and to be dependent on integrated communication between various areas of the brain.

In *The Comedy of Errors* Shakespeare seems to be tracing different spatial representations of subjectivity in relation to different versions of "home," usually the first environment to contain the embodied self and the environment in which it first comes to experience consciousness. Gaston Bachelard, moving out of psychoanalysis and phenomenology toward cognitive theory in his meditation on the "poetics of space," has suggested that "the house image would appear to have become the topography of our intimate being."[15] However, in addition to Bachelard's notion that images of "home" have a universal resonance, we must also consider the fact that this play was written at a moment when interiority, involving linked concepts of individual inner life and domestic privacy, was taking on new cultural significance.[16]

Significantly, marriage manuals and guides for regulation of households
in this period frequently use the house itself as a metaphor for the relationships or individuals contained within it. R.R., in "The House-holders
Helpe, for Domesticall Discipline," draws this analogy between a marital
relationship and the house that contains it, telling of "an honest-hearted
householder" who "compared himself and his wife to the couple pieces
of the house, which if they fall asunder, they cause other timber of the
house to shrink and to go out of order."[17] Similarly, Richard Bernard, in
"Joshua's Godly Resolution in Conference with Caleb, Touching Household Governement for Well Ordering a Familie," suggests that in order
to reform a disordered family, "the governor must do as in making a new
house, where an old stood. . . . The man and wife must be sound; they be
the two side posts. So their children, who are as the beams laid over-
thwart."[18] A prayer on "returning home" makes an even more direct connection between subjective interiority and a protecting home, noting that
"houses are builded for us to repair into, from the annoyance of the
weather, from the cruelty of beasts, and from the waves and turmoils of
this troublous world," and therefore asking that God "grant . . . our bodies may so resort unto them [homes] from outward doings, as our minds
may yield themselves obedient to thee without striving and that they may
the better and more quietly exalt themselves into that sovereign rest of
thine above."[19]

Cognitive theory suggests that while the basic human spatial sense of
self is universal to all (non-brain-damaged) human beings across time and
cultures, its representation, the importance it is accorded, and ideas about
the circumstances of its production change in relation to historical and
cultural conditions.[20] The proliferation of analogies between newly private domestic spaces and the individuals contained within them reflects
the fact that in the late sixteenth century both of these entities were just
beginning to be conceived in their modern forms. Shakespeare's premod-
ern self can seem uncannily postmodern because it does not *assume* the
coherence and integration of subjectivity that have come to be associated
with the modern "bourgeois individual."[21] But I would argue (from a
cognitive perspective) that neither does Shakespeare's version of the subject in this play assume that alienation and fragmentation are the sole
defining manifestations of selfhood. Instead, characters are made to represent both alienation and integration as possible trajectories for the self.[22]
In reading for signs not of a psychological complex but of a cognitive
process, we can offer a more open-ended account of cultural and physiological possibilities.

Several critics have recently argued that the material conditions of theatrical production in early modern England caused, in various ways, a
conception of character that strikingly resembles the postmodern Lacan-

ian subject. Harry F. Berger Jr., Margreta de Grazia, and Peter Stallybrass use Lacan to counter the traditional view that theatrical characters can be analyzed as if, in de Grazia and Stallybrass's words, they "developed prior to and independent of the plays in which they appear" and speak "a language that reflects this experiential and psychological history."[23] Instead, in Berger's apt formulation, "speakers are the effects rather than the causes of their language."[24] Berger implies that in this respect they resemble Lacanian subjects in their construction by language supplied to them by the Other (in this case, the author). These characters also share the fragmentation of the Lacanian subject since, as Stallybrass and de Grazia argue, inconsistencies of speech prefix, nomenclature, and orthography, as well as the practice of doubling parts onstage, create a situation in which "identities that modern critics would distinguish converge in a single mechanically reproduced image; identities that they would make uniform split into multiple names." The result is a radical lack of "fixity of character" in Shakespearean texts.[25] Barbara Freedman has similarly suggested that theater, and especially Elizabethan "theater in the round," with its subversion of "the truth of any private, individual, or fixed vantage point,"[26] has a particular affinity with postmodern theories of the self: "both mediums [theater and film] bear witness to our fascination with the spatial lure of the human form. The appeal of theater thus depends upon an uncanny awareness of a fundamental loss in relation to the mirror image through which subjectivity is procured" (56). As a result, "psychoanalysis and postmodernism alike employ theater to deny the possibility of an objective observer, a static object, or a stable process of viewing" (74).

From a cognitive perspective, Shakespeare's practice in *The Comedy of Errors* suggests that although theatrical characters do possess these postmodern characteristics of fragmentation, alienation, and lack of grounded relation to material reality, the human subjects that they represent are not necessarily imagined to share those qualities as fundamental and universal determinants of the nature of consciousness. This play seems to suggest that the verbal formation of a character in a play does not necessarily work in the same way as the linguistic formation of subjects in a culture. The spatial orientation of an author's perception of his own subjectivity obviously differs from his perception of the construction of his characters: he perceives himself as "inside" his own body, while he perceives his characters as being shaped from the outside by the language he provides for them to speak. A playwright who was also an actor would have yet another experience of the spatiality of theatrical characterization: he might feel confined by having to speak words written by another, and, as Meredith Skura has traced from a psychoanalytic perspective,

he might feel both dangerously exposed and safely contained within the
"wooden O" of the public theater stage.[27]

Thus, although theatrical characters are constructed by language
through a process resembling the Lacanian formation of the subject by
the symbolic order (or the related Althusserian process of interpellation),
human subjects both shape and are shaped by language. According to
cognitive theory, language is both innate and learned. As we have seen, it
is not an external symbolic system imposed on a child by parents and
teachers; instead, it is built *on* innate syntactic capacities and constraints
and builds *up* meaning based on experiences of living in the body in a
given culture. Language does, of course, carry cultural imperatives, but it
reflects traces of physiological imperative as well. In *The Comedy of Errors* Shakespeare explores the resemblances and, just as important, the
disjunctions between theatrical characters and early modern subjects, creating characters who seem at times almost to parody cultural processes
of subject formation. In this play, concepts of home and self are explored
from a distanced perspective, a distance produced by his experiences of
the material conditions of playhouse, stage, and theatrical practice as they
both resemble and contrast the experiences of living in a home and developing an embodied self-consciousness.

To the extent that characters are created by the words they speak, the
characters in *The Comedy of Errors* are shaped particularly by their almost obsessive references to their placement in society, in "house,"
"home," and, as a defining opposite of home, the "mart."[28] In the late
sixteenth century all of these words were undergoing shifts in their semantic registers that can be broadly linked to larger social changes but were
also motivated or structured by extension from basic spatial schemas.
These words all represent a particular kind of semantic change, undergoing what might be described as a prototype shift since the changes in
meaning seem to have been produced by an alteration in what most speakers would consider to be the prototypical example of a house or a home.
Although some linguists would not consider a prototype shift of this kind
to constitute real change in meaning, cognitive theorists, as we have seen,
argue that the meanings of words form complex webs, being linked together by associational chains and structured by prototype effects, and
thus they would recognize a shift of this kind.[29] For many speakers of
American English today, for instance, *home* would probably have as its
prototype a suburban house containing married heterosexual parents
with two children; but the web of possible meanings would include
"homes" for the aged and mentally ill, a "home" country, city, or state,
"home" plate in baseball, a "homepage" on the Internet, and many other
examples, including the knowledge that families and family homes do

not always resemble the prototypical example. Indeed, as conservative politicians attest, the last twenty years have seen a significant shift in expectation about the nature of the prototypical family that can define a "home."

The period when *The Comedy of Errors* was written was also a time of changing expectations about what might constitute a prototypical home or house. In this period the words *house* and *home* were changing in ways that can be clearly tied to the now-familiar narrative of the construction of the bourgeois individual. Generally speaking, the prototypical house shifted from a place of business that also housed a family to a private residence. Between 1570 and 1640 the structure of English houses at all levels of society changed dramatically. Peasant dwellings, which had housed people and animals under one roof and human inhabitants in a single open room, changed to a separate house and barn and included a loft for storage and sleeping. The homes of more wealthy people began to substitute private dining spaces for great halls and to include smaller spaces like studies and closets. In Lena Cowen Orlin's words, these changes generally provided "a higher standard of living, increased physical comfort, more individual privacy, the segregation of laboring and domestic life, and more household spaces, each with specialized functions."[30] During this period, then, the visual image of a prototypical house would have changed significantly.

A change in material culture thus caused conceptual change, which motivated linguistic change. Under a more strictly feudal system, for example, a *householder* was a man who had achieved the freedom of his guild and thus the right to establish his own household shop, which consisted of family, servants, and apprentices for whom he was responsible. In this context, *house* refers to an urban dwelling, usually with a shop and workshop on the ground floor, a vault for storage beneath, and living areas located on one or two floors above.[31] Such households were the central unit of urban production under feudalism and represented the means by which guild regulations affected not just "free" adult males, but also the women, children, servants, and apprentices placed under their jurisdiction.[32] In the late sixteenth century, however, *householder* came to mean anyone who was, in the modern sense, a "head of household," still responsible for its varied inhabitants but no longer necessarily tied to the guild hierarchy and its regulations.[33] This shift in usage reflects a change from viewing a house as an economic unit to viewing it as essentially a place for private domestic life apart from work. Advice and marriage manuals proliferated to provide guidance for the control of this "new" version of home, as a domestic space still but often including servants and nonfamily members and, in the absence of the guild structure, in need of new and more personal forms of regulation.[34]

The role and status of women within both upper- and working-class households was also changing as the nature of the households themselves altered. Lawrence Stone and others have argued that women in this period lost power and autonomy both within their households and outside them.[35] Both upper- and lower-class women experienced a redefinition of their relation to "work" and to the home: "The role of the former is defined by her status as psychological helpmeet to her husband and mother to her children; her work in the household is not considered real because it does not directly contribute to capitalist production. The lower-class woman's work also becomes increasingly invisible during this period" as production moved outside households into essentially male public spaces.[36] Indeed, Alice Friedman has shown how upper-class women in this period often led lives that were "dull" and "confined."[37] With little domestic responsibility, limited freedom of mobility even within their husbands' great country houses, and uncertain financial security due to changes in inheritance and dowry laws, "the position of upper-class women was clearly in transition."[38]

These changes may be reflected in the curiously double meaning of the word *housewife* or *huswife*, which originally meant "a woman (usually a married woman) who manages or directs the affairs of her household . . . a woman who manages her household with skill and thrift" but in the late sixteenth century also came to mean its opposite: "a light, worthless or pert woman or girl" (now *hussy*).[39] The temporary lessening of women's control over the domestic sphere may have made the laudatory sense of the word less applicable, while (as we shall see in moralistic tracts from the period) anxiety over women's changing roles made the term of opprobrium a useful tool of control. Interestingly, the correlative term *husband*, which originally meant "the male head of a household," usually a small farmer who held his land by freehold, did not take on a pejorative sense in this period but shifted to mean generally either "a man joined in marriage to a woman" (a correlative of *wife*, not *housewife*) or "one who tills or cultivates the soil." Interestingly, too, *The Comedy of Errors* plays repeatedly on *husband* but does not use *huswife* at all, relying instead on *minion* and *harlot*, which were themselves part of a pattern of semantic shift whereby insulting (or neutral) terms applied originally to males or to both sexes came, in the early modern period, to be directed primarily against women.[40]

This period also marked a decline in the direct regulatory influence of religious "houses" over domestic households. Catherine Belsey has argued that the "transition to the liberal-humanist family" in this period marked the beginning of "a mechanism of regulation more far-reaching but less visible than the repressive ecclesiastical courts."[41] Although church courts still tried and punished various domestic offenses, the

breakdown of religious consensus necessarily lessened the moral authority of the church.[42] Indeed, the dissolution of religious "houses" beginning
under Henry VIII made available lands with which the monarch could
reward rising "new men" in his service with suitable homes. In addition,
as Lena Orlin has noted, the destruction of monastic buildings provided
a store of materials such as "worked stone and timber as well as roof
and paving tiles," and the "sheer quantity of newly available resources"
encouraged the trend of rebuilding, improving, and enlarging domestic
houses. The new secular householders retained their courtly orientation
and, as moralists and political commentators lamented, did not ade-
quately observe the charitable, ceremonial, and regulatory responsibilities
accruing to manorial households under feudalism.[43] Building materials
gleaned from former monasteries allowed the renovation of old manor
houses, replacing large great halls for public meals with newly fashionable
private dining chambers. At the same time, as we will see later in more
detail, new "houses on purpose built" for theatrical performances threatened to lure householders away from religious houses, and apprentices
from their work in mercantile households. Critics of the playhouses also
complained that these structures removed performance from the regulated patronage system of noble households and transformed it into a
dangerously volatile public market.[44]

   Home had for several centuries been shifting its prototypical meaning
from the household, village, or town of a person's origin to simultaneously larger and smaller units of nation and individual domestic household. In the late sixteenth century a sense of national identity seems to
have developed and intensified in the wake of Tudor centralization and
alongside increased mercantile contact with other countries.[45] Significantly, the *OED* cites Shakespeare (in *King John* and *All's Well*, but I
would add *Comedy of Errors*) as among the first to use *home* in this
newer sense of nationality. Although *home* had ceased to mean primarily
"village" or "estate" in the Middle English period, it continued to narrow
its emphasis from the full (economic) household to the nuclear family.
Thus, as the role of kinship bonds and extended family decreased as a
determinant of identity, *home* seems to have shifted from meaning primarily a village cluster of related families to meaning both smaller (individual
household) and larger (national) units.[46]

   Mart, which is important in this play as defining an opposite of *home*,
was originally used to describe trade fairs held in the Netherlands. It came
to describe such fairs held even in other countries and in this play was
extended for the first time to mean "marketplace," in the sense of the
regular and regulated space where goods were bought and sold on certain
days of the week. *Market*, of course, as Jean-Christophe Agnew has
shown, changed even more significantly around this time from delineating

a place for selling to describing "acts of both buying and selling, regardless of locale, and to the price or exchange value of goods and services. . . .
By thus revealing the gradual separation of a market *process* from the
particularity of a market *place*, etymology makes its own modest contri-
bution to the critique of political economy; that is, it traces out, as a
matter of popular idiom, a critical transformation in the productive and
distributive relations of early modern England."[47] In choosing *mart* rather
than *market* this play perhaps signals a desire to reterritorialize and rereg-
ulate the marketplace.

On one level, *The Comedy of Errors* seems to depict a simple thematiza-
tion of the changing conceptions of home and self in the period, illustrating what might appear to be an Althusserian process of interpellation as
each important character literally "speaks" a different conception of
home and each version of home seems to be the originary site of a different
kind of self. The conflicts in the play could be read as a conflict between
these different theories of the social contexts for subjectivity, and the
comic resolution adjudicates, if abruptly and not quite satisfactorily, between them.[48] Although it is possible, initially, to see within the play a
narrative progression toward more "modern" ideas about subjectivity,
further examination reveals that narrative to be complicated by the persistence of older forms of selfhood, by characters' resistance to newer forms,
by an almost uncanny prescience about the disadvantages of individualism, and by awareness of the role of the public theater itself in constructing and representing the private subject. Although the linear plot
structure of the play accords with the trajectory of a historical narrative
about changing forms of domesticity and subjectivity, alternate insights
about the formation of subjectivity emerge from the spatial structures and
images that inflect the meanings of *house*, *home*, and related words in
this play. All of the characters' concepts of home and self can be linked
to experiences of space, which are more multiple and ambivalent than
historically produced discursive formations.[49]

The opening clash between the Duke of Ephesus and Egeon of Syracuse
introduces the first competing definitions of home. The Duke reflects the
burgeoning nationalism of early modern Europe and seems primarily to
define *home* in its newer sense, as "native land." He asks Egeon "why
thou departedst from thy native home" (1.1.29) to enter a foreign state.
For the Duke, the defining fact about an individual is his home state,
whether he is "born at Ephesus" or "Syracusian born" (1.1.16, 18). In
his desire to regulate the balance of trade between these rival states, he
attempts strictly to control the relatively open space of "Syracusian marts
and fairs" (1.1.17). Of course, as *market* shifts in meaning from an easily
regulated place to a vaguer, more elusive function, it becomes harder to
maintain control, especially on a stage space delineated by a "mart" on

one side and a "bay" (offering easy access to any foreigner) on the other. The play bears this out in the confusion occasioned by the unregulated and unplaced sale of the gold chain.[50] Thus, the penalty for foreign infringement on the Ephesian home mart is either a stiff fine or death.

Egeon, on the other hand, has the more cosmopolitan view that was becoming prevalent in England toward the end of the Tudor period. The power and status of the guilds, which represented a highly regulated market tied to households, began their long decline in the face of the increasing attractions of foreign trade. By the late sixteenth century it had become possible for merchants to make a fortune, rather than just a modest living, by engaging in the import and export of goods. The speech headings of the folio text identify Egeon not by name but as "merchant" even though he is present in Ephesus, not to engage in any commercial transactions, but simply to search for his missing sons. This persistent identification underscores the importance of mercantile cosmopolitanism in constructing his identity.[51]

As a result, Egeon seems to view "home" as a potentially dangerous and constricting space—whether it refers to nationality or a fixed household. He seems to attribute the loss of his family to his wife's narrower definition of the word. They set out on their fatal journey because his wife, having given birth to twin sons while accompanying her husband on one of his "prosperous voyages" to Epidamium, becomes anxious to return to Syracuse:

> My wife, not meanly proud of two such boys,
> Made daily motions for our home return:
> Unwilling I agreed
>
> (1.1.58–60)

When the mast to which the family is clinging is split and they are picked up by different ships, their final separation is described as the "homeward" (1.1.117) turning of one of the ships. Indeed, Egeon is in his present fix (under penalty of death for infringing Ephesian space) because in the process of "coasting homeward" (1.1.134) on his search for his missing son he has ventured into Ephesus. Although Egeon expresses some desire to be reunited with his missing family, he does not associated this desire with a longing for "home" in any positive sense. It is not surprising that he is in conflict with the Duke, whose desperate need to fix and control "home" and "mart" are in strong contrast with his own essential homelessness.

His twin sons, the two Antipholi, and their families are also delineated (and distinguished) by different views of home. Antipholus of Syracuse (the son who grew up with his father and has set out to find his lost brother) holds initially to the paradigm of kinship as a determinant of

home and self. He feels that without his family (defined as his brother
and mother) he lacks both home and self:

> I to the world am like a drop of water,
> That in the ocean seeks another drop,
> Who, falling there to find his fellow forth
> (Unseen, inquisitive), confounds himself.
> So I, to find a mother and a brother,
> In quest of them (unhappy), ah, lose myself.
>
>   (1.2.34–40)

Like Damasio's anosognosiacs, Antipholus seems to lack a sense of his
skin as a visceral boundary of a body within which consciousness is safely
contained.[52] This Antipholus experiences home and identity without the
ties of kinship as insubstantial, boundless, and frighteningly unstable. It
is no surprise that having grown up with his father's peripatetic homelessness, he describes lack of identity as a radically deterritorialized ocean
voyage. So powerful is the spatial analogy between home and body for
this Antipholus that he seems to feel that without a nurturing familial
home, he lacks a substantial, material body to contain his "self."

This Antipholus does not, however, embrace his selfless state. He experiences it as threatening and longs to recreate his family, presciently identifying it as a potential source of the "individual identity" he lacks (in the
sense that ego psychology looks to early family relations as the source of
the individual's psychic profile or that a cognitive theorist like Gerald
Edelman posits higher consciousness that "depends upon building a self
through affective intersubjective exchanges").[53] When it seems to him that
the constitutive ties of kinship cannot be recreated, as they increasingly
could not be in the early modern period, when dislocations and urbaniza-
tion separated individuals from extended family, he is willing to settle for
the emerging paradigm of companionate marriage.[54] He fixes on Luciana,
the sister-in-law of his twin brother, and links his love and "homage"
(with a pun on *home*) to her ability to create for him both home and
identity: "Spread o'er the silver waves thy golden hairs, / And as a [bed] I'll
take [them], and there lie" (3.2.48–49). Here the threatening emptiness of
the ocean is transformed into a cozy bed through a companionate relationship. Lacking a childhood home in which to develop an inner life,
Antipholus nevertheless manages to secure one when he hits upon the
kind of focused, heterosexual relationship to which (again, according to
ego psychology) a secure family life is supposed to lead.

Adriana, the wife of the other Antipholus, sees an intimate and companionate domestic relationship as the necessary basis for her own selfhood. She mirrors S. Antipholus's water image in describing her sense of
herself as lacking an individual body boundary, while she and her husband together form some sort of combined self:

undividable, incorporate,

. . . .

. . . as easy mayst thou fall
A drop of water in the breaking gulf,
And take unmingled thence that drop again,
Without addition or diminishing,
As take me from thyself and not me too.

(2.2.122–29)

She is obsessed with his dinner plans and clearly associates the domestic bond of the shared meal at home with their sexual intimacy and thus with their shared selfhood. Her sister, on the other hand, believes that a man's place is not in the home: "their business still lies out a' door" (2.1.11). She argues that a man's business is in the mart, and what he does there is not the business of his wife, who should wait at home for him to return.

Antipholus of Ephesus seems to agree with Luciana, rejects his own wife's passionate desire for a truly companionate marriage, and defines himself and his home through his possessions and his place in the community. His home is always "my house" (5.1.234), "my wife and house" (3.1.9), "the house I owe" (3.2.42), or "mine own doors" (3.1.120), and he married his wife not out of love but to cement his place in society. He has evidently felt no longings for his lost family, and it never occurs to him that his uncanny double might be his lost twin. Antipholus of Ephesus avoids his wife's version of an intimate domestic "home," and it comes to be experienced by him literally as a prison:

Then all together,
They fell upon me, bound me, bore me thence,
And in a dark and dankish vault at home
There left me and my man, both bound together

(5.1.246–49)

The repetition here of *home* and *bound* picks up a pervasive imagery, associated in the play with this Antipholus, of ropes and golden chains, ownership and bondage.[55] Indeed, proximate repetitions of *house, bond, bondman,* and *husband* (e.g., at 5.1.287–341) seem to imply a false etymology for *husband* as one "bound to a house." In fact, *band* is derived from OE through ON *bondi,* past participle of *dwell.* Its initial meaning implied the opposite of bondage; a husband was a free head of household who did not owe service to a lord.

Antipholus of Ephesus, his wife, and her sister Luciana all strongly contrast the "mart," his place of business, with "home," just as an early exchange between Antipholus of Syracuse and Dromio of Ephesus contrasts "marks," or money, and "home." There, Antipholus of Syracuse clings to the money that he, as a "stranger," needs to procure a temporary

home, while Dromio represents the claims of a more permanent household. Indeed, in that exchange, "marks" in the sense of disciplinary beating becomes a kind of fulcrum between money and home, as Antipholus
seeks to create a home and identity for himself by asserting mastery over
his portable household (consisting of Dromio and his money).[56] Here he
has something in common with his brother and sister-in-law, who also
use violence against their servant to assert a fragile sense of identity as
"master" and "mistress" (just as the Duke uses violence to regulate his
home "mart").[57]

According to this reading of the play, then, each character can be seen
to locate him- or herself differently along the spectrum of cultural possibilities for delineating a sense of home and self, ranging from nationality
to kinship to nuclear family, involving social ties, personal ties, or a sense
of an inner self. Language in this instance might seem to be working according to a Lacanian or Althusserian paradigm, constructing subjects as
they name their relations to home and family. To a certain extent this
rubric could be used to argue, as many critics have, that the play in the
end delineates a more "modern" sense of self and its place in culture and
that language begins to interpellate subjects as "bourgeois individuals."
Thus, the Abbess repudiates Antipholus's sense that home, marriage, and
selfhood are confining containers when she recognizes the imprisoned
Egeon as her long-lost husband and describes a version of marriage that
is liberating or at least offers a kind of liberation in bondage: "Whoever
bound him, I will loose his bonds, / And gain a husband by his liberty"
(5.1.340–41). Egeon's cosmopolitan mercantilism seems to win out over
the Duke's exclusionary nationalism, and while the claims of companionate marriage are qualified, they are to some extent upheld. Nevertheless,
the radical separation of work and home espoused by Antipholus of Ephesus is also upheld, as it would be increasingly in the modern world.

There are, however, other signs that the play does not espouse what we
might think of as more "modern" theories of the self-contained, stable
individual and in fact clearly complicates its representation of home and
self in several important ways. Barbara Freedman has pointed out some
of the ways in which the play uses the uncanny to imply that "identity
and meaning can never be stable."[58] The play, she argues, "requires a
more dynamic and dramatic model of reading based on the progression
of the subject in relation to its discourse—a model of reading based on
decentering and positionality, on splitting and attempting to recuperate
that loss" (110). A cognitive reading of the play also explores "the progression of the subject in relation to its discourse" but, unlike Freedman's
Lacanian reading, does not assume that "decentering," "splitting," and
"loss" are the only conditions of subject formation. I want to focus on
the ways in which language, in this case through the shifting senses of

house and *home*, offers a range of spatial possibilities for imagining the self as variously split and integrated, constructed from without and formed from within.

Despite their radically different conceptions of home and self, the twin brothers are, as Freedman emphasizes, in many ways indistinguishable, even at the end of the play. The folio text notoriously confuses them, since Antipholus of Syracuse (in modern usage, S. Antipholus) was originally called Antipholus Erotes, while the Ephesian brother (E. Antipholus) was, after Plautine usage, called Antipholus Sereptus (i.e., also S. Antipholus). The folio text confusingly uses "S. Ant." sometimes to mean the Syracusan Antipholus and sometimes to mean his brother, Antipholus Sereptus. Although earlier textual critics took this confusion as an indication that the play was printed directly from Shakespeare's "foul papers," and thus as a sign of authorial presence and control, de Grazia and Stallybrass would, of course, take this nominal instability in the text as a sign of a basic instability and indistinguishability of character. In this sense, the Syracusan Antipholus's longing for a unique and stable inner self is defeated by a text that conflates him with a brother who has no such longings and thus removes even the illusion of such a self.[59] On the other hand, it is important to remember that the twin brothers could not be "doubled" in performance and would thus (in the absence of identical twin actors) appear to be distinct onstage. In fact, the humor of the play depends in part on the ability of the audience to perceive the Antipholi as separate individuals and to tell them apart.

Adriana's desire for a self actualized in an intimate companionate marriage is also problematic. Although in this she might seem to resemble the Syracusan Antipholus in longing for a more modern version of home and inner self, both her sister and the Abbess argue forcefully that her expectations are unrealistic and against the dictates of hierarchy. Indeed, a more satisfactory conclusion to the play might pair her with her brother-in-law, who shares her longing for companionate marriage and also uses similar imagery (the water drop) to describe it. Since she is already "bound" to his less suitable twin, the play may be suggesting that the bond of companionate marriage involves a foreclosure of possibilities. Her own language in fact suggests uncertainty about the possibility of developing a self through an intimate relationship with her husband. She several times uses the word *homage* to refer to what she believes her husband owes her. *Homage,* of course, originated as a term in feudal law meaning "the formal and public acknowledgment of allegiance, wherein a tenant or vassal declared himself the man of the king or the lord of whom he held, and bound himself to his service" (*OED*). The term had broadened as early as the fourteenth century, especially in contexts of courtly love, to mean "reverence, dutiful respect, or honor shown." But the institutional mean-

ing of this word is appropriate in the context of the marriage of Antipholus and Adriana since, as we learn in act 5, she has actually been given to
her husband, presumably along with her substantial property—her sister
believes Antipholus married her for her "wealth"—as a reward for military service: "Long since thy husband serv'd me in my wars" (5.1.161);
"She whom thou gav'st to me to be my wife" (5.1.198). The contiguity
of the word *homage* with her repetitions of *home* suggests a play on the
similar sounds of these words, even though they are not etymologically
related. This suggests that in a deeper sense she views her home (and
herself) as requiring homage rather than intimate reciprocity.

In another revealing pun, Adriana claims that while her husband has
been pursuing his interests and business in the mart, she has become
"homely" (2.1.89) as a result of staying within the domestic sphere. Here
the word *homely* seems to retain its original meaning (suggesting plain
but cozy domesticity) but also to shade over into its more pejorative modern sense (plain and ugly). Thus, doubts about the kind of self to be constructed within an intimate domestic space seem to surface even as she
longs for it. When taken in conjunction with her radical separation of
"mart," or place of business and home, her homeliness may indicate a
sense of loss attendant upon the removal of business from the home and
women's loss of a role in the marketplace. It may also signal a new concern in this period to keep women confined within the home, as new
spaces (playhouses in particular) were opening to them.[60] The shift in
meaning of *homely* seems related to that of *huswife*, both indicating the
changing status of women within the home in this period and revealing a
kind of cultural double bind: a woman is "homely" if she remains within
the home and a "hussy" if she ventures outside it.

Adriana's husband, Antipholus of Ephesus, does not share his wife's
confused longing for an inner self and an intimate family life and seems on
the surface to be wholly content with his externally constructed identity.
However, the threats to that identity occasioned by the arrival of his twin
can also be seen as outward manifestations of threats already immanent
in his position, which seems strangely constructed through different and
conflicting systems. Despite Antipholus's reliance on his role in the mart
as a source of identity, for example, we never learn precisely what he does
for a living. Unlike his father (or Balthazar, or the other merchants in the
play), he is never explicitly identified as a merchant, although this would
be the most likely occupation for a foreigner who so radically dissociates
his home and his occupation. And yet, as editors of the play almost universally note, Antipholus's home is named the Phoenix because, like many
houses in late-sixteenth-century London, it is considered to be also a place
of business.[61] There is no evidence in the play that any business is being
carried out there—indeed, both Antipholus and Adriana radically sepa-

rate "home" and "mart"—and yet the name would suggest that Antipholus is a "householder" in the older sense implying guild membership.

On the other hand, although his house seems to contain a dining chamber on its (imaginary) upper floor ("Husband, I'll dine above with you today" [2.2.207]), we never learn anything about a shop or other commercial space on its ground floor. Antipholus's household seems to consist of his wife, his sister-in-law, seven female servants, and a male "slave" or "bondman." Although the configuration of this household and other domestic details are, of course, partly derived from Shakespeare's classical source, elements of contemporary English social structures emerge, if only in the language. Although the presence of Luciana and the servants would be typical of an urban household in the period, the absence of apprentices, and the presence of a "bondman" (a term usually applied to a dependent agricultural worker, a "villain" or "serf," rather than to a domestic servant) would not be.

There are in fact indications in the play that Antipholus's social position is also determined in relation to a quasi-feudal rather than mercantile or emerging capitalist economy. We learn at the end of the play that his place in Ephesian society is actually a result of a quasi-feudal bond: the Duke granted him a rich wife and home because he "serv'd me in my wars" (5.1.161). As we have seen, his wife several times refers to his failure to pay "homage" to her, a term suggesting feudal allegiance but, as used by her, also punning on her desire to make an intimate domestic "home." She also seems to see his role as "husband" as at least partly related to the agricultural sense of that word: "Thou art an elm, my husband, I a vine," while any "usurping ivy, brier, or idle moss" deserves "pruning" (2.2.174–79). Here he seems to be her "husband" in the sense that he is bound to her and his home through his bond with the Duke, a meaning at odds with the sense of a free "husband" in charge of his own "bondman" retainer. Under a feudal arrangement of the first kind, or, indeed, under the terms of "householding" through a guild, Antipholus would not "own" his house; he would "hold" it under the terms of either a lease or feudal tenure of some kind.[62] Thus, the ownership so important to him as an indicator of identity may be illusory, while the bonds of society he would eschew are an integral (but contradictory) part of his identity as "husband."

When this Antipholus is forced to descend into the "dark and dankish vault at home" in order to recognize and exorcise the "Sathan, hous'd within" himself, he is offered an opportunity to supplement his shifting and uncertain role in society with a psychologically complex inner self. The metaphoric mapping of house onto self here reflects the sense, evident in the domestic-advice books cited above, that a new kind of home could nurture a new kind of subject. However, Antipholus resists the development of bourgeois individualism as fervently as any late-twentieth-century Marxist critic. Unlike his brother, he seems unaware of and unwilling to participate in the cultural changes that would have him internalize the determinants of selfhood that had previously (for him) been external. The "dark and dankish vault" (5.1.248) and the "Sathan hous'd within" (4.4.54) might both be read as metaphors for the unconscious mind, and Antipholus resists not only this Freudian self but also his would-be analyst (Dr. Pinch) and the conditions of family life that would create such a self for analysis. Antipholus experiences a different emotional reaction to the related spatial paradigms of domestic container for the body and the body itself as it is imagined to house a complex inner life, responding with profound claustrophobia, revulsion, and violence:

> My master and his man are both broke loose,
> Beaten the maids a-row, and bound the doctor,
> Whose beard they have sing'd off with brands of fire,
> And ever as it blaz'd, they threw on him
> Great pails of puddled mire to quench the hair;
> My master preaches patience to him, and the while
> His man with scissors nicks him like a fool;
> And sure (unless you send some present help)
> Between them they will kill the conjurer.
>
>   (5.1.169–77)

As he so clearly rejects this attempt at forced domestication, his desires are in conflict with those of his wife, who wants to create herself entirely in a domestic context and seems, with slight misgivings, to welcome the version of subjectivity that it would bring.

The conclusion of the play similarly complicates what might have seemed to be its forward drive toward the development of modern homes housing characters with complex inner lives. The resolution of the errors occasioned by the characters' conflicting views is achieved not by any kind of inner growth or change on the part of the characters, nor is it facilitated by the power of the state. Instead, a figure of religious authority, a celibate mother who has lived in a religious "house" rather than a family home for thirty years, adjudicates between the rival claims of Antipholus and his wife, and Egeon and the Duke.[63] As noted previously, she speaks against companionate marriage and in favor of the ties of hereditary kinship. Thus she seems to assert in a retrograde way values and social conditions that were becoming obsolete. The final "gossip's feast" could be seen by Harold Brooks as unproblematically uniting elements of church, state, and family as determinants of identity: "The gossips' or baptismal feast affirms relationship and identity: the kin are united, the Duke is patron, all are friends and godparents, witnesses to the new identities truly established and christened into the family and community."[64] It is strange, however, that the final feast of the play does not take place in either home or inn (two poles of domesticity and commerce that have been in conflict throughout) but rather in an abbey. And since the play has shown forces of church, state, kin, market, nationality, and household to exert conflicting pressures on subjectivity, it seems unlikely that a single dinner could provide much more than a tenuous and symbolic resolution of that conflict.[65]

If certain words in the play are central to its depiction of a range of possibilities for the formation and location of the self, there is another material constituent of the play that similarly complicates its representation of house, home, and character. The nature of the stage—its physical construction and the way in which domestic scenes are located on it—also participates in the exploration here of the spatiality of the self. However, as in the case of other kinds of material evidence about Shakespearean texts, *The Comedy of Errors* seems to reflect complex and contradictory staging practices. Critical speculation over the years about the staging of this play reveals how little we actually know for sure about the material structures and practices related to any of the multiple staging venues that were possible in early modern England. It seems possible, however, that the text of *The Comedy of Errors* as we have it reflects mixed provenance, for it contains traces of at least two performances: an unrecorded earlier performance in a public theater as well as a private performance on 28 December 1594 at Gray's Inn. Such flexibility is by no means unique to this play. Andrew Gurr has emphasized that most plays had to be adaptable to different conditions for staging: "Throughout the Shakespearean era companies retained the capacity at the end of an afternoon's playing to take their plays off to a nobleman's house or to Court and play again there with no more aids to performance than the arena itself and what they could carry to it."[66] However, the critical controversy surrounding the staging of this play also reveals how staging practices affect the representation of character: if the play itself reveals how different homes shape different subjects, critics' desire to imagine particular configurations for the staging of domestic scenes in this play suggests that different stages could shape different kinds of theatrical character. The same spatial concepts (of interiority, containment, and privacy) that inflect Shakespeare's exploration of subject formation in the play are also crucial to thinking about the relationship between particular stages and the construction of characters of different kinds.

Expanding on the ideas of Stallybrass and de Grazia, we might see the mixed provenance reflected in the text of this play as further evidence that its characters are homeless, fragmented, and alienated; they do not even have a single playhouse to call "home." If the different spatial conditions of different stages represent character differently, then an inability to pin the play down to a particular stage home would suggest that its characters are similarly unlocatable. However, the words *house* and *home* are also relevant to issues of staging—in a "playhouse," possibly reflecting academic stagehouses, as well as the Roman comic *domi* (houses); these theatrical senses of the words were also a part of Shakespeare's mental lexicon, his conceptual system. So although the text is clearly fragmented by its need to accommodate several kinds of stage, we can see some level of integration in an internalized lexical system that inescapably puts playhouses, stagehouses, and issues of staging domestic scenes into the conceptual and verbal web that defines house, home, and subject in the text of the play. In a practical sense, the author of a play in this period would be aware of the need to produce a text that could be staged in several different ways as well as of the implications of each space for the representation of character. Thus, although the play would have been split by its physical location on different stages, it was also at least provisionally integrated within Shakespeare's brain by a conceptual system that contained knowledge of possible contemporary stages and their material conditions.

Modern editors of the play have generally argued that *The Comedy of Errors* is unique among Shakespeare's plays in using what Renaissance writers believed to be the conventional setting of Roman comedy. In this set, the rear wall of the stage contained three openings or doorways, called *domi*, meaning "houses." Each *domus* was meant to represent a character's house, and these houses were usually identified by name. In this case, editors have usually followed E. K. Chambers's conclusion that the three doors are labeled as the Priory, the Phoenix (house of Antipholus), and the Porpentine (the Courtesan's house).[67] Some have conjectured that the play uses this Plautine set because it was initially staged in the great hall of Gray's Inn, where an educated audience would have been familiar with the conventions of Roman comic staging and where the openings in the wooden screen at the rear of the hall would have provided a ready-made version of the set.[68] Alan Nelson and others, however, have argued that hall screens (located at the upper end of the hall) were rarely, if ever, used in dramatic productions; instead, stages in academic settings tended to be built at the lower end of the hall, near the dais. These academic stages were usually flanked by boxlike structures called stagehouses, which "provided curtained entrances and exits as well as recessed spaces and raised areas above."[69]

Both of these "older" staging practices (older in the sense that they precede the public theater stage, although both probably continued to be used in private and academic settings) represent, in different ways, the illusion that domestic life is "contained" in a space set apart from the open platform stage. Traditional Plautine "houses" actually have no interior space at all. All action takes place on the street in front of the houses, a space conventionally delineated as bounded by a marketplace on one side and a seaport on the other. The houses themselves simply serve as means of entrance onto or exit from the stage.[70] It makes sense that Roman comic characters have conventionally been described as "one-dimensional" types since they are represented as living in one-dimensional houses. Academic "stagehouses" did constitute a literal interior space, but that space sometimes served as a tiring-house, and thus the "house" itself, like the Roman "house," was principally a stage door. Although characters could sometimes speak briefly from within these houses, no interior actions would be visible to the audience.[71] Thus, in this case too all significant action had to take place outside the house structure. As we have seen, the subjectivity defined and analyzed by ego psychology needs a home and family life for its development. If dramatic characters are represented as living in houses with no interior space, no privacy, and no domestic intimacy, if all of their exchanges must take place in the street and they are seen in the context of their roles within the community (in relation to the market and the seaport), it is no surprise that they have been seen as lacking in depth, with an identity that was "principally a matter of establishing parentage and social class."[72] It is the great misfortune of Antipholus of Ephesus that he has been made to inhabit a different kind of play.

For while *Comedy of Errors* uses this set, it also goes beyond it in ways that have been seen as a movement toward giving its "houses" audible, if not visible, inner space and its characters inner life. Editors have long recognized various staging difficulties in act 3, scene 1, all generally growing out of indications that characters are actually living and speaking inside the Plautine "house." This scene depicts the attempts of Antipholus of Ephesus to gain entrance to his house while his wife, who has locked the door and stationed Dromio of Syracuse as guard, dines with his brother inside. The scene begins conventionally, with Antipholus and his friends in the street outside the house. But as they knock and demand to enter, various characters who are inside the house answer them. The folio text gives the stage directions "Enter Luce" (3.1.47) and "Enter Adriana" (3.1.60), even though they are clearly within the house and thus, at least conventionally, offstage. Modern editors usually amend these to "Enter . . . [within]," but this does not solve the problem, compounded by Dromio's contributions to the conversation from within the house, of how offstage characters could speak so that they would be intelligible to the audience. Foakes cites Dover Wilson as describing this situation as "extremely awkward from the theatrical point of view, since the audience would be greatly puzzled by three unseen characters."[73]

Editors have offered various solutions to this "problem." C. Walter Hodges, for example, has suggested both a doorframe at right angles to the audience so that characters can be visible as they speak on both sides, or, alternatively, a set of three "self-standing 'houses' " placed in the middle of the hall.[74] Characters evidently sometimes spoke from "within" academic stagehouses, so some such structures may have been built for the occasion. The possibility of public stage (rather than private) performance makes the problem more difficult for some: Dorsch "cannot suggest just how the play might have been staged if it had been performed in a public theatre," finally arguing for some form of freestanding "houses" in the center of that stage even though there seem to be no recorded instances of such stagehouse structures on the public stage.[75] Dover Wilson's solution, however, was that despite the probable private performance of the play, the stage directions for this scene were holdovers from a public theater performance, where it could be placed on the so-called inner stage.[76] Although stage historians have long since rejected the theory of an inner stage, Wilson's argument is worth pursuing since the desire for an inner-stage space reveals a great deal about why the staging for this scene has been so problematic to theater historians, as well as what is at stake in this scene and in the spatial depiction of domestic scenes generally on the Elizabethan stage. The issue of private versus public stage performance can be seen to be bound up with the changing boundaries between public and private life in early modern culture.

Richard Southern and John Cranford Adams were among the scholars who advanced and tenaciously defended the idea that the facade of the tiring-house at the rear of the Elizabethan stage contained a large recessed area (23 × 8 ft.) framed by a rudimentary proscenium arch and used to stage almost all of the interior scenes in the plays of that period.[77] Indeed Adams believed that there were two such spaces, the better to reproduce with verisimilitude the interior of a typical London house, which had a shop or public area on the ground floor and bedrooms above. Dover Wilson seemed to accept something like this when he argued that Adriana and Luce were to speak from inside such a space, or perhaps from its upper gallery, while Antipholus and his friends remained without. Nevertheless, there is virtually no evidence—either internal or external—that such a space actually existed or was used to stage domestic scenes.[78]

Adams, however, placed almost all Shakespearean domestic interior scenes in what he called the "chamber," the upper, recessed space that was removed from the open front of the stage both vertically and horizontally. His desire to place such scenes within a space that corresponded to actual urban domestic arrangements suggests a need to imagine Shakespeare's characters as individuals living and developing within real homes.[79] Adams located this home within what Robert Weimann has identified as the hierarchically ordered *locus*, regulated by its associations with throne (royalty), bed (patriarchy), and a "repertoire of signs and significations of the house and household and the power therein of parental authority."[80] Adams's plan of the Globe stage in fact reduced the depth of the open stage, giving more space to the ordered *locus* and less to the dangerously exposed and open *platea*.[81] Also, and Richard Southern especially stressed this, the inner stage was separated from the rest of the stage by a small proscenium arch, marking off domestic interiors as a site of framed, illusionistic theater in which characters representative of rounded "individuals" might well feel at home. An anachronistic desire for privacy also lies behind the inner-stage theory. Although Lawrence Stone and others have argued that a sense of domestic privacy as we know it did not really develop in England until the later seventeenth century, Adams especially seemed uneasy about placing domestic scenes out in the open.[82] Adams preferred that the domestic scenes take place not just in a regulated and illusionistic space but—even in a public theater play—in a private space virtually screened off from public scrutiny. Bedroom scenes predictably cause the most anxiety, and he argued, oddly, that beds were often placed in a passage behind the upper chamber so that the rear curtains of the space constituted bed curtains that could be drawn to screen the bed from the audience's view. Thus, he believed that in the final act of *Othello* "Desdemona's bed was back there, and that the act of smothering her was to that extent shrouded."[83] The audience would be unable to see her murder or the suggestion of marital intimacy (doubly threatening because of the characters' difference in race) implied by their final embrace in death.[84] In countering Adams's theory, C. Walter Hodges perhaps inadvertently reveals what Adams was so nervous about, arguing that beds were not behind the stage but "thrust forward onto it" and that the "thrusting in and out of beds" was common on the Elizabethan stage.[85]

Most scholars now reject the notion of an inner stage and accept Hodges's thrusting beds.[86] The inner stage is now described as a shallow discovery space used only for the staging of brief, silent tableaux. Interior scenes in most Shakespearean plays—*Comedy of Errors* is an interesting exception—are thought to have been most likely located on the open stage, delineated by properties carried on and off in full view of the audience. In *The Comedy of Errors* I believe that we *can* see Shakespeare working out how best to represent characters who manifest the complex interiority that was beginning to be valued as a defining characteristic of the human self. A playwright considering how such characters might be represented on the stage would necessarily think about selfhood in slightly different ways than someone who was simply taking for granted his own experiences of subjectivity. To some extent, the spatial concepts that are integral to the experience of subjectivity would be reversed: an audience can only see this inner life if both homes and characters are turned inside out. Characters, as Berger so astutely notes, are turned inside out by their construction from outside through language given them by the playwright in order to reveal nonexistent inner states; appropriately, these characters must live in "homes" that have no real interior. In *The Comedy of Errors* Shakespeare is still working out the spatiality of domestic scenes in relation to the spatiality of homes in early modern England. As increasingly private homes produced increasingly "inward"-looking selves, public playhouses began to open out even the most private experiences of home and self for audiences to see. Ironically, this public representation of fictional "outward" characters was a constituent part of the new emphasis on the inner self.

In subsequent plays by Shakespeare, then, domestic scenes were relatively exposed, lacking the illusionistic frame of the proscenium arch, thus, as Barbara Freedman has suggested, "subverting the truth of any private, individual, or fixed vantage point on the action or characters."[87] Steven Mullaney has discussed the location of the playhouses themselves in the "Liberties," an area outside the walls of London proper not subject to regulation by city ordinances and thus the home of brothels, bear-baiting pits, and theaters. Mullaney describes the Liberties as "an ambiguous realm, a borderland whose legal parameters and privileges were open-ended and equivocally defined," and argues that the placement of theaters here allowed "a different kind of license. . . a freedom to experiment with a wide range of available perspectives on its own times"[88] Similarly, placement of domestic interiors on the open stage, with its multiple perspectives, put the home—and thus the very origin of the individual and its representation in theatrical character—in an ambiguous and equivocal space.

The Comedy of Errors, however, seems located at a transitional point in Shakespeare's movement toward the practice of opening up domestic scenes to public view. The "problems" that modern editors have found in the stage directions for act 3, scene 1, can thus be seen as a function of its representation of domestic scenes as taking place both within the Plautine "house" (or academic stagehouse) and on the open stage in front of it. Paradoxically, the glimmerings of inner life and domestic intimacy imagined for these characters go hand in hand with opening the inside— of the self and of the house—to public view.[89] Rather than depicting a clear and coherent narrative movement toward domestic privacy and bourgeois individualism, this play enacts a more problematic dialectic between public and private, institutional and personal, staged and "real," determinants of subjectivity.

The place of the stage within the lexical and conceptual network defining *house* and *home* was especially complicated since theaters in this period were *both* houses and marts, and although the anxieties attendant upon their role as markets have been traced, their status as unconventional households has been less noted. As Douglas Bruster has shown, the public theaters themselves were markets as well as houses.[90] In the period when the nature of houses and homes was changing, the building of new kinds of "houses," to be the locus of a new kind of household, could occasion great anxiety. As Bruster has noted, antitheatrical tracts of the period cry out against "houses of purpose built with great charges for the maintenance of them, and that without the liberties, as who woulde say, there, let them saye what they will say, we will play."[91] The anxiety seems to have been occasioned in part by elaborate "houses" built specifically for the staging of plays; Thomas White saw these "sumptuous Theatre houses" as "a continuall monument of Londons prodigalitie and folly."[92]

Whereas plays had previously been controlled by the necessity of putting them on in structures already placed within and regulated by social norms, these new "houses" would have no such discursively determined place. Innyards, spaces that were the subject of intense scrutiny by manorial courts concerned about their potential as an alternative to the sanctioned marketplace, were the site of clearly public performances.[93] Performances in private houses were clearly private and were staged in spaces (halls or chambers) that were already marked and controlled by elaborate structures of ceremony and hierarchy.[94] But the newly built playhouse combined aspects of both kinds of performance, mixing elements of public and private, ceremonial and commercial, in ways that existing social structures could not easily accommodate. Richard Hosley has argued that public playhouses combined elements of the baiting house (the roughly circular shape composed of multiple bays with a central, open yard), the innyard (the platform stage) and the great hall of a private house (the tiring-house facade), thus mixing elements of public and private space, low and high status.[95] If, as Hosley argued, the facade of the tiring-house of the public theater stage was modeled on the screened entrance at the rear of the great house hall, the conditions of performance would have differed significantly: in a public theater access to the hall was based on one's being, not a follower or guest of the lord, but a paying customer.[96] On the other hand, if, as Alan Nelson has suggested, the public theater had "a functional antecedent in the stage at the *upper* [or dais] end of the hall, with a gallery behind the stage for noble spectators,"[97] which contributed to the practice of seating prominent persons in a "Lord's Room" over the stage or on the stage itself, the public theater stage would

have been a space with mixed status associations. The ideological implications for the actors traversing this space would thus be extremely complex.

These new playhouses not only contained unruly and unordered households within an ambiguous space but also were seen as posing a threat to
the regulation and containment of more conventional domestic households. First of all, as the antitheatrical tracts suggest, the elaborate playhouses, with their strange households, sent conflicting signals about class
hierarchy. As in the case of Antipholus of Ephesus, elements of feudal
service, guild membership, and entrepreneurial endeavor provided a
mixed context for identity. Originally, troupes of players grew up within
the households of wealthy patrons. Although the role of these players
within the household hierarchy was not as clear as the role of other servants, their status as servants attached to a specific household nevertheless
involved some stability and regulation.[98] Public theater players continued
to wear the livery of household servants of a great patron as protection
from vagrancy laws, but their status as retainers was tenuous. In 1580
one writer complained that players were not "servants" but "Caterpillers
. . . which cannot liue of them selues." Instead, "vnder the title of their
maisters or as reteiners, [they] are priuiledged to roaue abroad." Rather
than serving their masters, their purpose was "to iuggle in good earnest
the monie out of other mens purses into their owne handes."[99] This writer
was clearly concerned that men who appeared to be servants were actually
freed from confinement to their household and also free to engage in commercial endeavors.

Another critic of the theater, Stephen Gosson, criticized the unregulated
household of the theater because of its violation of the semiotics of status:
"Ouerlashing in apparel is so common a fault, that the very hyerlings of
some of our players . . . iet under gentlemens noses in sutes of silke, exer-
cising themselves to prating on the stage, and common scoffing when they
come abrode, where they looke askance over the shoulder at every man,
of whom the Sunday before they begged an almes." He admitted that
some players "are sober, discreete, properly learned honest housholders
and citizens well thought on amonge their neighbours at home," but said
that their own good reputation was destroyed by the servants they could
not control, "those hangebyes whome they succour with stipend."[100] For
Gosson, respectability was tied to one's placement within the network of
regulated households of the city and could be easily destroyed by failure
to discipline servant–apprentice players and to reign them within accepted
norms of class. It seems not to have mattered whether players were "men
of occupations, which they have forsaken to lyve by playing," or had been
"trayned up from theire childehood to this abhominable exercise & now
have no other way to get theire livinge"—in the first case, proper household regulation and education to a trade had been abandoned, and in the

second, it had been perverted. In Gosson's eyes, both versions of the new household would lead to a larger disruption of the body politic: "If priuat men be suffered to forsake theire calling because they desire to walke gentleman like in sattine & veluet, with a buckler at their heeles, proportion is so broken, vnitie dissolued, harmony confounded, that the whole body must be dismembred and the prince or heade cannot chuse but sicken."[101]

Critics of theater were also worried about the potential confusion of playhouses, religious houses, and houses of prostitution—all buildings that contained nonfamilial households but had the potential to influence the conduct of domestic households for good or ill. As long as theatrical performances were allowed on Sundays, there would be concern that "more have recourse to Playing houses, then to Praying houses."[102] In a treatise against "Vaine playes, or Enterluds, with other idle pastimes . . . commonly used on the Sabboth day," John Northbrooke urged that "those places also, whiche are made vppe and builded for such playes and enterludes, as the Theatre and Curtaine . . . should be forbidden, and dissolued, and put downe by authoritie, as the brothell houses and stewes are."[103] The author of *A Second and third blast of retrait from plaies and Theaters* (1580) called playhouses "mere brothel houses of Bauderie," which "bring both the Gospel into slander; the Sabboth into contempt," and have made "of honest women light huswives," once again conflating playhouses with houses of prostitution as a threat to both the religious houses and the proper conduct of "honest women," here threatening to turn them into their opposite, "light huswives," by luring them out of their households.[104]

Playhouses also threatened the order of households because of their paradoxical conflation of public and private. As the adherents of the inner-stage theory revealed, plays were threatening because they represented publicly the intimate moments of domestic life. Such a confusion of public and private was perhaps an endemic feature of a space that mixed elements of public inns and baiting houses and private residences. But theatrical houses could also be dangerous because they lured servants away from their own place in a regulated household into spaces that were more dangerously private—because away from the regulatory household. Thus, although the public nature of plays could be damaging when "under the title of their masters or as reteiners [players] are priuiledged to roave abroad and permitted to publish their mametree in euerie Temple of God, and that through England," some critics thought private performances were worse: "If [dangerous] on a stage, & in open courtes, much more in chambers and priuate houses. For there are manie roumes beside that where the play is, & peraduenture the strangenes of the place, & lacke of light to guide them, causeth errour in their way, more than good Christians should in their houses suffer."[105] Plays "entice seruants out of their maisters houses" but also transform homes into places of sin: "These goodly pageants being done, euery mate sorts to his mate, euery one bringes another homeward of their waye verye freendly, and in their secret conclaues (couertly) they play the *Sodomits*, or worse."[106]

In a period when the nature of the household was changing, the addition of a new kind of "house"—the playhouse—was interrelated with those changes in complex ways. The addition of "playhouse" and "stage-house" to the web of meanings for *house* necessarily would have inflected the whole complex conceptual structure, especially for a playwright and actor who would have lived the experience of this other kind of house every day. Like the household of Antipholus of Ephesus in *The Comedy of Errors*, playhouses in this period represented households that confusingly retained some elements of both feudal and guild households but also violated many of the regulatory mechanisms of both. Players wore livery as retainers but were able to "own" their own house and make a profit.[107] The shareholders in a theatrical company were, after all, termed *housekeepers* because their profit accrued from the receipts of the "house," a term both similar to and different from the guild-sanctioned *householder*.[108] Players were apprenticed in a quasi guild system but had freedom from sumptuary laws and other guild regulations that the "freemen" of London lacked. More dangerously, playhouses represented a rival to the religious houses, which shored up and regulated the conduct of domestic households, although with decreasing effectiveness. Playhouses were viewed as luring the inhabitants of such households into a space that was threatening both because it was public (exposing them to evil influences and disease) and because of its perceived power to transform private behavior (by opening actions that should be private to public view).

It is not surprising, then, that Shakespeare's *Comedy of Errors* represents houses and homes in such complex and contradictory ways. It shows us characters that are being shaped within widely different concepts of home. It does not show a clear movement "forward" to a unified individual subjectivity nurtured within an intimate and private domestic space. Instead, it shows a web of contradictory possibilities that are articulated through discourses of feudal law, nationalism, guild regulation, and theatrical practice but also through a spatially structured language of personal feelings and desires. Characters are shaped largely by the institutional parameters of their language, but the playwright seems to have been able to imagine different combinations and implications of house and home. This limited agency was possible in part because the playhouse was itself recognized as a kind of house, not simply a place in which to represent the changing nature of home and subject but an alternate home intimately involved in the changes that were taking place. As a denizen of that new "house," a playwright, constrained of course by its collective nature as well as by the cultural parameters of language, nevertheless had the power to conceive a text that gave full play to the complex web of concepts and associations he called "home." He might also imagine the spatial orientation of the self from a different perspective—not just as an individual with an inner self nurtured in a private home but as the creator of fictional selves, constructed by language, living in fictional homes that were, like the characters themselves, literally turned inside out for public display. In *The Comedy of Errors* we can trace the limited freedom that the playwright claimed both for his characters and for himself as he constructed them out of existing materials in a complex relation to both ideology and physiology.

Freud's essay on the uncanny offers an uncanny commentary on the issues discussed in this chapter. Freud, like Shakespeare in *The Comedy of Errors*, locates a complex etymology centered on usages of the word *home* at the center of his theories of subject formation. The German word that we translate as "uncanny" is, of course, *unheimlich*, literally "unhomely." As Freud says, "The uncanny [*unheimlich*] is something which is secretly familiar [*heimlich heimisch*], which has undergone repression and returned from it." He goes on to argue that the *heimlich* and the *unheimlich* are closely related, that what is familiar and "homely" to us is always the scene of the repressed memories that haunt us in the form of the uncanny.[109] Barbara Freedman uses Lacan and film theory to argue that the effect of theater is based in the uncanny: "The appeal of theater thus depends upon an uncanny awareness of a fundamental loss in relation to the mirror image through which subjectivity is procured."[110] Cognitive theory, as we have seen, problematizes the visual basis of subjectivity and also its implication in loss. In this sense, theater is uncanny because it seems to represent human experience but can only do so by turning it inside out. Cognitive theory might also see the uncanny as involving not just the return of the repressed but also a coming into awareness of the hidden links of the lexical web or of the preverbal spatial conceptions of the self. *The Comedy of Errors*, then, might also seem uncanny (as it has to so many critics) because of its structural basis in the usually unconscious web of verbal and spatial associations that define house, home, and subject. It can be seen as a function of cognition as well as psychology that both Shakespeare in this play (through the character Adriana) and Freud in his essay use a form of the word *homely* to express the idea that an intimate domestic home is always both a nurturing source of identity and a stifling container for it. In this play, Shakespeare, from the perspective of the theater, sees into the private spaces of home and self and opens them both to public view. That openness offers both liberation and disintegration. Shakespeare's earliest play, then, represents neither "flat" farce characters, "rounded" modern characters, nor fragmented modern subjects: its meditation on all these and other possible felt experiences of the self is perhaps more interesting to contemplate because of its uncertainty.

2

Theatrical Practice and the Ideologies of Status in *As You Like It*

IN *As You Like It*, even more directly than in *The Comedy of Errors*, Shakespeare explores the relationships between theater, language, and ideology in the formation of early modern subjectivity. In *As You Like It* Shakespeare seems to be interested in words that are directly implicated in the mediation of ideological structures, in Marxist terms, in the "reproduction of the conditions of production,"specifically the shift from feudal to capitalist ideologies of social mobility and status hierarchy.[1] In this play, as in *The Comedy of Errors*, the material practices of theatrical production are an integral part of the lexical web on which Shakespeare's attention seems focused. Here Shakespeare seems fascinated by the changing connotations of the words *villain* and *clown*, especially as they are inflected by the possibilities for upward or downward mobility within a theatrical company. Although most critics have seen this play as clearly working to reproduce the currently dominant ideologies of limited mobility and social hierarchy, I find that its relation to those ideologies is actually uneven and at times problematic.

Cognitive theory might seem initially to support this current critical orthodoxy since it suggests that the concept of hierarchy and a sense that it is better to be up than down are based in early image schemas and are therefore powerful discursive formations in most cultures because of their grounding in fundamental mental structures.[2] Certainly this play seems especially focused on forms of social hierarchy in a range of cultural settings. However, Shakespeare's interest in the ways words can work to shore up hierarchical discursive structures seems to be shaped significantly by feelings of anger, sympathy, and regret. In this play the issue of authorial agency is directly addressed, but this too is both ambivalently presented and marked by mixed feelings. Cognitive theory has begun to suggest how affect or emotion shapes the very nature of human thought and conceptualization. *As You Like It* provides an especially useful example of the ways in which the power of language to shape the subject (in a process like Althusserian interpellation) is itself shaped and complicated not just by cognitive structures and motivations but also by feeling.

Hamlet's famous complaint, probably performed in the year after *As You Like It*, about William Kemp's style of clowning ends with a significant phrase that glances back at and sums up the issues of agency and social mobility that are of central concern in the earlier play. Having urged the players to "let those that play your clowns speak no more than is set down for them, for there be of them that will themselves laugh to set on some quantity of barren spectators to laugh too, though in the mean time some necessary question of the play be then to be consider'd," he concludes: "That's villainous, and shows a most pitiful ambition in the fool that uses it" (3.2.38–44). We should be cautious in taking Hamlet's words here to be Shakespeare's, but the collocation of *clown, villainous,* and *ambition* returns us to the preoccupations of *As You Like It,* where the words *villain* and *clown* are used both to justify and to apologize for Shakespeare's own attempt to gain control over the text by banishing Kemp from the Globe stage. The meditations on *villain* and *clown* in *As You Like It* must thus be read in the context of the social implications of Kemp's jig performances and the ambitions of the Chamberlain's Men around 1600.

In 1612 the general sessions of the peace for Middlesex added yet another document to ongoing attempts at regulation of the theater, this time ordering suppression of the jigs that usually followed performances of plays:

> Whereas Complaynte have [*sic*] beene made at this last Generall Sessions, that by reason of certayne lewde Jigges songes and daunces vsed and accustomed at the play-house called the Fortune in Gouldinglane, divers cutt-purses and other lewd and ill disposed persons in greate multitudes doe resorte thither at th'end of euerye playe, many tymes causinge tumultes and outrages wherebye His Majesties peace is often broke and much mischiefe like to ensue thereby, Itt was hereuppon expresslye commaunded and ordered by the Justices of the said benche, That all Actors of euerye playhouse in this cittye and liberties thereof and in the County of Middlesex that they and euerie of them vtterlye abolishe all Jigges Rymes and Daunces after their playes.[3]

C. R. Baskervil speculated that the infamous jig "Garlic," probably performed by the clown named Shank, was the immediate catalyst for this order.[4] But the scattered references to jig performances that survive suggest that most of them were boisterous and obscene and that large crowds of vagrant and criminal persons who could not afford (or were not interested in affording) the minimal price of groundling admission to the featured play gathered outside the theater and somehow gained admission to the postperformance jig.[5] These jigs evidently involved plots centered on cuckoldry or rustic wooing, bawdy songs, and exuberant (and sometimes obscene) dances; there was a fashion around 1612 for dances performed by a man in a baboon costume, and *The Two Noble Kinsmen* describes "the beast-eating clown, and next the Fool / The Bavian [baboon], with long tail and eke long tool, / *cum multis aliis* that make a dance" (3.5.131–33).[6] The jig probably also included exchanges with the audience, who in any event by all accounts participated in the performance through shouts, loud laughter, and applause.[7]

Evidence suggests that by 1612 jigs (and the clowns who performed them) were held in contempt by some audiences because of their obscenity, rowdiness, and, to use Baskervil's term, "low art." Hamlet, of course, denigrates Polonius's taste in theater when he says that "he's for a jig or a tale of bawdry, or he sleeps" (2.2.500). Similarly, a contemporary satirist describes the audiences for the jigs of the celebrated clown William Kemp as decidedly lower class: "Whores, Bedles, bawdes, and Sergeants filthily / Chaunt Kemps Iigge."[8] Nevertheless, jigs remained enormously popular, especially in the theaters of the northern suburbs, from the opening of the first theaters until at least 1612.

During William Kemp's tenure as lead clown of the Chamberlain's Men from 1594 until around 1599, Shakespeare's plays, like most other plays performed in the period, would have been followed by such a jig, in this case one written and performed by Kemp himself. David Wiles, in his excellent study of Kemp's career, persuasively argues that these jigs had a complex relationship to their preceding plays, tending toward an anarchic "deconstruction" of the values of the main play.[9] In addition, a role appropriate for Kemp's popular persona of rustic clown had to be included in each play; once onstage, Kemp was notoriously liable to improvise. Shakespeare was, of course, probably thinking of Kemp when he had Hamlet voice the complaint about improvisation cited above. The presence of the clown and the jig, then, assured that plays would be subject to interruption and qualification by unruly voices that were not under the control of the author of the play. And there is evidence that Shakespeare, far from accepting this collaborative structure, took steps to regain a measure of authorial control over his texts by replacing Kemp with a clown who would speak his lines as written.

Concern over the unruliness of the audience (and the performing clown), as well as a desire to appeal to a more exclusive audience may have led the Chamberlain's Men to decide to abolish or curtail performances of jigs when they moved south to Bankside and the new Globe Theatre in 1599, well before the court order suppressing them. What we know for sure is that Kemp, a shareholder in the company and perhaps its most popular actor, suddenly sold his share and left the company at that time. *As You Like It*, probably first performed in 1599, introduces Kemp's replacement, Robert Armin, as the fool, Touchstone. Kemp subsequently made some (unsuccessful) attempts at raising money through spectacular solo performances, for example, an attempt to dance from London to Norwich, and ultimately appeared with Worcester's men, a

company located in the northern suburbs, where jigs remained popular
until their suppression.[10] But he never again regained the prosperity and
standing that he had achieved with the Chamberlain's Men. A number of
scholars speculate that Kemp left the company because of a decision to
curtail the role of the jig.[11] Certainly the Lord Chamberlain's company
had by this time begun to set its sights on a slightly different audience,
and as Wiles has argued, "the jig did nothing to raise the status of the
company, and increased the risk of crowd trouble."[12] With the purchase
and renovation of the Blackfriars Theatre in 1596 (although the company
could not perform there until 1608), and with a move south to Bankside
in 1599, the Chamberlain's Men dissociated themselves from the existing
public theaters in the north and created a repertory that could ultimately
be performed at both the public Globe and the private Blackfriars. The
move to the Globe, then, marked a point of upward mobility for the
Chamberlain's Men and one of downward mobility for the excluded
Kemp and his jigs.

David Wiles and Richard Helgerson have noted the important implications of these jigs for our understanding of authorship in the period.[13]
With the exception of Wiles and Helgerson, however, arguments over subversion and containment and over Shakespeare's role in the cultural work
of reproducing differences in social class have for the most part proceeded
based on assumptions about the nature of Shakespeare's authorship alone
rather than an uneasy collaboration with Kemp or, for that matter, the
rest of the company.[14] Those who argue that the dominant (hierarchical)
ideologies of early modern culture essentially construct and contain both
author and play correlate cultural work in the interests of the ruling hierarchies with lack of authorial agency.[15] On the other hand, those who
want to see Shakespeare's plays as furthering the interests of lower- or
working-class persons correlate that alignment with a high degree of authorial independence, individuality, and agency.[16]

Helgerson, on the other hand, allies authorial agency with support of
class hierarchy. He argues that the Shakespearean history plays written
around the same time as As You Like It "purge" the common, the festive,
and other lingering signs of the collaborative popular "player's theater"
from his plays. In comedy, however, Shakespeare treated the potential
conflicts between high and low, elite and popular, rulers and ruled, in a
different and less clearly purgative way. A cognitive reading may also offer
a more flexible way to think about the competing interests represented in
the play than does Helgerson's New Historicism. While a historicist or
materialist reading such as Helgerson's can note the presence of competing ideologies in a text—for example, his admission that Shakespeare's
history plays do offer some "exposure" of the "brutal and duplicitous
strategies by which power maintained itself," as well as some limited "fes-

tive power of inversion"—such readings seem to feel obligated to identify a text with some dominant ideological position.[17] A cognitive reading, with its broader sense of agency and its assumption that all meaning is polysemic, allows greater weight for multiplicity and the coexistence of competing interests. It also acknowledges a factor that is of particular importance in this play, namely, the central role of feelings—of regret, anger, envy—in inflecting the ideological forces present in the play.

An examination of the representation of relations between different social classes in *As You Like It* thus reveals that the connection between ideology and agency is neither simple nor uniform. The performance of Shakespeare's *As You Like It* marked a pivotal moment in the status negotiations of the Chamberlain's Men; it was perhaps the first play performed at their new Globe Theatre, and in what seems to have been an attempt to appeal to a "better" audience it was the first play to be performed with the new, more refined clown Robert Armin (and probably without an attendant jig). More importantly, the play links the exclusion of the rustic clown and jig from the Globe to the social mechanisms that helped to justify the exclusion of lower-class persons from the limited upward mobility then becoming possible in the culture as a whole. These mechanisms included the semantic shift of what previously had been status terms (e.g., *villain*, *churl*, and *clown*) to almost exclusively ethical connotations, a linguistic change that was deeply implicated in the reformulation of attitudes toward social class that accompanied the decline of the feudal system. The play uses these terms, however, in ways that reveal the implication of language in the reproduction of the ideologies of class, just as it uses the figure of the clown and several jig motifs to reveal the problematic ambitions of the play itself.

The "divers cutt-purses and other lewd and ill disposed persons in greate multitudes" who provided the jig with its unruly audience were most probably members of the group of persons identified as "vagrants" or "vagabonds," whose numbers were increasing significantly as a result of far-reaching changes in social and economic organization in this period.[18] Many of these vagrants were descended from the feudal "villein" class, the serfs or "churls" who were "unfree" workers bound to till their lords' fields and subject to burdensome manorial fees and royal taxes. By the end of the sixteenth century, villeage was in practice obsolete in England, having been replaced in most cases by copyhold tenures, which left workers free to move from place to place and protected, in some instances, by royal courts. The end of villeage, so long sought by English peasants, actually left many of them in an even less desirable condition, as vagrants lacking land and work. While feudal custom bound peasants to the land, landowners in the early modern period realized that the enclosure of tenantless land for sheep farming could bring greater profits. Thus, many villeins formerly attached to the land became vagrants, whose new prominence was reflected in the Elizabethan period by increased legislation attempting to control them.[19]

As semanticists have noted, and as the play makes clear, language itself played a role in mediating the changing attitudes toward class and social mobility in this period. Of particular interest in *As You Like It* is a set of terms that were in the process of shifting from essentially neutrally designating status to indicating something about a subject's personal character. In contrast to the prototype shifts that were a center of interest in *The Comedy of Errors*, the kind of semantic change that Shakespeare seems to have emphasized in *As You Like It* has been widely noted. C. S. Lewis described it as the "moralisation of status-words," whereby "words which originally referred to a person's rank—to legal, social, or economic status and the qualifications of birth which have often been attached to these—have a tendency to become words which assign a type of character and behaviour. Those implying superior status can become terms of praise; those implying inferior status, terms of disapproval. *Chivalrous, courteous, frank, generous, gentle, liberal,* and *noble* are examples of the first; *ignoble, villain,* and *vulgar,* of the second."[20] The second type of shift, from inferior status to moral disapproval, was categorized by the semanticist Gustaf Stern as "depreciative specialization," a category that also includes words such as *huswife* and *gossip,* which depreciate on the basis of gender rather than class.[21]

Of central concern in *As You Like It* are the terms *villain, churl,* and *clown.* By the time Shakespeare wrote that play *villein* had become *villain* and had lost most of its legal imputation of status, having come to mean instead "an unprincipled or depraved scoundrel" (*OED*). Lewis attributed such shifts to essentially benign and apolitical causes: to "optimism" that social superiors were also superior in ethical behavior and to a desire to encourage the socially ambitious to act in ethically acceptable ways (22–23). But more recent work on the ideologies of class in the medieval and early modern periods reveals the extent to which this semantic shift can be implicated in the strategies of changing social orders to constitute and reproduce themselves.[22] Lee Patterson has traced the medieval ideological formation insisting that "serfdom is a permanent condition of moral inferiority inherent in the peasant's very being rather than a social status capable of being both assumed and (at least in theory) left behind."[23] This concept of inferiority was based on the idea that peasants were descended from Cain or from Noah's son Ham and thus were especially tainted by sin.[24] The revolutionary slogan "When Adam dalf and Eve span / Who was thanne a gentil man," perennially cited by English peasants, especially during the revolts of 1381, 1450, 1536, and 1549, can thus be seen as an attempt to counter the dominant ideology of status

by establishing a common ancestry for all people.[25] Of course, such assertions of equality prompted attempts to oppose this revolutionary doctrine
with reassertions of orthodoxy: "A bonde man or a churle wyll say, 'All
we be cummyn of Adam.' So Lucifer with his cumpany may say, 'All we
be cummyn of heuyn.' " In fact, because of his sin "did Cayn become a
chorle and all his ofsprung after hym."[26] Such statements reveal the extent
to which the correlation of inferior moral and social status was a highly
charged ideological maneuver.

Increased possibilities for social mobility in the early modern period
necessarily changed how ideologies of status were articulated. In order to
accommodate upward mobility, the idea that people are born with qualities suitable to their permanent station in life shifts slightly to suggest that
each person's status will ultimately suit his qualities. Richard Halpern,
among others, has identified the role of such a "discourse of capacities"
in this period, which associated upward mobility with such personal qualities as "intelligence, talent, creativity . . . industry, parsimony, and persistence." Halpern argues that this discourse took on new significance in the
sixteenth century, when it was used "to explain *downward* mobility and
to cope ideologically with the swelling tides of the new poor," created in
part by the deterritorialization and displacement that followed the end
of villenage and widespread enclosures.[27] The upwardly mobile Edmund
Spenser illustrates a typically mixed ideological formation when he describes the witch's son in book 3 of the *Faerie Queene* as a "chorle" and
"villain" on the basis of low status (he and his mother live in "a little
cottage, built of stickes and reedes / In homely wize" [3.7.6]), natural
moral baseness (he feels "no love, but brutish lust" for Florimel [3.7.15]),
and inferior capacity (he would not "ply him selfe to any honest trade /
. . . Such laesinesse both lewd and poor attonce him made" [3.7.12]).

The word *clown*, though related in some ways to words such as *villain*
and *churl*, has a semantic history that differs in significant ways. *Clown*
was not an official status term during the feudal period and in fact seems
not to have occurred at all until the sixteenth century.[28] When it did begin
to appear, it had simultaneous status and ethical connotations, meaning
both "countryman, rustic, or peasant," and "an ignorant, rude, uncouth,
ill-bred man" (*OED*). Wiles argues, persuasively I think, that "the concept of a 'clown' emerged within a neo-chivalric discourse centered on
the notion of 'gentility.' The word 'gentle' has ambiguously genetic and
ethical connotations, and to be a 'clown' is the obverse of being 'gentle.' "[29] As *villain* came to be applicable, in its ethical sense, to upper-class
subjects, the term *clown* was needed to convey the special connections
between rusticity, low status, and lack of "gentle" qualities.[30] Also unlike
villain and *churl* in this period (although something similar happened to
villain in the nineteenth century), *clown* appreciated rather than depreci-

ated as it became a technical theatrical term for a particular (and very popular) kind of actor. In its theatrical sense the term initially retained connotations of low status, but at almost precisely the moment when this play was performed, it began to lose those associations and began to denote simply a comic actor without reference to status. Although in Kemp's persona rudeness and rusticity were inextricably linked to his role as clown, Armin, who appears first in *As You Like It*, preferred to represent a learned "fool" who had courtly and even gentle status.[31]

In general, critics of *As You Like It* have argued that the play represents upper-class concerns. Louis Montrose, for example, has argued that the romance plot and the pastoral genre of this play function to align it with the concerns about status and mobility that were current in the late sixteenth century for its essentially upper-class audience.[32] Montrose sees both the play and the pastoral mode in general as addressing issues of status at the upper end of the social scale and shows how *As You Like It* specifically works through anxieties about social class raised for younger sons by the practice of primogeniture. Similarly, Richard Wilson has traced the assimilation into the play of motifs of popular revolt current during the enclosure riots of the 1590s, arguing that the play finally works to "depoliticize Carnival" and neutralize "the rites of collective action," again associating the play with conservative and upper-class interests.[33]

But it is also possible to see in the play signs of sympathy with lower-class interests, though in an essentially contestatory relationship to the cultural work of the play as a whole.[34] On a verbal level, the insistent and ideologically charged uses of such shifting status terms as *villain* and *clown* insinuate into the play questions about the implications of upward (and downward) mobility for precisely those "poorest laborers and indigent" who were largely absent from the main play (although evidently sometimes present for the jig). Although these questions are for the most part not explicitly raised in the play, they are persistently suggested from its margins and are sufficiently present to ruffle the surface of the romance plot. The play repeatedly hints at the counterideologies of the peasant or vagrant class but usually diffuses these potentially disruptive ideas either by shifting the class referent to gradations of status within the "gentle" classes or by means of a distancing and neutralizing layer of classical allusion.[35] Nevertheless, because the play calls attention to the linguistic strategies at work in the culture to manage the threat of disruptive mobility from below, its representation of lower-class concerns is, finally, incompletely contained.

The negotiation of issues related to social mobility in *As You Like It* is complicated by theatrical practice in ways that remind us of the extent to which text and performance cannot be separated. The evidence of theater history suggests that in using a more refined clown designed to appeal to a more exclusive audience the play itself enacts the very mobility it examines and, at times, enables. Just as it uses words like *villain* and *churl* to allude to the concerns of those for whom upward mobility was largely impossible, the play also gestures toward the missing "clown" Will Kemp and his jig; the play is in part about the replacement of the clownish (but popular) Kemp with the more refined "fool," Robert Armin.[36] Just as the play includes partially managed bits of peasant ideology, it also incorporate some incompletely assimilated elements of the jig within itself. Like the "villains" to which the play alludes, Kemp is absent from the text, but his absence is treated in such a way as to raise a hint of discomfort about the implications of upward mobility for those left out and for those who benefit. In its emphasis on shifting terms and the changing conditions of theatrical production, *As You Like It* seems to question the self-justifications of hierarchy that it seems concerned, in other ways, to uphold.

The relationship between these potentially subversive moments and the agency of Shakespeare as author is, however, more complex than we might expect. On the one hand, the assimilation of elements of the jig into the play itself and exclusion of the extemporizing Kemp increased authorial agency since the author could now count on controlling the words spoken by the actors during the play and end the play as he liked, without facing the possibility of a disruptive coda. At the same time, however, this act of exclusion and assimilation transformed what had been an unruly lower-class voice into a "gentled" critique over which a single author now had more control. In this sense, increased authorial agency is not, as some have argued, to be inevitably associated with a more subversive text. On the other hand, wordplay focused on the ideologies of hierarchy and limited mobility as manifested in language seems to mark an attempt to evade interpellation with irony, to play on the language of the dominant classes in such a way as to render transparent the linguistic strategies at work to reproduce the conditions of their dominance. Whether an author can, in fact, attain a measure of control over the ideological workings of language is not only questioned by many critics today but significantly questioned in the play itself. What we do seem to see in the play is an increase in authorial control and agency coupled with various kinds of upward mobility—for the author himself, for the theatrical company, and, indirectly, for the audience. Along with its ambition, however, the play seems to manifest an awareness of and a sense of regret about what it must exclude to achieve its ambition, including the incipient rejection of the theater's festive roots and established tradition of collaborative work.

The emotional shadings inextricably attached through individual experience to words such as *villain* and *clown* complicate their ideological functions. Althusser has described ideology as a condition of "obviousness" that, "like all obviousnesses, including those that make a word 'name a thing,' or 'have a meaning' (therefore including the obviousness of the 'transparency' of language), the 'obviousness' that you and I are subjects—and that that does not cause any problems—is an ideological effect, the elementary ideological effect."[37] Individuals are interpellated as subjects when family structures inculcate in them "the rituals of ideological recognition, which guarantee for us that we are indeed concrete, individual, distinguishable and (naturally) irreplaceable subjects" (173).

This Althusserian theory of interpellation was, of course, influenced by Lacanian subject formation and is thus open to similar critique from a cognitive perspective, namely, that we perceive ourselves to be "concrete, individual, distinguishable" because of our physiologically based spatial and sensory experiences of selfhood as well as because our culture "hails" us as such. Daniel Stern's work on the development of selfhood in infants stresses the centrality of affect to all early learning, including the formation of this "core sense of self": "Affective and cognitive processes cannot be readily separated. In a simple learning task, activation builds up and falls off. Learning itself is motivated and affect-laden."[38] Antonio Damasio stresses the necessary involvement of feeling in the most rational decision-making processes, and Gerald Edelman similarly argues that feeling and "value" play a central role in the cumulative history of an individual "self": "Meaning takes shape in terms of concepts that depend on categorizations based on value. It grows with the history of remembered body sensations and mental images. The mixture of events is individual and, in large measure unpredictable. When, in society, linguistic and semantic capabilities arise and sentences involving metaphor are linked to thought, the capability to create new models of the world grows at an explosive rate. But one must remember that, because of its linkage to value and to the concept of self, this system of meaning is almost never free of affect; it is charged with emotions."[39] The Althusserian "transparency of language," then, must be complicated by a cognitive sense of the lexical field that defines the meaning of even the simplest word, as well as by the necessary inflection of that field by feelings that will be different (and not always consistent) for each individual.

It is in the context of Orlando's concerns about the relationship between social status, natural capacity, financial means, and education that the play introduces its concern with the ideological uses of status terms. Throughout the play, Orlando seems confused by his culture's contradictory ideologies of status and social mobility. On the one hand, he feels that he has been relegated to "peasant" (1.1.68) status by his brother's

failure to educate him and provide him with the means to live as a gentleman, complaining that his brother "keeps me rustically here at home"
and "mines my gentility with my [lack of] education" (1.1.7, 20). Here
Orlando seems to distrust his native capacities and to assume that gentle
status depends upon suitable education and financial resources. His desire
to "go buy my fortunes," however, plays on the contemporary shift in the
meaning of the word *fortune*, from an original sense of "chance" to a new
meaning, emerging in the late sixteenth century, "amount of wealth."[40] As
such, it works as a part of the "discourse of capacities" so important in
justifying the limitation of upward mobility to the already privileged.

It is no surprise, then, that Orlando also insists that he possesses gentlemanly capacities conferred by birth: "the spirit of my father, which I think
is within me, begins to mutiny against this servitude" (1.1.22–24). He
subsequently suggests that his "gentleman-like qualities" have been
merely hidden from him rather than undermined, by his lack of education.
Thus, Orlando's seemingly egalitarian belief in the importance of education for the achievement of true gentility is based on a more conservative
sense that someone born to the gentle class possesses both an innate superiority and an innate right to development through education.[41]

In *As You Like It* the status and ethical senses of *villain* are separated
and recombined in ways that seem motivated by powerful feelings and
that call attention to its role in the mediation and limitation of social
mobility. It is always used to indicate a person of gentle status, and it is
almost always used by one brother to describe another in an emotionally
charged situation; as a result, questions are raised about the connections
between birth, social class, and ethical worth. It is Oliver who prods Orlando toward a bolder claim to a natural capacity for gentle status when
he first calls him a "villain" (1.1.55). Oliver uses the term angrily, in its
ethical sense (Orlando has just threatened him with violence), but he also
intends to taunt Orlando with his own perception that a lack of education
has lowered his social status. Orlando responds indignantly, as if this were
the case. He clearly perceives an accusation of "villainy" to be an insult
with particular force in his case, asserting indignantly that "I am no villain; I am the youngest son of Sir Rowland de Boys. He was my father,
and he is thrice a villain that says such a father begot villains" (1.1.56–
59). Caught up in their intense and emotional rivalry, these brothers fail
to see the irony that their exchange makes clear to an audience. Since the
two are brothers, according to an ideology of inherited capacity and status, if one is a villain, the other must also be a villain. Just as clearly,
however, if Orlando has been relegated to "villain" or "peasant" status
by lack of education and means, Oliver reveals himself to be the true
"villain" in the ethical sense.

The troubled brothers in the play continue to repeat emotionally laden accusations of "villainy" in ways that reinforce its ethical sense and stress the ironies of its connection with status. The irony works to reveal the ways in which language is complicitous in the self-serving attitudes of the supposedly "gentle." Oliver, for example, twice describes Orlando as "villainous" (1.1.144, 154) to Charles the wrestler but in soliloquy admits that his brother is in fact by nature just the opposite: "gentle, never school'd and yet learned, full of noble device" (1.1.166–67). Here Oliver admits the confluence in Orlando of both status and ethical "gentility" and "nobility" while revealing that "my own people" recognize his own lack of those capacities: "I am altogether mispris'd." In similarly ironic uses, Duke Frederick, who has dispossessed his own older brother, believes that "some villains of my court" (2.2.2) must have helped Rosalind and Celia escape, and he terms Oliver "more villain" (3.1.15) because he admits that he hates Orlando.

These uses of moralized status terms initially seem to function as a part of the negotiation of upper-class issues in that they uphold both meritocratic and nativist views of status. By implying that some supposedly gentle persons behave as villains, the play opens the possibility of the converse: that some persons of lower status might possess the capacities for advancement. On the other hand, by insisting on the correlation of status and capacity in Orlando's case, the play obscures the question of how far down the social scale such gentle qualities might extend. The word *villain* thus participates in the play's negotiation of limited mobility by smoothing over contradictions in the system and allowing education and money to erode the status system, but only to a limited extent.

On the other hand, repetition of words such as *villain* in emotionally charged familial disputes emphasizes the purposeful use of such words to shore up one's own position at the expense of another. This insistence on their semantic shift and resulting double meanings calls our attention to their implication in the ideologies that both protected hierarchy and promoted limited individual ambition (at the upper end of the social scale) within it. The very presence of the word conjures up the plight of former feudal "villeins," many of whom were now vagrants and criminals, and what this ideology means for them. The control of just such "Roges Vacabonds or Sturdy Beggars" was the object of repeated statutes during this period, typically ordering, for example, that "all and everye persone and persones beynge whole and mightye in Body and able to labour, havinge not Land or Maister, nor using any lawfull Marchaundize Crafte," shall be considered vagabonds and "grevouslye whipped, and burnte through the gristle of the right Eare with a hot Yron of the compasse of an Ynche about."[42] It was also against such people that the "discourse of capacities" worked, justifying their downward mobility as resulting from a lack of the natural capacities that enabled others to rise. Whether such persons attended the public theaters has been debated, but clearly they lacked the financial means to make up a significant portion of the paying audience for the main play.[43] There is evidence that they attended jigs, but the decision of the Chamberlain's Men to curtail the jig suggests an attempt to discourage such an audience. Despite this, or perhaps because of it, *As You Like* continually hints at the situation of real "base" persons and a revolutionary ideology of class leveling.

As in many plays by Shakespeare, the upper-class characters of the main plot coexist with various characters lacking gentle status; this play includes the old servant Adam, the shepherds Corin, Silvius, and Phebe, the goatherd Audrey, and the "clown" William. In each case pressing issues of status and material conditions of life are suggested but for the most part undeveloped. Old Adam, the faithful servant, for example, represents a person who clearly possesses the prized capacities of the upwardly mobile merchant class: thrift, persistence, prudence, and temperance. He has a nest egg saved "by thrifty hire" during his years of service, he has provided for his old age, and he has avoided strong drink. Nevertheless, he realizes that his fate, once "service should in my old limbs lie lame," will be to become a masterless man, describing the ultimate fate of the geriatric servant in the period as "unregarded age in corners thrown" (2.3.38–51). Despite these capacities, he feels no compulsion to use his means "to mutiny against this servitude" (as Orlando does); instead, recognizing Orlando's natural status as his "master," he not only gives him all of his money but promises to do him "the service of a younger man" (2.3.54). Orlando recognizes Adam's attitude as that of a prior age, before the possibility of upward mobility:

> O good old man, how well in thee appears
> The constant service of the antique world,
> When service sweat for duty, not for meed!
> Thou art not for the fashion of these times,
> Where none will sweat but for promotion.

> (2.3.56–60)[44]

Orlando and Adam both attempt to rename Adam's lack of interest in promotion as a virtue: "loyalty." But since the rest of the play depicts Orlando's own striving for (and attainment of) a higher place in the world, it makes sense that after Orlando demonstrates a reciprocal loyalty to Adam (by refusing to abandon him to starve), Adam disappears from the play. His combination of capacity and inability to get ahead disrupts the ideology that would correlate low social and ethical status.

The biblical Adam was, of course, a central figure in the competing accounts of the role of inheritance in determining social class.[45] Louis Montrose and Lee Patterson have both noted the contradiction between the aristocratic belief that base persons were descended from Cain and a peasant belief in the common ancestry of all persons: "When Adam dalf and Eve span, who was then the gentle man."[46] Adam's presence in this play as a worthy person who seems to be relegated to servitude by birth and without regard for his capacities alludes to the revolutionary slogan. *As You Like It* conjures up the orthodox myth of class ancestry (Cain and Abel) as a parallel to the destructive intraclass rivalries between the gentry and the nobility; it brings in Adam to show a worthy but slighted servant.

The questions raised by Adam are given emphasis by the oblique presence of a spinning Eve (who, in a strategy typical of the play, is transformed into a classical spinster). When Celia and Rosalind discuss their own differences in status, they seem similarly concerned with the relationship between "Nature" (native gifts and inherited status) and "Fortune" (formerly "chance" but now "money") (1.2.42, 41). Rosalind and Celia both seem disturbed that Rosalind, who is the daughter of the rightful Duke, has been displaced by Celia, who has less inherited right to that status. As in the case of Oliver and Orlando, Rosalind's birth claim to higher status is also correlated with superior capacities: even Celia's father admits that "thou wilt show more bright and seem more virtuous / When she is gone" (1.3.81–82). Rosalind implies that Celia's upward mobility is the result of superior (but undeserved) financial means, punning on the new financial meanings of words like *estate* and *fortune*: "I will forget the condition of my estate to rejoice in yours"; "Fortune reigns in the gifts of the world, not in the lineaments of Nature" (1.2.15, 42). Celia brings in the spinster, here named "Fortune" rather than "Eve," although her take on social status seems similar: "Let us sit and mock the good huswife Fortune from her wheel, that her gifts may henceforth be bestow'd equally" (1.2.31–33). Celia calls not for a return to their former situation, with Rosalind as superior and she inferior, but rather for a more equitable distribution of fortune. It is Rosalind who insists that "Nature" is superior to "Fortune" even though her fortune is temporarily in decline. Of course, the implication of social leveling in Celia's invocation of Fortune is, literally, "gentle," since it only calls for a slight redistribution of resources among the nobility. But her spinning "Fortune," taken in tandem with Adam, similarly gestures toward more radical implications of a truly equitable bestowal of fortune in the monetary sense.

The play makes another covert gesture toward a counterideology of the peasant class when it mentions the myth of Robin Hood.[47] Rodney Hilton has argued that the popular Robin Hood ballads of the Middle Ages must be seen in the context of peasant insistence that the products of nature itself, particularly wood and game, should belong to all men, not only to the nobility.[48] The unlawful gathering of "the lord's wood," which was necessary for warmth and shelter, is frequently recorded in manorial court records, and royal proclamations into the sixteenth century abjure "you our loving subjects, from henceforth to abstain and forbear to murder, kill, or destroy, chase or hunt, any of our said deer."[49] Hilton suggests that the Robin Hood ballads represent at least in part a "Utopian vision of free communities of hunters eating their fill of forbidden food."[50] In "A Gest of Robin Hode" (ca. 1492–1534), for example, Robin addresses the king himself, who is disguised as an abbot:

We be yemen of this foreste
Under the grene-wode tre;
We lyve by our kynges dere,
Other shyft haue not we.[51]

The disguised king is impressed by Robin's "courteysy" and the "wonder semely syght" of his followers kneeling before him; he shares a meal with them—"Anone before our kynge was set / The fatte venyson"—and ultimately pardons them, and he invites Robin to come to his court (lines 385–417). This ballad clearly represents a fantasy involving gentle qualities ("courteysy") among men of low status that are recognized by the king himself, as well as an assertion of a right to eat the king's deer.[52]

When it appears in *As You Like It*, however, the ideological content of the Robin Hood myth is blunted—"made gentle"—in several ways.[53] In the first place, as Richard Wilson notes, it is an exiled Duke and "many young gentlemen" who "live like the old Robin Hood of England" and "fleet the time carelessly, as they did in the golden world" (1.1.116–20).[54] In this case, the Duke is probably killing deer that would be rightfully his if his position had not been wrongfully usurped. The insistence on the outlaws' leisured existence ("fleet the time carelessly") signals that these exiles retain that mark of nobility even in the forest. Their hunting bears a resemblance closer to the sanctioned hunt as aristocratic pastime than to the poacher's illicit hunt.[55] Thus, when the "civility" of the Duke's banquet is emphasized by Orlando's rude interruption, the class logic of the meal in the Robin Hood ballad is reversed: here it is the nobleman who represents courtesy in the forest and a person of (slightly) lower status who recognizes it. At the same time, the reference to "the golden world" distances class issues by transposing them onto a classical landscape.

The Duke's account of his misgivings about hunting in the forest of Arden curiously inflects these class issues, introducing relations between nobility and the merchant class and downward mobility among merchants. He claims to be distressed ("it irks me") that

> the poor dappled fools,
> Being native burghers of this desert city,
> Should in their own confines with forked heads
> Have their round haunches gor'd.

                                                              (2.1.21–25)

An attendant lord cites Jacques's opinion that "you do more usurp / Than doth your brother that hath banish'd you" (2.1.27–28) when he wrongfully kills the animals "in their assign'd and native dwelling place" (2.1.63). The lord further quotes Jacques's description of the deer who abandon their wounded comrade: "sweep on, you fat and greasy citizens, / 'Tis just the fashion. Wherefore do you look / Upon that poor and broken bankrupt there" (55–57). Here the lord's right to game is questioned, but it is rather oddly seen not as the right of peasants (who live close to nature) but as that of a bourgeois economy of the animals themselves. On the one hand, these animals are described as free "burghers" and "citizens," who nevertheless disregard the downward mobility of a fellow citizen who is "bankrupt." On the other hand, they have an "assign'd and native dwelling place"—assigned, like that of peasants tied to their lord's land. Until the sixteenth century the word *native* meant "one born in thralldom," and *nativus* was the Latin word used in manorial court records for "villein."[56] Whatever their putative class affiliation, these deer rather fancifully reflect the effects of usurpation and downward mobility both within a class and between classes.

The human inhabitants of the forest of Arden are depicted as having a similarly ambivalent status. Here again the play hints at the problems of "base" persons in the period and in some cases deflects direct treatment of such problems. Corin, Silvius, and Phebe are all identified as "shepherds," yet they seem to bridge several important social gaps: Corin is a wage laborer, while Silvius is a potential purchaser of the flock and seems relatively leisured; Corin is a "natural philosopher" who eschews courtly ways, while Silvius and Phebe seem versed (or rather saturated) in courtly love conventions. In this sense, these "shepherds" seem a part of what Montrose has identified as the role of the pastoral in the "mediation of status distinctions."[57] Their classicized names and participation in such literary conventions as Petrarchan love discourse, formal debate, and the "beatus ille" topos suggest that questions about their social status may be irrelevant.

And yet, at other points the text clearly foregrounds issues of status and the material realities of these characters' existence. Corin, for example, calls attention to the plight of the shepherd as wage laborer at the mercy of an absentee master:

But I am shepherd to another man,
And do not shear the fleeces that I graze.
My master is of churlish disposition,
And little reaks to find the way to heaven
By doing deeds of hospitality.
Besides, his cote, his flocks, and bounds of feed
Are now on sale, and at our sheep-cote now
By reason of his absence there is nothing
That you will feed on.

                                                        (2.4.78–86)

Significantly, Corin uses a depreciated status term—*churlish*—in its ethical sense to describe his "master."[58] His description of this particular gentleman shepherd works against the pastoral negotiation of status difference by pointing up the sharp *difference* between the shepherd who owns the sheep and the real shepherd who does the work. Corin's use of *churlish* to describe his master is a more pointed critique of depreciation than Oliver's use of *villain* to describe his brother since Corin is (most probably) a "churl" in status who suffers because of churlish treatment by his (ostensibly) "gentle" master. Corin suggests that his master fails in the duties of a truly "gentle" manorial proprietor since he does not take care of his workers and does not practice hospitality. In this he resembles the newly rich courtiers of the period, who neglected traditional country practices in order to spend time at court and who often were forced to sell lands to finance conspicuous expenditures in London.

Even Corin's critique is partially deflected by the romance plot, however, when Celia and Rosalind purchase the sheep farm and proceed to demonstrate truly "gentle" shepherd behavior. They will "mend" Corin's "wages" (2.4.94), and they plan to spend their time, at least for the time being, in the country and not at court. Of course, like all the gentle people in the forest, they plan a leisured existence ("I like this place, / And willingly could waste my time in it" [2.4.94–95); as in the case of Orlando and Adam, Corin recognizes their superior gentility and offers to serve them faithfully ("I will your faithful feeder be" [2.4.99]). Once again the play raises the possibility of "villainous" or "churlish" behavior on the part of those of high status, only to suggest that this is an exception rather than the rule. Once again it raises the issue of a worthy servant mistreated by a less worthy master, only to suggest that the servant simply needs a better, more "gentle" master.

Below the classicized shepherds are the truly menial rustics Audrey and William. Montrose has argued that the pastoral, because wealthy sheep owners could describe themselves as shepherds and also because of the traditional association of shepherds with a leisured life, was a form easily assimilated to courtly interests. In order for the pastoral to perform the cultural work of the upper classes, however, shepherds had to be rigorously separated from truly lower-class "plowmen," the traditional agricultural workers of the villein class.[59] It was in this context that the word *clown* arose in the sixteenth century to define civilized gentility with reference to its opposites. The roles of Audrey and William, then, must be seen in connection with Touchstone, and with the changes in personnel and policy relating to clowns that the Chamberlain's Men seem to have made when they moved to the Globe, changes that first surface in *As You Like It*.

David Wiles has argued that Kemp was a rustic clown, characterized by boorish behavior and derived, after the fashion of his predecessor Richard Tarlton, from festive traditions of the Lord of Misrule and the Vice.[60] Unlike most of the Globe shareholders, Kemp experienced a downward social mobility after he left the company in 1599. Unlike Shakespeare, Pope, Phillips, and Heminges, all of whom achieved financial success and applied for coats of arms (and gentle status), Kemp was unsuccessful in various subsequent ventures and did not leave a will when he died.[61]

Robert Armin, who proved to be a very different kind of comic character, replaced Kemp as company "clown." While Kemp clung to a rustic and boorish persona, Armin tended to play "fools" of indeterminate or higher social status. Armin's fools are attendants to gentle or noble persons, they are educated (quoting Latin and Italian), and they seem more closely related to the Renaissance tradition of "wise folly" than to the rustic Lord of Misrule.[62] As noted above, with Armin's introduction of this new, educated clown, the term began to lose its derogatory status implications and appreciated to suggest any comic performer, while the play as a whole makes an appeal to a more elite audience. A measure of its success may be the tendency of critics over the years to describe it as "refined and exquisite," "a play in which cruder humors would be out of place."[63]

However, as several historians of the stage have noted, *As You Like It* calls attention in various ways to the absence of Kemp, and in the process uses *clown*, as it does *villain*, to suggest both the costs and the advantages of social mobility. In addition, the play assimilates a number of jig elements, including but only partially controlling the unruly voice of the clown.[64] When Touchstone leaves the court and enters the rustic environs of the forest, he takes pains to stress his discomfort: "Ay, now am I in Arden, the more fool I. / When I was at home, I was in a better place" (2.4.16–17). Unlike one of Kemp's clowns, Touchstone is emphatically not a rustic, yet he points up the irony attendant upon a nonclownish fool by asserting that he is "the more fool" in the forest. Audiences would

expect the clown to be at home in a rustic environment; Touchstone, ironically, is more a fool not because he is now in the clown's natural rustic
environment but because he has left the court.

The appearance of two actual rustics, Silvius and Corin, leads Touchstone to attempt to distinguish himself from them. Touchstone addresses
Corin as "you clown!" and Rosalind's immediate reply puns on the theatrical and status connotations of the term: "Peace, fool, he's not thy kinsman" (2.4.67). When Corin responds "Who calls?" Touchstone replies
"Your betters, sir," to which Corin answers "Else are they very wretched"
(2.4.68). The play has been concerned all along with the relationship between status and kinship, persistently questioning whether the villainy of
one family member entails the villainy of another. Here Rosalind point-
edly calls Touchstone "fool" and differentiates him from a rustic clown.
Her tone seems to denigrate Touchstone rather than Corin, however, and
to imply that the rustic enjoys potentially higher ethical status than the
courtly fool. Similarly, Corin's barbed answer to Touchstone's preten-
sions reminds the audience that the hard life in the forest about which
Touchstone complains is Corin's daily lot.

Touchstone's appellation, appearance, and manner and the reactions
of other characters to him would all underscore his differences from the
traditional clown. Throughout the folio text he is identified as "clown"
in stage directions and speech prefixes, but he is generally called "fool"
in dialogue. The two exceptions are both in contexts where Touchstone's
status at court is at issue. Rosalind's early reference to him as a "clownish
fool" (1.3.130) may be intended to help the audience connect this new
kind of fool with the older clown tradition. The second lord's identification of "the roynish [paltry] clown" (2.2.8) in response to Duke Frederick's query concerning which "villains of my court" were involved in
Rosalind's escape clearly links the terms *villain* and *clown* in an ironic
context: that "villains" and a "clown" could originate in the court suggests that there is something wrong with the gentility of the court.

Not only is the "clown" a person of higher status in the play but unam-
biguously gentle characters sometimes speak with the voice of the clown.
Rosalind herself seems to borrow elements from the jig in some of her
exchanges with Orlando; however, the unruly voice of the jig is incompletely present, and thus the jig's critique of social institutions (such as
marriage) is in this instance largely blunted. Significantly, Rosalind's expressions of virulent misogyny in act 4, scene 1 (usually explained as a
test of Orlando's love), closely resemble an anonymous jig entitled "Clods
Carroll: or, A proper new Iigg, to be sung Dialogue wise, of a man and a
woman that would needs be married."[65] The situation in each text is the
same; a man who desires to be married consults another person (in the
jig, a woman; in the play, a "woman" disguised as a man), who argues

vehemently against marriage by enumerating the many faults of woman-
kind. In the jig, the man (who, in a line similar to Orlando's "I can no
longer live by thinking," has asserted that he "cannot live alone") is told
that no age is good for marriage:

> To marry with a yong wench,
> shee'l make thee poor with pride:
> To marry with one of middle age,
>   perhaps she hath been try'd:
> To marry with an old one,
>   to freeze by fire side;
>   both old and young are faulty.

(390, lines 29–35)

There is an obvious resemblance to Jaques's "seven ages of man" speech
here, which Rosalind picks up when she argues that "men are April when
they woo, December when they wed; maids are May when they are maids,
but the sky changes when they are wives" (4.1.147–49). In the jig, the
man concludes that "Ile marry with a yong wench, / of beauty and of wit,"
only to be told that "It is better tame a yong Colt, / without a curbing bit"
(lines 36–39). Rosalind, of course, predicts that as a wife she will resemble
a number of wild animals: "I will be more jealous of thee than a Barbary
cockpigeon over his hen, more clamorous than a parrot against rain, more
new-fangled than an ape, more giddy in my desires than a monkey"
(4.1.149–53). The jig concludes by calling the still amorous man "a Cuck-
old in reuersion," while Rosalind responds to Orlando's desire to marry
"a wife with such a wit" with the suggestion that he will meet his "wive's
wit going to your neighbor's bed" (4.1.168). Celia's response to Rosalind
after Orlando has left describes a gesture that would be at home in the
obscene dances that often were part of jigs: "We must have your doublet
and hose pluck'd over your head, and show the world what the bird hath
done to her own nest" (4.1.202–4).

Rosalind, of course, surely did not perform this gesture. And the play,
significantly, does not incorporate the second part of the jig, where the
man, now married, ruefully admits that his adviser's misogynist predictions have all come true:

> W. What griefe doth most oppresse thee?
>   may I request to know?
> M. That I have got a wanton.
> W. But, is she not a shrow?
> M. Shee's any thing that evill is.

(392, lines 99–103)

In *As You Like It,* Rosalind's advice works in part to establish her relationship with Orlando as real and durable and to smooth over the status difference between them; she may be superior in status (and capacities), but allusion to the supposed natural inferiority of women works to offset these features. This is important, since marriage with Rosalind is Orlando's means of upward mobility and, as Montrose has argued, deflection of anxiety about powerful women is a key to the "atonement" among men and the mediation of status differences that the play finally achieves. There is no hint in act 5 that the difficulties described in the jig will actually disrupt their marriage.[66] Instead, predictions of marital disharmony are reserved for Touchstone and Audrey in a move that simultaneously shifts the consequences of jig "wisdom" onto appropriately lower-class subjects and reflects disapproval of the one marriage that broaches the crucial divide of gentle and base. The potentially disruptive voice of the jig has, in this case, been largely assimilated into the cultural work of the play.

Touchstone's scene with the "clown" William, where he bests his rustic rival for Audrey's love, has been read by Wiles and others as a pointed dismissal of the Kemp style of clowning, and it too incorporates elements of the jig.[67] In this instance, however, the unruly force of the jig as a focus for lower-class concerns is not completely managed. William, of course, was Kemp's name, and the character William here is represented as a lumbering rustic whose slow wits are no match for Touchstone. Kemp's trademark malapropisms (made famous by Dogberry) are, significantly, transferred to Audrey in this play. This William stands silently while Touchstone runs verbal circles around him: "Therefore, you clown, abandon—which is in the vulgar leave—the society—which in the boorish is company—of this female—which in the common is woman; which together is, abandon the society of this female, or, clown, thou perishest; or to thy better understanding, diest" (5.1.46–52). Touchstone's emphasis on the pejorative language of inferior status here—*clown, vulgar, boorish, common*—seems extreme, especially since William is perfectly courteous throughout the scene. Like Adam and Corin, William seems naturally to recognize his social superior and to yield to him. The irony here is that Touchstone is himself a clown.[68] Like the earlier pointed references to upper-class accusations of "villainy," Touchstone's extreme emphasis on ethicized status terms to assert his superiority (and William's inferiority) reveals, in a comically hyperbolized manner, the role of such words in the emerging ideologies of limited social mobility.

This scene, like the wooing scene between Rosalind and Orlando, recapitulates jig motifs in a slightly altered form. This time, however, the elements of jig as incorporated into the play may represent a more subversive view of class relations than the original jig. That jig, called "The Wooing of Nan," which probably dates from the late sixteenth century, represents a common jig (and folk game) motif of wooing by rival suitors to be resolved by a dance contest. The jig begins with the rustic Rowland (evidently a stock jig name but especially associated with Kemp), who laments the fact that his beloved has been stolen from him by a "farmers sonn" who has been able to give her fancy gifts:

> Oh but he gives her gay gold rings.
> & tufted gloves to were vpon a holly day
> and many other goodly things,
> that hath stolne my love away[69]

Significantly, the "wench" in question denies having been influenced by gifts and instead offers to marry whoever has the best capacity in dance:

> I will no[t] forsake
> my bony rowland for any gold
> if he can daunce as well as perce [the farmer's son]
> he shall have my hart in hold
>
> (434, lines 29–32)

The implications of the jig as a focus for issues related to social status become more complex and more conservative when the dance contest is interrupted by the arrival of a "gentleman," who offers the wench "both land & tower" if she will marry him. Significantly, the wench refuses even to entertain his suit:

> I thank you for yo'r good will
> But one of thes my love must be.
> I ham but a homely countrie maid
> & farr vnfitt for yo'r degree
>
> (435, lines 48–51)

At this point the jig seems to be reinforcing class divisions and working against marriage across class lines. Suddenly, however, a "fool" of indeterminate class enters, begins to dance in a more lively (and possibly obscene) fashion, and wins the wench for himself, as she announces: "wellcom sweet hert & wellcom my tony [a stock fool name] / wellcome my none true love wellcom my huny / this is my love that my husband must be" (436, lines 60–62). The gentleman, clearly put out by this final insult, attributes a sexual motive to the wench: "I thought she had but Iested & ment but to fable / but now I doe see she hath play[d] wth his bable" (436, lines 68–69). "The Wooing of Nan," then, ends with the triumph of the least likely candidate over three variously qualified suitors. Although the jig introduces the issue of upward mobility through marriage, its punch line involves the substitution of sexual vigor for wealth or class as the central criterion for marriage and thus deflects direct treatment of issues related to social status and mobility.

The wooing of Audrey is, of course, both similar and different in its treatment of status. On the one hand, Audrey, like Nan, rejects a rustic Kemp-like clown for someone primarily identified as a "fool." However, the jig makes no attempt to differentiate the rustic and the fool because of status; the fool seems to win because of superior vigor in dancing (with the implication that this can be associated with superior sexual vigor). Unlike Nan, who rejects both the wealthy farmer's son and the even wealthier "gentleman," Audrey chooses the courtly Touchstone over William. She does not seem disturbed by the recognition of status difference, which led Nan to reject the gentleman out of hand; on the other hand, she does not seem interested in the physical and sexual superiority, which explain the fool's appeal to Nan. Thus, Touchstone wins not with a display of physical ability but with his verbal agility, a gift that Audrey in any case seems poorly equipped to appreciate. In general, however, the jig's festive ethos—that sexual prowess is a better basis for marriage than wealth, love, or social standing—is shifted to make Audrey, like Orlando and Oliver, marry "up" the social scale. Audrey's upward mobility through marriage is thus present in the play as a disturbing parallel for the other, more acceptable unions.

Throughout, the play's dismissal of the traditional rustic clown is complicated by its pastoral topoi, which suggest that the country is at least ethically better than the court.[70] When Touchstone, employing a comic catechism characteristic of Armin's new paradoxical humor, "proves" Corin to be damned because he has never been at court, part of the humor arises from Corin's echo of classical commonplaces about the superiority of country life: "I earn that I eat, get that I wear, own no man hate, envy no man's happiness, glad of other men's good, content with my harm" (3.2.73–76). Indeed, Touchstone admits that Corin is "a natural philosopher" (3.2.32), a phrase that puns on Armin's own imitation of a "natural" fool. Similarly, it is Audrey who asks a pointed question about the nature of poetry ("Is it honest in deed and word? Is it a true thing" [3.3.17–18]) and who more straightforwardly echoes Celia's comment about the inequity of Fortune's gifts to women—Celia: "Those that she makes fair she scarce makes honest, and those that she makes honest she makes very ill-favoredly" (1.2.37–39); Audrey: "I am not a slut, though I thank the gods I am foul" (3.3.39). Despite Touchstone's insistence that he belongs at court, he is repeatedly associated with rustic women—with Audrey, of course, but also in his fanciful account of wooing "Jane Smile," involving "kissing of her batler and the cow's dugs that her pretty chopp'd hands had milk'd" (2.4.49–50). As Wiles has pointed out, Kemp's clowns were not included in the marriages at the ends of plays. Instead, the concluding jig, as we have seen, provided a radically different view of sexuality and marriage. In *As You Like It*, however, Touchstone and Audrey marry within the play and alongside the gentle characters, thus including a less idealized view of love within the play itself.[71] Of course, Rosalind and Orlando (and Oliver and Celia) have married across a significant status demarcation (noble/gentle), but no one questions the potential success of these unions. However, when Touchstone and Audrey attempt to bridge the separation of base and gentle, their union is depicted as a potential disaster ("thy loving voyage / Is but for two months victuall'd"). This observation may serve to question the concept of upward mobility through marriage, but it also works to justify it among those of gentle status by stressing that it should not go too far. In this case, the potentially disruptive force of the jig is essentially harnessed to work toward the ideological interests of the play as a whole.

In other ways, however, the play seems to let questions about the excluded clown retain their disruptive force. Wiles has argued that "the social origins of Armin's stage fools are always left mysterious" so that the plays can explore the universality of folly.[72] But *As You Like It* seems to insist on Touchstone's status as a courtier in relation to the rustics in Arden and suggests that success in his case (in gaining Audrey) necessarily means that someone else (William) must fail. Thus, although the central focus of the play is on upward mobility and the preservation of gentle status, it also introduces instances of downward mobility (Corin, Adam, and William) that seem to be its corollary. Focus on shifting terms such as *villain* and *clown* and the ironies repeatedly attendant on their usage calls our attention to the ways in which the depreciative or appreciative specialization of these terms can be used to justify both upward and downward shifts in social status. The balance of plot and mode certainly works toward the negotiation of issues that would be of concern to a generally privileged audience. But the play also gestures toward the concerns of wage laborers, servants, and clowns.

Given that the paying audience for the play was most likely composed of more privileged persons, that Shakespeare and the other members of the company had aspirations of financial success and status mobility, and that this very play marks a new attempt by the company to appeal to an audience of higher status, why would the play even indirectly question the ideological strategies that enabled the maintenance and attainment of privilege?[73] For one thing, however hard the Chamberlain's Men might try to reduce the number of vagrants in their audience, they could not forget that the actors onstage were in perennial danger of falling to that status. Indeed, the *Acte for the punishment of Vacabondes,* cited above, specifically orders that all "Fencers Bearewardes Comon Players in Enterludes & Minstrels, not belonging to any Baron of this Realme . . .

shalbee taken adjudged and deemed Roges Vacaboundes and Sturdy Beg-
gers."[74] However many possibilities for a movement upward in status
were offered by shareholding in the Globe, the case of Will Kemp would
suggest that movement in the other direction was also possible. Ironically,
the Chamberlain's Men seem to have decided that their best chance of
success (and thus of avoiding designation as vagrants themselves) lay in
excluding or severely curtailing the jigs that attracted crowds of unruly
vagrants to the playhouse. Thus, their own upward mobility was enabled
by the exclusion of Kemp and all he stood for.

Also at issue, as Hamlet's words remind us, and as Helgerson has argued, was the author's control over the words of the play and the relation
of that control to his own ambition and the ambitions of the actors.[75] It
is easy for us to assume that such control was desirable, and indeed, as
Peter Stallybrass and Margreta de Grazia have recently pointed out, our
apparatus of bibliography and scholarly editing is designed to efface the
collaborative elements of Shakespeare's theater and to construct a (nonexistent) "pure" Shakespearean text. It is true that throughout the seventeenth century there was steady movement toward a "modern" concept
of authorship, and the replacement of Kemp by an actor more likely to
perform the lines as written, along with the exclusion of the potentially
subversive jig, may have been one small step along that path.[76]

What is less clear, at least in *As You Like It*, is how control over words
relates to social as well as ethical status. Touchstone's victories over the
rustic characters (Corin, Audrey, William) are based on his superior control over words. Unlike Dogberry (the archetypal Kemp clown), he can
make words do what he wants them to do. However, Corin, Audrey, and
William sometimes, in their seeming lack of control, appear to gain a
dignity that the manic Touchstone lacks. Touchstone points out to William that "the fool doth think he is wise, but the wise man knows himself
to be a fool" (5.1.31–32), and as always, Armin's paradoxical wit under-
mines itself. Similarly, getting rid of Kemp was seemingly a way for the
author to gain control over characters, to make sure that the words were
spoken as they were written, to let the author have the last word. In the
case of *As You Like It*, these changes appear to have facilitated, at least
initially, the play's being used to justify the very kinds of mobility it sought
for itself and its author.

Despite this measure of newly achieved control over the verbal register
of the performance, the author still had to contend with the ideological
implications of language. He could use such terms as *villain* and *clown*
without introducing into the play the workings of ideology to reproduce
the propertied classes at the expense of those below. Furthermore, many
critics would argue that he could not use those terms without implicating
himself in their ideologies, so that to gain control over dialogue (by assur-

ing that it would be spoken as written) was to put himself under the control of language itself. Like Touchstone, he could try to regain control by using those words ironically, by using them, as I believe Shakespeare does here, in ways that call attention to their functions within the ideologies of status and mobility. Of course to do so was to risk undermining the ideological formations at work in enabling his own nascent identity as successful author and would-be gentleman.

Beyond the ironies of this play, however, I think a note of regret can be felt—regret over the loss of Kemp and the jigs, over a gain in authorial control at the cost of distance from comedy's festive roots and the theater's collaborative fertility. It is this emotional shading, the subtle inflection of concepts by complex social feelings, that both Antonio Damasio and Leslie Brothers have emphasized as an integral part of human cognition.[77] It is also this affective content that Marxist and New Historicist criticism, with their tendency to focus on ideology and power relations, can sometimes fail to note. Shakespeare's ability both to participate in the mobility made possible by the cultural changes mediated by words such as *villain* and *clown* and, at the same time, to perceive the uses of these words as if from a distance and to regret the work that they do might, in more traditional criticism, be seen as a characteristic of his famous "negative capability." It might be possible here to redefine that capability as involving an unusual awareness of the complexities of thought and feeling that lie behind the lexical and conceptual structures in the brain—an awareness that prevents meaning from seeming transparent or obvious.

That such awareness might complicate interpellation within family structures may be suggested by Shakespeare's representation in the play of hostility located in both older and younger brothers. Although Montrose emphasizes reasons why Shakespeare might represent the plight of younger sons with more sympathy in order to appeal to an audience that probably contained a large proportion of those disinherited by primogeniture, psychoanalytic critics have tended to emphasize Shakespeare's own family position as an oldest son displaced by several younger brothers (and effectively "disinherited" by his father's financial failure).[78] Shakespeare's feelings about the failure of Will Kemp may have been colored by his feelings about another actor who, like Kemp, died in poverty and without a will. Edmund Shakespeare evidently followed his successful older brother to London, where the Parish register of St. Giles Cripplegate records him simply as "player, base born." William Shakespeare, of course, is recorded in the Stratford register as "Will Shakspere, gent." when he died in 1616, nine years after his younger brother, the base-born player. These complex events suggest that for Shakespeare, conceptions of status, mobility, brotherhood, and brothers who accuse each other of villainy were shaped and colored by mixed and contradictory emotions.

As You Like It thus takes us to the forest in order to sever, or at least to transform, the connection between drama and rustic festivity; later Shakespeare comedies have urban or country-house settings more appropriate to Armin's "gentle" fool. Finally, the play uses the question whether "nature" or "fortune" plays a greater role in the attainment and maintenance of status simultaneously to obscure and reveal the real issue: that those terms and other status terms were changing in ways that could be beneficial to those who had the power to use them, with full awareness of their double-edged ironies, for their own benefit. Shakespeare was preeminently able to do so, and the play reveals his dexterity, but also his misgivings about that project.

3

Twelfth Night: Suitable Suits and the Cognitive Space Between

Twelfth Night, Or What You Will, as almost all critics have noticed and as its subtitle attests, is about desire, especially as it relates to identity and disguise.[1] Most have read the play as showing the characters experiencing a movement from false or obstructive desires to acceptable ones and thus simultaneously clarifying their identities. The defining characteristics of acceptability differ depending on each critic's approach; a New Critical reader such as John Hollander sees limitation of excessive appetite as the key, while in Coppélia Kahn's psychoanalytic reading each protagonist must move from narcissistic desire for a similar object to a more mature relationship with someone different.[2] New Historicist approaches have focused on the need to channel desire toward someone of appropriate social status.[3] Relatively few critics have suggested that desire or disguise in the play remains uncontrolled; however, Barbara Freedman's Lacanian reading stresses the ways in which the play represents desire as inextricably related to loss, while Geoffrey Hartman celebrates language in the play as coining "its metaphors and fertile exchanges beyond any calculus of loss and gain."[4]

In seeking modern or postmodern terms for the movements of desire in the play, these critics have failed to notice the ways the play itself calls attention to a contemporary means of conceptualizing the simultaneous expression and control of desire and the assumption and revelation of identity through disguise. In this play Shakespeare explores multiple senses of the word *suit*, which in the early modern period named a nexus of ways in which desire was both satisfied and controlled, as well as ways in which clothing was used both to reveal and to conceal the self. Like *house* in *The Comedy of Errors* and *villain* in *As You Like It*, *suit* in *Twelfth Night* delineates another set of spatially structured concepts for understanding how subjects become themselves by interacting with other subjects and with their material environment; suits of various kinds thus form the interface between self and other and between physiological and cultural components of identity. Critics have generally pointed to a trajectory from one state of desire or identity to another, but in my view the play emphasizes cognitive process rather than historical or personal progress; in fact, the play uses the spatial schemas on which concepts of *suit* are based to problematize the traditional link between movement through space and the attainment of a goal.

In *Twelfth Night* Shakespeare again plays on the margins of polysemy, this time exploring a case that, according to classical linguistic categories, would include some instances of homonymy (different words with the same spelling, e.g., law *suit* and *suit* of clothes) as well as polysemy (e.g., law *suit* and *suit*, or wooing, of a woman). But cognitive linguistic theory stresses, as I think the play also does, that all senses of *suit* here are linked, possibly by a "family resemblance" chain, based on their relation to spatial concepts of following or pursuit.[5] The differences between these versions of *suit* are based, in interesting ways, on the degree and nature of agency involved: whether the subject is actively pursuing what he desires or following someone else's desires; whether clothing "follows" or matches social status or conceals it. Pushing the boundaries of polysemy, the play also insists on instantiations of the word that call on seemingly opposite versions of agency; *suit* in the sense of wooing suggesting active pursuit of desire and *suit* in the sense of accommodating oneself to the needs and desires of another person.[6] By exploring the ability of a single linguistic form to refer to what Taylor calls "incompatible attribute specifications" (120), Shakespeare investigates the logic of meaning itself. Challenging the boundaries of polysemic categories as he does here, Shakespeare offers not a narrative of channeling and discovery but rather a focus on what the complex linkages of meaning within the network of *suits* can tell us about the nature, causes, and achievement of both identity and desire.

According to Lacanian theory, desire emerges from the constitutive lack at the center of the human subject. The outwardly directed desire for the Other thus represents an attempt to recover the parts of the self lost when the subject is split by entry into the symbolic. As we have seen, however, cognitive theory represents the formation of the subject in slightly different terms. Emphasizing the somatosensory "feeling" of self-presence as the center of consciousness (rather than Lacan's hollow and illusory visual image), cognitive theory posits a self that feels itself to be at least bodily a partially integrated whole. Cognitive theory acknowledges that this feeling of integration may be illusory, a product of temporal rather than spatial concurrence. But a cognitive approach nevertheless emphasizes a feeling of presence (rather than lack) as the basis of the self. As we have also seen, cognitive theory suggests the importance of spatiality as the basis of this human sense of self and of conceptualization. Lakoff's "kinesthetic image schema" of containment, for example, is based on infants' experiences of their "own bodies as containers. Perhaps the most basic things we do are ingest and excrete, take air into our lungs and breathe it out."[7] This and other image schemas stem from basic bodily experiences in space and time and are extended to form metaphoric representations of abstract concepts.

Desire too has a different role in the formation of the cognitive subject. Rather than emerging from the fragmentation of the self, desire is seen to be bound up with the emergence of both consciousness and thought. We can recall Daniel Stern's observation that in infants "learning itself is motivated and affect-laden," deeply influenced by feelings and desires.[8] Gerald Edelman argues that higher consciousness itself is dependent upon desire: the brain must learn to delay its responses, which happens "by comparison and reward during social transmission and learning. During the acquisition of semantics, that reward arises by relating speech symbols to the gratification of affective needs by conspecifics in parental, grooming, or sexual interactions."[9] Rather than a Lacanian scenario of desire emerging from a sense of loss in the mirror stage that is intensified by the acquisition of language (which necessarily carries cultural prescriptions for the channeling of desire), cognitive theorists posit subjectivity, physiologically and affectively based desires, and cultural norms acquired together and inextricably linked. As F. Elizabeth Hart has put it, "Subjectivity, language, text, and culture are bound up in a matrix of cause and effect, each affecting others and being affected by others in a dynamic of exchange that is both accretive and infinitely circular."[10] In *Twelfth Night* Shakespeare uses the complex lexical network of *suits* to explore a range of spatial concepts placing the self in relation to others and its cultural environment. The traditional narrative movement toward a goal is just one of several spatial manifestations of self and desire in the play.

Nevertheless, an element of historical narrative is relevant to the concepts of desire expressed in the play because several of the cultural domains relevant to defining *suit* were undergoing significant change in the early modern period. As with *villain* in *As You Like It*, play on *suit* in *Twelfth Night* alludes to changes in legal and social institutions attendant upon the shift from the hierarchical controls of feudalism to burgeoning individual autonomy under emergent capitalism. Like *clown* in *As You Like It* and *house* in *Comedy of Errors*, *suit* in *Twelfth Night* also glances at the material practices of theater, in this case at the suits of livery that actors wore to delineate their status as servants and the elaborate suits worn onstage as costumes that sumptuary laws would otherwise forbid the players to wear. In both cases, the changing conceptualizations of *suit* reveal that desire and constraint are interconnected on the most basic levels and that the movement of the play is not toward the control of desire and disguise but toward an acceptance of the constant flux between loss, desire, and control that forms the basis of the cognitive self.

Critics may be so ready to see a trajectory of desire in the play because of the basic role of Lakoff's "source-path-goal" schema in our thinking about that concept. From the spatial experience of embodied movement we learn that "every time we move anywhere there is a place we start from, a place we wind up at, a sequence of contiguous locations connecting the starting and ending points" (275). When we metaphorically map this schema onto abstract concepts, "purposes are understood in terms of destinations, and achieving a purpose is understood as passing along a path from a starting point to an endpoint. Thus, one may *go a long way toward* achieving one's purposes, or one may get *sidetracked*, or find something getting *in one's way*."[11] Freud's term *trieb* (drive) reflects the forward movement associated with desire according to this spatial schema. The word *suit* participates in this schema through its derivation from the past participle of the Latin word *sequere* (to follow). It is in all its senses extended from various concepts of following or pursuit.

Stephen Greenblatt has noticed the importance of spatiality and movement to the treatment of desire in this play, citing Shakespeare's own use of a metaphor (from the game of bowls) of "bias," or curved movement, to suggest that "to be matched with someone of one's own sex is to follow an unnaturally straight line; heterosexuality, as the image of nature drawing to her bias implies, is bent."[12] Greenblatt goes on to suggest that this "deflection," represented thematically as "an essential life-truth—you reach a desired or at least desirable destination not by pursuing a straight line but by following a curved path" (71), "can only be revealed in movement," which the play provides by embodying "a structure whose realization depends upon temporal unfolding, or *rolling*" (68). This analogy between movement through space and the passage of time is another common example of metaphoric extension from a concrete, observable phenomenon (movement of an object through space) to form a concept of an invisible abstraction (time).[13] And yet, time is not necessarily imagined in this way, as Viola demonstrates when she uses a static metaphor to describe the process of time: "O time, thou must untangle this, not I, / It is too hard a knot for me t'untie" (2.2.40–41). Time is imagined here as suspended in a web, which it attempts to sort out. So, too, in the play, for while plot must unfold lineally through time, emphasis on the semantic web of suits at various points throughout the play can work against our perception of its progressive movement. *Suit* does not mean one thing at the beginning of the play and something else at the end, nor do characters learn to replace a false meaning with a true one. Instead, its multiple meanings are equally present throughout. In insisting on the different spatial references of various forms of "suit" (and in what I argue is a sort of visual pun on the similarly structured words *gate* and *gait*), Shakespeare makes evident the spatiality inherent in our thinking about desire and questions the adequacy of those spatial metaphors. History and plot may proceed in a linear fashion, but meaning (and perhaps identity), the play reveals, is not necessarily structured in this way.

When Viola is first introduced, in act 1 scene 2, she and the captain suggest the complex ways in which suits of various kinds are integral to her sense of herself and her desires. When the captain tells Viola that Olivia "will admit no kind of suit, / No, not the Duke's" (1.3.45–46), he uses *suit* in such a way as to conflate an older sense, "the action or an act of suing, supplicating, or petitioning," a meaning that was current from the fifteenth century, and a new specialized meaning, extended from the original sense in the late sixteenth century, which indicates the "the wooing or courting of a woman" (1.2.50–51). Viola's repetition of the same linguistic form four lines later ("I will believe thou hast a mind that suits / With this thy fair and outward character") calls on a quite different meaning, namely, "to make consonant or accordant with," a meaning that first appeared around 1600 (perhaps in *As You Like It*) and that, despite its extension from the same concepts of following or pursuit as the desiring kind of suit, might nevertheless be considered a homonym rather than a different sense of the same word. The proximate repetition of the word in two different senses (or two homonyms extended from the same basic sense) seems strange, as, indeed, does Viola's little unmotivated digression on the possibility that the captain might not be as good as he seems. *Suit* here is used to designate both a means of obtaining one's desire and also a form of self-regulation that inhibits desire to what is appropriate. In the next few lines Viola alludes to her "disguise" as a male servant, conjuring up *suit* as servant's livery as well as theatrical costume, that is, a suit that reveals its wearer's social status, position, and gender, as well as a suit that conceals them. These tensions between active attempts to achieve what one desires and constraints that ensure that desires and behavior are "suitable" and between clothes that reveal and conceal a person's nature and status are moving forces throughout the rest of the play. The complex cultural matrix surrounding the word *suit* becomes centrally relevant to the spinning out of these concepts in the text.

All forms of *suit* retain an etymologically based kinship with spatial schemas of following, accompanying, or pursuing. As noted above, Lakoff's "link" and "source-path-goal" schemas seem relevant to the ways in which complex polysemic chains, possibly structured as a "family resemblance" network or as a heterosemic category, spread out from this initial concept.[14] Various cultural changes seem relevant to understanding how meanings have been extended in this particular network. A basic meaning of the word proceeds from feudal institutions. Under the feudal system, retainers (followers) owed "suit and service" to their lords. The meaning of *service* (a word that is also of interest in the play) depended on the way in which their land was held; villeins owed labor, while those on a higher level might owe a pair of gloves or, in one memorable case, the obligation to jump into the air and fart on Christmas before the lord. *Suit* meant "suit of court," the retainer's obligation to attend periodic manorial courts, where social and agricultural customs were enforced and fines collected.[15] *Suit* could also refer to a tenant's obligation to use only the lord's mill (with attendant fees) for grinding his corn.

Those "followers" who owed "suit" were thus placed under the control of the manorial court and were subject to its fines and responsibilities. Thirteenth-century village records indicate a number of cases when retainers attempted to deny their suits and were "distrained," that is, had belongings taken as a guarantee of attendance, to enforce it. Court roles of the manor of Hales in 1280, for example, record that "Nicholas de Monte defaulted and denied suit of court. The jury say that he does owe suit. The accused is distrained for default."[16] Similarly, in 1301 William de Yieldingtree acknowledged "a rent of 4d. a year paid in lieu of all services, and one pound of cumin for right of common pasture for his pigs and cattle," but he was "accused of failing to do fealty properly in that he omitted mention of suit of court" but "produced his charter, as evidence that he never owed suit of court."[17] In this period, then, a suit was not a means to pursue something desirable but rather was a means to enforce obedience among one's followers.

As early as the fifteenth century, however, *suit* also came to describe a court action undertaken (or pursued) by one person in order to obtain something from another. The changing and uncertain state of land and inheritance laws, combined with the ambitions of upwardly mobile gentry, made the late medieval and early modern periods extremely litigious—perhaps even more so than today. A study of the legal dealings of an upwardly mobile Norfolk family, the Townshends, in the fifteenth century reveals the extent to which an attempt to amass landholdings almost inevitably led to lawsuits as the Townshends sought to make their fortune by exploiting the financial difficulties of aristocratic families and those families used conservative inheritance laws to try to get back land they had sold in difficult times.[18] This family, like others in the period, was more likely to pursue legal action against social inferiors than against equals or superiors, and records from the period show that lawsuits accompanied by various forms of intimidation were often the means that powerful families used to maintain their position.[19] Law "suits," then, could be a means for ordinary people to pursue justice or desire, but they were more likely used by the already wealthy and powerful to protect their position. Nevertheless, the different spatial metaphors implied by the idiomatic expressions *owe suit to* and *bring suit against* suggest a difference in the nature of the agency implied by different senses of the word.

By the sixteenth century, perhaps because of the increasing importance of the royal court, *suit* became a common term for the attempt to gain favor from the monarch. In this sense, the word takes on connotations almost opposite its original feudal meaning since the Elizabethan court found it necessary to limit, rather than enforce, the attendance of suitors. In 1593 a proclamation "Prohibiting Access to Court Because of Plague" ordered that "all private suitors shall forbear to come to court where her majesty shall reside until the 9th day of October next."[20] Another proclamation reveals that even when the plague was not a threat, there was concern about "idle vagrant persons . . . [who] haunt about the court, using a color of suits to her majesty or to her council or to others attendant on her majesty; whereas in truth many of them have no just cause of suits, or, though some of them have, yet when they have received their answers do not depart but live idly about the court as vagrants." The proclamation directs that as "a remedy hereof her majesty forbiddeth all persons that are not servitors to her majesty in her court, or that are not attendant servitors upon the council or upon other lords and ladies or gentlemen attending on her majesty, to forbear to come to the court or near the court."[21]

The word *suit* was not used to describe romantic courtship until the late sixteenth century; thus, *suitor* originally meant "follower" or one who owed suit, then "petitioner or suppliant" at court, and only later one seeking to satisfy erotic rather than material desires. The word thus shifted through various forms of category extension from suggesting a means of enforcement, constraint, and feudal allegiance, to describing a legal means of obtaining material desire (or of curbing others' desires), and finally to a more personal and private solicitation. As the word in this sense moved toward freedom and individual self-expression from social control, however, another sense of the word brought control back into the lexical web. The use of *suitable* to mean "acceptable" developed from its sense as "follower,"—one follows or accords with some norm—but suggests self- rather than external control. The contours of the etymology of *suit* in this regard thus seem roughly to follow Foucault's trajectory from external regulation (punishment) to internal self-discipline.[22] The etymology suggests, however, that regulation is bound up with desire and that in fact the possibility of unruly desire can only be recognized when efficient means of both external and internal regulation already exist as part of the mechanism for its satisfaction.

Suit of clothes in this period had two potential meanings, each with different implications about the relationship between attire and the representation of social status or position. The phrase originally designated "a livery or uniform . . . clothed in the same garb or colour as the members of a retinue or fraternity" (*OED*). Here again by extension from a basic sense of *follow*, the clothing is a "suit" because it accords with—"follows"—that worn by others who are members of the same group or are of the same status. As Peter Stallybrass has pointed out, this kind of livery was itself polysemic in that it could denote both "servitude and freedom from such servitude. To oversimplify, livery in a *household* was a mark of servitude whereas livery in a *guild* was a mark of freedom."[23] The livery worn by players in this period was related, according to Stallybrass, to both guild and household liveries. It was only in the fifteenth century that *suit* came to mean "a set of garments or habiliments intended to be worn together at the same time"; in this sense the "suit" matches or follows itself, and not the clothing of others. *Suit* is often used in this sense for a theatrical costume. Costume inventories of the period list "Antik sutes" and "Clownes Sewtes and Hermetes Sewtes" and specify such costumes as "Roben Hoodes sewtte," "Perowes sewt, which Wm Sley wore," "Longeshankes seute," and many others.[24] Jean MacIntyre cites Henslowe's reference to the making of "ij sewtes a licke [alike]" as a possible analogue to the identical suits of Viola and Sebastian in *Twelfth Night*.[25] Sumptuary laws expressly allowed players to wear elaborate clothing onstage that they would otherwise not have had sufficient rank to wear. Thus, players routinely wore two kinds of "suits," both livery that designated their mixed status in relation to guild and household servitude and elaborate costumes that represented their status as higher than it actually was. Suitable suits for players could both reveal and conceal their gender, status, and position in extremely complex ways.

Several senses of *suit* came together in discussions of the changing relationships between master and servant in late-sixteenth-century England. Around this time a pamphlet entitled *A Health to the Gentlemanly Profession of Serving-Men* (1598) was written to deplore the various social changes that had, in the author's opinion, caused the situation of gentlemen servants to decline. Cristina Malcolmson has argued that *Twelfth Night* is "searching to articulate a new social bond between 'master' and 'servant,' one which would acknowledge choice and ensure a new kind of 'dependability,' based on contract rather than feudal obligation."[26] Many traditional ideas about loyalty, service, and liberality that surface in *Twelfth Night* are expressed in the pamphlet through articulation of different senses of *suit* and help to provide a sense of its place in the cultural lexicon at this time. The author, identified only as I.M., believed that gentlemen servants were being turned out of their jobs in the late sixteenth century as a result of the decline in the keeping of country houses and their masters' prodigal expenditure on fancy clothes in London instead of traditional hospitality at home. The gentleman servant's traditional remuneration of four marks and livery was being spent instead on ostentatious display: "The Taylors Bill, so much for such a Sute of laced Satten, and such lyke superfluous charges, amounting in one yeere to more then the reuenues of his Landes, the charge of House-keeping, and other necessaries undefrayde."[27] Thus, when a master bought elaborate "suits" for himself, he was unable to provide wages and suits of livery for his servants. Under these circumstances, I.M. complained, masters were no longer liberal in rewarding their servants, and servants were forced to "sue" for what had previously been given to them freely: "To crouch and Kneele now duetie bindes, / Though Sutor nought but righte doth begge" (E2v). This was a more personalized from of "suit" than the original feudal obligation, and in this context it became degrading as it became more personal. I.M. contrasted "former ages," when "Potentates and Gentlemen of worth, spent their whole Rentes and Reuenues in hospitalitie and good House-keeping" and "held Coyne in utter contempt," with the present, when "Money is the marke whereat they all shoote . . . Golde they grope after, Gayne they groane for" (G2v–G3r). That is, I.M. contrasted an age of generosity with an age of untrammeled selfish desire; as might be expected, he used spatial metaphors ("whereat they all shoote," "grope after") to describe the new age of desire.

The complex polysemous network of the word *suit* encodes the ways in which concepts of gratification and control, pretense and manifestation of actual status, were closely interconnected. By the late sixteenth century, ideas about what might be desired and how those desires might be achieved, as well as about how attire might express or conceal desire, were conceptualized through this set of words, which related desire and control in terms quite different from those used in the twentieth century. *Twelfth Night* seems most concerned to explore the multiple ways in which "suits" simultaneously control and enable desire and also the multiple gradations of agency encoded through the varying saliency of following and pursuit, self-containment and self-expression.

Whereas *The Comedy of Errors* is anchored spatially by its representation of three houses, *Twelfth Night* turns around only two poles, the court of Orsino and the house of Olivia.[28] A number of critics have noted the apparent suitability of a union of these two households, an expectation that the play notoriously thwarts.[29] The play as a whole examines what might be described as the "suit and service" relationships within and between these two households, with *suit* often representing the movements of desire between them and *service*, often discussed in terms of "suitability," suggesting the depiction of loyalties and ties within each one. As characters interact in both these senses, repetition of the word *suit* and related puns on *gate* and *gait* (both spelled *gate* in the folio text) underscore the complex relationships between desire and control (both societal and internal) that seem central to the representation of identity and relationship within the play. Rather than tracing a trajectory of desire that comes under control as a stable core of identity is confirmed, the play reveals that the mechanisms for achieving and controlling desire work together to determine the shape both of desire and of the self that experiences it. Spatial possibilities of imagining the self include not just pursuit of a goal but also attempts to contain (and hide) what is already within, keep out what is outside, or generously give out (or reveal) what is within.

Barbara Freedman has argued that Olivia's household is defined by absence or loss.[30] Its organizing principle, however, seems to be an attempt to preserve what it still possesses and to keep out what is outside it. A sign of this principle is Olivia's much-remarked attempt to use her tears as a pickling agent to "season / A brother's dead love, which she would keep fresh / And lasting in her sad remembrance" (1.1.29–31). This household is repeatedly depicted as closed off from the desires or suits of the outside world, and Olivia is especially concerned to enforce what she sees as suitable behavior within her stronghold. Olivia is associated with a concept of home as container that preserves the integrity of the self by keeping the outside out. Ironically, however, Olivia's attempt to keep suitors out leads to a proliferation of suits for her hand from within her household as well as from outside it, and her attempts to regulate suitable behavior on the part of its inhabitants lead to extreme and inappropriate behavior. In addition, Olivia seems unable, partly because of her lack of generosity, to retain the loyalty of one significant servant, her fool, who is frequently to be found in the Duke's household. Although some critics have argued that the play is concerned to discipline Olivia's unruly desire to run her own household, it perhaps goes even further in insinuating that she is not quite competent to run it herself.[31]

Olivia attempts to use her house as a fortress to exclude what she sees as unruly and inappropriate desire. She bears out the captain's prediction that she will "admit no kind of suit" when she directs Malvolio that if a visitor "be a suit from the count, I am sick, or not at home,—what you will, to dismiss it" (1.5.108–9). Described as a "cloistress" within her home, she is hidden by and confined within several shielding layers: her garden gate, the walls of the house itself, and the veil that conceals her face until Viola persuades her to lift it. The garden gate surfaces several times as an emblem of her confinement; Viola waits "at the gate" (1.5.99) to prefer the Duke's suit and later describes how she would "make me a willow cabin at your gate" if the suit were her own. Here the enclosed space of Olivia's house functions to preserve unviolated the enclosed space of her own body.[32]

The enclosed space that Olivia initially attempts to use to close out desire, however, becomes a private space that encourages desire once she has fallen in love with the Duke's messenger. In this sense, Olivia's house replicates the complex dialectic of public and private encoded in the physical structures of the public playhouse (and explored by Shakespeare in *The Comedy of Errors*). In act 3, scene 1, Olivia ensures that she is alone with Viola when she orders, "Let the garden door be shut, and leave me to my hearing" (3.1.92). Unlike houses in *The Comedy of Errors*, Olivia's enclosed house is depicted not behind a closed door but as existing in fluid space on the open stage. The confinement, then, is largely a function of language rather than of the actual physical structure of the stage. Peter Thomson notes that when Olivia gives that order to close the garden gate and create a private space for herself and Viola, "the Folio carries no stage direction for the exit of Sir Toby, Sir Andrew, and Maria," who also were previously onstage. He argues that Olivia's request causes the space to be "transformed from public to private, from generalized 'platea' to specific 'locus,' by the shutting of the stage door. . . . Rather than moving Olivia and Viola to a private place, Shakespeare has moved a private place to them."[33] This "private" place is doubly illusory since it is located on the open stage without clear spatial separation from the rest of the set and is also in full view of the audience. Olivia's attempts to close herself off from desire, then, create a private space where desire can flourish. The analogy between this private space and her own body becomes clear when she acknowledges her growing love for Cesario as a similar penetration of enclosed space: "Methinks I feel this youth's perfections / With an invisible and subtle stealth / To creep in at mine eyes" (2.1.296–98).

Her attempts to regulate the behavior of those who live in her household have similarly mixed success. She approves of her steward Malvolio because "he is sad and civil, / And suits well for a servant with my fortunes" (3.4.5–6). She would like to extend this suitable behavior to the other inhabitants of the household, and her servants Maria and Malvolio echo her language of suitability and confinement when they try to extend her rule over her kinsman Sir Toby and his friends. Maria fruitlessly urges Toby to "confine yourself within / the modest limits of order" (1.3.8–9), and Malvolio incurs his wrath by urging "respect of place, persons, [or] time" (2.3.91). This attempt at regulation fails, however, and both Maria and Malvolio are themselves, in different ways, moved to unsuitable behavior.[34] Gail Paster has argued that Malvolio's reference to Olivia's "great P's" functions to disrupt her attempts at self-enclosure: "Olivia's declared withdrawal from the gaze of men into the confines of her house and the enclosure of her veil—an enclosure already penetrated by the importunate Cesario—is a presumptuous individualistic claim not only to social but to bodily autonomy. But that claim is contradicted by the 'open' evidence of her great P's, which robs her of her difference from the common fate, the common bodiliness of woman."[35]

In fact, Olivia's ability to manage her household must, to some extent, be questioned. Although Sebastian is reassured of her sanity by her ability to "sway her house, command her followers, / Take and give back affairs, and their dispatch, / With such a smooth, discrete, and stable bearing" (4.3.17–19), in fact her household is not at all orderly. Sir Toby's freedom with Olivia's food and drink at all hours is behavior explicitly at odds with contemporary ideas about the containment functions of a well-regulated household. The Willoughby household orders of 1572, for example, instruct the usher to control "all disorders in the hall . . . and if there shall be any stubborn persons, he is to expell them out of the hall." Similarly, the underbutler "is to suffer no household servant to remain tipling, or to be at all in the buttery." The buttery, a special container within the house itself, was to be locked at 9:00 P.M. "and after by no means to be opened that night without special cause. The discretion of that officer is to foresee that no filching of bread or beer be suffer'd, nor yet any want where reason doth require may be greatly both for his master's profit and worshipp, for it is an office both of good credit and great trust."[36] Olivia's servants attempt to enforce these regulations, but the atmosphere of her household is such that all efforts at control seem destined to fail.

Although (under Toby's influence) her household does meet and even exceed the requirements of liberal housekeeping so valued by I. M., what he calls "the spirit of the Butterie,"[37] Olivia herself is less generous and seems less skilled at recognizing when, and how, to pay servants and thus is unable to retain the "service" and physical presence of her own fool. In this case her principles of conservation work against her since by eschewing generous giving she loses the loyalty of her servants. By the late sixteenth century, despite a century of inflation, wages for upper servants remained frozen at the traditional "5 marks and liverie" per year.[38] Servants were unable to live on this wage and relied on tips to survive. I.M. describes several circumstances when, at least in a former, more liberal age, tips might be expected. For example, if a gentleman servant "were sent to this Maisters friende . . . with a present or friendly remembrance," it was customary for the friend "to shew his thankfulnesse towardes his Servant, in liberally rewarding him for his paynes." Similarly, if a servant performed some duties for his master's friend while visiting in that household, "some pence redounded to their profite." Indeed, a master was expected to tip his own servant if "duetie and diligence, did merite and deserue it before he had it, though it was ouer and aboue his couenant and bargayne."[39] In *Twelfth Night* the tipping of servants is frequently commented upon. Viola, Sebastian, Toby, and Orsino all tip Feste; Toby and Orsino specifically pay him for singing a song, but Viola and Sebastian simply offer reward for witty dialogue (e.g., Viola: "there's expenses for thee" [3.1.43]).[40] Olivia, significantly, never gives him money in the play; of course she has no interest in hearing him sing, but neither does she reward his witty dialogue with her in act 1, scene 5. This lack of generosity on her part may explain why, as Viola has noticed, he spends much of his time at Orsino's house.[41] Indeed, Maria warns Feste that "my lady will hang thee for thy absence" (1.5.4).

Unlike Olivia and her constitutive efforts at enclosure, Orsino defines himself, at least nominally, through the outward trajectory of desire. It is his "suit" that she refuses to admit; his version of I.M.'s arrow metaphor for desire ("shoot at the mark") takes on overtones of phallic aggression: his love is "the rich golden shaft" that will kill "the flock of all affections else" (1.1.34, 35). It is also Orsino who is willing to take in (music, food, and suitors) and also to give out (generous tips). As critics have often noted, he repeatedly uses imagery of gluttonous eating to describe his desires: "If music be the food of love, play on, / Give me excess of it" (1.1.1–2); "mine is all as hungry as the sea, / And can digest as much" (2.4.100–101). And it is he who accepts into his household the stranger, Cesario, and has soon "unclasp'd / To thee the book even of my secret soul" (1.4.13–14). In contrast with Olivia's ideal of closed, impermeable boundaries, Orsino thus represents himself as both open and directly expressive of his desires.

As in Olivia's case, Orsino's self-representation is not entirely accurate since he does not in fact pursue his desire himself, employing Viola/Cesario as a proxy, nor is he able (at least for most of the play) to recognize or accept Viola's love for him. Jean Howard has argued that Orsino "initially poses a threat to the Renaissance gender system by languidly abnegating his active role as masculine wooer," although in the end he "emerges from his claustrophobic house" and assumes his proper masculine role.[42] Although Orsino does, like Olivia, remain within his house, he is at least able to use the language of desire and pursuit. While Olivia uses her garden "gate" to refuse his suit, Orsino directs Cesario to "address thy gait unto her, / Be not denied access" (1.4.15–16). In the folio text *gait* is spelled "gate," another instance of this play's signature type of polysemy, in which a single linguistic form can have opposite meanings: Olivia uses a "gate" to bar the "gate" of Orsino's suit. Viola's pun "I will answer you with gait and entrance" (3.1.82) insists on the family resemblance that links the two seemingly opposite senses of the word. As in the case of *suit* this resemblance is based on a spatial schema. *Gate* was originally the only available linguistic form and could mean both "way, road, or path" and "an opening in a wall, made for the purpose of entrance and exit, and capable of being closed by a movable barrier." Both of these forms emphasize movement *through* space, and they may be derived from the root *get*, meaning either "receptacle" or "means of reaching." By metonymic extension from the second sense, *gate* could also mean "the barrier itself," a meaning that emphasizes its static, exclusionary force. *Gait* is also extended, to mean "manner or style of going," and in this sense, like a "suit," it can be indicative of character, as when Maria plans to fool Malvolio by praising "the shape of his leg, the manner of his gait" (2.3.156–57). *Gate* meaning "way or road" came to be spelled "gait" in the seventeenth century. Like *suit,* in the late sixteenth century these words were on the verge of homonymy but still linked (as Viola's pun makes clear) by association with concepts of movement through space. Like *suit, gate* emphasizes the extent to which personally revealing and desirous movement cannot be clearly separated from attempts to contain it or close it out.

Ironically, the outward-reaching Orsino is better able to retain loyal servants within his own household. Olivia's own fool, as we have seen, prefers Orsino's house to hers, perhaps because of Orsino's generosity and openness. And Orsino is surrounded, not by unruly hangers-on, but by retainers eager to flatter and serve him. Viola, of course, despite her initial wish that she "served that lady," remains loyal to Orsino throughout. Olivia's attempt to tip her at 2.1.283, "spend this for me," leads not to a Feste-like transfer of loyalty but to an indignant refusal, "I am no fee'd post, lady; keep your purse." Viola's response here may indicate her confused and confusing status in the play. It is Viola who both embodies the Duke's trajectory of desire (his "suit" and "gait" toward Olivia) and conceals or contains her "real" self more effectively than does Olivia.

Traditional criticism of the play has often commented on Viola's role as "a catalyst . . . who becomes the agent required to free Orsino and Olivia from the bondage of their self-delusions."[43] Viola does seem uniquely able to see the problematic aspects of the spatial orientations of Orsino and Olivia or of suits of various kinds. She can see the containing function of the body (so important to Olivia) as potentially dangerous and deceptive in various ways. Her initial comment to the captain that "nature with a beauteous wall / Doth oft close in pollution" (1.3.48–49) suggests that a containing self can keep in bad as well as good. Her speech to the Duke about her own contained and concealed love suggests that feelings that are kept in can become self-consuming and self-destructive: "she never told her love, / But let concealment like a worm i'th'bud / Feed on her damask cheek" (2.4.110–12). She also comments on Olivia's lack of generosity when she tells her: "you do usurp yourself; for what is yours to bestow is not yours to reserve" (1.5.188–89). On the other hand, she represents the Duke's permeability and aggressive pursuit as similarly problematic; she notes the dangers of impressionability: "How easy is it for the proper-false / In women's waxen hearts to set their forms" (2.2.29–30). And Viola never directly "pursues" the Duke, preferring instead to disguise herself and wait for "time" to untangle the knot of confused suits and desires, hoping that somehow her disguise will "become the form of my intent" (1.3.54–55).

Of course, the spatial configurations of selfhood employed by Orsino and Olivia correspond to some extent with expectations about hierarchical and gendered behavior in the period, expectations that Viola is to some extent able to evade. Orsino's language of aggressive pursuit, generosity, and conspicuous consumption would seem to conform to upper-class male cultural models, whereas Olivia's enclosure and containment would preserve inviolate the chaste "classical body" of a noble woman.[44] Although any person who inhabits a body might conceivably experience all of these spatialities of selfhood, it is clear that in the cases of Olivia and Orsino cultural norms are seen as limiting the spatial experiences that are considered suitable in relation to gender and class roles.

Viola, on the other hand, articulates a sense of both desire and identity as an ongoing process rather than either pursuit of a static goal or the stasis of self-enclosure. In act 5, for example, she characterizes her experiences in the course of the play as a movement "between this lady and this lord," a description that not only sums up her position as a mean between their two extremes of spatial orientation but also captures her sense of herself as constantly in motion between two points (rather than moving toward a goal or standing still). Her relatively static sense of time, as noted above, seems relevant to her sense of herself in space. Her initial statement of intent to assume "such disguise as haply shall become / The form of my intent" is, as Cristina Malcolmson has pointed out, ambiguous in several ways: "The word 'form' reproduces the riddles about inner and outer identity that pervade the scene, and the word 'become' increases the dilemma."[45] *Become* here, like *between* in the passage just cited, suggests Viola's sense that her identity, like her desire (or "intent"), is always in a process of becoming true to its spatial experience of its own "form." This sense of "becoming" or "betweenness" is what informs Viola's willingness to wait for time to untangle her problems. Indeed, even at the end of the play, when she is reunited with Sebastian and her "true" identity (in terms of class and gender) is revealed, Viola expresses a sense that she is not yet quite herself: "do not embrace me till each circumstance / Of place, time, fortune, do cohere and jump / That I am Viola" (5.1.251–53). Once again, Viola's ideal of time is static rather than based on a metaphor of linear movement through space: she will only be herself when place and time cohere in the same, still space.

It may be that the complex polysemy of Viola's "suit" of clothes provides her with an ambiguous space from which to observe and judge the spatiality of others' suits. Much has been written about the implications of cross-dressing for the distinction or confusion of gender boundaries.[46] From the time that Viola asks her own suitable servant the captain to hide her dress and procure for her a man's suit (for which service she tips him "bounteously"), she ambivalently wears that suit as a costume, concealing her gender but also, in more complicated ways, both concealing and revealing her social status. Thus, Viola, as she pursues the Duke's suit, is wearing a suit that is unsuitable in as many as three different ways. Malcolmson rightly suggests that the play "veils and manipulates" Viola's social status, but critics have not acknowledged the extent to which her "suit" is a crucial factor here.[47]

As G. K. Hunter, Jean MacIntyre, and others have argued, it was important that theatrical costume in the early modern period function as a visual emblem of its wearer's status and profession so that the character's role in the play would be immediately obvious to an audience accustomed even in everyday life to assessing status quite precisely through clothing.[48] Lisa Jardine has explained in detail the ways in which "dress, in the early modern period, was regulated by rank, not by income."[49] And as MacIntyre notes, "Stage costume showed its wearer's sex, rank, occupation, and often his age and marital status."[50] In Viola's case, of course, her gender is in one sense actually obscured by her costume. Status and occupation, however, are also only ambiguously delineated since Viola never appears in servant's livery.

When Viola first decides to assume "such disguise as haply shall become / The form of my intent," she immediately articulates at least part of that intent: "I'll serve this duke; / Thou shalt present me as an eunuch to him" (1.2.55–56). The costume she assumes, however, is a gentleman's suit identical (or nearly so, otherwise they could not be so easily mistaken) to that worn by her brother, Sebastian.[51] When the Duke is confronted, in act 5, with Viola and Sebastian together, he comments that their clothes appear to him as "one habit" worn by "two persons" (5.1.216–17). Viola thus rather surprisingly continues to wear that suit even after she has obtained a position as a page in the Duke's household, the kind of large, noble establishment where liveries would almost certainly be worn.[52] Such a gentleman's suit would probably be fairly elaborate; Henslowe's lists of properties include many fine and fashionable gentlemen's "sewtes" designed to contribute to the spectacular nature of a performance.[53] Indeed, Peter Stallybrass has argued that "the commercial theater is directly *derived* from the market in clothes," as pawnbrokers discovered the stage as a means to derive value from elaborate clothing pawned by nobles and not to be worn by anyone of lower rank.[54] When onstage, players were, of course, expressly exempted from sumptuary laws so that they could wear clothing indicative of higher status.

A gentleman servant in a large household would not usually wear a fashionable gentleman's suit. Instead, he would wear the livery of the house he served, usually a bright blue or tawny coat embroidered with an emblematic badge. The author of *A Health to the Gentlemanly Profession of Serving-Men* may have exaggerated the status of such gentlemen servants, asserting that "even the Dukes sonne preferred Page to the Prince, the Earles seconde sonne attendant upon the Duke, the Knights second sonne the Earles Seruant, the Esquires sonne toe weare the Knightes lyuerie, and the Gentlemans sonne the Esquiers Seruingman.' Nevertheless, he associated the "Blew coate and Badge," with all such servants, and evidence from a number of plays suggests that servants on-stage routinely wore it to indicate their role.[55] Other servants in *Twelfth Night*, Malvolio and Feste, wear clothing emblematic of their roles. Feste refers to his traditional fool's costume when he tells Olivia, "I wear not motley in my brain" (1.5.56–57), and Malvolio's transgression of his steward's livery with yellow stockings and crossed garters is an important visual joke (as is his inability to imagine himself, even as Olivia's husband, without his chain of office). In smaller households where servants did not wear livery, a page would nevertheless wear older, less fashionable clothes to set him apart from the gentleman of higher status whom he served.[56] Viola, however, wears a suit identical to that worn by her brother, a gentleman whom everyone considers to be a suitable match for Olivia.

Viola, then, does not wear livery (or inferior clothing) indicating her status as page to the Duke. This may explain Olivia's repeated questioning of her status even before she falls in love with her. Having been told by Maria that "there is at the gate a young gentleman much desires to speak to you," Olivia nevertheless asks Toby, "what is he at the gate, cousin" and when Toby replies "a gentleman," she asks, "a gentleman? What gentleman?" (1.5.116–18). At the end of their conversation after she has fallen in love with her, Olivia again questions Viola's status: "What is your parentage?" to be told yet again that it is "above my fortunes, yet my state is well: / I am a gentleman" (1.5.278–79). Viola here asserts that her status as servant is at variance with her true "estate" in life, yet her clothes, while concealing her gender, accord with and reveal that "estate." Olivia may be confused that a servant can appear in a gentleman's suit rather than in livery. Thus, although Viola's "suit" masks her true gender, it points toward her "gentle" status.

Of course, as playwright, Shakespeare would have had in mind an even more complicated sense of the "suitability" of Viola's suit with regard to gender and status because he would necessarily have been aware of the actor who played the role and of the complex and contradictory semiotics of that actor's various suits. Players like Viola wore suits that both revealed and concealed gender and social status; thus, like her, they occupied a social space that might well have provided a distanced vantage from which to view the spatial configurations of other people's suits. The fascination with different kinds of suits in this play reveals, I would argue, a process of thinking through the implications of several aspects of the material conditions of theatrical production—the use of boy actors to play women's roles, as well as the difference between the elaborate costumes worn onstage and the livery or plainer clothes worn by actors on the street. As many commentators on cross-dressing have noted, on one level Viola's male attire would have revealed the "truth" about the gender of the boy actor who played the role.[57] However, such a costume would not have revealed the boy's social status since a boy actor would normally have worn gentleman's suits only onstage. In the first place, sumptuary laws forbade him to wear such elaborate apparel on the street, and if he did, moralists inveighed against the breach of decorum: "Overlashing in apparel is so comon a fault, that the very hyerlings of some of our players . . . iet under gentlemens noses in sutes of silke."[58]

The elaborate costumes were probably the most valuable property owned both by a theatrical company and its individual sharers. As Stallybrass has pointed out, some company managers, such as Edward Alleyn and Christopher Beeson, began their theatrical careers by investing in costumes, which they could wear themselves, rent out to other actors, pawn in times of need, or resell.[59] The boy actors who played women's parts were usually apprenticed to regular sharers in the company and did not own their costumes. In many cases the principal actor would own the costumes used by his boy.[60] Since even principal actors were enjoined from wearing company costumes on the street, it seems even less likely that boy actors would regularly wear on the street expensive costumes owned by their masters. These boy actors were not even entitled to wear the liveries awarded to company sharers. We can only assume that since they were usually apprenticed to actors who belonged to some established guild like the grocers or goldsmiths, they were expected to wear the usual attire prescribed for apprentices: a flat woolen cap, no "ruffles, cuffs, loose collar . . . no doublets but what were made of canvas, fustian, sackcloth . . . only white, blue or russet hose to be worn . . . little breeches . . . a plain upper coat of cloth or leather."[61] The contrast between Viola's onstage gentleman's suit and the plain clothes deemed suitable for the apprenticed boy actor would have been marked.

Like the words *suit* and *gait*, the costumes of the play participate in a complex polysemy. Some costumes, such as, presumably, the gentlemen's suits of Orsino and Sebastian, would reveal their wearer's gender, status, and condition in quite straightforward ways, although, of course, they would conceal the status of the actor underneath. Others, like Malvolio's steward's coat and crossed garters or Olivia's mourning veil, reveal a more complex and double truth about their wearers. And in Viola's case, her polysemic costume verges on homonymy; that is, her gentleman's suit indicates a different identity, Cesario the page, while her "woman's weeds" reveal her to be Viola. Identity in the play is revealed to be as complex and multilayered as the meanings of polysemic words.

In a period in which sumptuary laws required "suits" that were suitable in that they were emblematic of status, the play suggested a more complex relation between identity and clothing. At times characters comment that clothing does indeed reveal something important about its wearer; recall Viola's inference that the captain has "a mind that suits / With this thy fair and outward character" (1.2.50–51) or the identification of Sebastian through reference to his suit in the recognition scene: "so went he suited to his watery tomb. / If spirits can assume both form and suit, / You come to fright us" (5.1.234–36). Sebastian responds by describing his body as a kind of "suit" for his spirit: "A spirit I am indeed / But am in that dimension grossly clad / Which from the womb I did participate" (5.1.236–38). Viola is wearing the same suit of clothing but a different bodily suit. For her, that same suit causes her to lament the gap between self and costume—"disguise, I see thou art a wickedness" (2.2.27)—experiencing guilt about the very act of cross-dressing never felt by either Rosalind or Portia. Viola also differs from the other two disguised heroines in her inability to resume her proper clothes, significantly because the captain "upon some action / Is now in durance, at Malvolio's suit" (275–76).

Malvolio, in fact, never releases the captain from his suit. Orsino sends someone to "pursue him, and entreat him to a peace" (5.1.380), but we are not optimistic, I think, about the success of this particular pursuit. Malvolio's lawsuit, like the fate of Antonio, who is also threatened with imprisonment, is left notoriously unresolved by the play. Like Viola, Malvolio to some extent occupies a liminal position in the play, wholly associated neither with Olivia's emphasis on the suitable nor with his Orsino-like desire to marry her. Unlike Viola, however, Malvolio refuses to accept the darker side of the self and its desires. After all, the disruptive "great P's" erupt from him and not from Olivia herself, revealing (along with the unconscious reference to "cut") a hidden reservoir of sexual desire that he refuses to acknowledge but that shapes his language all the same. Like the Ephesian Antipholus in *The Comedy of Errors*, Malvolio is confined in a place of "hideous darkness" and forced to undergo a mock exorcism, speaking, like Adriana in that play, "within" what he calls a

"house" : "this house is as dark as ignorance" (4.2.45). By this point
Shakespeare represents Olivia's complex enclosed house on the open
stage and reserves a truly enclosed space (like a "stagehouse" or discovery
space) for Malvolio's narrower version of subjectivity. Like Antipholus,
Malvolio refuses to accept the presence within himself of the darkness he
so vehemently insists pervades his prison. He firmly maintains his own
sanity—"I tell thee I am as well in my wits as any man in Illyria"
(4.2.107)—and believes that with the aid of "a candle, and pen, ink, and
paper" (4.2.81) he will be able to achieve a rational communication that
will solve his problem and obtain his release.

If Malvolio is too optimistic about the possibilities for self-possession
and self-expression, Feste, the fool and third go-between character in the
play, is perhaps too pessimistic. In his exchange with Viola in act 3, scene
1, he suggests a theory of language untethered by reference to any stability
of meaning: "a sentence is but a chev'ril glove to a good wit. How quickly
the wrong side may be turn'd outward" (3.1.11–13). And words, Feste
claims, "are grown so false, I am loath to prove reason with them"
(3.1.24–25). Viola, however, sees the cognitive process behind the fool's
seemingly slippery signifiers:

> He must observe their mood on whom he jests,
> The quality of persons, and the time;
> And like the haggard, check at every feather
> That comes before his eye. This is a practice
> As full of labor as a wise man's art.

> (3.1.62–66)

Significantly, Viola, echoing Malvolio's call for suitable "respect of place,
persons, [or] time," suggests that even the fool's language is "motivated"
by a desire to achieve suitable communication. Surely the tips he receives
provide material proof that he is at least partly successful in matching his
words to others' needs. It is Viola, once again, who sees with Feste the
ungrounded and seemingly random movement of language even as she
recognizes the shaping force of the process behind the fool's discourse.

Although cognitive theory posits a self that is to some extent more stable than the Lacanian subject, it nevertheless recognizes that language is
a "double-edged sword." In Daniel Stern's words, it "makes parts of our
experience more shareable with others," "permits two people to create
mutual experiences of meaning that had been unknown before," and
"permits the child to begin to construct a narrative of his own life," but
it also "makes some parts of our experience less shareable with ourselves
and with others," driving "a wedge between two simultaneous forms of
interpersonal experience: as it is lived, and as it is verbally represented."[62]

Olivia, Sebastian, and Malvolio all, in different ways, imagine their "suits" as narratives they direct toward a desired goal. But as Stern notes, and as Viola knows, "how much the act of making an autobiographical narrative reflects or necessarily alters the lived experiences that become the personal story is an open question" (182). Viola's openness to the process of "becoming" rather than a drive toward a completed narrative may reflect the complex spatial and lexical components of her concept of self unreduced to a single narrative line.

Most critics want to see that someone in the play has been taught a lesson, usually about desire or identity. The requirements of the comic plot do, on one level, suggest such a resolution: "Nature to her bias drew in that" (5.1.260). But the play, like Viola's concept of self, is structured around a polysemic category, and polysemy is not linear, even though chains of meaning are based on spatial concepts that can include linear movement. *Suit* in this play constitutes both a movement outward toward what one wants and confinement within what one has (a structure also echoed by *gate*). *Suit* similarly means a covering that both reveals and conceals what is within. As such, it replicates structurally the ways the embodied self interacts with what is around it—how it reveals and conceals itself, protects itself, seeks what it needs and desires.

Thus, the various linear movements of the play, from confusion to clarity, obscured identity to revealed identity, false desire to true, are disrupted by the fact that *suit* still refers to both poles of each binary even at the end of the play. The point here is not, however, as Feste might argue, the endless play of language. Rather, concepts of identity and desire are constructed through words with complex networks of meaning. Lacan recognizes something like this when he notes that "the linearity that Saussure holds to be constitutive of the chain of discourse, in conformity with its emission by a single voice and with its horizontal position in our writing—if this linearity is necessary, in fact, it is not sufficient. . . . There is in effect no signifying chain that does not have, as if attached to the punctuation of each of its units, a whole articulation of relevant contexts suspended 'vertically,' as it were, from that point."[63] Lacan calls such points of vertical suspension "anchoring points," or *points de capiton*, suggesting that the slippages of signification along the linear chain are tacked or anchored by human conceptualization. In this sense, Shakespeare's fascination with the inclusion of opposites within a polysemic web, his interest in ways that language, by embodying contradiction, leaves a space for a range of possibilities, does not indicate uncontrolled play of meaning but rather points to the very means by which meaning is anchored, like Feste's words, by its motivation. The characters in the play must not necessarily make a correct choice between a goal to pursue, a line to be toed, a path to follow, and a suitable place within which to be confined: all of these are possible constitutive manifestations of the self in relation to the world, all are possibilities expressed by the multiplicity of "suits." Meaning in *Twelfth Night*, like desire, is neither a rigidly confining system nor a slippery field of play; both meaning and desire offer both possibilities, a field of choice anchored by the plenitude of conceptualization itself.

4

Cognitive *Hamlet* and the Name of Action

HAMLET's claim to have "that within which passes show" (1.2.85) has become one of the most debated lines in early modern literature since it seems to make a definite statement about a highly contested topic, the nature of subjective interiority and its relation to the existence (or nonexistence) of the human "individual." Katherine Eisaman Maus, who recently summarized critical controversy over the cultural significance of Hamlet's "contrast between an authentic personal interior and derivative or secondary superficies," takes issue with those critics who have argued that such a sense of self did not exist until the later seventeenth century.[1] In her examination and defense of the "epistemology of inwardness" in the period Maus rightly insists that the sometimes contiguous concepts of "privacy," "inwardness," and "individuality" were not always associated, nor did their contiguity add up to a fully formed concept of modern subjectivity.[2] However, most critics have been ready to assume that what Hamlet has within is some version of the modern subject, either fully formed or still in the process of formation.

Like the other plays discussed so far, *Hamlet* asks precisely what it is that lies within the human subject; however, *Hamlet* is more directly concerned with early modern cognitive theory than the others and explores a number of cognitive processes that might suggest an answer to this question. These processes are imagined differently at different points in the play, and various versions of the ways in which the inner self comes into being delineate different relationships between the self, its actions, and its environment.[3] The words *act, action, actor,* and the coinage *enacture*, unique to this play, form the lexical category through which Shakespeare meditates on these questions in this play, and his sense of the word *action* has been significantly inflected by his reading of a near-contemporary cognitive treatise, Timothy Bright's *Treatise of Melancholie*.[4] In my view, Bright's treatise uses the word *action* to investigate the relationships between the soul, the body, and the mind and to describe the processes by which external and internal forces give rise to the actions that both define and express the self.

Modern critics' sense of what Hamlet has within has proceeded, as such concepts must, from the critical perspectives that they bring to the text. Ellen Spolsky has usefully demonstrated how cognitive linguistics helps us understand the determining effects of assumptions about the category of tragedy on readings of the play.[5] Francis Barker's Foucauldian reading, for instance, finds within Hamlet a tentatively sketched "essential interiority" that "prematurely" articulates "the figure that is to dominate and organize bourgeois culture."[6] In his reading, "Hamlet utters, against the substance of the spectacular plenum which is now reduced in his eyes to a factitious artificiality 'that a man might play', a first demand for the modern subject" (36). Psychoanalytic critics assume the complicated inner apparatus of the Freudian or Lacanian subject, a form of interiority that Hamlet's oedipal preoccupations predict with almost uncanny prescience.[7] In its emphasis on the processes by which action creates the self, the play might also seem to predict Judith Butler's theory of the performativity that brings the gendered self into being. Butler uses the word *act*, much as Shakespeare does in this play, as a fulcrum on which definitions of *act* shaped by phenomenology, speech-act theory, and theater can turn to create her theory of a subject constituted by its actions.[8] Arguing that "the feminist appropriation of the phenomenological theory of constitution might employ the notion of an *act* in a richly ambiguous sense," Butler uses that ambiguity, as Shakespeare does in *Hamlet*, to explore the relationship between the self and its actions.

Of course Hamlet's claim to possess an interiority that "passes show" and preexists those "actions that a man might play" would seem to argue, against Butler's denial of "a stable identity or locus of agency"—within— "from which various acts proceed" (519). On the other hand, his suggestion to his mother that "the use of actions fair and good" can "almost change the stamp of nature," his belief that the player has been able, through acting, to "force his soul . . . to his own conceit," and Laertes' embarrassed belief that his tears for Ophelia turn him into a woman come close to articulating a theory of performativity. Rather than espousing a single theory about the relationship between action and self, the play tries out a range of spatially delineated possibilities: there is, or is not, an essential self (variously the soul, rational faculty, heart) that works as a stable locus of agency; this self can, or cannot, be altered by influences from outside; this inner self can, or cannot, be reliably expressed; actions do, or do not, create the self. The famous images of poison and disease, as well as an almost obsessive repetition of clinical descriptions of the physiological manifestations of emotion, an interest in performative utterances, the structuration of scenes around an organizing principal of inside and outside, the much-remarked inactivities of the plot, all centering around the lexical category of "acts" and "action," are the means by which the play explores these issues.

The problem of manifesting subjective interiority onstage was, as we have seen, an issue in *The Comedy of Errors*. Most critics would agree that *Hamlet* marks a significant advance in this regard, a result of several years of experimentation with representing domestic scenes and individualized characters on the open platform stage. This play famously employs soliloquy as one way to create the illusion that Hamlet has a hidden inner life.[9] It also further develops a technique that appeared briefly in *Comedy of Errors*, namely, using language to create an analogy between the interior life of a central character and aspects of setting or plot, as when Antipholus's confinement in the vault reflects on a larger scale his feelings about companionate marriage and his nervousness about possession of an inner life. In *Hamlet* the central problem of the plot, Hamlet's inability to take external action, is a larger version of the problem of Hamlet, his felt lack of a stable and consistent interior self. Further, the play uses imagery—of breached fortification and bodily penetration, of weeds and disease—to suggest that Elsinore and Denmark are larger projections of the psychic structures of old Hamlet, Hamlet, Claudius, and the other characters.

The nature of subjectivity is, of course, directly explored in the character of Hamlet himself, the Shakespearean persona who most insistently embodies the contradictions and paradoxes inherent in an attempt to explore the human subject and its actions through "actions that a man might play," and does, onstage.[10] James Calderwood has argued that Hamlet is "conscious of his dual identity" as character and actor and that he "puzzles over the fact that as a character he is fully equipped for revenge but that as an actor, or instrument of the plot, he is not allowed to proceed with it."[11] I want to argue the reverse: that Hamlet is initially unable to act because of his resistance to his role in the play, as theatrical character and as instrument of a revenge plot. His concern to define what he has within is, in a sense, bound to fail because as a fictional character he has no inner self.[12] Howard Felperin has suggested that for most of the play Hamlet "has tried to be a two-dimensional character in a three-dimensional world," but, again, I believe that the reverse is true. Although he is preoccupied with locating such a self for most of the play, in the end he comes to accept his own implication in the plot and to act in accordance with his existence as a relatively conventional dramatic character shaped performatively through his words and actions. Significantly, Hamlet's preoccupation throughout most of the play with cognitive process disappears after the graveyard scene, the point at which, as others have noted, he stops speaking in soliloquy. Hamlet's final acquiescence in destiny might be seen to mark, not a religious conversion, but simply an acceptance of his role in a plot scripted by someone else and of a self that is as a result shaped by his actions.[13]

Shakespeare's overlapping categories of "act," "action," and "actor" seem initially quite close to modern senses of those words; however, the end of the sixteenth century and beginning of the seventeenth marked a period of striking shifts and extensions of meaning, with several new meanings for these words seeming to appear for the first time in various of Shakespeare's works. The shifts seem to incorporate a paradox that is of central concern in *Hamlet*: the contrast between purposeful action that proceeds from and expresses the inner character of its agent and achieves something in the world and the various new theatrical senses of *act* and *actor*, which suggest nongenuine, imitative, fictionalized activity.

Around the turn of the century the word *act* seems simultaneously to have been changing in ways that emphasized both purposeful agency and empty pretense. By 1600 the noun *act* had long had as its primary sense "a thing done, a deed, a performance (of an intelligent being)" (*OED*), encoding concepts of activity and purposeful agency. New at this point, however, were both the use of *act* as a verb meaning "to bring into action, bring about, produce, perform, work, make, do" and, more importantly, the theatrical sense of the word as both noun and verb "a performance of a part of a play" and "to carry out or represent in mimic action." The similar development of the word *action* may help to clarify the significance of the shifting meanings of *act*. *Action* had also long meant "process or condition of acting or doing . . . (distinguished from *passion*, from *thought* or *contemplation*, from *speaking* or *writing*)." New around the time that *Hamlet* was written were both the quasi-theatrical sense "mode of acting . . . gesture or attitude as expressive of the sentiment or passion depicted" and the sense of "active operation against, or engaging an enemy, fighting," which first appeared in *Othello*.

The history of *actor* may fill in the middle ground between the senses of strong agency and pretended action by suggesting the importance of special senses of these words in particular professional contexts. The primary meanings of *actor* before the late sixteenth century—"manager, overseer, agent, factor," and "a pleader; he who conducts an action at law"—suggest concepts of proxy, or acting at the behest, instructions, or on behalf of some other person. *Actor* only came to mean "one who personates a character or acts a part" in the latter years of the sixteenth century and "one who acts or performs any action" in the early seventeenth, perhaps first in Shakespeare's *Measure for Measure*. The sense of action at one remove from the originating agent seems halfway between concepts of strong agency and theatrical representation. In 1600, then, the category of "act" would include as its primary sense the concept of agentive actions in the world, but our own sense of violent activity would have been very new. (For me, as the mother of two boys, "action figure," and "action adventure film" are prototypical senses that would have been on the fringes of the category in 1600.) The contours of the category would instead have been shaped by a sense, foreign to us, of *act* as a secondary, indirect form of agency (a legal sense preserved now in "act" of Congress). And the theatrical senses were all quite new, probably not even firmly established.

Act and *action* thus encoded a range of versions of agency and authenticity. The sense of *act* as a complex process rather than a simple material fact was intensified by another, technical use of the term particularly relevant to *Hamlet*, that is, the philosophical sense of *action* as "the exertion of force by one body upon another." Faculty psychology and humoral physiology provided quite complex accounts of the "actions" within the body and brain that enabled any action in the world. The accounts of these inner "actions" provided in Timothy Bright's *Treatise of Melancholie* (1586) represent common late-sixteenth-century beliefs about cognitive process and therefore might be relevant to *Hamlet* whether Shakespeare ever read that work or not. But as noted above, several scholars have argued that Shakespeare had read the *Treatise* and that he had it in mind when writing *Hamlet*.[14] Although critics have tended to use the parallels between Bright's treatise and Shakespeare's play to argue that Hamlet is suffering from some form of melancholy, I want to argue that Shakespeare took from Bright not a specific clinical diagnosis but instead contradictory accounts of the cognitive processes "within" that result in (or prevent) purposeful action in the world.[15]

As both a medical doctor and a Protestant minister, Bright was concerned to find a synthesis of Galenic materialism and Christian faith.[16] Writing before Descartes, Bright was interested in a central preoccupation of modern cognitive science and philosophy of mind, the mind-body problem, or, in terms of Bright's concern with Christian theology, the soul-body problem.[17] Although Galenic physiology offered the possibility that even the soul was shaped and influenced by the material conditions of its embodiment, Bright, while accepting most tenets of humoral materialism, argues that the soul is superior to the body, that it functions (under ideal conditions) as its sovereign and controlling influence, that it is materially unaffected by bodily ills. In Hardin Craig's words, Bright tries to establish that "although the Galenic therapeutics of melancholy was excellent and applicable, it might not be extended to include contrition and those stings of conscience which God himself chooses to inflict on the sinner" (xiii). In his attempts to uphold both a material theory of humoral psychology and an idealizing theory of an immaterial and transcendent soul, Bright includes lengthy, often contradictory descriptions of the internal workings of body, soul, and mind. In my view, it was this sense of interior process and preoccupation with the spatiality and direction of agency that strongly influenced Shakespeare. Bright's repetition of *action* to denote the internal workings of the body, soul, and mind had a formative influ-

ence on Shakespeare's sense of the relationship between the subject and
its acts and thus on his sense of what Hamlet had within.

In accordance with faculty psychology and humoral physiology, Bright
argues that the spirits (animal, vital, and mineral) mediate between soul
and body. According to Bright's account, the soul uses the spirits as "instruments" to cause the three "seats" of the body—brain, heart, and
liver—to perform their functions (47–48). Concerned to demonstrate that
the material body can perhaps influence but not materially alter the soul
and mind, Bright provides a complex account of the nature of inner
agency involving various "actions" and "instruments." The soul itself has
a "nature eternall and divine, not fettered with the body" but joined to
the body by the spirits, which mediate between the material and the immaterial, being risen "from earthly creatures; yet are they more excellent,
then earth, or the earthie parts of those natures, from which they are
drawne; and rise from that diuine influence of life, and are not of them
selues earthie: neither yet comparable in purenesse and excellencie, vnto
that breath of life, wherewith the Lord made Adam a living soule" (37).
The immaterial soul cannot be affected or "impressed" by the body and
uses the spirits as "the chiefe instrument" by which it "bestoweth the
exercises of her facultie in her bodie" (35).

Bright's treatise argues that the "spirit and body" are "without any free
worke or action, otherwise then at the mindes commandement" (61), and
attempts to distinguish various forms of "instrument" that can carry out
action at second hand. Interestingly, Bright distinguishes a kind of instrument "dead in it selfe and destitute of all motion: as a saw before it be
moved of the workman" and another kind that is "lively, and carrieth in
it selfe aptnes, and disposition of motion: as the hound to hunt with, and
the hauke to fowle with" (61). Hamlet's ability to distinguish "hawk"
from "handsaw" may thus involve a fine distinction between types of
instrumental agency: for Bright, "the spirit [is] the verie hand of the soule;
the body and bodily members like flailes, sawes, or axes in the hand of
him that vseth them" (64–65).

Any external action is thus the result of a complex string of internal
actions: the human hand acts, "not absolutely of it selfe, but by impulsion
of the mind" acting through its instruments, the spirits, a mind that in
Bright's optimistic view is "placed the only agent, absolute and soueraigne
not onely in respect of commaunding but also of facultie and execution"
(65).[18] Bright imagines a striking regress of hands and saws: the actual
hand holding a saw, impelled by the "sawe" or "flaile" of the hand, which
is in turn impelled by the "hand" of the spirits, which are controlled by
the soul, which is influenced, presumably, by the hand of God. The soul
can be altered or influenced by the material body and spirits only "as a

false stringed lute giveth to the musician, or a rough and evill fashioned pen to the cunning writer" (38).

In his attempts to delineate the relationships between soul, body, and mind Bright investigates the extent to which internal factors (e.g., the balance of humors within the body, the rational faculty of the mind, the soul itself) or external influences (habitual actions, emotionally upsetting events) shape thought and feeling. Interestingly, the example of poison is used several times to illustrate the nature of an external influence on the mind. To prove that external forces can have only a temporary effect on the mind, Bright adduces "the effectes of poisons in our natures, as of henbane, coriander, hemlock, night shade, and such like . . . by which the mind seemeth greatly to be altered, and quite put beside the reasonable vse of her ingenerate faculties during the force of the poysons: which being maistered, or at least rebated, by convenient remedies, it recovereth those gifts, whereof it was in daunger to suffer wracke before" (54). Even the natural "complexion," or balance of humors innate to each person, is difficult to alter: "Neither purgations of humour alter complexion, a fixed thing, ingenerate by nature and not ouerthrowne but by some venimous qualitie direct opposit against it, or long custome of other disorder, whereby nature is supplanted in time" (85–86).

The question whether habitual actions can alter the very nature of the self is also of interest to Bright, and his discussion of the influence of occupation on the mind has been cited as a source for Horatio's comment that the gravedigger's "custom hath made it in him a property of easiness" (5.1.67). Bright's comments on occupational influence have a broader relevance to the play, especially to discussions of whether action can shape the self. According to Bright, "custom of life" can influence behavior without substantially altering the mind: "for their instruments of action through continuall practice of such artes, maketh them in common sense, imagination, and affection, to deliuer thinges vnto the minde after an impure sort, always sauouring of their ordinary trade of life" (78). Thus, butchers are "accustomed with slaughter" and unfit to serve on juries in capital cases, while mariners are "rough, bold, hardie, inconstant" (78).

Like Shakespeare in *Hamlet*, Bright is interested in the processes behind the physiological manifestations of "passion": tears, sighs, blushing, and various symptoms of fear. Bright, like Hamlet, seems unsure whether these outward signs of emotion are necessarily accurate indications of inner states or can be counterfeited.[19] Bright argues that as "animall actions" (as opposed to involuntary "naturall actions" like digestion), such signs of emotion as "solitarines, morning, weeping . . . melancholie laughter, sighing, sobbing, lamentation, countenance demisse, and hanging downe, blushing" are all actions "which lie in our powers to doe" (124). He describes the internal processes behind these outward signs, however, in such a way that they do not seem to depend on conscious agency. Crying results when, occasioned by some cause of grief or sadness, the body "gathereth in one her spirits, and bloud," collecting them in the brain. The brain, overflowing with these additional humors and spirits, "expresseth that which by thinnesse is readie to voide, and forcing with spirit, and pressing with contracted substance, signifieth by shower of teares, what storme tosseth the afflicted heart" (146–47). The tears themselves are composed of "the excrementitious humiditie of the brayne" (144). Thus, despite Bright's classification of weeping as a voluntary "animall action," he concludes that "tears cannot be counterfetted, because they rise not of any action or facultie voluntarie, but naturall" (148).

Sighs, similarly, are a means by which the body purges itself of spirits and humors that have congregated unnaturally in one part of the body as the result of strong emotion. Sighs or sobs, actions that Bright argues are related, "by agitation of the chest expelling of the smothered vapours, and drawing in of fresh aire, geve also some comfort" (161). In a kind of reversal of the opening and purging manifested by sighs and tears, fear "restraineth teares" by stopping up the pores, which also "appeareth in such as are scarred: whose haire seemeth to stand vpright and stiffe through that contraction" (139).

Blushing, also classified as an "animall action," also seems difficult to control or feign. Bright argues that blushing is caused only by shame and "declareth a tender heart, and easily moued with remorse of that which is done amisse," as well as "a conscience quicke, and tender, and an vpright sentence of the mind, agreable to this engrauen maximes of good and euill" (170). The internal actions behind blushing are as complex as those behind tears and sighs: a blush occurs when "the heart discontented with the opennesse of the offence, maketh a retraction of bloud, and spirit at the first, as in feare and griefe; and because it feeleth no greater hurt then of laughter, or rebuke of worde, or such like touch, seeketh no farther escape, then a small withdrawing of the spirite and bloud by the first entrance of the perturbation: so that the necessitie being no more vrgent, the bloud and spirit breake forth againe more vehemently, and fill the partes about the face more then before, and causeth the rednesse" (168–69).

For Bright, then, the soul, which ideally forms a stable, essential, and unchanging center for the inner self, is linked to the body and mind through a complex chain of impulsive and instrumental actions that lead to both involuntary and purposeful acts. Human acts ought to express the truth of the unchanging inner self since the soul is supposed to be in control of both body and mind. But the inconsistencies of the treatise reveal that even Bright was unable to come up with a theory of human cognitive process that both posits a transcendent soul in charge and also accounts in any plausible way for the vagaries of human behavior. What stands out from a reading of Bright is the complicated account of what people have within and the multiple and complex agencies that inform their actions.

Why does Hamlet not act? Michael Goldman has argued that "the 'problems' of the play point, finally, to the subtle means it employs for manipulating one of our most fundamental theatrical appetites: the desire for action that makes sense, especially for action that seems complete and resolved."[20] Goldman traces the ways the play uses a technique of "frozen action" to make us question the very nature of action itself. But the play also, on several different levels, makes us question the nature of action by focusing on the processes behind it. *Hamlet* centers around two insistent questions: what do human subjects have within? and how is that inner self related to external action in the world? The play considers these issues not just directly, in speeches and soliloquies, but also structurally, in its organization around poles of inside and outside, in its delaying plot, and in its representation of character. Much like Bright's sense of agency as involving a regression of causes and instruments, Hamlet functions in the play both as a subject who contains within himself a chain of instrumental actions that controls his own actions and also as an instrument within a Denmark that is presented as in some ways analogous to a human subject.[21] This parallel is, of course, based on an analogy that was basic to political thought in the period, that between the human body and the "body politic."[22] On this level the plot of the play—Hamlet's movement toward revenge—is the action that old Hamlet, one embodiment of Denmark, wants carried out. The cognitive processes behind action and subjectivity are thus examined in the play on both the micro- and the macro-level—that is, within Hamlet and the other characters and, on a larger scale, within Denmark itself. As it proceeds, the play moves from outside the castle inward until it reaches the most private and interior space in Gertrude's closet, then moves back out to Fortinbras's approaching army and the graveyard. This movement is paralleled by Hamlet's initial preoccupation with what is within himself and other people, which is most intense in the closet scene but disappears as he begins to focus on his own instrumental role in Denmark.

As the play examines various versions of cognitive subjectivity in relation to action, the issue of the relationship between matter and the immaterial becomes important, as it was in Bright. Margaret Ferguson has noted that the word *matter* appears in the play twenty-six times, more than in any other play by Shakespeare, and that "the relation between matter and spirit, matter and art, matter and anything that is 'no matter,' is altogether questionable for Hamlet."[23] Although characters in the play are generally more skeptical about the immateriality and the transcendent nature of the soul than was Bright, the realm of "spirit" and the possible kinds of interface between matter and spirit are of crucial importance. The nature of language, that is, whether it is material and whether it can have material effects, is of particular concern. Although action in the world seems to require the participation of the material, matter, without the informing power of a divine soul, comes to seem easily contaminated and not so easily controlled.

The first act introduces, both structurally and spatially, an analogy between Denmark and Hamlet; images of ears and fortification help to establish this connection. The first two scenes in particular introduce the question, familiar from Bright, whether subjects are most shaped and influenced by innate, internal qualities or by external forces. Stephen Booth has traced ways in which the opening scene of the play wavers between offering a military assault or the ghost as an explanation for the sentries' anxiety.[24] Almost immediately the question whether Denmark is most in danger from external or internal forces is related to an image of threats to an individual human subject. We learn that Denmark is fortified against invasion just as Barnardo says to Horatio that he will "assail your ears, / That are so fortified against our story" (1.1.31–32) of the ghost. An image of a fortified human head, attempting to protect its cognitive machinery from outside influence, is introduced in this passage and recurs throughout the play. The opening scene leaves the audience, as Booth suggests, unsure about whether the greatest threat is Fortinbras's intended invasion or the appearance of the ghost or whether they are the same thing.

The first scene, placed outside Elsinore and directed largely against a threat from without, immediately gives way to a claustrophobic indoor scene that introduces Hamlet's sense that corruption in Denmark comes from within. Claudius begins the scene with an attempt to establish a direct correlation between sincere emotion and its outward signs: his hasty marriage to Gertrude is authorized by the fact that he possesses "an auspicious, and a dropping eye" (1.2.11), signs, he hopes to establish, of a sincere and simultaneous joy and grief. Hamlet counters this by arguing that signs of emotion—"windy suspiration of forc'd breath / . . . the fruitful river in the eye, / . . . the dejected havior of the visage" (1.2.79–81)— can be falsified and are not necessarily direct expressions of "that within which passes show" just as Gertrude's "most unrighteous tears" (1.2.154) are deceptive. On the other hand, Hamlet believes that the problems in Denmark *are* accurate manifestations of an inner evil, which he initially identifies as stemming from his mother's remarriage. Hamlet's description of Denmark as "an unweeded garden that grows to seed" because "things rank and gross in nature / Possess it merely" (1.2.135– 37) introduces into the play a recurrent image of plants or vegetation, which, unlike the outward signs of human emotion, accurately express their nature through their appearance.[25]

Claudius continues to insist on a direct link between inner feeling and outward manifestation when he decrees that his happiness at the fact that Hamlet agrees to remain in Denmark, which "sits smiling to my heart" (1.2.124), will be expressed in canon blasts every time he takes a drink. In this case his outward show of emotion is literally outward, revealed outside the fortifications of Elsinore with its engines of war.[26] It is clearly the person of the King that embodies the linkage between Denmark and individual Danes—his joy will reveal itself directly on the face of the castle and indeed on the face of heaven itself: "the King's rouse the heaven shall bruit again, / Respeaking earthly thunder" (1.2.127–28). Hamlet's comments on Claudius's noisy celebration, however, reassert the importance of what is *behind* this outward show and the possibility of an imperfect fit between inward and outward. Hamlet first objects to Claudius's "heavy-headed revel" because it is an outward show of drunkenness that falsely represents what is within Denmark: "the pith and marrow of our attribute" (1.4.22).

Moving easily from a discussion of the relationship between inward and outward in Denmark as a whole to a discussion of Claudius himself, Hamlet speculates on the causes of evil "in particular men." This passage is typical of many in the play in its lengthy and difficult description of inner processes and its offering of contradictory versions of the configuration of the inner self. On the one hand, Hamlet argues that "some vicious mole of Nature" can cause "o'ergrowth of some complexion," which can, in turn, break down "the pales and forts of reason" and cause "his virtues" to "take corruption / From that particular fault" (1.4.24–36). The chain of internal cause and effect—a mole of nature alters complexion, a change in complexion breaks down reason, corrupted reason destroys virtue—sounds very much like Bright. Departing from Bright, however, Hamlet includes within his account the potentially contradictory idea that external actions ("some form of habit that too much o'erleavens / The form of plausive manners" [1.4.29–30]) can also alter the self.[27] The word *o'ergrowth* links Claudius's inner fault with Denmark's current state as an "unweeded garden," suggesting that although Claudius's inner nature does express itself outwardly on the face of the country, it does not do so as he thinks it does or in a way that he can control. Vegetation continues to figure an outward manifestation of inner nature that cannot be falsified. For the most part, Hamlet cannot share Bright's certainty (or even his desire to be certain) that the human soul is divine, transcendent, and essentially unaltered by bodily disruptions and remains conflicted about the nature of the relationship between soul and body, spirit and matter.[28]

Hamlet's encounter with the ghost repeats many of the images of the opening scenes of the play and continues the exploration of the relationship between internal and external influences on the formation of the self. The scene begins with a discussion of what effect the ghost might have on Hamlet's soul or mind. To Hamlet's insistence (in agreement with Bright) that "for my soul, what can it do to that, / Being a thing immortal as itself" (1.4.66–67) Horatio replies by separating (in opposition to Bright) the soul from the rational faculty: the ghost could "assume some other horrible form / Which might deprive your sovereignty of reason / And draw you into madness" (1.4.72–74). The ghost seems to continue this debate about the relationship between body, mind, and soul with a lengthy clinical description of the harmful effects there would be on Hamlet if he were to describe to him the nature of purgatory. The story

> Would harrow up they soul, freeze thy young blood,
> Make thy two eyes like stars start from their spheres,
> Thy knotted and combined locks to part,
> And each particular hair to stand on end,
> Like quills upon the fearfull porpentine.
> But this eternal blazon must not be
> To ears of flesh and blood.
>
> (1.5.16–22)

The ghost argues that his discourse, if poured into Hamlet's ear, would have material effects on both soul and body. Horatio earlier described the physical effects of fear when he described to Hamlet the sentries' "fear-surprised eyes" and bodies "distill'd / Almost to jelly with the act of fear" (1.2.203, 204–5), and the ghost here echoes that description. Fear, unlike grief, seems to be an emotion that cannot be falsified and that shows itself through unmistakable physical effects.

The ghost then reiterates the analogy between Denmark and Hamlet by asserting that "the whole ear of Denmark / Is by a forged process of my death / Rankly abused" (1.5.36–38). The long and once again oddly clinical account of his own death provides a literal analogue for the dominant image of the poisoned ear:

> Upon my secure hour thy uncle stole,
> With juice of cursed hebona in a vial,
> And in the porches of my ear did pour
> The leprous distillment, whose effect
> Holds such an enmity with blood of man
> That swift as quicksilver it courses through
> The natural gates and alleys of the body,
> And with a sudden vigor it doth posset

And curd, like eager droppings into milk,
The thin and wholesome blood. So did it mine,
And a most instant tetter bark'd about,
Most lazar-like, with vile and loathsome crust
All my smooth body.

(1.5.61–73)

The ghost's use of the terms *posset* and *curd* has long been attributed to Bright's influence. However, this speech also seems to be profoundly shaped by Bright's interest in the nature of both internal and external causes of mental and bodily disturbance. We might recall his passage on the mental influence of "henbane" and other poisons and also a passage detailing such external signs of internal humoral imbalance as "soares, Emphostumes, or other such annoyances" (92). The fact that poison was poured into old Hamlet's ear allies it to the poisonous effects of discourse on the mind, much like the potentially frightening effects of the description of purgatory on young Hamlet or the lies with which Claudius has "abused" the ear of Denmark. The ghost insists that the external manifestations of corruption that appeared on his body in death were due not to some internal imbalance—some "mole of nature"—but solely to Claudius's poison. Of course, his own admission that he was "cut off even in the blossoms of my sin" (1.5.76) suggests that he had internal corruptions that appeared outwardly in plantlike form, much as the poison caused his skin to develop "bark." Hamlet reiterates this image of a vegetative externalization of internal corruption when he notes in act 3, scene 3, that Claudius killed old Hamlet "with all his crimes broad blown, as flush as May" (81); with these images Hamlet seems to link old Hamlet himself with Denmark's "unweeded" state, although he continues to try hard to deny this connection. The ghost here stresses not the mental effects of poison but physical ones, as he did in his account of the potential effects of his own discourse on Hamlet. The question remains, however, whether the ghost's discourse, and especially its attempts to set in motion an action leading to revenge, does not have a similarly corrupting effect on Hamlet's mind.

In asking him to "revenge his foul and most unnatural murther" (1.5.25), the ghost (or spirit) of the Dane is the impulsion that would cause Hamlet, as instrument, to take action. The ghost is thus to Hamlet, who is forced to become its "scourge and minister" (3.4.175), as the mind is to body in Bright: "The mind is the sole mover in the body, and . . . the rest of the parts fare as instruments, and ministers" (91). David Kastan has pointed out that the act of revenge is always at one remove from its inspiration: "The revenger is prevented from originating an action. He is allowed only to react to—and to reenact—the original crime."[29] The play

emphasizes not only the belated and necessarily imitative quality of the action that the ghost demands but also Hamlet's role as instrument. It suggests that in urging Hamlet to carry out this action the ghost has influenced him in some fundamental way. He has poured his disturbing discourse into Hamlet's ear, and Hamlet's immediate reaction is to imagine a material alteration in his mental faculties:

> From the table of my memory
> I'll wipe away all trivial fond records,
> All saws of books, all forms, all pressures past
> That youth and observation copied there,
> And thy commandement all alone shall live
> Within the book and volume of my brain
>
> (1.5.98–103)

In Bright's treatise the mind is able to "discerne betwixt good and badde, trueth and falsehood" because of both innate and acquired knowledge: "The soul hath certain principles of knowledge ingenerate, . . . and certaine taken from obseruation of sensible thinges" (73). Hamlet imagines the ghost's "commandement" replacing the knowledge acquired by reading and youthful "observation." But in erasing this knowledge, he runs the risk of losing his ability to judge good and evil, truth and falsehood. Thus, when Hamlet proposes to "put an antic disposition on" (1.5.172) and to feign madness, we must wonder whether this "act" does not reflect some version of an inner truth, that Hamlet's mind has been corroded by the ghost's speech.[30]

As the play proceeds, it continues to ask what internal state Hamlet needs in order to act, as well as what internal state Denmark needs in order for Hamlet to act. Denmark itself is full of "instrumental" acts other than Hamlet's movement toward revenge. Almost everyone in Denmark employs spies, messengers, or other proxies to act on their behalf. As Patricia Parker has noted, the play's emphasis on proxies reflects "the emergent world of statecraft contemporary with the play, one that historians describe as increasingly involving the mediation of agents, go-betweens, and representatives across bureaucratic as well as geographical distances, along with the corresponding multiplication of informers and spies."[31] Political life in Denmark seems for most of the play to operate at one remove from sources of power; in this sense, Claudius, with his reliance on messengers, ambassadors, and spies rather than direct single combat, seems almost an instrumental king who rules at one remove from old Hamlet, who remains the true source of royal authority in Denmark. The rest of the play proliferates with depictions of such action by proxy: Polonius's instructions to Reynaldo, Claudius's use of Polonius and Polonius's of Ophelia to spy on Hamlet, Claudius's of Rosencrantz and Guildenstern for the same purpose. Even Laertes, who seems contrasted with Hamlet in his ability to act, agrees to act as Claudius's "organ" (4.7.69). Only Fortinbras's accession to the throne of Denmark at the end of the play restores a direct link between agent and action. Fortinbras, the external threat to Denmark, seems to act largely for himself, although even he is partly motivated by a desire to revenge his father's death at the hands of old Hamlet. His name itself, which means "strong arm," suggests this ambiguity since he is indeed a powerful military leader but, like the arm to the body in Bright, not quite an independent agent.

Polonius and his family are in some ways centers for instrumental action in Denmark. Claudius assures Laertes in the second scene of the play that "The head is not more native to the heart, / The hand more instrumental to the mouth, / Than is the throne of Denmark to thy father" (1.2.47–49), but it is actually Polonius who is "instrumental" to the Danish king. Claudius's language here insists, as he tends to do early in the play, on a close connection between feeling and thought and between feeling and what is spoken. (It is only later that he acknowledges the distance between "my deed" and "my most painted word" [3.1.52]). Polonius, on the other hand, cautions a prudent distance between thought and deed: "Give thy thoughts no tongue, / Nor any unproportion'd thought his act" (1.3.59–60), advice that contrasts strongly with Hamlet's sense that such a distance between self and spoken word is tragic: "but break my heart, for I must hold my tongue" (1.2.159). Ironically, it is Polonius who believes that he can diagnose the nature of Hamlet's inner disturbance through observation. Based on Ophelia's description of Hamlet's behavior—including "a sigh so piteous and profound / As it did seem to shatter all his bulk / And end his being" (2.1.91–93)—Polonius confidently pronounces that

> this is the very ecstasy of love,
> Whose violent property fordoes itself,
> And leads the will to desperate undertakings
> As oft as any passions under heaven
>
> (2.1.99–102)

Claudius, on the other hand, is less sure that he can see exactly what is within Hamlet, suggesting only that there is

> something in his soul
> O'er which his melancholy sits on brood,
> And I do doubt the hatch and the disclose
> Will be some danger[.]
>
> (3.1.164–67)

Claudius does not doubt that Hamlet will "hatch" some threatening action that he imagines as "disclosing" the secrets within, secrets that Claudius believes to be either Hamlet's knowledge of his crimes or else hatred of him. Claudius is, however, unaware that Hamlet's conception of the relationship between self and action is much more complex and problematic and would not so easily move from brooding to action.

As the play proceeds, Hamlet continues to try out various theories about the relationship between the subject and action. The arrival of the players introduces the theatrical sense of the word and provides an occasion for Hamlet to consider the links between agentive action, action by proxy, and fictionalized acting, as well as the connection between inner feelings and processes and outward actions. When the player's histrionic speech describing the death of Priam is interrupted by a show of emotion ("look whe'er he has not turn'd his color and has tears in's eyes" [2.2.519–20]), Hamlet is moved to a further meditation on the relationship between such outward "actions" and inner feeling. He believes that the player has been able to

> force his soul so to his own conceit
> That from her working all the visage wann'd,
> Tears in his eyes, distraction in his aspect,
> A broken voice, an' his whole function suiting
> With forms to his conceit[.]
>
> (2.2.553–57)

This marks a change, however slight, from Hamlet's early theory about the falsification of the physiological signs of emotion. Whereas earlier Hamlet believed these symptoms to be always potentially false and to function as proof that "that within" could not be genuinely revealed, he now believes that the player's show of feeling is a result of an inner alteration: he has been able to "force his soul" to experience feelings of sadness occasioned by "a fiction . . . a dream of passion." Although the manifestation is outwardly the same, Hamlet imagines the inner processes differently, so that he now envies what he previously held in contempt.[32] At this point his guilty envy results from the player's seeming ability to control the inner processes that reveal themselves in the symptoms of emotion.

Perhaps in concert with this shift, Hamlet is now sometimes able to believe that the sight of the play will cause Claudius almost involuntarily to reveal the guilty truth that he has hidden within, although he does not consistently maintain this belief. Hamlet wavers between thinking that he will be able to see Claudius's guilt manifested through his actions or facial expression and that Claudius will be moved to admit his crime publicly and verbally.[33] Hamlet has heard that "guilty creatures sitting at a play" have been "strook so to the soul, that presently / They have proclaim'd

their malefactions" (2.2.591–92). Hamlet believes that by observing
Claudius's "looks," he will be able to "tent him to the quick" (2.2.597)
or reveal his secret, inner corruption, which is quite some distance from
the belief that inner feelings are almost necessarily other than what is
shown. When Hamlet discusses this plan with Horatio, he offers a slightly
(but significantly) different version of how Claudius's guilt will be revealed, suggesting that it will be spoken rather than visually manifested.
Horatio is to observe Claudius "even with the very comment of thy soul,"
but Hamlet now hopes the play will cause him to speak out: "if his oc-
culted guilt / Do not itself unkennel in one speech" (3.2.79–81). This
uncertainty about whether Claudius is more likely to reveal his inner secrets through looks or through speech may explain why Hamlet uses both
a dumb show and spoken lines in his mousetrap, offering both visual and
auditory stimuli.[34] Certainly Claudius seems to react not to the sight of
poison poured into Gonzago's ears but to Hamlet's verbal interpretation;
he rushes out, as Hamlet emphasizes to Horatio, "Upon the talk of pois'n-
ing" (3.2.289). Claudius, like both Hamlets, seems particularly vulnerable to something poured into his ears—although, strikingly, he does not
openly proclaim his guilt, leaving Hamlet still in uncertainty.

The Player King's longest speech is not, as we might expect, full of
references to his own murder designed to elicit Claudius's guilt but instead, quite in line with the preoccupations of the play, examines and
describes the cognitive processes attendant upon intention and will. Hamlet as playwright seems more concerned with working through one more
version of the inner processes of emotion, thought, and intention than
with catching the conscience of the King. Although the Player King does
not doubt the sincerity of his Queen's avowed intention not to marry
again, he argues that various internal factors can alter willed intentions:
"purpose is but the slave to memory," and

> What to ourselves in passion we propose,
> The passion ending, doth the purpose lose.
> The violence of either grief or joy
> Their own enactures with themselves destroy.
>
> (3.2.194–97)

Shakespeare here coins the word *enactures*—the only instance of its use
cited in the *OED*—to express intended action that is carried through to
completion, although the Player King's point is that a change in emotional
state can prevent intended actions from becoming "enactures." It is as if
by this point in the play the word *action* had become so distanced from
a concept of successful completion that a new word was necessary to
convey this idea. The King uses Claudius's oxymoronic conflation of emotion to very different purpose, arguing that "joy" and "grief" are easily

interchangeable and can alter the will "on slender accident." He concludes that cognitive process is easily interrupted and that the complicated chain of internal actions that lead to successful "enacture" of the will can be easily disrupted: "Our wills and fates do so contrary run / That our devices still are overthrown, / Our thoughts are ours, their ends none of our own" (3.2.211–13).

Hamlet is prevented, even after the evidence provided by Claudius's reactions, from his own "enacture" because he badly misinterprets the visual evidence offered in the prayer scene, assuming that because Claudius appears to be praying, he is in an appropriately devotional state of mind, engaged in "purging of his soul." Claudius, in soliloquy, reveals that his inner thoughts differ markedly from his outward act of kneeling in prayer and that his inner state effects his will: "Pray can I not, / Though inclination be as strong as will. / My stronger guilt defeats my strong intent" (3.3.38–40). Claudius here fears judgment in heaven, where

> the action lies
> In his true nature, and we ourselves compell'd
> Even to the teeth and forehead of our faults
> To give in evidence.
>
> (3.3.61–64)

He seems to realize that a corollary of his earlier belief that emotion is genuinely revealed on the surface of the body is that at the Last Judgment guilt will also be so revealed, "the teeth and forehead of our faults." Quite at odds with Bright, Claudius imagines a soul trapped within a sinful body: "O bosom black as death! / O limed soul, that struggling to be free / Art more engag'd!" (3.3.67–69). It is not surprising that at this point Claudius cannot see the immortal soul as a controlling force for good within the body. He has come to realize that he cannot control the inner processes of thought and emotion as handily as he claimed in his first speeches.

The closet scene moves the play into its innermost space in order to explore, most insistently, what Gertrude has within and the relationship between action and guilt. It is no accident that this matrix of guilt, secrecy, and seeing into a soiled interior space is most insistently associated with a woman. As with other issues, the play wavers between imagining gender as essentially performative and as based in some essential inward core of being. Hamlet accuses Ophelia, for instance, of enacting her femininity through culturally familiar gestures: "I have heard of your paintings, well enough. God hath given you one face, and you make yourselves another. You jig and amble, and you lisp, you nickname God's creatures and make your wantonness your ignorance" (3.1.141–46).[35] Hamlet's words here seem in line with the early modern cultural commonplace traced by Katherine Maus that "the woman's body, a fascinating surface further elaborated by cosmetic enhancements, has nothing to do with the essence con-cealed within, the soul or secret parts—if, indeed, there is anything inside at all."[36] Certainly Hamlet's emphasis in the mousetrap scene on the "nothing" between Ophelia's legs suggests that he imagines her, not as possessing the "fecundity dependent upon hiddenness" (190) that Maus finds in some contemporary accounts of female sexual organs, but instead as possessing an empty space that is given shape by her actions. *Frailty* is another name for "woman" because women's inner selves can be so easily molded or altered by what they do.

Gertrude, at least initially, is imagined as possessing perhaps the most clearly delineated interior self in the whole play, although the relationship between what she has within and what she has (or has not) done remains open to question. During the closet scene Hamlet variously imagines the hidden space inside Gertrude that he intends to penetrate with his spoken daggers. Initially he echoes language and fortification images from scene 1, moving fortification from the exterior to the inmost part of the castle and shifting focus from head and rational faculty to the heart, or seat of emotion:

> Peace, sit you down,
> And let me wring your heart, for so I shall
> If it be made of penetrable stuff,
> If damned custom hath not brass'd it so
> That it be proof and bulwark against sense.
>
> (3.4.34–38)

As in Bright, "custom," or habitual action, is thought to have an effect on perception, here imagined as a deadening of the emotions (like that experienced by butchers who become inured to slaughter). Unlike Hora-tio, who is ordered to sit down and admit the "assault" of his fortified ears with a story that his rational faculty would reject, Gertrude is prepared for an assault on her emotions. It is her fortified "heart" that Hamlet, at this point, imagines as the primary seat of her inner self.

In the course of his attempts to wring her heart, Hamlet voices a preoc-cupation with blushing, which he, like Bright, associates with outward manifestation of inwardly felt shame. However, for Hamlet, even blush-ing is not necessarily a straightforward indication of inner truth. He first accuses Gertrude of committing "Such an act / That blurs the grace and blush of modesty" (3.4.40–41), suggesting that her actions destroy shame itself and render blushing meaningless or deceptive. Within ten lines, how-ever, heaven is imagined as blushing at what she has done: "Heaven's face does glow . . . Is thought-sick at the act" (3.4.48, 51); and within another thirty lines Hamlet demands "O shame, where is thy blush" (3.4.81). Despite his habitual distrust of outward signs of emotion, Hamlet here seems to yearn for a blush as a sign of, in Bright's words, "a conscience quicke, and tender, and an upright sentence of mind" within Gertrude.

However, the blush never seems to appear, and therefore Hamlet continues to imagines various physiological and cognitive interiors for Gertrude. What he does not want to imagine, but what he is inevitably drawn toward, is the secret interior sexual parts that define women and their frailty. Lear, we might recall, had no difficulty in describing what women possess "down from the waist"—"There is the sulphurous pit, burning, scalding, / Stench, consumption" (4.6.124, 128–29)—but Hamlet persistently displaces the qualities he associates with female genitalia onto cognitive spaces: soul, heart, and mind. He first imagines various breakdowns in cognitive process that would provide a nonsexual explanation for Gertrude's inability to judge the difference between the two brothers:

> ha, have you eyes?
> You cannot call it love, for at your age
> The heyday in the blood is tame, it's humble,
> And waits upon the judgment, and what judgment
> Would step from this to this? Sense sure you have,
> Else you could not have motion, but sure that sense
> Is apoplex'd, for madness would not err,
> Nor sense to ecstasy was ne'er so thrall'd
> But it reserv'd some quantity of choice
> To serve in such a difference.
>
> (3.4.67–76)

Hamlet, finally, can find no acceptable cognitive account of Gertrude's faulty judgment. Dismissing bodily imperatives ("the heyday in the blood"), Hamlet embarks on a kind of process of elimination of potential cognitive causes: it cannot be that she lacks sense, nor can it be that her senses are depraved by mere madness or ecstasy. Hamlet runs through possible configurations of damaged sensory apparatus—"Eyes without feeling, feeling without sight, / Ears without hands or eyes, smelling sans all" (3.4.78–79)—returning in the end to the kind of bodily explanation he attempted to avoid with his cognitive catalogue, asking, "Rebellious hell, / If thou can'st mutine in a matron's bones" then "compulsive ardure" takes over and "reason panders will" (3.4.81–82, 86, 88). Even here, however, Hamlet imagines the inner space as Gertrude's bone marrow rather than explicitly sexual parts.

Hamlet is so obsessed with the nature of the internal processes behind Gertrude's shameful act that he never makes entirely clear what that act was. As in the Player King's speech in the mousetrap, his preoccupation with process impedes his stated purpose of awakening guilt. His answer to Gertrude's question "Ay me, what act, / That roars so loud and thunders in the index?" (3.4.51–52) is indirect: "Look here upon this picture." Hamlet has earlier implied that the "act" was to "kill a king, and marry with his brother" (3.4.29), but in this speech he suggests that the act in question was simply Gertrude's inability to judge the great difference between her two husbands. Thus, when Gertrude acknowledges some degree of guilt by describing her own soiled inner space—"Thou turn'st my eyes into my very soul, / And there I see such black and grained spots / As will not leave their tinct" (3.4.89–91)—it is not entirely clear what action has occasioned this guilt.[37] Hamlet's reply,

> Nay, but to live
> In the rank sweat of an enseamed bed,
> Stew'd in corruption, honeying and making love
> Over the nasty sty!
>
> (3.4.91–94)

suggests that it is specifically a sexual act, but he also reimagines the soiled space—the sweaty bed, the "nasty sty"—as external to Gertrude. Gertrude's response, that "these words like daggers enter in my ears" (3.4.95), shifts the focus from her soul to her mind and to the rational faculty that hears and is affected by Hamlet's discourse. Still, there is no indication that she ever blushes.

The appearance of the ghost refocuses attention on Hamlet's inner state and its external manifestations. Gertrude, who is unable to see the ghost herself, provides a clinical description of Hamlet's appearance and attempts to use it to diagnose his inner state:

> Alas, how is't with you,
> That you do bend your eye on vacancy,
> And with th'incorporal air do hold discourse?
> Forth at your eyes your spirits wildly peep,
> And as the sleeping soldiers in th'alarm,
> Your bedded hair, like life in excrements,
> Start up and stand on end.
>
> (3.4.116–22)

She urges him to "sprinkle cool patience" "upon the heat and flame of thy distemper" (3.4.124, 123), judging the vision to be a hallucination caused by "the very coinage of your brain, / This bodiless creation ecstasy / Is very cunning in" (3.4.137–39). Hamlet's symptoms—his extruding eye spirits, his erected hair—suggest to Gertrude some disorder of the spirits that has caused a "distemper," leading to "ecstasy" and a terrifying hallucination that causes the classic manifestations of fear that Hamlet exhibits. Hamlet once again suggests that his outward appearance does not provide a reliable indicator of his inward state; despite his appearance, "my pulse as yours doth temperately keep time . . . It is not madness / That I have ut-t'red" (140–42). Of course, Gertrude's account of Hamlet's symptoms reminds us that in act 1 the actual appearance of the ghost caused manifestations of fear ranging from trembling and paleness to, potentially, the same starting eyes and hair standing on end. Presumably the sight of the ghost, whether or not it is a psychotic hallucination, would cause Hamlet's heart to race. It may be that Gertrude's diversion of attention from her own inner state to Hamlet's is exactly what he does not want to occur, for he maintains that "I essentially am not in madness, / But mad in craft" (3.4.187–88), although the symptoms described by Gertrude suggest that he is undergoing some sort of internal "distemper."

For whatever reason, Hamlet makes one more attempt to imagine Gertrude's interior self and shifts to suggesting that she can transform that self through her acts. Still focusing on her "soul," Hamlet nevertheless describes it using images of bodily disease and corruption:

> Lay not that flattering unction to your soul,
> That not your trespass but my madness speaks;
> It will but skin and film the ulcerous place,
> Whiles rank corruption, mining all within,
> Infects unseen.
>
> (3.4.145–49)

Hamlet seems here to echo the cultural commonplace, noted by Maus, that women possess a hidden and corrupt interior masked by their outward appearance. Although he is still nominally talking about her soul, the physicality of the description suggests a more bodily form of corruption, perhaps similar to that which destroys the "pocky" corpses later to be described by the gravedigger.

Hamlet goes on to suggest, however, that this inner corruption of the soul can be altered by a change in customary action. He advises her:

> go not to my uncle's bed—
> Assume a virtue if you have it not.
> That monster custom, who all sense doth eat,
> Of habits devil, is angel yet in this,
> That to the use of actions fair and good
> He likewise gives a frock or livery
> That aptly is put on. Refrain to-night,
> And that shall lend a kind of easiness
> To the next abstinence, the next more easy;
> For use almost can change the stamp of nature,
>
> (3.4.159–68)

Having spent most of the scene in a desperate but futile attempt either to get Gertrude to blush (thus manifesting her inner purity despite seemingly evil acts) or else to discern exactly what cognitive processes might lie behind her actions, Hamlet seems to reverse the direction of his inquiry and argue that if she alters her actions, her inner self might also be altered. Like Bright, Hamlet suggests, first, that "monster custom" can affect the senses ("for their instruments of action through continuall practice of such artes, maketh them in common sense, imagination, and affection, to deliver thinges unto the minde after an impure sort" 78). He goes beyond Bright, however in arguing that "use almost can change the stamp of nature," although his image of custom providing the self with "a frock or livery / That aptly is put on" echoes the "trappings and the suits of woe" that Hamlet felt (in act 1) obscured his true self. Having projected Gertrude's soiled interior onto the bed she shares with Claudius, Hamlet is able to imagine that avoiding that space will somehow purify her soul. Or almost—for Hamlet still cannot quite give up his belief in an unchanging and unrevealed inner self that carries a "stamp of nature" and influences human action for good or ill.

Women in the play may seem safer if they are imagined as constructed, performatively, by their actions rather than as possessing a secret inner self from which their actions spring. However, it is Hamlet who may become mad by acting that way (if not by having the ghost's discourse poured in his ear or by something that his melancholy sits in brood on) and Ophelia who is actually mad. Ophelia's madness never seems to occasion the long clinical descriptions of cognitive and affective processes that other characters' behavior elicits. This may be in part because Hamlet, the character most prone to such speculation, never sees her symptoms of madness, although the characters who do see and describe it superficially (Claudius, Gertrude, and Laertes) are perfectly willing to speculate about their own and Hamlet's inner states. Claudius says briefly, "This is the poison of deep grief, it springs / All from her father's death" (4.5.75–76), perhaps the simplest account of a poisoning in the play. There is no mystery about what is inside Ophelia, and her madness, though thought genuine, seems to be all surface, all symptom. As Elaine Showalter has noted, "On the Elizabethan stage, the conventions of female insanity were sharply defined. Ophelia dresses in white, decks herself with 'fantastical garlands' of wild flowers," and "her speeches are marked by extravagant metaphors, lyrical free associations," and sexual imagery.[38] Ophelia's madness is presented as a product of these gestures rather than, as in Hamlet's case, as arising from an obsessively scrutinized inner self. The gentleman is contemptuous of attempts to "read" it:

Her speech is nothing,
Yet the unshaped use of it doth move
The hearers to collection; they yawn at it,
And botch the words up to fit their own thoughts,
Which as her winks and nods and gestures yield them,
Indeed would make one think there might be thought,
Though nothing sure, yet much unhappily.

(4.5.7–13)

This is the "nothing" between her legs externalized and transposed to symptoms of cognitive failure. As R. D. Laing has argued, from a different perspective, "In her madness, there is no one there. . . . There is no integral selfhood expressed through her actions and utterances. Incomprehensible statements are said by nothing."[39] Like Gertrude at the end of the closet scene, Ophelia is imagined as possessing no interior space, just externalized "gesture" which tempts others to read her. Other people are depicted as inevitably misreading her, not because (as in Hamlet's case) what is inside her "passes show," but because there is nothing there.

The catalogues of flowers that seem most emblematic of her madness recall the blossoms that are used metaphorically to represent an external manifestation of old Hamlet's secret inner guilt. In her case, however, the flowers she obsessively sings about and wears project her sexuality and her preoccupation with death outward, to the surface, where they become a part of the repertoire of gestures that make up her self, even in madness. When she appears before Laertes, Claudius, and Gertrude in act 4, scene 5, she hands out flowers, which she interprets, according to traditional symbolism, as emblems of the recipients' inner states: "There's rosemary, that's for remembrance; pray you, love, remember. And there is pansies, that's for thoughts. . . . There's fennel for you, and columbines. There's rue for you, and here's some for me" (4.5.175–77, 179–81). Laertes comments that her use of flowers is "a document in madness, thoughts and remembrance fitted" (4.5.178–79), a comment in line with his earlier claim that "this nothing's more than matter" (4.5.174). Critics often note that when Gertrude describes Ophelia's death, most of the passage is taken up with a catalogue of the flowers with which she decks herself:

   fantastic garlands did she make
Of crow-flowers, nettles, daisies, and long purples
That liberal shepherds give a grosser name,
But our cull-cold maids do dead men's fingers call them.

(4.7.168–71)

These garlands of flowers were part of a traditional iconography of madness, but in Gertrude's interpretation of them they represent Ophelia's ambivalent sexuality. These flowers do not metaphorically bloom from her body, however, like old Hamlet's sins, but must be plucked and put on externally.

Like his sister, Laertes seems largely defined by his external actions. Calderwood has perceptively argued that Laertes differs from Hamlet in his emphasis on and acceptance of the force of relationship and public roles in constructing the self.[40] As a result, Laertes is able easily to accept both his role as instrument in Claudius's plot against Hamlet and his role as hero of a conventional revenge plot. Although Claudius almost compulsively uses Hamlet-like language (images of ears as entrances to a hidden bodily interior) with reference to Laertes, Laertes himself seems uninterested in what he may, or may not, have within. Claudius worries about Laertes' secret arrival from France because he "wants not buzzers to infect his ear / With pestilent speeches of his father's death" and "will nothing stick our person to arraign / In eye and ear" (4.5.90–91, 93–94). Similarly, Claudius caps his self-serving account of Polonius's death with a request that Laertes "must put me in your heart for friend / Sith you have heard, and with a knowing ear" (4.7.3) that Hamlet has also tried to kill the King. When unfolding his plan to make Hamlet's death seem accidental, he seeks to spur Laertes' eager cooperation with a question similar to one Hamlet has asked of himself several times: "was your father dear to you? / Or are you like the painting of a sorrow, / A face without a heart?" (4.7.107–9). Laertes seems uninterested in all of these references to his interiority and untroubled by his role as "instrument" of someone else's action. Rather than taking offense at Claudius's suggestion that his anger at his father's death is superficial, he responds, simply, "why ask you this?"(4.7.109)—as if baffled by this concern with inner process. Throughout these scenes Laertes is completely unreflecting and easily speaks the conventional words of the revenger: "but my revenge will come" (4.7.29); "That drop of blood that's calm proclaims me bastard" (4.5.118); "Let come what comes, only I'll be reveng'd / Most throughly for my father" (4.5.136–37). When Claudius first raises the possibility of "the exploit, / now ripe in my device" by which Hamlet can be killed, Laertes says "My lord, I will be rul'd, / The rather if you could devise it so / That I might be the organ" (4.7.68–70).[41] To be an "organ," or instrument of any kind, however, is what Hamlet spends most of the play desperately avoiding.

Until his transformative experiences in the closet scene, on board the ship to England, and in the graveyard Hamlet continues to insist that he, at least, possesses a secret inner self from which his actions ought to proceed. In an angry exchange with Rosencrantz and Guildenstern he vehemently denies his instrumentality in language that links it to the possession of hidden interiority: "You would play upon me, you would seem to know my stops, you would pluck out the heart of my mystery, you would sound me from my lowest note to the top of my compass; and there is much music, excellent voice, in this little organ, yet cannot you make it speak" (3.2.364–69). However, Hamlet's references to inner cognitive process abruptly cease after the closet scene that is so packed with them, replaced in part by an obsession with digestive process, in part by a new acceptance of his own role as "instrument" in the larger plot, a kind of role-playing that, for Hamlet at least, seems to preclude or replace belief in a significant hidden self "within." Hamlet shifts from viewing "action" as something that grows out of the self and begins to accept the senses of "actor" as proxy and as theatrical character—to allow his inner self to be shaped by his actions. The paradox is that he can best take action in the "action hero" sense by giving up his obsession with the mechanics of human action.

Critics universally recognize that Hamlet changes in some fundamental way during act 5, most likely as a result of his experiences on board the ship to England and in the graveyard. That he moves from questioning and uncertain anxiety to some kind of resignation or acceptance seems undeniable. However, the nature and cause of the change have been much debated. Some critics see a religious conversion or a new acceptance of the fact of death. Others suggest that there is no consistent psychological explanation for the change, which in Calderwood's terms involves the union of "the person with the role, the character with the actor" (35) as Hamlet comes to accept his place in the ghost's revenge plot. Although Calderwood denies that Shakespeare simply "shifts dramaturgical gears and transforms the truant individual into the generic revenger demanded by the plot" (35), I think something like this does occur. Hamlet has, during the first four acts of the play, brought his inner self into being by talking about it. In act 5 he gives up his focus on inner process and accepts his role as instrument in the larger Danish plot.

Critics also argue about the relative roles of his experiences on board ship and in the graveyard in causing Hamlet to change. Change is, however, evident after the closet scene, when Hamlet insistently probes Gertrude's inner self only to end with the idea that she may shape what is within by her actions. Hamlet moves, that is, toward a performative theory of self-fashioning. It is not surprising, then, that he becomes willing to experiment with this version of the self. His final soliloquy (4.4.32–66) eschews examination of inner process and simply names the cognitive faculties—"reason," "oblivion" (a failure of memory), "will"—that, through some unknown process, have impeded action. He does note an abbreviated version of such a process in Fortinbras, whose "spirit with divine ambition puff'd" (4.4.49) represents an allusion to the physiology of bravery. That the "puff'd" spirits echo the hollow lightness of the "straw" and "egg-shell"—Hamlet's metaphors for the trivial causes of the Norwegian campaign in Poland—links Fortinbras's swollen spirits with "th' imposthume of much wealth and peace. / That inward breaks, and shows no cause without / Why the man dies" (4.4.27–29). Fortinbras has allowed his inner self, his very spirits, to be shaped by external causes: the hollow eggshell of honor, the broken abscess of wealth and peace. Although he scoffs at Fortinbras's willingness to risk death for "this straw" or "an egg-shell," Hamlet concludes that such a policy does make action possible. Thus, Hamlet's resolution—"O, from this time forth, / My thoughts be bloody, or be nothing worth!" (4.4.65–66)—signals his willingness at least to try on the language and role of the conventional revenger, as well as a willingness to let his external goal—the "bloody" murder of Claudius—shape his very thoughts.

The Hamlet who allowed himself to respond rashly on the boat was thus prepared to do so by his frightening confrontation with interiority in the closet. Whereas Gertrude's acts were caused by the inner "mutine" of hell within her bones, Hamlet, on board ship and bound for England, felt "a kind of fighting" in his heart that made him sleep "worse than the mutines in the bilboes" (5.2.4–6). Hamlet's "rashness" thus seems to come bubbling up from an inner conflict similar to the one he imagined within his mother. But Hamlet's internal mutiny is caused not by inner corruption but by external circumstance, some uncanny knowledge of the contents of the sealed message. He makes no attempt here to understand the processes behind his rash decision but simply concludes, on the basis of its success, that "there is a divinity that shapes our ends" and "our indiscretion sometime serves us well / When our deep plots do pall" (5.2.10, 8–9).

Hamlet describes his quick decision to alter the commission to call for the execution of Rosencrantz and Guildenstern in theatrical terms: "Or I could make a prologue to my brains / They had begun the play" (5.2.30–31). As Calderwood notes, these lines mark a shift: "Hamlet the individual is beginning to take a subordinate place within a larger context—the providential plot that governs human experience in Denmark and the revenge tragedy plot that governs dramatic experience in the Globe theater" (36). Here Shakespeare does seem to call attention to the theatrical plot and to Hamlet's role in it, and Hamlet, for the first time, explicitly replaces cognitive process with "actions that a man might play" in both senses of the word. But the appeal to providence is less clear. Although Hamlet speaks vaguely here of "a divinity" and later of "a special providence" (5.2.220), the play has all along questioned the extent to which the ghost's revenge plot is congruent with some larger plan. In the Denmark that we have seen so far, old Hamlet and Claudius vie for the role of destiny, shaper of the face of Denmark and of Hamlet's actions. So although it is clear that Hamlet here accepts his role as "instrument" in a way that he has not done before, it is not at all clear whose instrument he is agreeing to be. Hamlet's disavowal of guilt for the intended murder of Claudius articulates a new version of the relationship between interiority and action:

> is't not perfect conscience
> To quit him with this arm? And is't not to be damn'd,
> To let this canker of our nature come
> In further evil?

> (5.2.67–70)

In a reversal of Bright, who describes the complicated sequence of inner hands and instruments that leads to action, Hamlet imagines his inner quality of conscience as being shaped or perfected by the action of his arm. Further, the "canker," or sore, that was previously inside Claudius ("I'll tent him to the quick") and Gertrude ("it will but skin and film the ulcerous place") is now, as in the case of Fortinbras, externalized: Claudius has become the "canker of our nature." The issue is no longer an examination of the nature and sources of corruption within but an extermination of its external manifestation. Hamlet is no longer preoccupied with clinical description and diagnosis but with a radical cure.

The graveyard scene similarly suggests that inner cognitive process can never be known, and the play's previous preoccupation with such process is replaced by a focus on other biological processes, such as decay and digestion, or else on legal process, which attempts to define intentionality from outside. The gravediggers begin the scene with their famous discussion of the nature of Ophelia's "act" and the intention behind it. The first gravedigger uses a parody of legal and logical language, rather than a focus on cognition, to discuss Ophelia's suicide: "if I drown myself wittingly, it argues an act, and an act hath three branches—it is to act, to do, to perform; argal, she drown'd herself wittingly" (5.1.10–13). Although the clowns examine Ophelia's actions in legal, logical, ecclesiastical, and cultural terms (its relation to social class), they never approach any sense of what was "within" her when she drowned. Indeed, Gertrude's oddly lyrical description of her drowning, with its transposition of agency to the surrounding plants and her clothing—"an envious sliver broke"; "her clothes spread wide, / And mermaid-like awhile they bore her up"; "her garments, heavy with their drink, / Pull'd the poor wretch from her melodious lay / To muddy death" (4.7.173, 175–76, 181–83)—similarly leaves Ophelia's inner state opaque. She is only "*as* one incapable of her own distress" (4.7.178, my emphasis). This sense that Ophelia's intentions are formed from the outside in, by her gestures and songs, by the contesting official interpretations of her act, and finally by the rituals that accompany her burial, accord with the outward movement of the play.

Hamlet initially takes over the gravediggers' focus on the institutional acts and gestures that make people who they are when they are alive. As noted above, Horatio comments (following Bright) that the gravedigger himself has been shaped by his occupation: "custom hath made it in him a property of easiness" (5.1.67). Contemplating the skulls turned up by the shovel, Hamlet does not attempt to see inside them because they have been hollowed out by death. The skull is, of course, a traditional memento mori, but it particularly emphasizes the fact that the brain, seat of rational decision making and cognition, is literally gone, rotted away. Instead of contemplating what is no longer within, Hamlet imagines the actions that shaped them when they were alive: the courtier's words, the lawyer's "quiddities" and "action of battery," the land buyer's "fines, his double vouchers, his recoveries" (5.1.99, 103, 106, 105). Now the defining and clinically described processes are the physical facts of decay: "Faith, if a' be not rotten before 'a die—as we have many pocky corses, that will scarce hold the laying in—'a will last you some eight year or nine year. A tanner will last you nine year" because "his hide is so tann'd with his trade that 'a will keep out water a great while, and your water is a sore decayer of your whoreson dead body" (5.1.165–72). Like the gravediggers themselves, only in a more fundamental way, the tanner has been shaped by his occupation. But in death cognitive shaping is irrelevant; only something as basic as the permeation of the skin by tanning chemicals can have an effect.

Now, too, the rottenness and inward decay that had been, for Hamlet, a metaphor for inner psychological and cognitive corruption become literal: pocky corpses are literally "rotten" and therefore decay sooner. In this physical economy cognitive process is replaced by digestive process, as when Hamlet previously told Claudius that Polonius was "at supper. . . . Not where he eats, but where 'a is eaten" and that "A man may fish with the worm that hath eat of a king, and eat of the fish that hath fed of that worm," so that "a king may go a progress through the guts of a beggar" (4.3.17–19, 27–29, 30–31).[42] Now the mad Ophelia's use of flowers as gestures to create and express her sexuality and grief is also made literal through a process of decay: "And from her fair and unpolluted flesh / May violets spring!" (5.1.239–40).

The empty skull that most affects Hamlet is that of an actor, the jester Yorick, and Hamlet is here also struck by the fact that his gibes, gambols, and songs are reduced to a parody of his former grin. If the constitutive gestures of an actor are, in death, just as genuine as any others, Hamlet seems willing to conflate the two kinds of action. Picking up on Laertes' theatrical protestations of love for Ophelia and his melodramatic leap into her grave, Hamlet follows suit and identifies himself for the first time in accordance with his role in Denmark: "This is I, / Hamlet the Dane!" (5.1.257–58).[43] He explicitly identifies his language here as excessively theatrical: "I'll rant as well as thou" (5.1.284). The inner space of Ophelia's grave, soon to contain her rotting body, is the skull-grin parody of Gertrude's closet. In the closet Hamlet attempted to describe what might constitute the self, the causes of action, within his mother and himself. In Ophelia's grave Hamlet lets the role of "Hamlet the Dane" shape his actions and himself.

Although the final scene of the play takes place inside the castle, its images and themes return us to the opening scene of the play and shift our focus from Hamlet back to Denmark and to Hamlet's role as instrument of a larger plot. The scene as a whole emphasizes Hamlet's turn away from interiors by externalizing images and themes that throughout most of the play have been associated with hidden interiority.[44] Terence Hawkes has argued that the final scene of Hamlet echoes the first in significant ways and that these symmetries "suggest, not linearity, but circularity: a cyclical and recursive movement."[45] I want to suggest that there is a significant difference between the first and last scenes of the play—the difference in Hamlet himself, who at the end of the play is effectively recuperated into the Danish plot and comes to accept his own instrumentality, both of which he struggled against for most of the play.

The final sword fight with Laertes emphasizes and literalizes the instrumentality of both Laertes and Hamlet in the Danish court. Laertes is the "organ" of Claudius, and his hand is his own instrumental organ, the poisoned and unbated foil a further "treacherous instrument" (5.2.316). When Hamlet says "I'll be your foil, Laertes" (5.2.255), he accepts his own role as instrument in a scene that has already been written for him. The swordplay itself makes literal and external the chains of agency that previously were internal to Hamlet and the other characters.[46] Michael Goldman has argued that the sword fight represents the action an audience has been waiting for throughout the play: "All the significances are clear and we watch them explode into action. Every piece of inner villainy leaves its telltale outer mark and is repaid in fully emblematic action. ('The point envenomed too! / Then, venom, to thy work') The purpose of playing is achieved; acting and being are one."[47] Although I agree that the swordplay has this emblematic, externalizing effect, it seems rather to emphasize a split between being and acting, in the various senses of the word *act*. The nature and causes of "inner villainy" have become irrelevant to Hamlet. There is no longer any "heart of mystery" to probe or hidden ulcer to "tent." Instead, the point of the probing instrument itself is poisoned, and the sources of corruption are revealed. All is on the surface, and so it can become obvious, at last, that "the King, the King's to blame" (5.2.320).

The poison in the cup of wine similarly renders external and literal several central images from the play. Although in the earlier scenes of the play poison applied through the ear was a figure for the dangerous cognitive effects of corrupting discourse, Gertrude and Claudius ingest the fatal poison orally. As Jonathan Gil Harris has suggested, Hamlet's command that Claudius "drink off this potion" (5.2.328) invokes the double sense of "poison" and "medicine": "The 'potion' has a toxic effect on Claudius, and a medicinal one on the Danish body politic."[48] In keeping with the shift in the latter parts of the play from cognitive to digestive process, there is no suggestion here that this poison represents discursive contamination. Since its source is the "union" thrown into the cup by Claudius, it may in part represent the problematic union of Claudius and Gertrude in marriage.[49] But it is particularly important that when Gertrude drinks it and dies, we know nothing about her motives—was it an accident, an attempt to save Hamlet, or suicide?—nor do we hear anything about the workings of the poison. As she dies, the inner space that Hamlet so obsessively scrutinized in the closet scene remains completely hidden.

As in act 1, fear and anxiety remain emotions that are reliably revealed on the surface of the body, as Hamlet addresses the surrounding courtiers: "You that look pale, and tremble at this chance, / That are but mutes or audience to this act" (5.2.334–35). As many critics have noted, the pale and trembling audience here echoes Barnardo's comment to Horatio in scene 1 after the ghost has first appeared: "How now, Horatio? you tremble and look pale. / Is not this something more than fantasy?" (1.1.53–54). In the opening scene Horatio's involuntary physical signs of fear belie his skeptical denial that ghosts exist and signal that the ghost is "more than fantasy." The pale and trembling courtiers of act 5, however, are frightened by what Hamlet seems to describe as a play. And no one is concerned with the processes behind their display of emotion; indeed, its corporate nature—all of the courtiers manifest the same signs of fear—seems to detach it from any sort of private inner self.

Throughout this final scene, Claudius takes to almost frenzied extremes his penchant for registering emotion through external ceremonial displays. In the course of the scene the link that Claudius has desired to maintain between the King's sincerity and his power is completely broken. No longer content with simple cannon shots, Claudius piles up external signs of his (patently false) joy at Hamlet's success:

> If Hamlet give the first or second hit,
> Or quit in answer of the third exchange,
> Let all the battlements their ord'nance fire. . . .

And let the kettle to the trumpet speak,
The trumpet to the cannoneer without,
The cannons to the heavens, the heaven to earth,
"Now the King drinks to Hamlet."

(5.2.268–70, 275–78)

Claudius here attempts to replicate externally the kind of internal chain of instrumentality that Bright describes behind the expression of emotion. Instead of spirits affecting the brain, which in turn causes weeping or laughter, drum will signal trumpet, which will signal the cannon to fire. The drink, of course, we know to be poisoned, and the elaborate chain of celebration emphasizes its externality and its falsity. Like everyone else in this scene, Claudius becomes the product of his gestures, in this case grandiose gestures that reveal the hollowness of the power they would display. When the ambassador from England complains that "the ears are senseless that should give us hearing" (5.2.369) and Horatio notes that thanks will be forthcoming "not from his mouth" (5.2.372), they reiterate the loss of cognitive capacity in death. The choice, it would seem, is between a secret inner space liable to corruption and decay and a hollow shell formed by ritualized social gesture.

When Fortinbras appears, then, his arrival signaled by martial music and *a shot within*, and when he marks Hamlet's death with the order "go bid the soldiers shoot" (5.2.403), the triumph of outside over inside is complete. Fortinbras has always represented externality, the threat from outside, his soldiers gathered from "the skirts of Norway" (1.1.97). He is, literally, a "strong arm," an external instrument. Even in act 1, when everyone is described as having some sort of shaping interiority, Fortinbras's inner self is composed of digestive, rather than cognitive, processes: he is "of unimproved mettle hot and full," his soldiers gathered "for food and diet to some enterprise / That hath a stomach in't" (1.1.96, 99–100). Fortinbras's composition of hot "mettle" also suggests that he has internalized the molten metal from which the "daily cast of brazen cannon" (1.1.73) just described by Marcellus would be made. When Hamlet registers Fortinbras's essential hollowness in act 4, "puff'd" by ambition, he seems quite accurately represented by the cannon's blasts— part hot metal, part hot air. Fortinbras is thus the quintessential performative subject.

That Hamlet gives Fortinbras his "dying voice" (5.2.356) to become King of Denmark suggests the extent to which he has allowed himself to become like Fortinbras. His dying concern is not with his inner state— the state of his soul or conscience—but with his "wounded name" (5.2.344), as if the sword is not able to penetrate a nonexistent interiority but only his social role. He is concerned that Laertes remain alive to "tell my story" (5.2.349), suggesting that a narrative of his actions will be able accurately to represent him. Since Hamlet's concern is the repair of his "wounded name" and not the accurate representation of his true nature, Laertes' summary of events may not be as inadequate as critics have thought it to be.[50] Like Gertrude's account of Ophelia's death, it eschews agency, implying that the actions of the play have taken place either in spite of or without the direction of human will:

> So shall you hear
> Of carnal, bloody, and unnatural acts,
> Of accidental judgments, casual slaughters,
> Of deaths put on by cunning and forc'd cause,
> And in this upshot, purposes mistook
> Fall'n on th' inventors' heads.
>
> (5.2.380–85)

Except for the "deaths put on by cunning and forc'd cause," the rest of the "acts" of the play have been "accidental," "casual," a result of "purposes mistook."

Even the deaths "put on" suggest theatrical rather than actual deaths, just as Fortinbras's judgment of Hamlet—"he was likely, had he been put on, / To have prov'd most royal" (5.2.397–98)—implies that Hamlet could become king only by assuming the kingship as a role. Thus, Hamlet's body is borne onto a "stage," and Fortinbras is determined to use the gestures of military ceremony retrospectively to construct Hamlet as the kind of soldier-king he is himself: "the soldiers' music and the rite of war / Speak loudly for him" (5.2.399–400), transforming Hamlet's dying voice into a marching song. The concluding peal of ordinance and Fortinbras's longing reference to the field of battle, where so many dead would be suitable, mark the final stage of the movement outward that Fortinbras needs to make. Fortinbras literally "becomes the field" (5.2.402) insofar as he is shaped by his military actions, his "strong arm." As a Norwegian king of Denmark, he brings the outside in even as he epitomizes a subject formed in exactly that way.

Hamlet, then, gives up a great deal to achieve his readiness for action.[51] He gives up any sense that what is within is an immortal and transcendent soul untainted by its immersion in bodily matter; indeed, he was never able to do much more than entertain this as a possibility. What is more, he gives up the idea of subjective interiority, of a unique, private inner self that can be a source of meaningful and purposeful action in the world. A final attempt to articulate what his inner self contains, "how ill all's here about my heart—but it is no matter" (5.2.212–13), suggests that what he has within is immaterial, in both senses of that word. Since such a self had come to seem inevitably either a hidden source of corruption or a bar to action, Hamlet, largely through his contemplation of Gertrude's potential inner (and explicitly sexual) corruption, comes to believe in a self shaped, performatively, by its actions, actions that cannot easily be distinguished from actions that a man might play.

It might seem, then, that Hamlet invents not only the bourgeois subject but also its postmodern disintegration, discovering in its place the freedom afforded by performativity. This is, however, a tragedy, and Hamlet registers the hollowness of this version of the new self even as he embraces it. In the scene just preceding this final one, Hamlet describes Osric the courtier with open contempt and with language that echoes his earlier comments on Fortinbras. Like the hollow Fortinbras, "puff'd" with ambition, fighting over straws and eggshells, Osric "runs away with the shell on his head" (5.2.186). Furthermore, Osric is seen as representative of a current trend: courtiers' subjectivity is "a kind of yesty collection, which carries them through and through the most profound and winnow'd opinions and do but blow them to their trial, the bubbles are out" (5.2.191–94). Such people are formed "out of an habit of encounter" (5.2.190), by the gestures required by courtly life. That Hamlet himself gives up his attempts to understand his cognitive processes and instead embraces this mode of being is hardly positive, although it does make defining action possible.

As Hamlet is a theatrical character, his dream of subjective interiority was always futile, since he has always been, literally, a product of his gestures and words. Hamlet attempted at one point to narrow the gap between theatricality and reality by espousing a more naturalistic kind of performance, one where actors "suit the action to the word, the word to the action" (3.2.17–18), bringing gesture into congruence with language and both in line with "nature." In this passage Hamlet's relatively straightforward image of drama as holding "the mirror up to nature: to show virtue her feature, scorn her own image" (3.2.21–23) shifts to a strangely material sense of drama as a pliable substance that can take a kind of cast or impression of the surrounding culture to show "the very age and body of the time his form and pressure" (3.2.23–24). *Pressure*, meaning "impression" is used by Shakespeare only in this play and seems here to suggest that actors are a malleable medium, materially shaped, like Osric, by what they imitate.[52] In act 1 Hamlet imagined the interior of his brain as similarly containing "all forms, all pressures past / That youth and observation copied there" (1.5.100–101). Theatrical performance as imagined by Hamlet at this point has at least the potential to mediate between what is inside and what is outside, as external actions leave an impression on the brain and theatrical actions similarly take the impression of actions in culture. This sense of *matter* as a substance that can be shaped by the "form and pressure" of external actions seems here to depend upon a congruence between words and acts. Shakespeare has been interested throughout this play in exploring whether discourse can constitute an "act" and in so doing have some effect on surrounding material culture or else on the subjects that hear and speak it. In this sense as well, the play seems to anticipate Judith Butler's connection between a phenomenology of constituting acts (actions that "form" the subject) and speech act theory (language that "impresses" or affects those who hear it).

Margaret Ferguson has argued that the play literalizes words, turning them into "matter that kills." Just as it is about the interface of soul and body and intentionality, it is also about whether discourse is material or can have material effects. The mousetrap includes both a dumb show and a "speech of some dozen lines, or sixteen lines" in part because of Hamlet's uncertainty about whether gesture or speech is more likely to function performatively in the sense of having an effect on Claudius. Throughout the play, Hamlet is interested in what speech-act theory would term "performative utterances," speech acts such as vows, oaths, and commands, which actually perform what they say.[53] Hamlet wants very badly, in J. L. Austin's words, to "do things with words," just as he would like to take physical action against Claudius; he wants to believe in efficacious and binding speech acts that are made valid by the sincerity of the speaker. Thus, Hamlet's and other characters' interest throughout the play in the validity of performative utterances resembles their interest in the physiological signs of emotion: both conjure up and call into question the presence of an authorizing interiority.

Katherine Maus aptly summarizes Austin's argument that speech-act theory "renders irrelevant a secret, ontologically prior realm of intention."[54] This Austinian position differs, she notes, from early modern "casuists," who "imagine utterances matching up, well or badly, with authoritative internal propositions; and so the promise is only binding upon its maker if it properly expresses what [the English Jesuit Henry] Garnet calls its preexistent mental 'essence.'"[55] In general, religious belief in this period placed new emphasis on questions of sincerity. Hamlet, however, seems torn between a hope that sincerity can guarantee the efficacy of performatives and a fear of its corollary, that insincerity renders them inefficacious. He spends most of the play hoping that he will be able to suit the intention to the words, the word to the intentions. By the end, however, the only successful performative utterances are those that have behind them not sincere intentions but rather power itself, however insincere. Paradoxically, as Hamlet comes to accept that his very self is created, performatively, by his words and actions, both word and act are hollowed out and reduced to the products of a strong arm.

In the early acts of the play, performatives proliferate, and many characters, including Hamlet, place great trust in the power and efficacy of
words to effect action. The sentries, for example, rely on an exchange of
passwords in order to distinguish friend from enemy. The ghost, a firm
believer in the power of words to cause strong emotional effects, also
assures Hamlet that his own love for Gertrude "was of that dignity / That
it went hand in hand even with the vow / I made to her in marriage"
(1.5.48–50); the ghost also seconds Hamlet's insistence that Horatio and
Marcellus "lay your hands again upon my sword. / Swear by my sword /
Never to speak of this that you have heard" (1.5.158–60). For the ghost
and for Hamlet at this point, vows and oaths have an instrumentality akin
to both hands and swords: like the sword, they are tools wielded by
human hands in order to achieve effective action in the world. Both Hamlets seem to believe that sincerity can ensure the efficacy of speech acts
and also that the breaking of such oaths and vows is an unusual and
heinous crime.

The Polonius family, on the other hand, sets no such trust in promises.
Laertes warns Ophelia that Hamlet's vows cannot be performative unless
seconded by the voice of power in Denmark:

> Then if he says he loves you,
> It fits your wisdom so far to believe it
> As he in his particular act and place
> May give his saying deed, which is no further
> Than the main voice of Denmark goes withal.
>
> (1.3.24–28)

For Laertes, words cannot do anything unless authorized by "act and
place," by the cultural circumstances in which they are uttered. Polonius
goes further and warns that vows are meaningless because they are almost
invariably insincere: "I do know, / When the blood burns, how prodigal
the soul / Lends the tongue vows" (1.3.115–17). Polonius sees vows as
produced by a process similar to (but much more pessimistic than) those
described by Bright: blood burns, moves the soul to prodigality, and
causes the subject to make false vows. Polonius further warns:

> Do not believe his vows, for they are brokers,
> Not of that dye which their investments show,
> But mere implorators of unholy suits,
> Breathing like sanctified and pious bonds,
> The better to beguile.
>
> (1.3.127–31)

Judith Anderson has suggestively noted the complex polysemy of these
lines, combining images of money, clothing, and religion.[56] Polonius em-

phasizes, again, the gap between what might be within and the vows that purport to manifest it. For Polonius, however, even the inner states behind the vows are "investments," linked, as Anderson suggests, by the pun on *vestments* with the "unholy suits" without.

Hamlet eventually comes to share their suspicion of vows and oaths. As noted above, the "speech" he inserts into "The Murder of Gonzago," the dialogue between the Player King and Queen, is largely about the efficacy of oaths and vows, with the Player King providing an almost Austinian account of conditions of intentionality that might cause such vows to be "infelicitous." Indeed, the Player King's coinage *enacture* is almost a synonym for Austin's "perlocutionary" utterance since it suggests words that actually carry out the action that they intend.[57] Of course, Austin notoriously excepted such fictional performatives from the status of actual performativity—as Hamlet says, "they do but jest, poison in jest" (3.2.235), quite different in effect from actual poisoning. However, what Hamlet eventually learns is that real oaths and vows are no more or less efficacious than his fictional versions.

In act 3, scene 3, when Hamlet misrecognizes Claudius's insincere and "infelicitous" prayer as effectively performative prayer (which would "purge" his soul and ensure that it went straight to heaven), he briefly returns to his earlier belief in the authorizing power of sincere intentions. It may be that the religious context of the scene causes this shift, since the sight of Claudius at prayer seems briefly to enable Hamlet to believe that the most important feature of human interiority is an immortal soul. Claudius, on the other hand, feels his soul to be completely imprisoned by corporeal matter—"O limed soul, that struggling to be free / Art more engag'd" (3.3.68–69)—and sees in this imprisoning matter the cause of his inability sincerely to repent. Interestingly, Hamlet's belief here in the perlocutionary force of Claudius's prayer is clearly perceived by the audience to be mistaken; however, its falsity is based on our knowledge of Claudius's insincerity and therefore on an assumption that intention *can* determine the force of an utterance.

In the closet scene, however, the link between sincere inner feeling and performativity seems less clear. Hamlet tells Gertrude that her "act" has not just destroyed "the blush of grace and modesty" but also "made marriage vows / As false as dicers' oaths" (3.4.44–45). Hamlet continues to see performative utterances as similar to the involuntary outward effects of emotion, although here he believes that both have been falsified (or rendered infelicitous) by Gertrude's actions. At the end of that scene, although he asks Gertrude not to tell Claudius that his madness is feigned, he does not ask her to swear. Significantly, she does swear an oath that connects the words she speaks to her very life:

Be thou assur'd, if words be made of breath,
And breath of life, I have no life to breathe
What thou hast said to me.

(3.4.197–99)

It is Claudius who begins the next scene by attempting to read the truth in Gertrude's breath: "There's matter in these sighs, these profound heaves—/ You must translate, 'tis fit we understand them. / Where is your son?" (4.1.1–3). Claudius still believes that signs of emotion point to some kind of inner truth, although he here admits that it must be "translated" by the person who experiences it. Gertrude's answer, that Hamlet is "Mad as the sea and wind, when both contend / Which is the mightier" (4.1.7–8), clearly preserves her oath, but we know nothing about the intentions behind it. Does she believe Hamlet to be sane and lie to Claudius? Or does she believe that Hamlet is truly mad and tell a partial truth here? She certainly lies when she tells Claudius that Hamlet "weeps for what is done" (4.1.27).

Hamlet's experiences on board ship teach him the efficacy of a different kind of performative: a command rather than a vow or oath. A command is preeminently the kind of performative whose success is dependent not on sincerity but on the authorizing power behind it. Opening the "grand commission" or "exact command" (5.2.18, 19) sent to England by Rosencrantz and Guildenstern and learning that it orders his own death, Hamlet uses a sign of power that he happens to have with him to authorize a counter command:

I had my father's signet in my purse,
Which was the model of that Danish seal;
Folded the writ up in the form of th'other,
Subscrib'd it, gave it th'impression, plac'd it safely,
The changeling never known.

(5.2.49–53)

It is now the King's seal that is able to alter the "form" and "impression" of the time. Rosencrantz and Guildenstern "go to't" (5.2.56) because Hamlet has been able to wield the "General voice of Denmark" and not because of any authorizing sincerity on his part. Indeed, "they come not near [his] conscience" (5.2.58).

In the final lines of the play, then, Claudius's elaborately performative chain of command—his order will prompt the trumpets, which will signal the drums, which will cause the cannon to fire—is an empty gesture because his power is gone. There is a kind of circularity here: Claudius's gestures cannot create a powerful self because there is no powerful self behind the gestures. But where has his power gone? The evidence here is mixed since Claudius's power seemed partly to depend on a smooth rhetorical surface and an ability to persuade others to serve as his instruments, qualities that are in no way diminished during the final scene of the play. It may be that his own admissions in soliloquy and aside to a gap between his confident performance and inner feelings of guilt and inadequacy are a cause, in which case what he has "within" would seem to be of central importance. But Claudius seems mostly diminished here by Hamlet's assumption of his role as "Hamlet the Dane," the "mighty opposite" who sees Claudius as a "king of shreds and patches" (3.4.103). Hamlet's "dying voice," on the other hand, has managed to accumulate power achieved by assuming this role, using the late King's signet to reverse Claudius's command, and finally by killing Claudius. Fortinbras's final line is a command, "go bid the soldiers shoot," which resembles Claudius's gestural claim to power. But whereas Claudius used military symbols to represent personal emotion, Fortinbras uses them simply to manifest his own military power. Although he assures Horatio that "with sorrow I embrace my fortune" (5.2.388), his power is in no way authorized by the sincerity of that claim or rendered null by its insincerity.

The play may conclude with a paradox. On the one hand, it seems to suggest that language can be performative, can "act," only when it is based in pure power. On the other hand, the final scenes of the play suggest that language and gesture or action create the subject performatively. The tragedy of the play may be its final coalescence of this reduced sense of language and an increased sense of its power to construct the self. Hamlet is able to act at the cost of hollowing out his sense of self and his sense of language. The play suggests that this hollowing out is an inevitable consequence of political power.

On the other hand, this hollowing out can be registered as tragic (rather than simply a fact of history) because for much of the play we at least partly believe in Hamlet's dream of a prior and authorizing interiority from which efficacious language and action proceed.[58] Indeed, the play itself uses language to conjure up multiple versions of what is within and multiple versions of the effects that language can have. The polysemic web of "acts" is not hollow but resembles Hamlet's imagined pliable matter reflecting the form and pressure of culture, as well as the cognitive systems within Shakespeare's brain. The idea that language creates this "web" within which Hamlet is caught for most of the play provides an alternative to the narrowly instrumental sense of language that emerges in the final acts of the play.

The play works through its interest in the bourgeois subject from a particularly theatrical point of view. Its sense of the nature of agency and of the power of language is markedly shaped by the material conditions of theatrical production. Thus, although Shakespeare in Hamlet evinces a fascination with the nature of inner processes explored by Bright, he cannot escape the realization that without belief in a controlling soul, these processes inevitably turn to decay and digestion. An alternative to this depressing fact of biological life, however, is the example offered by theatrical characters, who lack the easily corrupted core of biological matter and are formed by external gestures around an empty center. Theatrical characters are thus performative subjects, but the play registers the shortcomings of this version of subjectivity as well as its appeal. The question whether words can be performative, can do anything, remains unanswered, as does the question of the relationship between words and "real" subjects in the world. A cognitive Hamlet who binds himself up in a tangle of imagined inner processes is no less tragic than a politically or psychologically crippled prince. In suggesting that the polysemic webs that offered multiple possibilities in the comedies can also foreclose and obscure them *Hamlet* questions and qualifies the creative powers of human thought and language even as it demonstrates them.

5

Male Pregnancy and Cognitive Permeability in *Measure for Measure*

Measure for Measure was an early favorite of New Historicist critics, and no wonder: it clearly treats changing technologies of power, especially the appropriation by the state and stage of internalized methods of control that had previously been the property of other institutions, most notably the Catholic Church. Steven Mullaney describes the play as "a searching exploration of the shape a more intrusive form of power might take," a form of power that he calls "apprehension" and Steven Greenblatt calls "anxiety."[1] All agree that the play is about the power of ruling ideologies to shape early modern subjects and that the unruliness of those subjects is to be interpreted for the most part as a self-justifying construction of power. In Jonathan Dollimore's words, "We can indeed discern in the demonising of sexuality a relegitimation of authority."[2] In these readings the unruly materiality of the subject itself is to some extent shortchanged; what seems important is external cultural interpretations of the body and bodily behavior.[3] Indeed, both psychoanalytic and New Historicist readings have seen the process of subjectification represented in the play as involving a kind of disembodiment. Janet Adelman, for example, argues that "the last scene is constructed to make invisible male power, rather than the visibly pregnant female body, the site of revelation," so that "in the end, the replacement of the bodily female by the spiritual male dispensation seems complete."[4] According to Mullaney, "The power of the stage was precisely the power of fiction, the power to induce an audience or an Angelo to view themselves as actors in their own lives, as artificial and artfully manipulated constructions, as indeed they were, whether they existed on-stage or off, whether they were constituted by a playwright or by larger cultural forces of determination."[5]

While Greenblatt, Mullaney, and other New Historicist readers of the play imagine immaterial and ubiquitous manifestations of power that are able to construct human subjects invisibly, the play emphasizes the physicality of both the body and the mind and the necessarily material forms that power must take in its attempts to shape them. By vesting the power of the state in the all-too-human Duke, the play insists on depicting power as it is embodied in a particular human agent who is vulnerable to the

very kinds of discursive penetration with which he would control his subjects.[6] In focusing on the role of embodiment in Shakespeare's play I join
a number of critics who have recently used such an emphasis to consider
subject formation and agency within culture at the material site where the
subject is formed and agency must begin—the human body. Gail Kern
Paster's work on humoral physiology in the period, studies by Jonathan
Sawday and others on anatomy and dissection, and a recent collection of
essays, *The Body in Parts*, all attest to the salience of this approach.[7] However, while these critics have generally theorized the body using Bakhtin-
ian, Foucauldian, or Lacanian paradigms, I believe that cognitive theory
offers a particularly useful way of reading this preeminently cognitive play.

Just as *Hamlet* called on the early modern cognitive theory of Timothy
Bright's treatise in attempting to imagine the inner processes behind
human action and speech, *Measure for Measure* alludes to contemporary
medical discourse in its more physical representations of the embodied
mind and its vulnerabilities. It is important to recall here that current
cognitive theory entails an assumption shared by the pre-Cartesian psychology of the early modern period, namely, that the mind is inextricably
part of the material body. We should also remember that although psychoanalytic approaches also see the body, and especially the gendered body,
as an essential part of psychic formation, both psychoanalytic and contemporary materialist theories about the nature of subject formation differ from cognitive approaches in emphasizing the fragmentation of body
and mind and in positing a more thoroughgoing and pervasive role for
language and the symbolic in the process of forming a conscious and
speaking human subject.

Like psychoanalytic readings, my cognitive reading of the linguistic,
imagistic, and plot structures of *Measure for Measure* claims to offer some
limited access to deeper processes of authorial thought that gave rise to it.
Similarly, my cognitive study of these characters looks for ways in which
Shakespeare represents fictional subjects that serve as complex images of
the processes that constitute real subjects. Thus, a cognitive reading of
Measure for Measure lets us tell a different story about the interrelationships between power, language, and bodies in the play, one that gives
more weight to the constitutive power of the body itself. *Hamlet* turned
inward in an attempt to figure out what processes might constitute the
self that inhabits the body and directs its outward actions. *Measure for
Measure* might be seen as based on a central image from *Hamlet*—that
of language as poison poured into the ear—since it pushes further than
that play the disturbing implications of the physicality of the mind, emphasizing not its relation to action in the world but the potentially corrupting grounds of its own creative thought.

In insisting on the materiality of the humoral body, Gail Kern Paster has rightly emphasized the pre-Cartesian interpenetration of body and mind to be found in humoral physiology. Paster's concern is the extent to which theories of humoral physiology shaped early modern somatosensory awareness and provided a focal point for representations of unruliness and control. Paster resembles New Historicist critics like Mullaney and Greenblatt when she focuses on the ways in which the unruly humoral body was subjected to the emerging disciplinary strategies of embarrassment and shame, particularly as its unruliness was assimilated "to external hierarchies of class and gender."[8] Elsewhere, Paster emphasizes that these early modern bodies were "*epistemically* though not *biologically* different from our own,*" an insight that allows her to stress the "ideological texture of early modern somatic experiences."[9] A cognitive reading does not deny the "epistemic" differences, but it shifts the emphasis slightly to focus on where the spatial and metaphoric structures of cognitive process intersect with, and exert pressure against, the ideological forces of culture.

Building on Paster's work, I argue that *Measure for Measure* is largely about the terrifying permeability of the human body and the embodied brain and thus about the internal properties that made the early modern self both vulnerable and resistant to the workings of disciplinary power. If *Comedy of Errors*, *As You Like It*, and *Twelfth Night* began to explore how early modern subjects thought about the grounds of their own existence in space and time, and if *Hamlet* examined more insistently the inner workings of such subjects, *Measure for Measure* takes very literally the physicality of the embodied mind. In this play Shakespeare focuses on a lexical oddity rather than a complex polysemic category—the strange etymology of the word *pregnant*—to explore the cognitive implications of the humoral body in culture, especially as it thinks and speaks.[10]

Rather than simply displaying the beginnings of a process of Foucauldian discipline, in which a dominant ideological formation learns ever more effective ways to infiltrate and shape the subject, Shakespeare traces the physical as well as the cultural conditions that make such infiltration and shaping possible. The unruly bodies of this play are not just instruments in the exercise of power but also serve as an analogy for its workings; thus, the play shows ideological construction to be dependent upon the very permeability it seeks to control.[11] Because language, the very medium of disciplinary technology in this play, is itself shown to be based on analogies with bodily experience, the process of subject formation seems circular rather than progressive. While a narrative of movement toward a more efficiently disciplined future is present, it does not tell the whole story, which seems to take the shape of a complex and interlinked web of possibilities, a lexical web that is itself vulnerable to a fertilizing contamination. Like contemporary cognitive theory, the play emphasizes how it feels to inhabit a body and how those feelings of embodiment shape thought, language, and even power itself.

For Shakespeare, *pregnant* was a word that named the multiple ways that bodies are penetrated by the external world and produce something—offspring, ideas, language—as a result of that penetration. Strikingly, in a play that has as its central image a pregnant female body the word is never used to describe a woman but is instead used exclusively to denote the mental processes of men. Gender is certainly relevant to the depiction of penetration and productivity in the play since male and female bodies undergo them differently, and with different results. But both male and female bodies are finally shown to be penetrable and productive, with equally problematic results.[12] In the world of *Measure for Measure* penetration is seen as almost invariably contaminating; its products are in turn powerful but also capable of spreading contamination. This procreative process reshapes the body that is penetrated and rendered productive and also the bodies that its product has contact with once it is released. At the same time, however, attempts like those of Angelo and Isabella to avoid penetration and contamination are both deeply problematic and probably futile. The new technologies of interpellation, of course, depend on this permeability and impressionability of the body and mind, but the play suggests that they cannot control it.

To a modern linguist, Shakespeare's definition of *pregnant* would appear hopelessly contaminated by etymological confusion and conflation and idiosyncratic personal feeling. Like instances of pregnancy in the play, this lexical contamination is fruitful, producing a surplus of meaning and yielding a radially structured web of concepts about the intermeshed workings of body and brain. Like most speakers of English in 1604, the Shakespeare who sat down to write *Measure for Measure* thought of the word *pregnant* as referring primarily to a mental condition, "of a person or his mind: teeming with ideas, fertile" (*OED*). The *OED* comments that "*pregnaunt* was used in 1413, and was apparently common in the 15th century in the transferential sense [i.e., 'of a person or his mind']. It is remarkable that this should appear so much earlier than the literal sense." Shakespeare and other educated speakers of English would have been well aware that the Latin word *praegnans* meant "with child," and, indeed, Thomas Raynalde's *Byrth of Mankynde* (an English translation of a German obstetrical treatise) used the English word *pregnant* in this sense as early as 1545; the reproductive sense of the word did not enter common usage until the mid-seventeenth century. The reasons for this "remarkable" preference for what seems to us to be a metaphorical sense of the word are complex: Shakespeare, I think, was interested in, or perhaps obsessed with, the interconnected web of bodily and cultural factors that contributed to the complex polysemy of early modern pregnancy. He explores them in *Measure for Measure*.

For Shakespeare, *pregnant* was a site of early modern cognitive theory on two counts: first, the word itself constitutes a category that is clearly based on images of the body as a container; second, it provided a way to explore analogies between bodily and mental production that were fundamental to early modern psychology. In *Twelfth Night* (3.1.88–89) the word *pregnant* seems to be considered an affectation—a Latinate inkhorn term that many theorists of language in the period criticized. It may simply be that a formal term was considered more appropriate for describing processes of thought than for describing the bodily functions of women (for which the simple English phrase *with child* was most commonly employed). But conflation of this term with an adjectival form of *pregnant*, derived from the Old French word *preignant*, meaning "pressing," and commonly used to describe a convincing argument, was probably the main reason for its application to mental rather than reproductive processes. The *OED* notes that this term "ran together with the later *pregnant* . . . and it is probable that in later times the two were viewed merely as senses of the same word, and that this was hence apt to be confused with some of the figurative uses of the next." A "pressing" argument was probably also "pregnant," or filled with matter, so the two senses of the word become intertwined. Thus in *Measure for Measure* when Angelo identifies his example of the "jewel that we find, we stoop and take it" as "very pregnant" (1.4.23–24), and when the *Riverside Shakespeare* glosses the word as meaning "readily perceived, obvious," it is unclear whether the example is obvious because it is "pressing," because it is "full of meaning, highly significant," or both.

Shakespeare uses "pregnant" in yet another sense, that of being "apt to receive or be influenced; receptive; disposed, inclined." The *OED* identifies this sense as appearing "chiefly in Shakespeare" (the only other cited example is from one of Donne's sermons). Cesario's use in *Twelfth Night* (which so impresses Sir Andrew) is in this sense: "My matter hath no voice, Lady, but to your own most pregnant and vouchsafed eare" (3.1.87–88). Similarly, the fawning courtiers in *Hamlet* who "crooke the pregnant hinges of the knee" (3.2.61) reflect this unusual meaning. It seems clear that Shakespeare conflates *pregnant* with *pregnable*, meaning "assailable, vulnerable," a word that was current in the sixteenth century and that Edward Topsell uses erroneously in *Four-footed Beasts* to mean pregnant (in the sense "full of matter"). The polysemic category comprising Shakespeare's sense of the word *pregnant* was thus complex, including interconnected concepts of plenitude, ability to make an impression, and vulnerability to penetration or impression.[13] In *Measure for Measure* the word is also linked to images of coining, stamping, and biological pregnancy, making clear the importance of spatial image schemas of the body as a container, vulnerable to various kinds of penetration and impressionability, as structuring principles for this lexical category.

Shakespeare's mental model for pregnancy seems shaped in several different ways by the experience of living in a humoral body. As we have seen, cognitive theory suggests that neurologically normal human beings experience a basic somatosensory awareness, a feeling that they inhabit a body that contains internal organs and is bounded by the skin.[14] Paster acknowledges this universal experience of embodiment but also argues that our "*internal* habitus," or sense of the body, includes "the enshrouded domain of the body's internal workings and the locally determined explanatory framework within which those workings are always understood."[15] Shakespeare's experience of embodiment would thus have been shaped, as Paster demonstrates, by his culture's dominant theory of physiology, which involved a belief that the internal functions of the body depended on the balance of the four humors, or body fluids (blood, phlegm, choler, and black bile), and the presence of *spritus*, the airy substance thought to animate or vivify the body. In Paster's words, every early modern subject "grew up with a common understanding of his or her body as a semipermeable, irrigated container in which humors moved sluggishly" (8). This bodily permeability involves not only penetration of the body by environmental substances such as air, food, and liquids but also the physical interpenetration of mind and body.

Cognitive theory, as we have seen, does not deny the force of the "locally determined explanatory framework" in shaping early modern experiences of the body; nor does it deny the complex ways in which the framework of Galenic medicine established "an internal hierarchy of fluids and functions within the body which is fully assimilable to external hierarchies of class and gender."[16] At the same time, it argues that humor theory's particular narratives about the nature of the body as a container are built on subsymbolic experiences of embodiment (which give rise to the concept of containment) and that its hierarchizing constructs are so easily assimilable to "external" hierarchies because those hierarchies are themselves ultimately built on embodied experiences. Thus, the representations of embodiment in a play like *Measure for Measure* reflect not only how discourse shapes the body in accordance with dominant cultural formations but also how those very formations and mechanisms of control are literally built on the body. The question becomes, then, not to what extent the play exerts an unquestioned normative force in the formation of early modern subjects but rather in what ways conditions of embodiment are imagined as contributing to the creation of cultural norms.

The role of the brain in early modern anatomical theory was controversial; it was believed to be a cold, phlegmy organ inferior to the heart, which many anatomists considered to be the true controlling and animating seat of the body. The brain, the spinal cord, and the nervous system were nevertheless considered to be "responsible for mental activity, motion, and sensation." These parts of the body were animated by "*spiritus* . . . conveyed from the heart by the arteries to the *rete mirabile*, where it underwent further refinement into special animal spirits to which were ascribed a role in brain function and the process of vision."[17] The connection between thought and sexual reproduction—the two kinds of "pregnancy" discussed above—was reinforced by the belief that semen contained the same "spiritus" that animated the brain, that it may even have been manufactured or "concocted" in the brain, that the uterus resembled a brain (in its cold, phlegmy nature as well as in size and shape), and that therefore, as Thomas Laquer puts it, "conception is for the male to have an idea, an artistic or artisanal conception, in the brain-uterus of the female."[18] The use of the word *pregnant* in sixteenth-century England to describe mental conception was thus, strictly speaking, a literal rather than a metaphoric usage, the *OED* to the contrary notwithstanding.[19]

A cognitive reading of *Measure for Measure* might begin by focusing on different spatial configurations of the self and on the ways in which different characters stake out a range of possible versions of that self. The operative spatial configuration in this play centers on a sense of the body as a container that is variously impermeable or permeable to outside influences.[20] The play is about characterization in the literal sense of *character* as "a distinctive mark impressed, engraved, or otherwise formed, a brand, stamp" (*OED*), and about the impressionability that forms the subject into a distinctive self. As cognitive theory suggests, subjects are formed when the physiological structures of the organism (e.g., neurons in the brain) interact with sensory impressions of the environment surrounding the body; language itself is created from this experience of impressionability. The characters in the play might initially seem to divide themselves into two clearly demarcated groups: Claudio, Juliet, and the characters who inhabit the brothel world are (to differing degrees) open to penetration, whereas Angelo, Isabella, and the Duke attempt to close their bodies and brains off from it. However, it soon becomes clear that this binary division of the characters is overly schematic and that Angelo, Isabella, and especially the Duke are both attracted to and repelled by the possibilities of mental and bodily interpenetration. The language and imagery of pregnancy in the play represents the conception of children and ideas as deeply analogous processes and the body as subject to impression or penetration by sexual organs, disease, and language. The self is imagined variously as stamped unalterably at conception and walled off from influence or as impressionable and subject to reshaping by physical and cultural forces. In general, the state seems relatively powerless to control the mental and bodily processes that form this substrate of the play; indeed, as embodied in the person of the Duke, it is itself shown to be subject to a reciprocal penetration and impression.

The much-noted imagery of disease in the play is an obvious register of the consequences of humoral permeability. Syphilis, like bubonic plague, actually posed an initial challenge to the humoral tradition of Galenic medicine since both diseases seemed to be new developments, unrecorded in the authoritative ancient texts on which doctors still relied, and both were clearly spread by contact with infected people (rather than by an imbalance of humors caused by bad diet or natural disposition). "Bad air," leading to a humoral imbalance, could be adduced as the cause of plague, but by the beginning of the seventeenth century it was clear that syphilis was spread directly by sexual contact.[21] Some medical experts developed a virtual germ theory of contagion by "seeds" of disease in the case of syphilis, while others imagined that the disease developed in the uterus of a prostitute either when it became overheated or because of the unnatural confluence of semen from many different men.[22] In either case, sexually transmitted disease can be seen as an especially striking example of the consequences of bodily penetration that corrupts both parties involved.

In act 1, scene 2, of *Measure for Measure* we first hear about the circumstances of Juliet's pregnancy from the crowd of unruly brothel frequenters who intersperse their commentary on it with descriptions of their own permeability to disease. The first gentleman initially seems to admit having "purchas'd . . . diseases" (1.2.46) from Mistress Overdone but then denies Lucio's accusation that he is diseased in lines that equate the penetration of disease and mistaken ideas: "Thou art always figuring diseases in me; but thou art full of error, I am sound" (1.2.53–54). Lucio's retort that "thy bones are hollow; impiety has made a feast of thee" (1.2.56–57) suggests that in this culture the capacity of the body to serve as a container is altered as the result of disease, which hollows it out in order to make it into a capacious container for yet more diseases. As I noted earlier, the word *pregnant* is never used to describe a woman in this play, although Juliet remains throughout a visible reminder of its reproductive sense.[23] Instead, these characters multiply colloquial euphemisms for sexual penetration: "groping for trouts in a peculiar river" (1.2.90); "filling a bottle with a tun-dish" (3.2.172). Constable Elbow's wife is described in this context as being "great with child" (2.1.89) and has the cravings associated (then as well as now) with that state. Her "longing . . . for stew'd pruins" (2.1.89–90) doubly represents the porousness of the humoral body since prunes were believed to function both as an aphrodisiac and as a laxative.[24]

Descriptions of Juliet's pregnancy include the images of penetration, eating, productivity, and impressionability that are central to the play. Lucio, perhaps the most vocal representative of the brothel world, articulates a relatively positive and productive account of her state:

> Your brother and his lover have embrac'd.
> As those that feed grow full, as blossoming time
> That from the seedness the bare fallow brings
> To teeming foison, even so her plenteous womb
> Expresseth his full tilth and husbandry.
>
> (1.4.40–44)

The image of eating ("as those that feed grow full") glances at the more negative eating imagery of the gentleman's "hollow bones," where impiety has feasted; the verb *expresseth* continues the connection forged throughout the play between the production of language and sexual reproduction. Here, as in the humoral theory of pregnancy resulting from a man's idea thought in the medium of a woman's brain/uterus, Claudio "expresses" himself through Juliet's body. Claudio, interestingly, offers a less positive description of Juliet's permeability and its result: "The stealth of our most mutual entertainment / With character too gross is writ on Juliet" (1.2.154–55). It is the secret and stealthy nature of their sexual act that seems here to lead, paradoxically, to its public revelation, as if the most private penetration inevitably and indelibly marks its participants. *Character* here has the meaning "distinctive mark impressed, engraved . . . a brand, stamp," and thus contributes to establishing the concept of pregnancy as the result of an impressionability that marks or changes the person who suffers it. That the character is "gross" conjures up Juliet's physical appearance and perhaps relates her pregnancy to the obesity of "those that feed" and grow full.[25]

It is the Duke, however, in an exchange with Juliet herself, who most damagingly describes the results of Juliet's productivity: "Repent you, fair one, of the sin you carry?" he asks, and Juliet replies, "I do; and bear the shame most patiently" (2.2.19–20). The Duke describes Juliet as literally pregnant with sin and shame, which indelibly mark or "character" her body. Greenblatt argues that the Duke's disciplinary technology of shaming, in this scene as elsewhere in the play, fails to arouse a salutary anxiety in Juliet since she also insists that she bears "the shame with joy" (2.2.36).[26] What seems important here is the sense that sin and shame, although named by the Duke, are produced within Juliet's body and remain open to varying interpretations, namely, repentance or joy. Katherine Hayles has argued, from a partially cognitive perspective, that while "it is the body that is naturalized within a culture" and is subject to Foucauldian discipline, individual experience of embodiment is not: "As soon as embodiment is acknowledged, the abstractions of the Panopticon disintegrate into the particularities of specific people embedded in specific contexts. Along with these particularities come concomitant strategies for resistances and subversions, excesses and deviations."[27] According to Hayles's theory, then, while Juliet's body can be "charactered" with shame, her experience of embodiment can produce a resistant feeling of "joy."

The characters who try to prevent permeability in themselves and others are also depicted as vulnerable to it. The Duke most clearly voices the mistaken belief that in his case, no "dribbling dart of love / Can pierce a complete bosom" (1.3.2–3). Harry Berger Jr. notes that the Duke is engaged (with Angelo and also with Isabella) in a "contest for the title of Vienna's most complete bosom."[28] The *Riverside Shakespeare* glosses "complete" as suggesting "fully defended as if in complete armor," and this image takes its place in a system of related images that seek to see the human body as constructed from an invulnerable metallic substance, indelibly and unchangeably stamped with its defining "character" at birth.[29] The Duke's decision to disguise himself as a friar functions in part as an attempt to provide himself with just such an armor, as do Isabella's similar intention to confine herself within convent walls and Mariana's, within her moated grange.[30] When the Duke tells Angelo that there is "a kind of character in thy life, / That to th' observer doth thy history / Fully unfold" (1.1.27–29), he suggests that in his case, unlike in Juliet's, an initial shaping inscription of character will be unchanged by any subsequent impressionability. Angelo seems to pick up this image but, significantly, suggests its vulnerability when he asks that "there be some more test made of my mettle / Before so noble and so great a figure / Be stamp'd upon it" (1.1.48–50). By figuring his appointment as stand-in for the Duke as a restamping of his "mettle" with the Duke's authority, Angelo suggests that his "character" is not a permanent and unchanging inscription but capable of taking the impression of a new stamp.

These male characters attempt (and fail) to formulate a concept of pregnancy that retains its productivity and plenitude but avoids contamination. The first use of *pregnant* in the play comes when the Duke praises Escalus:

> The nature of our people,
> Our city's institutions, and the terms
> For common justice, y'are as pregnant in
> As art and practice hath enriched any
> That we remember.

> (1.1.9–13)

With these lines, the Duke attempts to appropriate *pregnant* as a term to describe successful interpellation of subjects by the law; Escalus's mind has literally been so filled with knowledge of institutions and laws that it has become pregnant and "enriched" with this matter. Significantly, Escalus's pregnancy is seen as productive in monetary rather than agricultural terms, so the potential biological contaminations of eating are kept at bay and are replaced by the fantasy of metallic coinage. Contamination may reinsinuate itself even here, however, since Escalus is seen as pregnant both with "the nature of our people," a nature the following scene reveals to be unruly and disease-ridden, and with "common" justice, again implying intimate contact with his subjects. Indeed, Escalus will later be thwarted in his attempt to sort out the case of Mrs. Elbow since justice there seems too confused, "common," and contaminated to be easily controlled.

Angelo similarly imagines biological pregnancy as a process of monetary stamping: they "that do coin heaven's image / In stamps that are forbid" (2.4.45–46). As Janet Adelman comments, Angelo believes that "the male stamps his will—and his image—upon an unresisting female matter. Given the extent to which Angelo feels contaminated by the process of sexual exchange, this must be a consoling image for him."[31] I would further emphasize that through this image Angelo tries to produce a version of sexual penetration that would, like Escalus's pregnancy, produce monetary enrichment, an unchanging metal substance, rather than porous organic matter. For his part, the Duke pictures himself undergoing a metallic pregnancy in which he carries, but then fails to give birth to, Angelo's reputation:

> O, your desert speaks loud, and I should wrong it
> To lock it in the wards of covert bosom,
> When it deserves with characters of brass
> A forted residence 'gainst the tooth of time
> And razure of oblivion.
>
>   (5.1.9–13)

The Duke first sees his own body, or "bosom," as containing Angelo's reputation, or "desert," in a kind of parody of pregnancy. That the Duke's containing bosom is "covert" as it carries and conceals Angelo's "desert" reminds us of the "stealth" that impregnates Juliet. The birth image that we might expect after the Duke suggests that he will not continue to contain Angelo's "desert" within his body never appears. Instead, the Duke imagines his covert pregnancy as giving way to another metallic enclosure, "a forted residence" (perhaps similar to Mariana's "moated grange"), which is able to withstand the altering impression of the "tooth of time" but is itself composed, not of solid walls, but of brass characters or inscriptions impressed in metal. This image thus attempts to refigure a vulnerability to inscription (or character) as a sign, not of weakness and impressionability, but of fortification.[32] The Duke here echoes humanist educational theorists, who tended to conflate the inscription of moral precepts on the "walls" of memory with images of fortifying the mind against evil influences.[33] The alternation between impregnability and impressionability in this passage is dangerously unstable, and of course this whole passage is ironic: by this point in the play the Duke knows very well that Angelo has no such "desert" and no such unchanging brass character.

Although Angelo seems to be the center for the breakdown of these fantasies of enclosure and metallic pregnancy, Isabella also shows signs of permeability, and the Duke proves to be a hidden source for the vulnerabilities of all three. While these characters generally manage to wall themselves off from sexual penetration, they are penetrated by language, their own and that of other characters, and this linguistic permeability is shown to have implications that are related to and perhaps even more troubling than sexual permeability. Claudio introduces this possibility when he imagines that Isabella's speech will be able to permeate and "soften" (1.4.70) Angelo:

> There is a prone and speechless dialect,
> Such as move men; beside, she hath prosperous art
> When she will play with reason and discourse,
> And well she can persuade.

> (1.2.183–86)

Claudio's characterization of Isabella's "speechless dialect" as "prone" seems closely related to Shakespeare's concept of pregnancy, since, like Shakespeare's odd sense that *pregnant* could mean "easily impressed" or "pregnable," *prone* involves mapping a spatial concept, "having a downward or descending inclination of slope," onto an ethical one, "said of an action compared to following a downward sloping path, easy to adopt or pursue" (*OED*). In both cases a physical movement (involving the concept of inclination) is taken to denote someone who is either subject to impression or easily able to impress someone else.[34]

As many critics have noticed, it is Angelo himself who persistently describes the effects of Isabella's language on him using metaphors of conception and pregnancy. Critics have tended to see in this language a fantasy of "male parthenogenesis."[35] But we can also interpret his language as an attempt to believe that the desire he wants to disavow results from penetration by some external contaminant. That is, he perceives his desire, not as self-produced, but as implanted by Isabella's words. Angelo's lust for Isabella may indeed be caused by a deeper desire to locate the source of his own sexuality outside his body. The metaphor of implantation first appears when Angelo speaks to Isabella of the necessity for law to control his subjects' "future evils, / Either now, or by remissness new conceiv'd, / And so in progress to be hatch'd and born" (2.2.95–97). As Isabella begins to argue on her brother's behalf, Angelo is moved by the very cogency of her argument: "She speaks, and 'tis such sense that my sense breeds with it" (2.2.141). His pun on *sense* conflates her words with feelings that he continues to believe himself incapable of experiencing.

Angelo brings these metaphors of inseminated sexuality to a literal conclusion when he refers in his soliloquy at the beginning of act 2, scene 4, to "the strong and swelling evil / Of my conception" (2.4.6–7). In a figure that reverses the humoral theory that biological impregnation is the implantation of a male idea in the female body, Angelo says that Isabella's language has penetrated and impregnated him with his own evil desire for her. At the same time, however, Angelo continues to cling to his vision of bodily impermeability, figuring his intended sexual act with Isabella in monetary terms that recall earlier imagery of coinage ("you must lay down the treasures of your body" [2.4.96]) or, oddly, in a metaphor that involves dressing rather than undressing ("If you be one [a woman] . . . show it now, / By putting on the destined livery" [2.4.136–38]). But his fantasies of metallic invulnerability and containment are contradicted by his desire to evade responsibility for his actions by believing himself to be constructed by discursive penetration from without.

Our reading of Angelo's character might be deepened by the theory, outlined by Antonio Damasio and others, that rational thought is imbued with the most basic feelings and desires, that "emotions and feelings may not be intruders in the bastion of reason at all: they may be enmeshed in its networks, for worse *and* for better." Based on the study of subjects with a particular kind of damage to emotive centers of the brain that significantly impaired their decision-making processes, Damasio argues that "certain aspects of the process of emotion and feeling are indispensable for rationality."[36] Angelo believes that his reasoning processes must remain uncontaminated by personal feeling; his response to Escalus's plea that he allow human feeling to soften a rigorous and rational application of law in Claudio's case suggests the extent to which he attempts to think without feeling. Significantly, Angelo uses the idea of pregnancy to represent his fantasy of purely rational thought: he describes the exemplum of the jewel with which he denies Escalus's plea as "very pregnant," and later, when the threat of exposure makes him unable to think clearly, he describes himself as "unpregnant / And dull to all proceedings" (4.4.20–21).[37]

Ironically, of course, pregnancy throughout the play is a metaphor for precisely the kind of contamination by feeling that Angelo believes it can deny. Thus, it is not surprising that his rational processes are so easily disrupted by strong feeling inspired by Isabella, although Angelo continues almost frantically to insist that these feelings are the result of a contaminating penetration from outside rather than naturally produced within himself. Of course, Damasio suggests that the interpenetration of rational thought and emotion actually furthers reasonable and ethical decision making: "The fact that acting according to an ethical principle requires the participation of simple circuitry in the brain core does not cheapen the ethical principle. The edifice of ethics does not collapse, morality is not threatened, and in a normal individual the will remains the will."[38] In the dark world of *Measure for Measure*, however, Shakespeare seems to have imagined a human cognitive system in which not only is pure rationality impossible but the contamination of emotion seems necessarily unethical.

Isabella, by contrast, is far less permeable, despite a tendency to view herself as such. Women, she says, are "soft as our complexions are, / And credulous to false prints" (2.4.129–30), an image that calls directly on humor theory—the balance of humors in each person was called "complexion"—and echoes Viola's musings in *Twelfth Night* about how easy it is for "the proper-false / In women's waxen hearts to set their forms!" (2.2.29–30).[39] Even Isabella's adamant refusal of Angelo's offer is figured, in a reversal of Angelo's own metaphors, through the impressionability and nakedness, rather than imperviousness, of her body: "Th'impression of keen whips I'ld wear as rubies, / And strip myself to death, as to a bed" (2.4.101–2). Her intention to hide herself inside the protective walls of the convent may be motivated by her sense of herself as soft and impressionable, rather like a crustacean in need of a protecting shell.

Even Isabella, however, is penetrated by the Duke and, like Juliet and Angelo, made to conceive and bear her own shame. The Duke, perhaps sensing and in part sharing her fear of her own permeability, is careful, at least initially, not to represent his persuasive language to her in phallic terms. He urges her to "fasten your ear on my advisings" (3.1.197–98), depicting her as the active partner who "fastens" onto rather than is penetrated by his language. Nevertheless, once she has heard his planned "bed trick," in which Mariana will be substituted for her in Angelo's bed, she approves it with language that combines pleasure and growth to suggest an image of impregnation: "The image of it gives me content already, and I trust it will grow to a most prosperous perfection" (3.1.259–60).[40] Although Isabella is at this point able to view her ideational pregnancy as "prosperous" and potentially "perfect," it later becomes a source of shame when she is convinced to make a (false) public confession that she has herself had sex with Angelo: "the vild conclusion / I now begin with grief and shame to utter" (5.1.95–96). As she is taken off to prison for making what has been judged to be a false accusation, she imagines herself pregnant with a truth that in time will be delivered: "Keep me in patience, and with ripened time / Unfold the evil which is here wrapp'd up / In countenance!" (5.1.116–18).

The Duke might seem to go to the greatest lengths to avoid contamination. He hints that his withdrawal is motivated not only by his desire to have the law enforced more rigorously in his absence and to test Angelo but also by a desire to isolate himself even from his people:

> I love the people,
> But do not like to stage me to their eyes;
> Though it do well, I do not relish well
> Their loud applause and aves vehement;
> Nor do I think the man of safe discretion
> That does affect it
>
> (1.1.67–72)

The Duke realizes from the start what Angelo and Isabella learn only through experience: that an altering and contaminating penetration can result not just from sexual contact but also—as early modern cognitive theory suggested—through sight and language. Thus, although New Historicist readers of the play persistently associate the Duke with "surveillance" and see him as the wielder of a powerful and controlling gaze, early modern theories of vision did not allow a watcher to remain unimplicated in what he watched.[41] The faculty of vision was thought to involve the emission from the brain through the eye of a special kind of *spiritus* that took the form of a "luminous ray," enveloped the object seen, and returned into the brain through the eye carrying an image of the object.[42] The eyebeams of one person could become entangled with and influence those of another; for example, it was believed that obsessive love could result when the eye spirit of another person penetrated the eye of a gazer with a powerful version of his or her image. Thus, early modern optical theories were very far from positing a distant, disembodied and controlling gaze. Like sex, the act of looking involved a penetrating emission of vital spirit and also opened the looker to potentially contaminating penetration by what was seen.[43]

While the Duke's disguise as a friar, like Isabella's withdrawal into the convent, seems in some ways designed to protect him from potentially contaminating contact with other people, it also works to increase both visual and linguistic contact with his subjects since he uses it to spy on them, to hear confessions, and to authorize various collaborative deceptions. As Berger notes, the ostensible purpose of the disguise is to spy on Angelo, but through its means the Duke also watches the conversation between Isabella and her brother. Dressed as a friar, he hears the confessions of Juliet, Claudio, and Mariana, penetrating both prison and moated grange in order to have this intimate verbal contact with his subjects. He collaborates with Mariana, Isabella, and the jailer in his attempts to save Isabella's virginity, unmask Angelo, and save Claudio's life. There is evidence in his actions that the Duke desires this kind of potentially contaminating contact with other people as much as he fears it.

Unlike Angelo, whose fantasy of bodily impermeability is suddenly and rudely shattered when he is exposed to Isabella's language, the Duke is torn between belief in the possibility of maintaining bodily and mental integrity and acknowledgment that the permeability he exploits in others is a necessary condition of human embodiment and also of social control. The play to some extent indulges the Duke's fantasy of "completeness," resulting in the sense of his inconsistency as a character that has often troubled critics. Richard Wheeler has noted Vincentio's double existence both as a "providential figure of justice and authority" who seems oddly "bereft of an inner life" and as a figure deeply involved in the "psychological patterns" of the play.[44] Wheeler's sense of the Duke as "an empty center precariously holding at a distance, rather than holding together, the teeming life that threatens to overwhelm it" (139) reflects the Duke's own tendency to imagine himself as invulnerable and aloof. However, the tragedy of the Duke is that he also realizes the impossibility of being, literally, a "character," if he remains invulnerable, unpenetrated, and uninscribed. Just as sexual penetration is necessary to produce biological pregnancy and human offspring, linguistic and visual penetration are necessary to bring a human subject into being and to enable it to participate in discursive exchange. Cognitive theorists such as Daniel Stern, Gerald Edelman, and L. S. Vygotsky have emphasized the importance of interaction with other people as well as with an environment as an infant develops its sense of self. Stern, for example, argues that a kind of emotional prototypic image schema (which he calls Representations of Interactions that have been Generalized, or RIGs) form the basis of a child's sense of self in relation to others.[45] Edelman argues that such interactions literally inscribe the brain as "maps," or collections of neuronal groups, are formed in response to sensory and emotional experience.[46] So the Duke's sense that he cannot be a person without such interpenetration reflects cognitive theory, as well as the pragmatics of performance onstage. As Berger has suggested, a character is created by the words he speaks; if the Duke refuses to speak or interact with other characters, he can hardly function as a character in the play. Such contact is also necessary to inseminate the Duke with the plots, tricks, and speech through which he exercises his power.

The Duke's own penetrating use of language seems to open him up to the effects of other people's words. Language describing how gossip and slander penetrate the toughest armor seems concentrated around the figure of the Duke. It is he who imprisons Isabella in order, he falsely claims, to prevent "a blasting and a scandalous breath" (5.1.122) from touching Angelo. Slander's power to "blast" even someone with a "complete bosom" is borne out by Lucio's repeated accusations that "the Duke (I say to thee again) would eat mutton on Fridays. He's past it now, yet (and I say to thee) he would mouth with a beggar, though she smelt brown bread and garlic" (3.2.181–84).[47] Lucio emphasizes the verbal nature of the slander with which he assaults the Duke ("I say to thee again," "and I say to thee"), and his images of eating and intimate contact with a bad-smelling member of the people directly counter the Duke's own claim that he avoids the people. The Duke feels that he has been violated by this attack, describing it as "back-wounding calumny" (3.2.186), and Escalus uses familiar imagery of penetration through the ear (and may also glance at the bad breath of the beggar woman) when he accuses the friar of verbally attacking the Duke: "in foul mouth / And in the witness of his proper ear, / To call him villain" (5.1.307–9). For Richard Wheeler, Lucio's slanders highlight "the dramatic emptiness of Vincentio's character-ization, as if through Lucio Shakespeare is obliquely trying to fill a void he has created at the heart of the play."[48] It does seem that Lucio's language functions to include the Duke within the economy of violation and con-tamination experienced by other characters and that inscription or pene-tration by discourse is a necessary condition of existence as a character within the social world of the play.

To some extent the Duke may have propagated this slander by an earlier verbal deception of his own, when he covered his decision to vacate his throne and secretly observe Angelo's rule with a story that he had gone to Poland: "For so I have strew'd it in the common ear, / And so it is receiv'd" (1.3. 15–16). The Duke has been unable to resist a use of lan-guage that he imagines as entering his subjects' ears and affecting them in some way; however, such acts of penetration in the economy of this play always involve a reciprocal contamination of both agent and recipi-ent. One might argue that the Duke at this moment of contaminating penetration becomes pregnant with the rest of his stealthy deceptions— the bed trick, his decision to deceive Isabella about her brother's death, and, perhaps ultimately, his decision publicly to shame and then offer to marry her.

We may be able to hear the faint echo of a pun, one of those accidents of juxtaposition in lexical storage that seem so common in Shakespeare's writing, on *strew'd* and on another frequently repeated term in the play, *stew*. The Duke's act of strewing a lie in the public ear has the kind of contaminating effect associated in the play with the "stews," a slang term for brothel derived from the common euphemistic fiction that brothels were bathhouses. Stew originally meant "a heated room used for hot air or vapour baths: hence a hot bath" (*OED*) and thus seems a part of the humoral economy of the play, in which heat is associated with the connected images of penetration, contamination, and production. The humoral body was, of course, regulated by its "complexion," or relative degree of heat and moisture. Although heat was usually thought to be preferable to cold—thus, for example, women were inferior to men because their bodies were colder—an excess of heat, like any bodily excess, was thought to disrupt the balance of humors and to cause disease. "Stewing" in this play seems to represent the qualities of permeability, excess, and spreading contamination that are most deeply threatening to those who would like to maintain control. Mrs. Elbow's greedy longing for "stew'd pruins" during pregnancy leads her to a possibly contaminating visit to Mistress Overdone's brothel. To describe what he has observed while traveling around Vienna incognito, the Duke uses an image that associates heat, stews, and an overflow of corruption: "I have seen corruption boil and bubble, / Till it o'errun the stew" (5.1.318–19). The question is whether, as "a looker-on here in Vienna" (5.1.317), the Duke has himself been able to avoid contamination. The play suggests that he cannot do so.

The Duke has frequently been compared to a playwright: he tries to protect himself from reciprocal penetration by working behind the scenes, scripting little plays for others to act in so that they (not he) will bear the brunt of discursive exchange. Meredith Skura has stressed the vulnerability of actors onstage and the ways in which Shakespeare "narratizes the discrepancy between actor's and audience's power, points up the confrontation between the player's grandiose ambitions and the threat of humiliation, and infantilizes the player."[49] But as we have seen, a playwright's experience of the spatialities of performance was not the same as an actor's, and Shakespeare presumably experienced plays in both ways. A playwright may seem safely distanced from his own attempts to penetrate the audience and from their loud applause, but *Measure for Measure* suggests that he cannot remain untouched.[50] The Duke is perhaps most frequently criticized for his attempts to hide behind other characters and the manipulations that this entails. He is finally unsuccessful in avoiding contact with his audience since he is contaminated by the very message he "strews" in his audience's ear in order to escape from their "loud applause and aves vehement," just as, when playing the role of friar that he has scripted for himself, he feels penetrated by Lucio's slanders (ironically *because* his performance is so successful: Lucio would not say what he does he if were not completely fooled by the Duke's impersonation of a friar). That the playwright Duke also taints his actress (Mariana) and collaborator (Isabella) with shame suggests that the various exchanges involved in dramatic authorship and production could be mutually contaminating. *Measure for Measure* seems to express an attraction to an idea of powerful, self-contained authorship and uneasiness about it. Here, however, the physiological processes involved in thought and writing are seen as inextricably connected to concepts of authorship and as deeply implicated in Shakespeare's ambivalence about its nature.

It is no surprise that collaboration, like any linguistic exchange, is depicted in *Measure for Measure* as deeply problematic. Although most critics read the play as commenting on a shift of power from monarch to playhouse, it also seems to use shared rule as a metaphor for shared production of other kinds. The Duke imagines that in his absence Escalus and Angelo will be able to rule Vienna through a vaguely defined collaborative relationship: both receive written "commissions" from the Duke, and Angelo is told that "old Escalus, / Though first in question, is thy secondary" (1.1.45–46). Act 2, scene 1, provides graphic examples of the failure of this collaborative rule when, first, Angelo refuses to heed Escalus's advice about the need to show mercy in Claudio's case and, then, when both of them together prove unable to untangle the dispute between Elbow and Pompey and Angelo withdraws in disgust.

The Duke too figures considerable ambivalence about collaboration. As both Greenblatt and Mullaney argue, he succeeds only partly in his attempts to control his actors or shape his audience. The recalcitrance of the pirate Barnardine, who refuses to play the role the Duke and the Provost have scripted for him, represents, as Mullaney has argued, "the limits of even the Duke's power to control or contain, to induce and subvert the desires of his subjects." Mullaney reads Barnardine as a "figure of uncontained license" who also represents the marginal position of the Elizabethan stage itself.[51] But the play suggests an ambivalence about the varieties of exchange involved in writing and staging plays that extends beyond a fear that they might fail and encompasses the fact that the very act of collaboration itself can contaminate the author.

Like Escalus, Duke Vincentio in effect tries to collaborate with Angelo in ruling Vienna. He attempts to avoid "slander," as Laura Knoppers has pointed out, by leaving Angelo exposed to public view as the enforcer of the law while he works toward the same end behind the scenes.[52] As we have seen, the image of the Duke's stamping Angelo with his authority marks an attempt to represent this collaboration in safely monetary terms, but the Duke's fantasy of a metallic pregnancy that can protect Angelo's reputation gives way to his own and Angelo's penetration by the "blasting" breath of scandal. Although his disguise as friar seems designed to allow him to work alone and to script his interventions covertly and untrammeled by any accountability or collaboration, he is nevertheless forced to collaborate with Mariana, Isabella, and the Provost in order to carry out his plans. Similarly, although he tries to deflect all contaminating shame onto these collaborators, he is unable, most readers agree, to avoid a share in it. Indeed, his final decision to offer to marry Isabella represents his willingness to "share" a woman publicly thought to have slept with Angelo, perhaps reflecting an admission that collaboration, however problematic, is unavoidable.

Critics have given various explanations for this seemingly sudden decision to violate the completeness of his bosom and marry Isabella: that it represents "the last move in the Duke's successful campaign against Angelo";[53] that it provides a way for the Duke to undermine Isabella's threatening invulnerability;[54] that his willingness to marry a publicly shamed woman reflects his own guilty culpability. Robert Watson has argued that it marks the Duke's recognition of the necessity for biological procreation;[55] however, it might be more accurate to say that it reveals his realization that interpenetration and contamination are inevitable. Certainly his final words to Isabella edge away from the careful avoidance of penetration that he earlier used with her: "I have a motion which imports your good, / Whereto if you'll a willing ear incline, / What's mine is yours, and what is yours is mine" (5.1.535–37). Isabella's inclining ear seems to involve a spatial image that is similar to her "prone" dialect; in both cases vulnerability is imagined as involving leaning or bending over. These lines try desperately to put a positive spin on a nexus of images that has been deeply disturbing throughout the play: the possession of an idea ("a motion") that is implanted in another person's ear—here he asks her, once again, to willingly participate in this penetration of her ear—and then yields a shared fertilization or contamination ("What's mine is yours, and what is yours is mine"). Isabella's much remarked silence may be a sign that she still remains relatively impermeable; she does not seem to incline a willing ear or to produce further potentially contaminating language in response. However, as the Duke knows by now, the cost of eschewing contamination is exactly that silence, a silence that, if it can be read as resistance, also literally marks the end of her existence as a character in the play.

The language of pregnancy in *Measure for Measure* thus offers a representation of early modern power much more complicated than a state that merely posits an unruly but permeable subject and then penetrates it with language in order to control it. Rather, the play seems to suggest, there is no escape from penetration and contamination, which are properties of the human body, brain, and language systems. Cognitive theory helps us to see this permeability as reflecting the complex, multiple, and reciprocal ways in which the body and language produce each other. The play also suggests that in the process of trying to penetrate subjects, figures of authority are themselves penetrated, contaminated, changed, impressed, and made productive. Contamination here becomes a pessimistic figure for the interpenetrations of body and mind, for the ways all thought

and language are deeply marked by their bodily origins, and for the inescapable material effects of all human intercourse. Disciplinary strategies
thus seem, in effect, to work both ways; subjects are penetrated by the
state (as represented by the Duke and Angelo), but the Duke himself is
also penetrated in various ways by his subjects, and his mode of rule,
his decision-making processes, are shown to be influenced by reciprocal
coercion. It would be a mistake, however, to see this movement as a carnivalesque inversion with subversive results. The play does seem to insist
on permeability as a universal bodily trait, one that does not always bear
out cultural expectations about the ways in which bodily differences
ought to reflect the hierarchies of class and gender.[56] Although the play
seems to suggest that the body is on some level resistant to politicization
and control, no one in Vienna is liberated by the possession of an open
and vulnerable body.

Shakespeare here seems also to be thinking about the means though
which discourse is produced and the ways in which it shapes human subjects. Despite attempts to imagine the production of language as walled
off from cultural and collaborative contamination within an impermeable
metallic container, the vulnerability of the human brain to penetration by
the language of others seems powerfully unavoidable. Indeed, the very
formation of the self, and its "breeding" of words and ideas, seems dependent upon fertilization from these external sources. The variously linguistic and sexual collaborations of Claudio and Juliet, Escalus and Angelo,
the Duke and Angelo, Angelo and Isabella, Lucio and the Duke, and the
friar with Mariana and Isabella suggest not only the productivity but also
the possibilities for contamination and betrayal inherent in all acts of
exchange.

Thus, although *Measure for Measure* is, in part, about a movement
toward more subtle and coercive forms of power and about the role of
the stage in this new economy, it is also about the cognitive mechanisms
through which the human body and the embodied brain both originate
and succumb to the linguistic expressions of power. By insisting on the
physical parameters of thought and language in this play, Shakespeare
conveys a visceral sense of how it felt to think and write under cultural
(and perhaps personal) conditions that induced a deep distrust in the productive capacities of both men and women.[57] *Measure for Measure* does
not simply comment on or represent the external lineaments of new
modes of power; it describes how it felt to *think* them from within an
early modern body. It also offers an exploration of the spatial analogies
on which the body builds its sense of itself as a subject in culture. That
the vulnerabilities of the body and the mind cannot be fully controlled
even by more intrusive forms of power is not, finally, a comforting vision.
Ironically, the Duke, at least at times, would very much like to be an

abstract and inhuman agent of the state, able to penetrate and control his subjects with a disembodied surveillant and discursive apparatus. Similarly, Angelo would like to imagine that his behavior is controlled by, and that his innermost feelings are constructed by, a penetrating external discourse. A cognitive reading of the play, however, shows their Foucauldian fantasies to be unworkable when they confront the lived experience of embodiment. Critics have argued for years about whether the Duke represents a just and effective ruler or an odious Machiavel who, in William Empson's words, treats "his subjects as puppets for the fun of making them twitch."[58] From a cognitive perspective, it might be possible for the first time to pity the Duke, viewing him as a poignant figure, the character in the play who most fully understands the dilemma of embodied power, unable to maintain his fantasy of solitary "completeness" and inviolability, unable at the same time to accept the inevitable vulnerability and contamination that are the conditions of human selfhood, productivity, and exchange.

6

Sound and Space in *The Tempest*

ALTHOUGH critical interpretation of *The Tempest* has changed dramatically over the past fifteen years, virtually all critics, writing both before and after the shift occasioned by postcolonial theory, would agree that the play is preeminently about control, specifically Prospero's control over the island and everyone on it. The change, then, lies mostly in whether this control is considered to be good (before) or bad (now). Older interpretations of Prospero as benevolent ruler, humanist sage, and playwright who gradually comes to control his own unruly emotions assumed that the controlling ascendance of art over nature, and reason over passion, was almost always good. The island setting of the play, however, helped critics to see the more sinister aspects of Prospero's power, especially the ways the play reveals his implication in repressive early modern discursive formations. His use of discourses of colonialism, treason, masterlessness, and the New Science have all been traced, and in the wake of Freud, critics have come to see even his control over himself as problematic.[1]

The Foucauldian terms *discourse* and *discursive* have been crucial concepts in more recent readings of *The Tempest*, perhaps particularly important in the case of this play because Prospero's magic can so easily be read as a metaphor for the operations of discourse to reproduce and maintain power relations in a culture.[2] Yet it seems clear that the play represents discourse as larger and more complicated than Prospero's magical powers, constituting a metaphorically based radial category with fuzzy boundaries. The differences and connections between speech, music, human cries of pain, animal noises, and natural noises such as thunder in creating and attempting to control an environment greatly complicate the definition of discourse in this play. In addition, the spatial schemas of containment and confinement that structure Prospero's concept of his discursive powers reveal them to comprise the very material properties they claim to transcend and control.

Although there is considerable slippage in Foucault's use of these terms—he speaks of "the equivocal meaning of the term *discourse*, which I have used and abused in many different senses"—critics of this play have tended to emphasize certain features.[3] Paul Brown includes a helpful note: "By 'discourse' I refer to a domain or field of linguistic strategies operating within particular areas of social practice to effect knowledge and pleasure, being produced by and reproducing or reworking power relations between classes, genders and cultures."[4] Brown's definition is immediately striking for two reasons. First, it uses spatial metaphors ("domain," "field," "areas") to stabilize the complex and mobile workings of language; and second, it effaces the role of individual subjects in the production of language, attributing that production instead to "power relations."[5] *Discourse*, then, seems to have become a specialized term designed in part to simplify our sense of how the language of the text has its material existence in the world. Bruce Smith recently suggested that the very media of "academic discourse, operating as it does through books, articles, and conference papers (as opposed to the discussion afterward), assumes that words are disembodied signifiers. Like all autopoietic systems, academic discourse is equipped to read other systems only through its own terms. Academic *discourse*: the very word, in Foucault's formulation, points toward something incorporeal, an abstract force to which individual bodies become subject."[6]

Instead of taking into account the role of the author's brain in the production of language, its movement from script to spoken dialogue to printed text, the relationship between comprehensible dialogue and sound and visual effects of other kinds, we picture a uniform field or domain in which disembodied strategies can work themselves out. This simplification, of course, enabled readings of the play that took into account more fully its political and cultural embeddedness. But it is also dangerous to simplify in this way when reading a play that is so patently about the relationship between sound and space, about the ways in which language creates but is also created (and disrupted) by a physical environment.

Applying the perspectives of cognitive theory can help us to see another side of the play, namely, how it reveals (like *Measure for Measure*, but with more attention to extrabodily physicality) the failures of discourse to control the material world. Denise Albanese has suggested that the play marks an intersection of colonialism and the New Science, in which the perceived failure of older discursive forms to achieve mastery over the material was intensified by the colonial project: "It takes science proper to supplement the inquirer into nature with a technological armature." For Albanese, Prospero's island "begins, remotely, to figure the productiveness of colonial space in the making of modern epistemologies," an epistemological shift that she reads in Foucauldian terms as moving from a quasi-mystical belief in a system of analogical relationships in the material world to rational scrutiny and classification of differences.[7] While I would agree that the play can be located along the borders of a change in the very definitions of *order* and *control*, I believe that cognitive theory, with its different relation to those concepts, lets us attend more closely

and productively to the play's meditation on the difficult interrelationships between the "natural" and the "discursive." In my reading, the island (as well as its double, the stage) figures, not a space ripe for exploitation and control, but the fragile and pain-ridden human self as it uses
all its resources in an attempt to make sense of and survive within its
environment.

In this play, as in the other plays examined in this volume, Shakespeare
uses a nexus of words to provide a kind of counterpoint to the more
directed (and ordered) narratives of the plot. In *The Tempest* he calls on
a set of words that are linked primarily by sound and only secondarily by
associations of sense: *pinch*, *pitch*, *pity*, *pen*, and *pine* (and its cognate
pain). Although the most obvious connections here seem to be through
assonance and consonance of *p* short *i*, *t*, *n*, and *e*, these words also have
connotations that circle around concepts of painful confinement, dearth
or lack, and the ability of an environment to inflict wounds and defilement
on those who inhabit it. These words are also linked by their association
with inarticulate human or animal cries of pain. They form the center of
a group of images that explore the way human subjects exist in a body
and within a natural environment, perceive that environment, form themselves in relation to it, and attempt to gain control over it. The negative
connotations of these words, all centering on concepts of suffering and
restriction, imply that control is achieved only tenuously, if at all.

The linkage of words through sound is itself a feature of the human
cognitive system that cannot be easily assimilated to rationalist explanation. In this sense it may disrupt Foucauldian theories of discourse, which
do not seem to allow for alogical or nonsignifying elements of language.
And yet, cognitive theory recognizes that such links are neither accidental
nor special devices of literary language but a crucial feature of the storage
and retrieval of words in the brain. Studies of phenomena such as malapropisms and other word-retrieval errors as well as tests of word recall
and memory have shown that sound plays an important role in our ability
to understand the speech of others and to recall and produce words while
speaking or writing.

Human subjects seem to remember words in part as sequences of
sounds tied to a particular rhythmic structure of syllables, so that, for
instance, malapropisms like constable Elbow's "suspected" for "respected" involves substitution of a word with the opposite meaning for
one with the same number of syllables and similar sounds. The brain
makes retrieval errors of this kind because words are organized in the
brain by features of sound as well as meaning—although the humor of
such literary malapropisms may depend on subterranean associations of
meaning that work alongside a primary linkage of sound. While comprehension of spoken language seems necessarily to depend on a sound-based

organization of words, this structure may be less efficiently suited to the production of spoken language; hence the relatively frequent incidence of linguistic errors caused by similarities of sound. Experimental evidence also suggests that sound linkages have the same sort of weblike structure that linkages of meaning do. As Jean Aitchison notes, "Words which have similar beginnings, similar endings and similar rhythm are likely to be tightly bonded. 'Similar' in this context means either identical or coming from the same natural class. Words seem to be grouped in clumps rather than in a list, suggesting that, once again, we are dealing with a net-work."[8] Also, since it is sometimes quite difficult to distinguish errors of sound definitively from errors of meaning, it seems clear that these are radial categories with fuzzy boundaries.[9]

The evidence provided by malapropisms (and Shakespeare's interest in this phenomenon, as seen in comic characters such as Elbow) suggests that sound linkages are a feature of discourse that is not usually under conscious control but that underlies all speech and writing and interacts with meaning in complex ways. Of course, literary or rhetorical writing often makes conscious use of sound patterns for subliminal effects of various kinds, a practice codified in rhyme and also in the rhetorical tradition of "schemes" such as isocolon (parallel phrases with equal numbers of syllables), alliteration, anaphora, and so on. Russ McDonald has recently argued that *The Tempest* is particularly full of "musical repetition of vowels and consonants, reduplication of words, echoing of metrical forms, and incantatory effect of this musical design," and that these patterns of sound "are congruent with and supported by larger networks of reiteration, most of them narrative and structural." However, McDonald's conclusion that the function of these patterns is, finally, to frustrate interpretation and, as a result, to promote "in its audience a kind of moral and imaginative athleticism" seems only partly true.[10] From the perspective of the complex, intermeshed and largely unconscious structures of sound and meaning in the mental lexicon, the reliance of *The Tempest* on subterranean connections among words reveals, not a conscious attempt to give the audience a workout, but rather a bringing to the surface of the buried and often alogical ways in which we think and give meaning to things around us. The point is not that *The Tempest* shows itself to be "one of the most knowing, most self-conscious texts in the canon" but that it reveals what lies behind the process of knowing.

Nondiscursive sounds, which cannot be discriminated or made sense of as speech, play a crucial role in *The Tempest*, possibly in part a function of its performance in Blackfriars and a masquelike reliance on music and special effects that might appeal to audience tastes. Keith Sturgess has argued suggestively that music provides "the play's true scenery" and that in many instances it "enacts Prospero's magic power," while Caroline

Spurgeon identified sound as "the dominant image" in the play.[11] The play is noteworthy for its discordant sounds as well as for its beautiful music, beginning with the stage direction "A tempestuous noise of thunder and lightning heard" but also including several other references to thunder, such as "A confused noise within" and "a strange, hollow, and confused noise." Thematically, as we shall see, Prospero's pinches are often imagined as causing moans and groans that incite wild animals to respond with loud noises; the play stands out for its frequent use of *howl* and *roar*.

If Shakespeare in both *Hamlet* and *Measure for Measure* figured the vulnerability of the human body with images of ears penetrated by damaging sound, *The Tempest* assails the ears of its characters with sounds that are purported to have magical effects—while also assailing the ears of the audience with an alternation of beautiful and painful noises. The cognitive researcher Albert Bregman has argued that human perception of sound differs from visual perception in several crucial ways. Perhaps the most important difference, and the most relevant to Shakespeare's use of sound in this play, is that whereas visual perception relies on reflected light energy, auditory perception takes in sound energy directly. Thus, in Bregman's words, humans "use their eyes to determine the shape and size of a car on the road by the way in which its surfaces reflect the light of the sun, but use their ears to determine the intensity of the crash by receiving the energy that is emitted when the event occurs. The shape reflects energy; the crash creates it. For humans, sound serves to supplement vision by supplying information about the nature of events, defining the 'energetics' of a situation."[12]

Even if Shakespeare never performed Bregman's experiments in the perception of sound, as a playwright he would have given thought to the nature of visual and auditory effects on an audience. *The Tempest* is preeminently a play about how "energy" or force can be transmitted by visual displays (the disappearing banquet, the masque), by touch (cramps and pinches), and by sound (music, thunder, or other sound effects). A demonstration of the special vulnerability of the human cognitive system to influence by the more direct energies carried by sound is thus both a subject of the play and also a feature of its performance, as is the power of sound—as pure energy—to break through the limitations of a material environment. *Pinch*, *pitch*, *pine*, *pen*, and *pity* are doubly connected by sound, then, in ways that work against rational meaning: they tend to appear together in the play in part because they sound alike, and they are all associated with nonlinguistic cries, roars, or moans.

Shakespeare's odd fascination with the word *pinch* in this play and elsewhere has been noted by several critics, and it is worth pausing for a moment to note the different meanings attributed to this phenomenon from the perspective of different interpretive frames. Although not as noteworthy as the "dogs, licking, candy, melting" image cluster, *pinch* merited a chapter, "Pinch's Partners," in Edward Armstrong's *Shakespeare's Imagination*, first published in 1946.[13] Caroline Spurgeon, writing twelve years earlier, sought relatively straightforward intentional explanations for Shakespeare's idiosyncratic and repetitive image clusters, for example, that the "dog, licking" cluster arose from Shakespeare's observation of dogs begging for food at the table: "Shakespeare, who was unusually fastidious, hated the habit, as he disliked all dirt and messiness, especially connected with food."[14] Her goal was to illuminate Shakespeare's personality, and he emerges, as this example suggests, sounding a bit like the prototypical British spinster familiar from detective fiction— a lover of nature and especially gardening but finicky and having a surprisingly un-English dislike of dogs. Armstrong, on the other hand, influenced in a rudimentary way by Freud, argued that these image clusters were the products of associations in the unconscious mind. Like the recent cognitive theorist Wilma Bucci, Armstrong sought to establish a version of the unconscious that was not entirely conterminous with Freud's concepts of censorship and repression. Focusing on the proliferation of pinches in *The Comedy of Errors*, *The Merry Wives of Windsor*, and *The Tempest*, as well as scattered references in other plays, Armstrong places pinching in relation to a nexus of related images (beetles, darkness, chains, vaults, humming noises) that, he argues, Shakespeare unconsciously associated with death and confinement.[15] Armstrong's Shakespeare is a darker figure than Spurgeon's, preoccupied with the inescapable connections between life and death, sexuality and decay. Meredith Skura cites Armstrong in her more traditionally Freudian reading of the plays as exhibiting psychological traits and structures common to actors. For Skura, who for the most part ignores the pinches in *The Tempest*, pinching is associated most strongly with dog bites and linked, especially in *Merry Wives*, with the Actaeon myth, so that it comes to represent an exposed and defenseless actor's vulnerability to a potentially hostile audience.[16] Skura's Shakespeare exhibits psychological traits that she argues are typical of actors: he is narcissistic, ambivalent about performance, and fixated on powerful mother figures.

Curt Breight, on the other hand, writing from a New Historicist perspective, emphasizes the association of pinches in *The Tempest* with power rather than vulnerability, doubly so since he argues that the play not only depicts Prospero as the wielder of powerful pinches but also intervenes in and demystifies "various official strategies within the discourse of treason."[17] He associates the pinches in the play with contemporary descriptions of torture inflicted on traitors, including the rack and also the continental practice of using hot "pincers" to tear off bits of flesh from those convicted of regicide. In Breight's reading, Prospero's pinches are "euphemized," so that he achieves "the kind of euphemistic revenge that leads to the repossession of secure and legitimate political power" (27). Breight feels, however, that the play exposes Prospero's "psychological reign of terror" and reveals the strategies through which he masks "subjection of the body with a show of benevolence" (28). In keeping with post-Foucauldian theories about authorship, he does not speculate on what this imagery reveals about Shakespeare.

It probably is not immediately apparent that *pinch* and these other words are either so completely central to the play or connected to one another as I suggest here. Unlike the words I focused on in previous chapters, these are connected more obviously by sound than by meaning, there are many more of them, and they are not so clearly related to one another. The connections *are* tenuous, arising sometimes from juxtaposition (*pitch* and *piteous* within fifteen lines of each other in act 1, scene 1, *pinch* and *pitch* in adjacent lines at 2.2.4–5), sometimes from association (a confining *pine* is said to cause roars that make animals howl, a cramping *pinch* is later said to do the same thing). I shall begin by describing this web of connections in an attempt to establish that the play does indeed turn on a linking of these words. I shall then follow several strands of association that branch out from various of the words. As in other chapters, I believe that all these different word paths circle around an exploration of a kinesthetic and spatial sense of the human subject—in this case an exploration of its painful confinement on an island, on the stage, and in a mortal body and also of its yearning for control, escape, and transcendence of all these states. Again, although the plot may depict Prospero's successful mastery of discourse, the island, and other people, this web of words suggests his profound vulnerability, and his dilemma, as he attempts to imagine a powerful, immaterial mode of being in sound (including but not limited to discourse) and also realizes that this evanescent reality lacks the comforting (though confining) solidity of the material.

Perhaps the first image of painful confinement in the play does not actually involve the word *pinch* but centers instead on Ariel's imprisonment by Sycorax in the "pine." As Prospero describes it, Ariel was forced

> Into a cloven *pine*, within which rift
> *Imprison'd*, thou didst *painfully* remain
> A dozen years; within which space she died,
> And left thee there, where thou didst vent thy *groans*
> As fast as mill-wheels strike.
>
> (1.2.277–81, my emphasis)

This image of confinement causing extreme pain that leads to involuntary sounds will become a central one in the play. Prospero reiterates it a few lines later:

> Thou best know'st
> What *torment* I did find thee in; thy *groans*
> Did make wolves *howl*, and penetrate the breasts
> Of ever-angry bears.
>
> > (1.2.286–89, my emphasis)

In another image that will be repeated in the play, Prospero imagines that Ariel's cries of torment cause animals to suffer and also to vent their own inarticulate "howls." Interestingly, although the ever-angry bears are imagined here as feeling sympathy for Ariel's plight, Prospero himself does not seem to. He immediately goes on to threaten him with a renewal of his suffering:

> I will rend an oak
> And *peg* thee in his knotty *entrails* till
> Thou has *howl'd* away twelve winters.
>
> > (1.2.294–96, my emphasis)

It is not an accident that the word *pine* suggests not only a kind of tree but also suffering itself, being defined in the *OED* as "suffering, affliction, distress, trouble, physical suffering = PAIN." Derived, like *pain*, from the Latin word *poena* (punishment), *pine* suggests exactly what Ariel was undergoing during his twelve years of confinement. Thus, in a slippage common to this play, a feature of the landscape is imagined as so integrally a part of the infliction of pain that it becomes itself a way of naming or describing the pain. Elaine Scarry has argued that the otherwise inarticulable experience of pain is often brought into language through linkage with the agent of the pain or some wound that results. Thus, although "physical pain is not identical with (and often exists without) either agency or damage, . . . these things are referential; consequently we often call on them to convey the experience of pain itself."[18] The "knotty entrails" of the oak itself look forward to the "cramps," "aches," and other internal ills that Prospero is able to induce, so that the agent of injury is once again conflated with the damage that it causes in order to describe and emphasize the experience of pain.

As Elaine Scarry has suggested, the experience of extreme pain is fundamentally associated with inarticulate sounds: "Physical pain does not simply resist language but actively destroys it, bringing about an immediate reversion to a state anterior to language, to the sounds and cries a human being makes before language is learned," or, as here, to the sounds that animals make.[19] As we shall see, Prospero's persistent linking of pain that he causes with animal noises breaks down the distinctions between human and animal or savage that he insists upon in other contexts. These cries of pain are also as much a part of the atmosphere of sound in the play as the music, on which critics have tended to focus. Like the linkage by sound of seemingly unconnected words, cries of pain represent noise that is not easily ordered by rational ways of controlling and understanding the world and yet are integral to Prospero's control over the island.

As noted above, "pinching" also is linked to animal cries of pain. When Prospero sics Ariel on the conspirators Caliban, Stephano, and Trinculo in act 4, he commands, "goblins . . . more pinch-spotted make them / Than pard or cat o' mountain," to which Ariel replies, "Hark, they roar!" (4.1.260–62). Earlier Prospero threatens Caliban directly in two passages that link animals, pinches and cramps, confinement, pain, and loud sounds. He will inflict:

> Side-stitches that shall *pen* thy breath up; *urchins*
> Shall, for that vast of night that they may work,
> All exercise on thee; thou shalt be *pinch'd*
> As thick as honey comb, each *pinch* more stinging
> Than *bees* that made 'em.
>
> (1.2.326–30, my emphasis)

Like Ariel's torment in the tree, pain is associated with confinement, "pen thy breath up," animals "urchins," and "bees" here linked to pinching, a word that itself can figure confinement (also as in *Cymbeline*, where a cave is described as "pinching"). Prospero in this scene further promises to "rack" Caliban with "old cramps," another pain linked etymologically with confinement (as in a cramped space) and also, in the text, with noise: "Fill all thy bones with aches, make thee roar / That beasts shall tremble at thy din" (1.2.370–71).

A contemporary context for Prospero's pinches that has not often been noted by critics can shed light on the slippage between natural and supernatural causes for the pains imagined in the play. Prospero punishes people with invisible spirit pinches most obviously because fairies were traditionally thought to do so.[20] Shakespeare specifically alludes to this tradition in *Merry Wives*, where Falstaff is tormented by villagers dressed as fairies, who "Pinch them, arms, legs, backs, shoulders, sides, and shins" (5.5.54). In a story from his childhood (1633) John Aubrey tells how the curate of his grammar school "was annoy'd one night by these elves, or fairies." This Mr. Hart happened one night upon "one of the faiery dances," where he all at once saw an innumerable quantitie of pigmies, or very small people, dancing round and round, and singing and making all manner of small odd noises. He, being very greatly amaz'd, and yet not being able, as he sayes, to run away from them, being, as he supposes kept there in a kind of enchantment, they no sooner perceave him but they surround him on all sides, and what betwixte feare and amazement he fell down, scarcely knowing what he did; and thereupon these little creatures pinch'd him all over, and made a quick humming noyse all the tyme; but at length they left him.[21]

The pinches, as well as the emphasis on humming and other odd noises, suggest the spirit world of *The Tempest*, as does the allusion to a fairy ring, which Prospero describes as a "green sour ringlet."

These English fairies were often imagined as nature spirits, as are Oberon and Titania (and their followers) in *A Midsummer Night's Dream*. Lewis Spence, in *British Fairy Origins*, records the theory that fairies represented spirits "which are believed to animate nature, inhabiting or ensouling trees, rocks, rivers, waters and clouds, plants, grain—or any natural object."[22] If fairies are nature spirits, their pinches (and the related phenomenon of "elf shots," pains caused by pieces of wood injected into the body by elves) seem to function as supernatural explanations for otherwise inexplicable aches, pains, and bruises. Prospero's economy of punishment involves an alteration of this tradition since he claims a supernatural agency for his pinches but also persistently describes them in terms of natural features of the landscape. It is clear that the line Prospero attempts to draw between nature and his civilized "art" is fundamentally blurred. The language with which he describes his supernatural agency is imbued with images of its dependence on nature, a dependence that may derive not only from the strong connection between the natural and the supernatural in the folkloric roots of his powers but also from Shakespeare's sense of the difficulty of escaping or evading the limits of materiality.

It has been a commonplace of criticism that Caliban and Ariel represent, respectively, the material (elements of earth and water) and the spiritual (air and fire). As Sturgess puts it, "Ariel is a thing of spirit and without human sentience; Caliban a thing of matter, bestial and sensual. In an allegorical reading of the play, they act as linked cyphers."[23] However, in *The Tempest* Shakespeare does not seem to be able to imagine either spiritual or material entities as pure or self-contained, so that in the course of the play both Ariel and Caliban also enact some difficult intermixture of the two states. Spence records an English folk rhyme, "Fairy folks / Are in old oaks," as evidence of their role as nature spirits (100). Ariel's confinement in a tree represents a significant variation on this traditional belief, for he is imagined not as naturally inhabiting and animating the tree but as undergoing a painful punishment in his confinement there. Caliban, on the other hand, may to some extent be modeled on the tradition of the fairy "changeling," a fairy left in exchange for a human child who has been stolen away. Changelings were usually ugly and undesirable, characterized in Spence's words by "fractious behaviour and voracious appetite" (39) and also by a fondness for music. Thus, Caliban's attentiveness to the mysterious music of the island and his closeness to nature may be signs of his relation to a supernatural state of being not so different from Ariel's.

The case of Caliban most clearly reveals the circular logic of Prospero's definition of the natural. Prospero typically justifies his domination of Caliban on the basis of the latter's evil nature; he describes Caliban as "a devil, a born devil, on whose nature / Nurture can never stick" (4.1.188–89). Prospero's following comments to Ariel here suggest, however, that Caliban's "natural" depravity may be in part caused by Prospero's manipulations of nature against him: "As with his age his body uglier grows, / So his mind cankers. I will plague them all, / Even to roaring" (4.1.191–93). Here Prospero sees physical deformity and disease ("cankers") as signs of Caliban's innate inferiority even as he threatens to inflict him with diseaselike suffering. Similarly, Miranda associated Caliban's lack of civilization with his inability to use language, while Prospero here plans to reduce him to bestial "roaring." Prospero's initial description of Caliban emphasized his "freckled," or spotted, appearance as a sign of his imperfection, yet the text also suggests that it is Prospero himself who has made Caliban "more pinch-spotted . . . / Than pard or cat o' mountain" (4.1.260–61). Despite his own claims to attempt to teach and civilize Caliban, Prospero's tortures are relentlessly imagined as turning him into a beast—even while that beastlike nature is the justification for the torments.[24]

It is Caliban himself who links *pinch* and *pitch* when, with some bravado, he defies Prospero's "spirits" in act 2: "But they'll nor pinch, / Fright me with urchin-shows, pitch me i' th' mire" (2.2.4–5). Although the word here is used in the sense of "throw," it is nevertheless connected (by the "mire") with the proverbial quality of "pitch" or tar, which dirties whatever it touches, as in the common proverb "this pitch, as ancient writers report, doth defile" (*1 Henry IV* 2.4.455). In this passage Caliban associates pinching, as Prospero also does, with the vulnerability of the human body to penetration by sharp objects. As Prospero constantly links pinches with bee stings, hedgehog spines, and other sharp implements in nature, Caliban here thinks of "urchins" or hedgehogs in connection with pinches and goes on to mention "hedgehogs," which "Lie tumbling in my barefoot way, and mount / Their pricks at my footfall" (2.2.10–12). Yet another passage, spoken by Ariel, similarly links nature, pricking, animal sounds, confinement, and defilement. Ariel describes how he pursues the three conspirators through "Tooth'd briers, sharp furzes, pricking goss, and thorns, / Which enter'd their frail shins. At last I left them / I'th' filthy-mantled pool beyond your cell," where "the foul lake / O'erstunk their feet" (4.1.180–84). These punishments once again turn their sufferers into animals—"like unback'd colts they prick'd their ears," "that calf-like they my lowing follow'd" (4.1.176, 179)—and again their animality has a verbal connection with both their torments ("prick'd") and a loud noise (lowing).

Pity is the one of these linked words that does not directly name some form of pain or suffering; rather, it indicates a possible response to it. Pity is, for Shakespeare, at least in some contexts, a distinguishing feature of humane and civilized behavior, as when, in *As You Like It*, Orlando and Duke Senior exchange proofs of "smooth civility" and "nurture": "If ever from your eyelids wip'd a tear, / And know what 'tis to pity, and be pit-ied"; "True is it that we have seen better days . . . and wip'd our eyes / Of drops that sacred pity hath engend'red" (2.7.116–17, 120, 122–23). In *The Tempest*, however, it is repeatedly invoked as something that Pros-pero is unable to feel; it is instead deflected onto Miranda, Ariel, or nature itself. When Miranda describes the opening tempest as pouring down "stinking pitch," Prospero responds by asking her to "Tell your piteous heart / There's no harm done" (1.2.14–15). Pity is associated with sad sounds during Prospero's long narrative—the "winds, whose pity, sighing back again, / Did us but loving wrong"—and in Miranda's response that "Alack, for pity! / I, not remembering how I cried out then, / Will cry it o'er again" (1.2.150–51, 132–34). Paul Brown has suggested that Pros-pero's emphasis on his arrival on the island as a "helpless exile" works to mystify "the origins of what is after all a colonialist regime on the island by producing it as a result of charitable acts (by the sea, the wind and the honest courtier Gonzalo alike) made out of pity for powerless exiles."[25] Prospero himself, however, feels no pity for his island subjects; indeed, his storm represents the lack of pity he feels as he exploits nature to undertake his revenge.

Although Miranda asks Prospero to "have pity" (1.2.475) on Ferdi-nand, he does not do it, and he ultimately responds to Ariel's suggestion that he might feel sorry for his tormented enemies first with surprise and then with a kind of competitive determination to be as tenderhearted as Ariel and with a statement about the importance of "reason" and "virtue" but not, finally, with a *feeling* of pity:

Hast thou, which art but air, a touch, a feeling
Of their afflictions, and shall not myself,
One of their kind, that relish all as sharply
Passion as they, be kindlier mov'd than thou art?
Though with their high wrongs I am strook to th'quick,
Yet with my nobler reason, 'gainst my fury
Do I take part. The rarer action is
In virtue than in vengeance.

(5.1.21–28)

It is Miranda—and I believe the lines must for this reason be attributed to her—who associates pity with civilization when she chides Caliban, "I pitied thee, / Took pains to make thee speak" (1.2.353–54). Miranda here continues the association of pity with pain, but unlike Prospero, she attempts to link it also to articulate speech (as a civilizing force) rather than to animal cries.

If it now seems more plausible that these words and images are linked through tenuous interconnections of sound and sense, what are we to make of them in relation to the play as a whole? The words appear and reappear in scenarios in which Prospero inflicts pain or other characters describe it, where it is associated in various ways with confinement, penetration, and defilement. The sufferer of the pain emits inarticulate animal noises, which excite a sympathetic response in actual fauna of the island but not in Prospero himself. If a usual reading of the play has come to center on Prospero's clever use of various hegemonic discursive formations—language, education, books, music—in order to gain control over the island, its inhabitants, his enemies, and himself, it seems clear that the nexus of words and images traced here emphasizes instead the extent to which Prospero and all human subjects are trapped in and subjected to the material world. Although Prospero attempts, at times successfully, to use discourse to escape, master, or transcend his limited materiality, he is finally unable to achieve complete success. The play emphasizes three material spaces in which Prospero is trapped: the island, his body, and the stage. We now need to explore the ways in which *pinch* and its partners are implicated in these overlapping and confining spaces.

The landscape in *The Tempest* is perhaps more persistently present than is the locale of any other Shakespearean work. Its presence is, however, literally immaterial since in the absence of elaborate scenery or backdrops it is conjured up on the bare platform stage by the descriptive language of the characters and by the sound effects that are so unusually prominent in the play. Although the descriptions and sounds highlight its stubborn materiality—the rocks, fens, and storms that plague its inhabitants—these features have their existence in the immaterial medium of sound waves. Because this landscape exists only as it is known and described by different characters, its nature is radically ambiguous. Some characters describe a fruitful, nurturing paradise; others, a barren, thorny, swampy wasteland; still others, some combination of the two. This ambivalent view of the landscape may well have its source in the Bermuda pamphlets that Shakespeare clearly had in mind when writing the play, although the ambivalence is there resolved into a contrast between expectation and reality. The authors of A Discovery of the Barmudas, for example, contrast the islands' "ever esteemed, and reputed, a most prodigious and inchanted place, affoording nothing but gusts, stormes, and foule weather," with a very different reality: "Yet did we find there the ayre so temperate and the Country so aboundantly fruitfull of all fit necessaries, for the sustentation and preservation of mans life." [26]

In the play, however, this dichotomy between harsh and nurturing landscapes remains operative. It becomes clear that a given character's knowledge of the island is dependent upon his own nature and that landscape and subjectivity are represented as mutually constitutive. In act 2, scene 1, for example, the good characters Adrian and Gonzalo perceive a fruitful paradise, while the bad guys Antonio and Sebastian describe a hostile desert. Adrian comments that although the island seems deserted—"Uninhabitable, and almost inaccessible" (38)—"It must needs be of a subtle, tender, and delicate temperance" (43). To his remark that "the air breathes upon us here most sweetly" (46), Antonio retorts that it is "as 'twere perfum'd by a fen" (49). When Gonzalo suggests, perhaps echoing the pamphlet, that "here is every thing advantageous to life" (50), Antonio again answers "True, save means to live" (51). Even Gonzalo's exclamation "How lush and lusty the grass looks! How green!" is countered by Antonio's "The ground indeed is tawny" (54–55). To an audience trying to decide what sort of landscape to imagine, this conversation must be confusing indeed. In this scene, clearly, the virtuous Adrian and Gonzalo are able to see a welcoming landscape, while the villainous Sebastian and Antonio cannot. Which landscape is actually "there" remains an open question, however, since Gonzalo may be overly optimistic, the others may be overly pessimistic, or Prospero's magic may be influencing what they see. To use Michel De Certeau's distinction, the bare "space" of the platform stage in this instance resists competing attempts to delineate it discursively as a mapped and controlled "place." [27]

Prospero himself claims to know the island intimately and to have power over and through nature to dominate its other inhabitants. Environmental criticism would point out that in the absence of truly indigenous inhabitants it is the island itself that is most completely colonized, not just by Prospero but even, to some extent, by Caliban as well. This perspective on the play takes seriously Lawrence Buell's argument that "the ecological colonization of the Americas by disease and invasive plant forms is as crucial as the subjugation of their indigenous peoples by political and military means." In Buell's view, such ecological colonization is bound up with political subjugation: "Nature has been doubly otherized in modern thought. The Natural environment as empirical reality has been made to subserve human interests, and one of those interests has been to make it serve as a symbolic reinforcement of the subservience of disempowered groups."[28] Prospero's use of the environment itself to control his subjects and enemies illustrates this concept of a "doubly otherized nature." As Albanese suggests, in Prospero's final catalogue of feats performed through his "so potent art" almost all involve power over the weather or landscape—bedimming the sun, controlling wind and sea, pulling up trees (5.1.42–47).[29]

Prospero's pitiless technology of colonial domination, however, seems almost completely dependent on the harsher features of the island's landscape, despite his repeated claims that it is derived from books and "art." Descriptions of the natural torments he inflicts on his subjects seem, as we have seen, to circle around images of cramped confinement, penetration by sharp objects, and sounds of human distress, which are imagined as so awful that even animals are disturbed by them. While the direct agents of this physical torture are described as "spirits," the language used to describe the pain that they cause repeatedly relates it, as we have seen, to the plant and animal life of the island. Ariel, for example, is kept in line through frequent reminders of his painful incarceration in the "cloven pine" and the threat that this torment will be repeated in a different tree. Ariel's response to his confinement, the "groans" that "did make wolves howl, and penetrate the breasts of ever-angry bears," seems to conflate him with those very animals as he both causes wolves to howl and also howls himself. Like Caliban, the "freckled whelp, hag-born," Ariel seems less than human here, rendered worthy of domination precisely by the torment inflicted on him by his colonizer. Only the "every-angry" Prospero seems unmoved by these sounds.

Postcolonial and New Historicist readings of the play that have identified the "pinches" through which Prospero controls Caliban and others with various actual mechanisms of domination in the early modern period generally have not noted the extent to which these pinches are linked to natural phenomena or to features of the island landscape. Indeed, they are most persistently associated with the two aspects of environmental colonization identified by Buell, "disease, and invasive plant forms," although animal life is also often involved. When Prospero first threatens Caliban with painful coercion, he does so, significantly, in response to Caliban's own attempt to wish on Prospero environmentally caused diseases:

> As wicked dew as e'er my mother brush'd
> With raven's feather from unwholesome fen
> Drop on you both! A south-west blow on ye,
> And blister you all o'er!

$$(1.2.321-24)$$

Caliban associates these curses with his mother, but the use of the environment as a threat may also be something he has learned from Prospero, or their similar use of nature may reinforce the similarities, suggested elsewhere in the play though vehemently denied by Prospero, between Sycorax's magic and his own. Prospero responds with his own version of the same kind of curse:

> For this be sure, to-night thou shalt have cramps,
> Side-stitches that shall pen thy breath up; urchins
> Shall, for that vast of night that they may work,
> All exercise on thee; thou shalt be pinch'd
> As thick as honeycomb, each pinch more stinging
> Than bees that made 'em.

$$(1.2.325-29)$$

Notice here Prospero's obsession with confinement: "cramp," "pen," "pinch," as well as penetration by sharp objects, the urchins' spines and bee stings. Notice, too, the shift from pain that proceeds from the inside out, like a disease, to stinging pinches inflicted from outside. It is also significant that one natural feature that might be associated with a positive, nurturing landscape—the honeycomb—is linked by Prospero with pain. As with Ariel, Prospero anticipates that Caliban's "cramps" will "make thee roar / That beasts shall tremble at thy din" (1.2.369-71). Later in the play, Prospero will similarly torture the conspirators Caliban, Stephano, and Trinculo, as well as his old enemies Antonio and Sebastian, with natural torments. Alonso, Sebastian, Antonio, and Gonzalo, meanwhile, have bones that "ache" from the exertions of searching the island: "Here's a maze trod indeed / Through forth-rights and meanders!" (3.3.2-3).

Significantly, Prospero shares with the evil conspirators Antonio and Sebastian a sense of the island as hostile and uncomfortable. Perhaps Prospero views the island in this way because he wants to emphasize the superiority of his "art" and his own lack of dependence on the landscape. He suggests, for instance, that he and Miranda have been able to survive because they have brought the necessities of life with them—"Some food we had, and some fresh water . . . / Rich garments, linens, stuffs, and necessaries, / Which since have steaded much" (1.2.160, 164–65)—possibly eroding Caliban's claim that they could not have survived on the island without his help. As we have seen, Prospero's torments are based on exploitation of a harsh landscape; even his "cell" represents not a cozy nurturing space but a "hard rock," a prisonlike structure evidently so cold that it requires an almost infinite supply of firewood, carried by both Caliban and Ferdinand. These logs seem emblematic of Prospero's simultaneous colonization of the environment through deforestation and his use of elements of that landscape to punish and control its human inhabitants. Certainly the destruction of trees remains a powerful fantasy for him that seems integral to his magic.

The only fruitful landscape perceived by Prospero is that conjured up in his masque, with its representations of Ceres and a harvest scene. Contrasting Prospero's references to the harsh features of the island's landscape, the masque presents a cultivated (and therefore civilized) landscape: "turfy mountains, where live nibbling sheep," "bosky acres," "a short-grass'd green," not to mention "rich leas / Of wheat, rye, barley, fetches, oats, and pease" (4.1.63, 81, 84, 60–61). Prospero seems willing to admit a productive and nurturing nature only when it is firmly under the control of his art, and Ferdinand seconds this sentiment when, after viewing the masque, he comments, "Let me live here ever; / So rare a wond'red father and a wise / Makes this place Paradise" (4.1.123–25). Prospero's anxieties about the sexuality of Ferdinand and Miranda seem linked to his desire to control natural procreativity. Indeed, he threatens them with yet another version of the unproductive landscape should they give in to desire—"Sour-ey'd disdain, and discord shall bestrew / The union of your bed with weeds so loathly / That you shall hate it both" (4.1.20–22)—while the masque is an extended promise of the artificial "paradise" that awaits them if they remain chaste as he commands.

If Prospero is only able to know the island in its natural state as hostile and punitive, Caliban is famously possessed of knowledge of its nurturing side. He claims that Prospero and Miranda have learned to survive on the island because he has conveyed this knowledge to them: "then I lov'd thee / And show'd thee all the qualities o' th' isle, / The fresh springs, brine-pits, barren place and fertile" (1.2.336–38). Prospero performs a parody of this offer when he threatens to torture Ferdinand with the island's unpalatable produce: "Sea-water shalt thou drink; thy food shall be / The fresh-brook mussels, wither'd roots, and husks / Wherein the acorn cradled" (1.2.463–65). Significantly, Caliban is able to see the island as both hostile and nurturing, and he links the sharing of this knowledge with love. Newly impressed with Stephano and Trinculo, he offers the most detailed description of the provisions that he might glean from the island:

I'll show thee the best springs; I'll pluck thee berries;
I'll fish for thee, and get thee wood enough.

(2.2.160–61)

I prithee let me bring thee where crabs grow;
And I with my long nails will dig thee pig-nuts,
Show thee a jay's nest, and instruct thee how
To snare the nimble marmazet. I'll bring thee
To clust'ring filberts, and sometimes I'll get thee
Young scamels from the rock.

(2.2.167–72)[30]

Caliban knows a very different landscape from the one Prospero knows, and he uses it very differently, as a means of sustenance rather than a means of torture. In its practicality and specificity this passage is very different from the dream passage usually cited to illustrate Caliban's oneness with the island.[31] There he describes the "Sounds, and sweet airs, that give delight and hurt not" and his dreams of "clouds" that "methought would open, and show riches / Ready to drop upon me" (3.2.136, 141–42). This passage curiously connects Caliban to a supernatural rather than a natural abundance, more like Prospero's masque (or, for that matter, the feast that is revealed to his enemies and then snatched away by a harpylike Ariel). As such, it furthers a distinction that seems to be emerging between the solid matter of the landscape—emphasizing elements of earth and water—and the "insubstantial pageant" of sound and air.

Different characters on the island perceive it as differently implicated in their own freedom or entrapment. Prospero seems to imagine the whole island as a kind of prison. His home on the island is repeatedly called a "cell," and in his narrative of arrival on the island he uses the cell metonymically to name the whole island: "we came unto this cell" (1.2.39). Although Prospero claims to control the island and its landscape, it is Ariel who flies around it freely, while Prospero remains, for the most part, in his cave. And despite Ariel's subjugation to Prospero, he is the one repeatedly associated with air, transcendence of the material world, and freedom to journey over vast expanses of space. Ariel is able to fly over the island, travel even as far as the "still-vexed Bermoothes," and render himself invisible. He is most associated with music and sound, and Prospero describes him as composed of "air" (5.1.21). Even Ferdinand is better able than Prospero to see the "cell" for what it is and to imagine a freedom beyond it: "All corners else o'th' earth / Let liberty make use of; space enough / Have I in such a prison" (1.2.492–94). Caliban is also in some sense more free than Prospero since he sees most of the island as offering the possibility of freedom, considering Prospero's cell alone as confining, sharply differentiating "this hard rock" from "the rest o' th' island" (1.2.343, 344).

It seems clear that despite Prospero's almost desperate attempts to represent his power as power over the island derived from books, his very reliance on the landscape in controlling his enemies suggests that his "potent art" is itself dependant on a "nature" that he knows only imperfectly. Thus, his decision to "abjure" his magic and "drown" his book before leaving the island may simply be an admission that without the island his magic will lack the power to dominate. Earlier materialist critics like Brown, Greenblatt, Barker, and Hulme seem to agree with Prospero that his power over the island and over people is essentially discursive and cultural. Brown, for instance, argues that "Prospero's problems concerning the maintenance of his power on the island are therefore also problems of representation, of his capacity to 'forge' the island in his own image" through powerful narratives that "can be seen, then, to operate as a reality principle, ordering and correcting the inhabitants of the island, subordinating their discourse to his own."[32] Albanese, however, rightly suggests that Prospero's control needs to extend beyond the discursive level of humanist study to "instrumentality over the phenomenal world," a new technology that is made possible, she argues, by the colonial island setting and resembles the beginnings of modern science.[33]

The play, however, suggests that Prospero's knowledge of the island and its landscape is partial at best. He is, after all, only able to see the negative aspects of the island, and he seems oddly trapped within a limited and limiting landscape, finally refusing to venture much beyond his cell or to see the more positive side of the island that is evident to others. Although he is finally able to subdue his enemies and regain his dukedom, the play persistently suggests that he has been able to do so only through this inability to see nature as anything but hostile, through an obstinate blindness to nurturing qualities that other characters can see and enjoy. Thus, despite his attempts to turn the island into a "place" where nature is fully instrumental to the strategies of his "so potent art," other characters' experiences of it continually reassert its possibilities as a "space" that can be tactically deployed in a variety of ways. In some ways the play might seem to support the idea that the natural environment is as discursively constructed as everything else in a play where the landscape is quite literally a function of discourse. On the other hand, it strongly emphasizes physical experience of the environment and extradiscursive responses to those experiences, such as pain causing an inarticulate cry that prompts anguished howls from animals.[34] Despite Prospero's initial claims that nature—the sea and wind—pitied and preserved him on his way to the island, his obsessive repetition of the verbal web centered on *pinch*, *pitch*, and *pine* conveys a deep-seated fear of being trapped within, and vulnerable to, a hostile natural environment.

Although Prospero is at least potentially able to leave the island at the end of the play, there is a further sense that he is more inescapably trapped in his own body. Indeed, the play draws an analogy between the island and the human body as material spaces within which human subjects are confined. The sense of an island as analogous to the body is, of course, the governing metaphor of Phineas Fletcher's poem "The Purple Island, or the Isle of Man," of 1633, which describes the workings of the body/island at some length. Shakespeare himself uses this metaphor in reverse in *Richard III*, where England is described and personified as a "noble isle" that "doth want her proper limbs; / Her face defac'd with scars of infamy" (3.7.125–26). And if Prospero is able to leave the actual island to return to Italy, he is aware that, once there, he will remain trapped within his mortal body, while "every third thought shall be my grave" (5.1.312).

If Caliban perceives the island, in both natural and supernatural terms, as a nurturing haven, it may be, as Skura has argued, because he associates it so strongly with his mother and with the maternal body.[35] Prospero, not surprisingly, just as persistently links the island with images of painful childbirth rather than with subsequent maternal care, a connection that helps us begin to see how the island also represents a confining and pain-ridden mortal body. Critics have noted that Prospero's description of his relationship to Miranda as they make their way to the island seems to represent himself as giving birth to her, as he "under my burthen groan'd" (1.2.156). Similarly, Ariel's imprisonment in the pine resembles a pregnancy, and Prospero's emergency cesarean delivery, which "made gape / The pine, and let thee out" (1.2.292–93), follows within ten lines of his description of how Sycorax had a son "which she did litter here" (1.2.282). Prospero's enslavement of Ariel might almost be an allegorical representation of the entrapment of the soul or spirit in a mortal body. As noted above, Prospero's tortures center around a nexus of confinement, penetration, "cramps," and loud groans, which also conjure up images of pregnancy and childbirth, of painful birth out of a body as well as birth into a body that is vulnerable to pain and disease.

Rather than pursuing another psychoanalytic reading of these images, we might consider the spatial implications of Prospero's fear of confinement, both on the island and within a mortal and pain-racked body. A line from *The Merchant of Venice* can serve as a gloss on this play's images of embodiment as confining and defiling: Lorenzo argues that transcendent music of the spheres does exist and is matched by a similar "harmony . . . in immortal souls," which "whilst this muddy vesture of decay [the

human body] / Doth grossly close it in, we cannot hear it" (5.1.63–65).
Since *The Tempest* so often associates sounds with magical transcendence
of the material world, Lorenzo's contrast between heavenly music and
the gross materiality of the body seems especially relevant.

Lorenzo's description of the body as "muddy" is significantly echoed
in *The Tempest*, connecting the defiling properties of the landscape of the
island with the corruption to which mortal flesh is subject, a corruption
involving both the defilement of original sin and the decay that occurs
after the inevitable death that results from sinful condition. Both mind
and body are imagined as vulnerable to this taint. The supposed death of
Ferdinand by drowning is twice imagined as burial in the mud at the
bottom of the sea, an image that proleptically links the potential mortality
of the body with its actual death. Alonso bewails his death, lamenting
that as a result of his sin against Prospero, "my son i' th'ooze is bedded,
and / I'll seek him deeper than e'er plummet sounded, / And with him
there lie mudded" (3.3.100–102). He uses similar language again in act
5: "I wish / Myself were mudded in that oozy bed / Where my son lies"
(5.1.150–52). Prospero describes the insanity with which he has inflicted
his enemies in terms that conjure up a similar muddy beach:

> Their understanding
> Begins to swell, and the approaching tide
> Will shortly fill the reasonable shores
> That now lie foul and muddy.
>
> (5.1.79–82)

In this image the mind is like an island, surrounded by a sea of reason
that has been muddied by Prospero's physical torments.

The clouded minds of his enemies also are described by Prospero in
terms that recall another natural scene:

> as the morning steals upon the night,
> Melting the darkness, so their rising senses
> Begin to chase the fumes that mantle
> Their clearer reason.
>
> (5.1.65–68)

Mantle here links these fumes with Lorenzo's image of the body as clothing, or "muddy vesture," for the soul and also links Prospero's torture of
the nobles to the final punishment of his lower-class enemies. The confinement of Caliban and the other conspirators in "th' filthy-mantled pool
beyond your cell" (4.1.182) is closely followed by Prospero's famous description linking the disgusting nature of Caliban's mind and body with
his imperviousness to civilization:

A devil, a born devil, on whose nature
Nurture can never stick; on whom my pains,
Humanely taken, all, all lost, quite lost;
And as with age his body uglier grows,
So his mind cankers.

(4.1.188–92)

Ariel comments that the "foul lake / O'er stunk their feet," just as Prospero previously described their plot as a "foul conspiracy" (4.1.139). Prospero's imagery here effects a reversal similar to that effected by his references to animals. In that case Prospero's tortures were imagined as causing Caliban to become animal-like, even while his animal nature was adduced as justification for the torture. Here Caliban's defilement is both a product of and a justification for his punishment.

Sexuality, like death, is another feature of human embodiment that Prospero (and Ferdinand, as he increasingly adopts Prospero's views) conflates with the environment of the island and describes in terms of dirt and disgust. As noted above, Prospero threatens Ferdinand and Miranda with a bed full of "weeds so loathly" if they do not remain chaste until their wedding. Ferdinand reassures Prospero that

> the murkiest den,
> The most opportune place, the strong'st suggestion
> Our worser genius can, shall never melt
> Mine honor into lust,

(4.1.25–28)

"Murkiest den" seems to be an allusion both to Prospero's cave and also, potentially, to Miranda's body—but the word *murkiest* also connects them to the images of mud and foulness that have been associated with death and insanity. Sebastian, interestingly, reveals that like his view of the island, his view of sexuality may also resemble Prospero's: he describes Alonso's daughter's attitude toward marriage as "loathness" (2.1.131), foreshadowing Prospero's "loathly" weeds of inchastity.

In these passages Prospero once again seems to imagine that just as he controls the island itself, so also does he control the bodies of his subjects: it is he who muddies their reason, he who confines them within the disgusting pool, and he who makes Alonso imagine Ferdinand's oozy death so vividly. Prospero boasts that he is able to control death itself: "Graves at my command / Have wak'd their sleepers, op'd, and let them forth / By my so potent art" (5.1.48–50). But we must ask whether this claim constitutes an empty boast or perhaps a wistful fantasy. Significantly, the passage in which Prospero imagines the end of his magic powers echoes Alonso's description of Ferdinand's death. Like Ferdinand's body, Prospero will confine his magical implements to "earth" and to the bottom of the sea: "And deeper than did ever plummet sound / I'll drown my book" (5.1.55–57). This echo suggests that despite his claims, Prospero's magic is more subject to the limits of the material body than he has been willing to admit. Thus, his reliance on the natural environment of the island is mirrored by his ultimate subjection to the mortal body.

It is therefore no surprise that Prospero foretells his own preoccupation with death once he leaves the island and returns to Milan. Indeed, although Prospero has repeatedly described his magical torments as causing the pains of old age, these are pains to which he, more than anyone else on the island, would be subject. Thus, he threatens Caliban, "I'll rack thee with old cramps" (1.2.369), and he later orders his spirits to torment the three conspirators with "aged cramps" (4.1.260), both of which are glossed in the *Riverside Shakespeare* as "such as old people have." He uses the rough terrain of the island to induce a more natural version of these elderly pains in his other enemies, so that Gonzalo comments, "By'r lakin, I can go no further, sir, / My old bones aches" (3.3.1–2). Yet Prospero also associates his own internal disturbances with old age, so that his threats to inflict "aged" pains on others seems like another of his signature confusions of cause and effect, of the agent of pain for its result. When his masque is disrupted by the sudden memory of the conspiracy against him and the resulting anger that he feels, he excuses himself to Ferdinand:

> Sir, I am vex'd;
> Bear with my weakness, my old brain is troubled.
> Be not disturb'd with my infirmity.
> If you be pleas'd, retire into my cell,
> And there repose. A turn or two I'll walk
> To still my beating mind.

> (4.1.158–63)

Although Miranda and Ferdinand attribute Prospero's disturbance to "passion" and "anger," he sees it as an "infirmity" caused by age. Interestingly, his response is to escape, however briefly, from the "cell," which he seems to associate with a confining body.

Prospero repeatedly conceives of the internal psychological disturbances of others as involving confinement and constraint, perhaps as a projection of his own feeling that he and his powerful emotions are trapped within a small and fragile space. He gloats that "these, mine enemies, are all knit up / In their distractions" (3.3.89–90) and pictures their "brains, / Now useless, boil'd within thy skull" (5.1.59–60). Not surprisingly, the emotionally arid Prospero also sees the feelings of Ferdinand for Miranda as a kind of imprisonment; he boasts in asides, "The Duke of Milan / And his more braver daughter could control thee, / If now t'were fit to do't" and "They are both in either's pow'rs" (1.2.439–41, 451). Ferdinand, however, recognizes that it is Prospero himself who is "crabbed," pinched and confined by his own need for rigid control over himself and others. As much as Prospero attempts to project his own fears of old age, confinement, and pain onto the landscape of the island and onto other people, he is unable to free himself from them.

Interestingly, Prospero also seems to project onto others the qualities— including freedom—that he is unable to attain for himself. He repeatedly describes Ariel as a creature of "air" whose release from the pine seems also to have effected a release from the constraints of a mortal body or the material world. Miranda becomes the repository of feelings like "pity," love, and wonder, which Prospero, with his "crabbed" nature, is unable to experience. And Gonzalo is imagined by Prospero as transcending material limitations despite his old age: "Let me embrace thine age, whose honor cannot / Be measur'd or confin'd" (5.1.121–22). All of these unconfined attributes—pity, love, honor—are abstractions that in fact do not have material limits. The image of measurelessness, however, returns us to the repeated image of Ferdinand's body and Prospero's magic book sunk "deeper than did ever plummet sound" (5.1.56), reminding us that however much Prospero wants to imagine a magical or spiritual transcendence of the material world, the mortal body and the harsh environment are paradoxically without limit in their ability to confine and destroy.

Critics have noticed that Prospero, despite his triumph, seems oddly depressed at the end of the play. Although he will gain his longed-for freedom from the island, he looks forward to increased awareness of the limitations of his body. His final inability to free himself also surfaces in the epilogue when he confesses that his own strength is "most faint" and requests the help of the audience:

> Now 'tis true,
> I must be here confin'd by you,
> Or sent to Naples. Let me not,
> Since I have my Dukedom got,
> And pardon'd the deceiver, dwell
> In this bare island by your spell,
> But release me from my bands
> With the help of your good hands.
>
> (3–10)

Prospero represents himself here as trapped on "this bare island" through the "spell" of the audience, only able to escape through their applause. The applause of the audience now supplies the ethereal "breath," "spirits," "mercy," and "indulgence" that he attributed to Ariel, Miranda, and Gonzalo during the play. The epilogue makes another connection for us, however, identifying "this bare island" as representing also the stage. For in this passage, which, as epilogues often do, partially breaks the illusionary frame to allow an actor to speak half in and half out of character, Prospero appears as both the fictional magician of the play and also as an actor trapped onstage until the audience allows him to leave.

Both Keith Sturgess and Douglas Bruster have argued persuasively that *The Tempest* was written for performance at Blackfriars, the smaller indoor theater that James Burbage had acquired in 1596 but had been prevented from using as a second venue for the Chamberlain's Men by a petition of neighborhood residents.[36] The space was leased to the Children of the Chapel, who were allowed to perform there, until 1608, when a change in governance of the Liberties made it possible for the King's Men to buy back the lease and perform there themselves. By 1610 Shakespeare's company seems regularly to have divided the theatrical year into a summer season at the Globe and a winter season at Blackfriars.[37] Although the repertory seems to have been largely the same at the two houses, the smaller and more expensive Blackfriars would have encouraged the lavish use of music and sound effects that we see in *The Tempest*. Sturgess suggests that Shakespeare responded to the new opportunities and challenges afforded by the more intimate theatrical space with "an experiment in metatheatre," a play that "explores the baffling territory marked out by 'magic,' 'illusion,' and 'trick,' " words that, along with "quaint" and "strange," he sees as central to the play.[38]

If *The Comedy of Errors*, written near the beginning of Shakespeare's career, explored the spatial dynamics of representing domestic scenes and the new kind of characters needed for such scenes on the large, open, outdoor theater stage, *The Tempest*, written near the end of his career, similarly explores the new spatiality of the smaller Blackfriars stage. If characters in *The Comedy of Errors* felt dangerously unbounded and porous, characters in *The Tempest*, as we have seen, feel almost claustrophobic—on the island, in their bodies, and, as I shall argue, on the stage of Blackfriars. Certainly the dimensions might well make it seem cramped compared with the Globe. Where the Globe could seat probably close to three thousand spectators with a ground area of (probably) about 8,000 square feet and a stage (if it was similar in size to that of the Fortune) of about 43 by 27 feet, Blackfriars held probably between five hundred and a thousand spectators, with a total ground area of only 3,036 square feet and a stage of about 30 by 23 feet, with playing space further reduced by the presence of audience members sitting onstage.[39]

Although contemporary accounts praise private theaters like Blackfriars for freedom from the bad smells that came with the more plebian
public theater audience, the experience of playing in Blackfriars would
still have seemed much more crowded and potentially claustrophobic.[40]
The "bare island" stage from which Prospero asks to be freed in the epilogue would have seemed as "pinched" and cramped as the fictional island portrayed on it. The smaller stage, doubly hemmed in by spectators
(since there were probably galleries on both sides, as well as spectators
on the stage itself), the theater itself completely indoors rather than partly
open, probably lighted artificially—for all of these reasons the experience
and effect of playing would have been quite different. As Bruster suggests,
if the first scene of the play "is about a ship at sea, it is also about working
in a crowded playhouse."[41]

Most theater historians agree that Blackfriars did not rely on the elaborate scenery and special effects that were used for masques at court but,
like the Globe, with which it shared a significant repertory, used properties carried on by the characters, elaborate costumes, and verbal description to create scenic effects. Sturgess speculates that sounds would have
been more prominent and impressive in the enclosed space, and this
might explain the emphasis given to sound effects and music in *The Tempest*; indeed, he argues that "the scenery of the first scene is in fact largely
acoustical."[42] Bruce Smith concludes that "Blackfriars presented an altogether different acoustic environment" than that of the Globe and argues
that the use of consort music there situated "the audience within a wider,
more fully articulated field of sound than in the outdoor ampitheaters."[43]
I want to suggest that the thematic interests of the play in the contrast
between "pinching" confinement within a limiting and mortal material
world and various attempts to master or transcend that state are also
extended to issues related to its staging, most specifically in a contrast
between the cramped Blackfriars stage space and the possibilities for
extending it through language and sound. Here, as in other plays, Shakespeare treats the spatial issues of representing places and characters onstage in relation to the spatialities of human subjects within their environment. It is in the context of thinking about transcending the material
limitations of the stage that the difficulties of such a project become most
apparent.

Like *The Comedy of Errors*, *The Tempest* raises these issues in part
through a scene that appears to be stageable only with difficulty as written. The initial tempest illustrates not only a virtuoso ability to conjure
up impressive scenic effects verbally and aurally but also the limits of
doing so. That this tempest famously conflates Prospero's magic with the
resources of the stage makes clear the connection between Prospero's and

the playwright's attempts to use the discursive to control or transcend the material.[44] Sturgess has argued that an initial staging at Blackfriars probably led the audience to "believe in" the tempest as an actual storm and to accept its verisimilitude before suddenly learning, at the opening of act 1, scene 2, that it is an illusion caused by Prospero. He emphasizes the importance of the initial stage direction, "A tempestuous noise of thunder and lightening heard," as well as other, similar directions that work to create the storm, such as "A cry within" and "A confused noise within." Significantly, the direction "Enter Mariners wet" seems to be the only visual effect of the storm called for in the text. Sturgess further stresses the use of "nautically technical" language by the mariners to establish "ship, storm, nearness of land and imminence of shipwreck."[45] The storm, then, depends largely on a combination of dialogue and sound effect, so that the materiality of the play is, from the first scene, established by immaterial effects of sound.

However, other critics have argued that dialogue and sound do not seem to work together so seamlessly to create the storm. Roger Warren begins his essay on the play by noting that "the first of *The Tempest*'s many problems begins with the opening stage direction in the First Folio text: '*A tempestuous noise of thunder and lightening is heard.*' This has usually been taken as a cue for a great deal of noise from the very start, which may give a general impression of a storm at sea but which tends to obliterate the dialogue."[46] Taking a common approach to problematic moments in the plays, Warren argues that the stage direction in question was not written by Shakespeare but represents an addition by Ralph Crane and that the impression of "noisy chaos" that it conveys would prevent the audience from hearing the thematically crucial dialogue between the Boatswain and the nobles. Warren prefers instead a version of the scene staged by Peter Hall, which took "a more formalized approach," representing the sound effects as "more surrealistic," "stylized," creating a storm that is clearly an illusion (153).

In contrast, Sturgess describes the means by which the realistic sound effects of the storm would have caused an "assault upon the sense of the audience." Thunder would have been created by rolling cannonballs in a thunder run or by drums; and further sound effects might have come from a "sea machine (small pebbles revolved in a drum) and a wind machine (a loose length of canvas turned on a wheel)."[47] Given the presence throughout the play of stage directions calling for loud and discordant noises—"A noise of thunder heard" (2.2); "Thunder and lightening," "He vanishes in thunder" (3.3); "a strange, hollow, and confused noise" (4.1), and so on—Sturgess's sense that loud effects were necessary to create the storm seems right. On the other hand, rolling cannonballs, tumbling pebbles, and flapping canvas would have created quite a noise in the enclosed space of Blackfriars, so Warren's statement that the important dialogue of the first scene would have become at least partially inaudible to the audience seems correct, and subsequent productions have tended to bear this out. One might imagine a careful orchestration of these effects in which the sound level would rise and fall in relation to the dialogue, but it seems clear that sound and speech are not natural allies in this scene. Shakespeare has perhaps sacrificed the intelligibility of the dialogue for an experiment in sound effect and theatrical illusion, as he did in *Comedy of Errors*, where dialogue was also possibly sacrificed to an experiment in staging an enclosed domestic scene.

The dialogue in this scene, as many critics have noted, introduces a discussion of usurpation and control that is central to the play's imbrication in discourses of colonialism, treason, and political power. But if this dialogue is even partly obscured by the noise of the storm, the energies of sound do not seem to be so easily harnessed to the discursive reproduction of power relations. If Prospero's artificial storm is usually read as a revelation that "the natural" is discursively produced and employed in the service of power, the clash between sound effect and dialogue hints that this production—at least in the theater—is not seamless.

It seems clear that the loud version of this first scene would have opened the play with a shocking effect. The elite Blackfriars audience, some of them sitting on the stage itself, would find itself suddenly in the middle of a violent storm at sea, assaulted by loud noises, shouting, and confusion. If we remember that sound involves a direct (rather than reflected) perception of energy and that it is the means through which we assess the forcefulness or the energy of events, the bombardment of loud sounds at the beginning of the play seems to have been designed literally to extend the energies of the play beyond the stage. Shakespeare seems to have stretched the capacities of the small Blackfriars stage with sound effects, pushing out into the audience that hems in the action of the play. Douglas Bruster has argued that as the sailors scurry around and the Boatswain berates the nobles for getting in the way—"you mar our labor"—those sitting on the stage may have felt themselves to be also in the way.[48] However, a storm created entirely out of sound effects can vanish into nothingness in an instant, as this one does when Prospero decides to end it.

Albert Bregman has identified another property that differentiates the "ecology" of sound from that of vision: "auditory events are transparent" and therefore, unlike seen objects, "do not occlude energy from what lies behind them."[49] This transparency gives sound, despite its more direct transmission of energy, an appearance at least of being less material or substantial. While visual perception, like hearing, depends on reception and discrimination of differing frequencies of waves, vision conveys the solidity of the objects off of which light waves are reflected. Hearing, on the other hand, registers sound waves, which are invisible and do not convey the shape or solidity of objects that emit them. Sound, then, seems to be less imbued in the material world than visual or tactile signals; in Bregman's formulation, it consists more purely of energy rather than of energy in concert with matter.

This is why sound is imagined in the play, at times at least, as a way of transcending the limitations of the material world. Elaine Scarry has suggested that it is "through his ability to project words and sounds out into his environment [that] a human being inhabits, humanizes, and makes his own a space much larger than that occupied by his body alone. This space, always contracted under repressive regimes, is in torture almost wholly eliminated."[50] Sturgess has suggested that "music expresses both the functioning and effect of Prospero's magic" but I argue that it is manifested also in thunder, confused noises, and, at least hypothetically, in the various animal howls and roars that he believes it can cause.[51] At the end of the play, when Prospero gives up his magic, he must first make sure that he has called for music to carry out his last magical act:

> when I have requir'd
> Some heavenly music (which even now I do)
> To work mine end upon their senses that
> This airy charm is for, I'll break my staff,
>
> (5.1.51–54)

Music, in its insubstantiality, is the invisible substance of an "airy charm," and yet it is also carefully measured and controlled. Ariel, of course, is constantly associated with music, both sung and performed on tabor and pipe. His songs, indeed, are imagined as having the power to transform the "oozy" mud of mortality "into something rich and strange," as when he sings a song that describes a death by drowning in quite different terms than Alonso does:

> Full fadom five thy father lies,
>   Of his bones are coral made:
> Those are pearls that were his eyes.
>
> (1.2.397–99)

Paradoxically, though, unlike Alonso's own despair at Ferdinand's muddy death "deeper than did ever plummet sound," Ariel imagines a transcendence of decay that is nevertheless precisely measured: "Full fadom five." Both Ariel and Prospero realize, in different ways, that the various means of transcending the material with which they experiment are limited.[52] Although noise is technically sound that does not have a regular wave pattern, most instrumental sounds—both music and speech—must be constrained by ordered patterns. Although in *The Merchant of Venice* Lorenzo believes that our material bodies, or "muddy vesture of decay," prevent us from hearing transcendent music, that does not seem to be the case in *The Tempest*, where even Caliban can hear magical "sounds and sweet airs, that give delight and hurt not." Although Prospero (through Ariel) is to some extent able to use music to extend his control over others, he is himself subject to the constraints of melody and harmony. Perhaps, then, his fantasies about cries of pain and animal howls represent a yearning for sound that is unconstrained, pure energy. Such cries and animal vocalizations, or "visceral sounds," recent brain research indicates, are sharply different from controlled sounds such as speech and music in that they are involuntary, innate, and reflexive.[53] Such sounds have only limited instrumentality, however, since they cannot be controlled or produced at will. Prospero's bind is that sounds that have the power to extend his control beyond his own body involve limit and constraint, while unlimited sounds are unpredictable and uncontrollable.

The very immateriality of sound can also be a barrier to its use as a technology of control or expansion since it can seem dangerously insubstantial and evanescent. An island landscape created solely by descriptive dialogue does not really exist, or rather it exists in such contradictory multiplicity that it seems hard to get a fix on; hence, for example, critics' sense that it is somehow located in both the Mediterranean and the Caribbean. Prospero's famous speech at the end of his masque emphasizes the immateriality and impermanence of dramatic productions:

> These our actors
> (As I foretold you) were all spirits, and
> Are melted into air, into thin air,
> And like the baseless fabric of this vision,
> The cloud-capp'd tow'rs, the gorgeous palaces,
> The solemn temples, the great globe itself,
> Yea, all which it inherit, shall dissolve,
> And like this insubstantial pageant faded
> Leave not a rack behind. We are such stuff
> As dreams are made on; and our little life
> Is rounded with a sleep.
>
> (4.1.148–58)

Prospero here acknowledges, as he also does in the epilogue, that if a playwright uses sound and language to extend the limits of the stage, the imaginary world thus created is, like the island, as "baseless" and "insubstantial" as the spoken word itself. Significantly, this immaterial vision vanishes, leaving "not a rack behind." Although *rack* here probably means "cloud," we must also necessarily recall Curt Breight's argu-

ment that the play's pinches allude to the torturer's rack. Breight has suggested that Prospero's torture through invisible or psychological pinches
represents an "effacement of power relations through euphemization" by
translating real, material torture into a more powerful and unconstrained,
though seemingly less threatening, immaterial force.[54] Although the play
does show that discursively based psychological torments can have a powerful effect, it also reveals the inconsistencies and limitations inherent in
an attempt to use language to control the physical world.

In his attempts to find ways of extending control through space and
over his material environment and the people in it, Prospero finds himself
caught up in several different paradoxes. If sound seems able to extend
or transcend the limitations of material space, it nevertheless seems less
lasting than matter. The material world too is finally impermanent, and
it can at times be both defiling and confining. Prospero seems to imagine
a choice between the mortal, material world—"mudded in that oozy
bed"—and a sonic or spiritual extension of it that leaves "not a rack
behind." Shakespeare, in a way, faces the same set of problems as a playwright, for when the character Prospero is freed by the sound of the audience's applause, that freedom consists in his dissolution. However, if the
play seems to be forcing a choice between the earthy Caliban and the airy
Ariel, it is also true that it has shown that Caliban can hear spiritual music
and that Ariel can be trapped in a pine—suggesting, perhaps, that we
must make the best of our imperfect intermeshing of body and mind.

I am arguing, then, that Prospero's problem is exactly the problem of
the embodied mind. Terence Deacon has put it this way:

> We live in a world that is both entirely physical and virtual at the same time.
> Remarkably, this virtual facet of the world came into existence relatively re-
> cently, as evolutionary time is measured, and it has provided human selves with
> an unprecedented sort of autonomy or freedom to wander from the constraints
> of concrete reference, and a unique power for self-determination that derives
> from this increasingly indirect linkage between . . . mind and body, as well. So
> this provides a somewhat different perspective on that curious human intuition
> that our minds are somehow independent of our bodies. . . . The experience we
> have of ourselves as symbols is in at least a minimal sense an experience of
> this sort of virtual independence—it's just not an independence from corporeal
> embodiment altogether.[55]

Because of their capability for symbolic thought, human beings are able
to imagine that they can extend the limits of, or be free from, their bodies.
But they can also imagine the cessation of their own being. They can use
language to gain power over other people, and they can even gain some
limited power over the environment. But the state of embodiment remains
a fact against which symbolic discourse has only limited power.

This power is limited in part by the fact that kinesthetic and spatial experiences of living in a body are, as we have seen, themselves fundamental to the thought processes that might seem to transcend them. Thus, Prospero's discursive mastery of the material environment is only partially effective because his discourse itself shows traces of its dependence on space. Stephen Greenblatt's reading of linguistic imperialism in *The Tempest* argues that early modern colonialist discourses were able to categorize and dismiss native cultures with such ruthless efficiency because of a "fundamental inability to sustain the simultaneous perception of likeness and difference, the very special perception we give to metaphor." Shakespeare, he suggests, presents Caliban's simultaneous similarity to and difference from the Europeans in the play "as if he were testing our capacity to sustain metaphor."[56] Greenblatt seems to return us to Russ MacDonald's argument that the difficulties of the play are designed intentionally to test or exercise the cognitive capabilities of the audience. However, it is also possible to see its insistence on the metaphorical basis of discourse as simply reflecting, in unusually bold relief, the spatial structures that underlie our understanding of ourselves and our place in the world. Shakespeare's language in this play thus reveals the limitations of official discourses that gain their power by denying their metaphoricity, their implication in complex networks of image and feeling, their kinship with inarticulate sounds and cries.

Prospero's—and here I also want to say Shakespeare's—idiosyncratic linking of *pinch*, *pitch*, *pine*, and *pen*, in expressing an imagined relation to the landscape of the island, reflects subterranean cognitive structuring principles. The words delineate for us a way of thinking about space that is itself structured by sound and by spatial concepts derived from experiences of containment and invasion. The weird collocation of these words suggests that however we try to turn our concepts of space into "places," mental categories with firm boundaries and clear internal logic, a preconceptual spatial sense works to complicate and undermine our rationality. *The Tempest*, then, shows us that the relationship between places and systems of knowledge is complex and reciprocal and that although human discursive paradigms (such as colonialism) are indeed powerful, they are necessarily and imperfectly composed of the very environmental and cognitive structures that they attempt to harness and control.

Notes

Introduction
Shakespeare's Brain: Embodying the Author-Function

1. Michel Foucault, "What Is an Author?" in *Language, Counter-Memory, Practice: Selected Essays and Interviews by Michel Foucault*, ed. Donald F. Bouchard (Ithaca: Cornell University Press, 1977), 113.

2. G. Wilson Knight, "On the Principles of Shakespeare Interpretation," from *The Wheel of Fire*, as excerpted in *Modern Shakespearean Criticism: Essays on Style, Dramaturgy, and the Major Plays*, ed. Alvin B. Kernan (New York: Harcourt, 1970), 5.

3. A full bibliography of psychoanalytic criticism of Shakespeare is clearly beyond the scope of a single note. A very basic list might include C. L. Barber and Richard P. Wheeler, *The Whole Journey: Shakespeare's Power of Development* (Berkeley and Los Angeles: University of California Press, 1986); Meredith Anne Skura, *Shakespeare the Actor and the Purposes of Playing* (Chicago: University of Chicago Press, 1993); Janet Adelman, *Suffocating Mothers: Fantasies of Maternal Origin in Shakespeare's Plays, Hamlet to The Tempest* (New York: Routledge, 1992); Norman Holland, *Psychoanalysis and Shakespeare* (New York: McGraw-Hill, 1966); and Murray Schwartz and Coppélia Kahn, eds., *Representing Shakespeare: New Psychoanalytic Essays* (Baltimore: Johns Hopkins University Press, 1980).

4. As George Lakoff puts it, "Because concepts and reason both derive from, and make use of, the sensorimotor system, the mind is not separate from or independent of the body" (George Lakoff and Mark Johnson, *Philosophy in the Flesh: The Embodied Mind and Its Challenge to Western Thought* [New York: Basic Books, 1999], 555).

5. It would not be possible to acknowledge all of those working to apply cognitive approaches to literature. Ellen Spolsky and F. Elizabeth Hart have done important work on the relevance of cognitive science for reading Shakespeare. Spolsky offers a chapter on *Hamlet* in *Gaps in Nature: Literary Interpretation and the Modular Mind* (Albany: State University of New York Press, 1993) and more extended treatment of *Coriolanus* and *Othello* in *Satisfying Skepticism: The Evolved Mind in the Early Modern World* (forthcoming). Hart offers groundbreaking theoretical work as well as readings of Shakespeare in "Cognitive Linguistics: The Experiential Dynamics of Metaphor," *Mosaic* 28 (1995): 645–58, and "Matter, System, and Early Modern Studies: Outlines for a Materialist Linguistics," *Configurations* 6 (1998): 311–43. Bruce Smith's largely phenomenological approach to the materiality of sound in *The Acoustic World of Early Modern England: Attending to the O-Factor* (Chicago: University of Chicago Press, 1999) has much in common with the cognitive theories that I use here and calls on some

of the same sources. See also the important work of Reuven Tsur, esp. *Toward a Theory of Cognitive Poetics* (Amsterdam: North-Holland, 1992); Norman Holland, *The Brain of Robert Frost* (New York: Routledge, 1988); David C. Rubin, *Memory in Oral Traditions: The Cognitive Psychology of Epic, Ballads, and Counting-out Rhymes* (New York: Oxford University Press, 1995); David Herman, "Scripts, Sequences, and Stories: Elements of a Postclassical Narratology," *PMLA* 112 (1997): 1046–59; and essays by William Benzon on Shakespeare's sonnets, "Cognitive Networks and Literary Semantics," *MLN* 91 (1976): 952–82, and "Lust in Action: An Abstraction," *Language and Style* 14 (1981): 251–70. For work applying Lakoffian theories of metaphor to literary texts, see the series of extremely important books by Mark Turner, including *Death Is the Mother of Beauty: Mind, Metaphor, Criticism* (Chicago: University of Chicago Press, 1987), *Reading Minds: The Study of English in the Age of Cognitive Science* (Princeton: Princeton University Press, 1991), and *The Literary Mind* (New York: Oxford University Press, 1996); see also Donald Freeman, " 'According to My Bond': *King Lear* and Re-Cognition," *Language and Literature* 2 (1993): 1–18. For summaries and analysis of many of the works listed here, see Mary Thomas Crane and Alan Richardson, "Literary Studies and Cognitive Science: Toward a New Interdisciplinarity," *Mosaic* 32 (1999): 124–40.

6. Hart, "Matter, System, and Early Modern Studies." David Scott Kastan, *Shakespeare after Theory* (New York: Routledge, 1999), 30–31, makes the similar point that New Historicist methods "are not properly historical at all but rather formalist practices, discovering pattern and order, unity and coherence, in the culture (which is revealingly imagined and engaged as a 'text,' even if a 'social text') exactly as an earlier generation of formalist critics found them in works of literature."

7. Graham Holderness, "Bardolotry: or, The Cultural Materialist's Guide to Stratford-upon-Avon," in *The Shakespeare Myth*, ed. Graham Holderness (Manchester: Manchester University Press, 1988), 13. Holderness does list writers as part of "a collaborative cultural process" also involving "theatrical entrepreneurs, architects and craftsmen, actors and audience," but his emphasis is on the ways in which "the concept of individual authorship" is "misleading."

8. Margreta de Grazia and Peter Stallybrass, "The Materiality of the Shakespearean Text," *Shakespeare Quarterly* 44 (1993): 257. For similar views on the collaborative nature of drama in this period, see Stephen Orgel, "What Is a Text?" in *Staging the Renaissance*, ed. David Kastan and Peter Stallybrass (New York: Routledge, 1991): 83–87; and Jeffrey Masten, "Beaumont and/or Fletcher: Collaboration and the Interpretation of English Renaissance Drama," *ELH* 59 (1992): 337–56.

9. De Grazia and Stallybrass, "Materiality of the Shakespearean Text," 283. Masten seems to recognize and make explicit the pattern of both beginning and ending with Foucault's essay. He begins with the quotation from Foucault, "What does it matter who is speaking," and ends with a minor revision of the same line: "What, or rather how, does it matter who are speaking." (337, 352).

10. David Willbern, "What Is Shakespeare?" in *Shakespeare's Personality*, ed. Norman N. Holland, Sidney Homan, and Bernard J. Paris (Berkeley and Los Angeles: University of California Press, 1989), 229, interestingly associates the

Foucauldian author-function with the ghost in *Hamlet*, where "the principle of authorship thus displayed posits a ghostly and questionable narrator who is backed by a substantial and identifiable actor who authors his own player's speech."

11. As Paul Smith has noted, "Any ideology must lodge itself in the subject/individual in order to function as ideology" (*Discerning the Subject* [Minneapolis: University of Minnesota Press, 1988], 29).

12. Stephen Greenblatt, *Shakespearean Negotiations* (Berkeley and Los Angeles: University of California Press, 1988), 2.

13. For a hostile (and reductive) reading of the attribution of agency to the text rather than to the author in materialist criticism, see Richard Levin, "The Poetics and Politics of Bardicide," *PMLA* 105 (1990): 491–504.

14. Francis Barker, *The Tremulous Private Body: Essays in Subjection* (London: Methuen, 1984), 63.

15. Jonathan Sawday, *The Body Emblazoned: Dissection and the Human Body in Renaissance Culture* (New York: Routledge, 1995), 4.

16. Gail Kern Paster, *The Body Embarrassed: Drama and the Disciplines of Shame in Early Modern England* (Ithaca: Cornell University Press, 1993), 5–6.

17. In new work focused primarily on early modern theories of the nervous system Gail Kern Paster has begun to explore the implications of minds contained in bodies "*epistemically* though not *biologically* different from our own" ("Nervous Tension: Networks of Blood and Spirit in the Early Modern Body," in *The Body in Parts: Fantasies of Corporeality in Early Modern Europe*, ed. David Hillman and Carla Mazzio [New York: Routledge, 1997], 122, Paster's emphasis).

18. Judith Butler, *The Psychic Life of Power: Theories in Subjection* (Stanford: Stanford University Press, 1997), 2.

19. Hart, "Matter, System, and Early Modern Studies," traces this gap back through Derrida to Saussure and his "decision to isolate language from the very psychology that he himself admits must undergird it" (8–9). Paul Smith makes a similar claim about Marxist criticism in general, arguing that "orthodox Marxist theories about the hold that ideology seems to have over 'subjects' by and large neglect to specify the actual locus of that hold" and concluding that "the point of interaction between ideological pressures and subjective existence is still a relatively mysterious one in Marxist thinking" (Smith, *Discerning the Subject*, xxx).

20. Scott Manning Stevens, "Sacred Heart and Secular Brain," in Hillman and Mazzio, *Body in Parts*, 278.

21. Terence W. Deacon, *The Symbolic Species: The Co-evolution of Language and the Brain* (New York: Norton, 1997), 111.

22. On the culturally produced nature of symbolic systems, see ibid., 433–54. For a detailed discussion of the role of physical constraint in the evolution of linguistic universals, see 117–42.

23. See N. Katherine Hayles, "The Materiality of Informatics," *Configurations* 1 (1992): 153, where she attributes this conclusion to Scarry. See also Elaine Scarry, *The Body in Pain: The Making and Unmaking of the World* (Oxford: Oxford University Press, 1985).

24. Wilma Bucci, *Psychoanalysis and Cognitive Science: A Multiple Code Theory* (New York: Guilford, 1997), 143–47. Bucci is here relying on work by Ste-

phen Kosslyn, esp. "Seeing and Imagining in the Cerebral Hemispheres: A Computational Approach," *Psychological Review* 94 (1987): 148–75; Jean Mandler, "How to Build a Baby: II Conceptual Primitives," ibid. 99 (1992): 587–604; Lev Vygotsky, *Thought and Language* (Cambridge: MIT Press, 1986); Mark Johnson, *The Body in the Mind: The Bodily Basis of Meaning, Imagination, and Reasoning* (Chicago: University of Chicago Press, 1987); George Lakoff, *Women, Fire, and Dangerous Things: What Categories Reveal about the Mind* (Chicago: University of Chicago Press, 1987); and Ronald W. Langacker, *Foundations of Cognitive Grammar*, 2 vols. (Stanford: Stanford University Press, 1987–91), vol. 1, *Theoretical Prerequisites*.

25. R. N. Shepard and Jacqueline Metzler, "Mental Rotation of Three-Dimensional Objects," *Science* 171 (1971): 701–3. They measured the amount of time it took for subjects to solve the problem and concluded that "reaction time is a strikingly linear function of the angular difference between the two three-dimensional objects portrayed" (703).

26. Mandler, "How to Build a Baby," 591–92.

27. Gerald Edelman, *Bright Air, Brilliant Fire: On the Matter of the Mind* (New York: Basic Books, 1992), 94–101, 245–46.

28. Mandler, "How to Build a Baby," 598.

29. Lakoff, *Women, Fire, and Dangerous Things*, xiv–xv.

30. Turner, *Death Is the Mother of Beauty*, 12.

31. Antonio Damasio, *Descartes' Error: Emotion, Reason, and the Human Brain* (New York: Avon, 1994).

32. David Silverman and Brian Torode, *The Material Word: Some Theories of Language and Its Limits* (London: Routledge & Kegan Paul, 1980), 3–4.

33. As noted above, a number of critics have begun to explore the implications of cognitive science for literary study; indeed, it would be impossible to acknowledge all of them in a note. For summaries and assessments of some of the most important contributions to this field, see Crane and Richardson, "Literary Studies and Cognitive Science," esp. 132–37.

34. Stephen Kosslyn and Oliver Koenig, *Wet Mind: The New Cognitive Neuroscience* (New York: Free Press, 1992), 4.

35. See Leslie Brothers, *Friday's Footprint: How Society Shapes the Human Mind* (New York: Oxford University Press, 1997), 56–65.

36. N. Katherine Hayles, "Constrained Constructivism: Locating Scientific Inquiry in the Theater of Representation," in *Realism and Representation: Essays on the Problem of Realism in Relation to Science, Literature, and Culture*, ed. George Levine (Madison: University of Wisconsin Press, 1993), suggests that while scientific research is unavoidably constructed by cultural factors, its outcomes are nevertheless constrained by physical reality: "Consider how conceptions of gravity have changed over the last three hundred years. In the Newtonian paradigm, gravity is conceived very differently than in the general theory of relativity. . . . No matter how gravity is conceived, no viable model could predict that when someone steps off a cliff on earth, she will remain suspended in midair. This possibility is ruled out by the nature of physical reality. Although the constraints that lead to this result are interpreted differently in different paradigms, they oper-

ate universally to eliminate certain configurations from the range of possible answers" (33).

37. For an account of recent developments in cognitive science and artificial intelligence, including these two different approaches, see Howard Gardner, *The Mind's New Science: A History of the Cognitive Revolution*, rev. ed. (New York: Basic Books, 1987); and Daniel Crevier, *AI: The Tumultuous History of the Search for Artificial Intelligence* (New York: Basic Books, 1993). For the first view, see Kosslyn and Koenig, *Wet Mind*; and Steven Pinker, *The Language Instinct* (New York: Harper, 1994), and the works of many theorists of artificial intelligence (although some are now searching for more complex computer models for mental function). For a critique of the first view and articulation of the second, see Edelman, *Bright Air, Brilliant Fire*.

38. Francisco J. Varela, Evan Thompson, and Eleanor Rosch, *The Embodied Mind: Cognitive Science and Human Experience* (Cambridge: MIT Press, 1993), 6–7, distinguish three approaches: "cognitivism," which is based on the analogy with digital computers, and "emergence" and "enactive," which include "fuzzier," semantic-based theories. See Hart, "Matter, System, and Early Modern Studies," 16–21, for a more explicit discussion of the critique of Chomskian approaches to language from a semantic perspective. Hart follows more recent usage in designating Chomskian approaches as "generative" and semantic or metaphoric approaches as "cognitive."

39. See P. N. Johnson-Laird, "Mental Models," in *The Foundations of Cognitive Science*, ed. Michael Posner (Cambridge: MIT Press, 1989), 470–73. Kosslyn and Koenig, *Wet Mind*, 128–66, discusses in detail the relationship between "visual cognition" and actual visual perception, as well as the role of visual cognition in language, memory, and reasoning.

40. For the basis in Saussurean semiotics of such postmodern theorists as Lacan, Barthes, Derrida, Foucault, and Althusser, see Jonathan Culler, *The Pursuit of Signs: Theory and Criticism after Structuralism* (Ithaca: Cornell University Press, 1981); and Kaja Silverman, *The Subject of Semiotics* (New York: Oxford University Press, 1983). For a powerful critique of Saussure's lingering formalism and its influence on Derrida and other poststructuralist theorists, see Hart, "Matter, System, and Early Modern Studies," 2–16.

41. John R. Taylor, *Linguistic Categorization: Prototypes in Linguistic Theory*, 2nd ed. (Oxford: Clarendon, 1995), 6.

42. Ibid., 6–7.

43. Hart, "Matter, System, and Early Modern Studies," 6.

44. Taylor, *Linguistic Categorization*, 141.

45. Brent Berlin and Paul Kay, *Basic Color Terms: Their Universality and Evolution* (Berkeley: University of California Press, 1969).

46. Taylor, *Linguistic Categorization*, 9.

47. Kosslyn and Koenig, *Wet Mind*, 47–48.

48. Deacon, *Symbolic Species*, 117–21. His point here is that "the universality of color term reference is an expression of shared neurological biases, but—and this is the crucial point—the translation of this biological constraint into a social universal is brought about through the action of *nongenetic* evolutionary forces" (119–20).

49. Eleanor Rosch first demonstrated the existence of prototypes (see her "Principles of Categorization," in *Cognition and Categorization*, ed. Eleanor Rosch and B. B. Lloyd [Hillsdale, N.J.: Erlbaum, 1978]). For brief accounts of Rosch's work and later corroborating research, see Roy G. D'Andrade, "Cultural Cognition," and Edward Smith, "Concepts and Induction," in Posner, *Foundations of Cognitive Science*, 802–3 and 501–26, respectively; and Kosslyn and Koenig, *Wet Mind*, 366–70.

50. Ludwig Wittgenstein, *Philosophical Investigations*, trans. G.E.M. Anscombe (Oxford: Blackwell, 1978), perhaps first questioned the current logical interpretation of categorization, without, however, suggesting a cognitivist alternative; see Taylor, *Linguistic Categorization*, 38–39, for Wittgenstein's relation to cognitive theory.

51. For the theory of mental spaces, see Gilles Fauconnier, *Mental Spaces: Aspects of Meaning Construction in Natural Language* (1985; reprint, Cambridge: Cambridge University Press, 1994). For scripts, see Roger Schank and R. P. Abelson, *Scripts, Plans, Goals, and Understanding: An Inquiry into Human Knowledge Structures* (Hillsdale, N.J.: Erlbaum, 1977).

52. Lacan again anticipates elements of cognitive theory in recognizing the centrality of metaphor and metonymy to signification (see Jacques Lacan, "The Agency of the Letter in the Unconscious," in *Ecrits: A Selection*, trans. Alan Sheridan [New York: Norton, 1977], 166–67); his reliance on metaphor and metonymy alone is overly schematic and probably reflects the influence of Roman Jakobson's structuralist linguist theory.

53. Taylor, *Linguistic Categorization*, 81–141.

54. Eve Sweetser, "Mental Spaces and the Grammar of Conditional Constructions," in *Spaces, Worlds, and Grammar*, ed. Gilles Fauconnier and Eve Sweetser (Chicago: University of Chicago Press, 1996). For pioneering work on the motivation of grammar by cognitive structures, see Langacker, *Foundations of Cognitive Grammar*, vols. 1 and 2, *Descriptive Application*.

55. Spolsky, *Satisfaction*, ms. p. 28.

56. See Judith Anderson, "Translating Investments: The Metaphoricity of Language, 2 *Henry IV*, and *Hamlet*," *Texas Studies in Literature and Language* 40 (1998): 236; and idem, *Words That Matter: Linguistic Perception in Renaissance England* (Stanford: Stanford University Press, 1996). Her reading in the essay (242–53) of Shakespeare's complex and metaphorically packed use of the word *investment* is similar in many ways to the kinds of reading that I attempt here.

57. Anderson, "Translating Investments," 232.

58. Michel Foucault, *The Order of Things: An Archaeology of the Human Sciences* (New York: Vintage, 1973), 55.

59. F. Elizabeth Hart has suggested the same of Derrida.

60. See Lakoff and Johnson, *Philosophy in the Flesh*, esp. 404–9, for the origins of Cartesian rationalism and a critique of it.

61. See Kosslyn and Koenig, *Wet Mind*, 13–14, for parts of the brain.

62. Pinker, *Language Instinct*, 307–13, summarizes evidence associating language with this area of the brain. Kosslyn and Koenig, in *Wet Mind*, 266, provide a more cautious account of cerebral localization of language but do summarize a study conducted by C. W. Wallesch, L. Henriksen, H. H. Kornhuber, and O. B.

Paulson in 1985 measuring "regional cerebral blood flow while subjects performed a variety of tasks, some of which engaged the mechanisms underlying
speech production," which seemed similarly to locate some of these functions
in the "left frontal and left anterior thalamic/pallidal regions" (Wallesch et al.,
"Observations on Regional Cerebral Blood Flow in Cortical and Subcortical
Structures during Language Production in Normal Men," *Brain and Language*
25 [1985]: 224–33).

63. Mark Turner and Gilles Fauconnier offer an important theory of "conceptual blending," in which new concepts are formed by combining already existing
ideas (see Turner, *Literary Mind*, 57–84; and Mark Turner and Gilles Fauconnier,
"Conceptual Integration and Formal Expression," *Journal of Metaphor and Symbolic Activity* 10, no. 3 [1995]: 183–204).

64. Jean Aitchison, *Words in the Mind: An Introduction to the Mental Lexicon*, 2nd ed. (Oxford: Blackwell, 1994), provides a helpful introduction to the
human word store and its organization.

65. Jacques Derrida, *Of Grammatology*, trans. Gayatri Chakravorty Spivak,
5th paperback ed. (Baltimore: Johns Hopkins University Press, 1982), 3–4, identifies science's distrust of natural language as the beginning of a dislocation within
logocentrism.

66. John Searle, *Minds, Brains, and Science* (Cambridge: Harvard University
Press, 1984), 14.

67. Antonio Damasio calls his book *Descartes' Error* because he attributes to
Descartes "the abyssal separation between body and mind" (249). David Hillman, "Visceral Knowledge: Shakespeare, Skepticism, and the Interior of the Early
Modern Body," in Hillman and Mazzio, *Body in Parts*, notes that "selfhood and
materiality, then, were ineluctably linked in the pre-Cartesian belief systems of
the period, which preceded, for the most part, any attempt to separate the vocabulary of medical and humoral physiology from that of individual psychology" (83).
See Hardin Craig's introduction to Timothy Bright, *A Treatise of Melancholie*
(New York: Columbia University Press, 1940), ix–xiv, for an account of tensions
in the period between Platonic and religious theories of the difference between
soul and body and Galenic materialism.

68. Hart, "Matter, System, and Early Modern Studies," has also suggested that
cognitive linguistics provides a more thoroughly materialist approach to language
than does Marxist theory, though from a slightly different perspective.

69. Johnson-Laird, "Mental Models," 471.

70. See Hart, "Matter, System, and Early Modern Studies," 313 n. 9, for more
careful and nuanced attention to the word *material* and its implications in Marxist, poststructuralist, and scientific discourse. She also argues, in slightly different
terms, that cognitive metaphorics can offer a more truly materialist theory of language.

71. Ibid., 342.

72. Michel Pecheux, *Language, Semantics, and Ideology* (New York: St. Martin's, 1975), 51.

73. Smith, *Discerning the Subject*, 22. Smith argues that psychoanalysis can
provide the theoretical basis for this clarification; however, cognitive theory pro-

vides another way of conceiving the "place where agency and structure are fused," the human brain.

74. From the perspective of computer models for mental function Marvin Minsky argues that "the reputation of self-awareness is not so well deserved, because our conscious thoughts reveal to us so little of what gives rise to them" (*The Society of Mind* [New York: Simon & Schuster, 1986], 56–57). Minsky later argues that consciousness is always of events in the recent past, not the present (151–52). Neuroscientific research seems to support the idea of a lag between events in the brain and consciousness of them (see Benjamin Libet et al., "Response of Human Somatosensory Cortex to Stimuli below Threshold for Conscious Sensation," *Science* 58 [1967]: 1597–1600).

75. Damasio, *Descartes' Error*, 240.

76. Bucci, *Psychoanalysis and Cognitive Science*, 2. She usefully summarizes Freud's changing theories about the structure of the mind, from his early "topographic" system, in which the mind is divided into conscious, preconscious, and unconscious "regions," and a later "structural" theory, with its division into id, ego, and superego (17–30).

77. Ibid., 173–77. These coding formats correspond to Mandler's stages of perceptual analysis, image schema, and language.

78. Lacan, "Agency of the Letter," 163. However, see Hart, "Matter, System, and Early Modern Studies," for the useful suggestion that "Lacan's turn late in his career to mathematics . . . suggests a life-long commitment to the principles of formalism," a shift that might "imply if not the direct influence of, then perhaps a response parallel to, Chomsky's own turn in the late 1950s and 60s toward the rationalist program of mathematical logic as a revolutionary new method of formulating linguistic analysis" (323 n. 31).

79. On the relationship between psychoanalysis and cognitive sciences, see Sherry Turkle, "Artificial Intelligence and Psychoanalysis," in *The Artificial Intelligence Debate: False Starts, Real Foundations*. ed. Stephen R. Graubard (Cambridge: MIT Press, 1988), 241–68. Turkle argues that object-relations theory offers a way to link these two approaches to the mind. Andrew W. Ellis, "On the Freudian Theory of Speech Errors," in *Errors in Linguistic Performance: Slips of the Tongue, Ear, Pen, and Hand*, ed. Victoria A. Fromkin (New York: Academic Press, 1980), 123–32, argues that while "the evidence for Freud's theory of speech errors is not strong," it is nevertheless compatible in some ways with cognitive theories of language production (129–30).

80. See Hart, "Matter, System, and Early Modern Studies," for a slightly different argument that cognitive science offers new ways to theorize "the ideological means by which the human subject is constructed and the limits to agency imposed on the subject through its interpellation by the cultural system" (312).

81. The Marxist/psychoanalytic definition is from Smith, *Discerning the Subject*, xxxv; Lakoff and Johnson define *subject* and *self* in *Philosophy in the Flesh*, 268.

82. Smith, *Discerning the Subject*, xxxv.

83. Mandler, "How to Build a Baby," 596.

84. Lars Engle, *Shakespearean Pragmatism: Market of His Time* (Chicago: University of Chicago Press, 1993), 61.

85. The philosopher Daniel Dennett has most persistently challenged the "homunculus" theory (see Daniel Dennett, *Consciousness Explained* [New York: Little, Brown, 1991]).

86. Minsky, *Society of Mind*, 50.

87. Kosslyn and Koenig, *Wet Mind*, lists division of labor, weak modularity (including functional relations among subsystems and localization in the brain), constraint satisfaction, coarse coding, concurrent processing, and opportunism as five principles of brain function. These all suggest ways in which neurons are able to work within networks, and networks within larger brain systems, to accomplish many complex tasks at the same time (without a single directing "intelligence").

88. Damasio, *Descartes' Error*, 238.

89. George Lakoff, "Sorry, I'm Not Myself Today: The Metaphor System for Conceptualizing the Self," in Fauconnier and Sweetser, *Spaces, Worlds, and Grammar*, 118.

90. Frederic Jameson, "Imaginary and Symbolic in Lacan: Marxism, Psychoanalytic Criticism, and the Problem of the Subject," in *Literature and Psychoanalysis: The Question of Reading: Otherwise*, ed. Shoshana Felman (Baltimore: Johns Hopkins University Press, 1982), 363–64.

91. On this evidence, see Pinker's summary of the work of Derek Bickerton on creolization in Hawaii and also among deaf children learning sign language (Pinker, *Language Instinct*, 32–39).

92. On various possible applications of the Silverstein hierarchy, see Paul W. Deane, *Grammar in Mind and Body: Explorations in Cognitive Syntax* (New York: Mouton, 1992), 200–222.

93. Transcript of an interview with a patient suffering from Broca's aphasia, cited in Aitchison, *Words in the Mind*, 107.

94. For a summary of this controversy in the field of cognitive psychology, for example, see Jeanette Altarriba, ed., *Culture and Cognition: A Cross-Cultural Approach to Cognitive Psychology* (New York: North-Holland, 1993), v–viii. Altarriba espouses what she calls a "universalist" position, which assumes both "commonality in experience" and the importance of cultural differences (vi).

95. The most notorious attempt to correlate intelligence and race is Richard J. Herrnstein and Charles Murray, *The Bell Curve: Intelligence and Class Structure in American Life* (New York: Free Press, 1994). For a strong restatement of Chomsky's position that language is innate, see Pinker, *Language Instinct*, 297–331. Pinker, interestingly and perhaps predictably, uses Shakespeare as an example of a genetic predisposition to use language effectively (330–31).

96. Taylor, *Linguistic Categorization*, 81–98, sketches out various accounts of the cultural domains, schemas, or scripts that have been posited as the mechanisms for establishing the meaning of linguistic forms.

97. Ibid., 11–12.

98. Pinker, *Language Instinct*, 428.

99. Hayles, "Materiality of Informatics," suggests that Lakoff insufficiently acknowledges the influence of the "specificities of physically diverse and differentially marked bodies" on the production of image schemas: "Just as the schemata would vary for different physiologies, so would they for the different experiences of embodiment created by historically positioned and culturally constructed bodies" (154). It seems possible that basic image schemas are relatively the same for all embodied minds but that they might carry quite different emotional valences depending on historical and cultural positioning.

100. Edelman, *Bright Air, Brilliant Fire*, 174.

101. Hart has argued the same in "Matter, System, and Early Modern Studies."

102. See G. L. Brook, *The Language of Shakespeare* (London: Andre Deutsch, 1976), 26–64, for a general description of Shakespearean word use. See also S. S. Hussey, *The Literary Language of Shakespeare* (New York: Longman, 1982), 37–60, on Shakespeare's vocabulary.

103. For a brief cognitive account of Shakespeare and the expanding early modern vocabulary, see Hart, "Matter, System, and Early Modern Studies," 333–43.

104. New Critical studies often discuss these repeated words and images. On the use of *honest* in *Othello*, see William Empson, *The Structure of Complex Words* (London: Chatto & Windus, 1951), 218–49; on *nature* in several Shakespearean plays, see C. S. Lewis, *Studies in Words*, 2nd ed. (Cambridge: Cambridge University Press, 1967), 43–74; on clothing and infants in *Macbeth*, see Cleanth Brooks, "The Naked Babe and the Cloak of Manliness," in *The Well-Wrought Urn* (New York: Harcourt, 1947).

105. Critics have previously tended to study Shakespeare's words and images separately. Cognitive theory, as we have seen, suggests that many concepts are based in metaphor and that, as a result, words cannot be strictly separated from images. The words on which I focus in this book are variously intertwined with metaphorical concepts and structures. See chapter 6 below for a longer discussion of different approaches to Shakespeare's use of imagery, including Caroline Spurgeon, *Shakespeare's Imagery and What It Tells Us* (1935; reprint, Cambridge: Cambridge University Press, 1971); Edward A. Armstrong, *Shakespeare's Imagination: A Study of the Psychology of Association and Inspiration*, rev. ed. (1963; reprint, Lincoln: University of Nebraska Press, 1982); Wolfgang H. Clemen, *The Development of Shakespeare's Imagery* (London: Methuen, 1951); and, for a psychoanalytic approach to selected image clusters, Skura, *Shakespeare the Actor*.

106. Eve Sweetser, *From Etymology to Pragmatics* (Cambridge: Cambridge University Press, 1990), 5.

107. Nancy G. Siraisi, *Medieval and Early Renaissance Medicine: An Introduction to Knowledge and Practice* (Chicago: University of Chicago Press, 1990), 106.

108. For Lewis and Empson see above, n. 104. See also Raymond Williams, *Keywords: A Vocabulary of Culture and Society* (London: Croom Helm, 1976); and Patricia Parker, *Shakespeare from the Margins: Language, Culture, Context*

(Chicago: University of Chicago Press, 1996). To these might be added even studies of imagery, such as Spurgeon's *Shakespeare's Imagery* or Clemen's *Development of Shakespeare's Imagery*. Judith Anderson charted the relationship between
metaphor and polysemy in "Translating Investments."

109. Aitchison, *Words in the Mind*, 223. Aitchison describes the various kinds
of tests used to obtain data about how words are linked, including word-association tests (in which subjects are given a word and asked to name the first word
that comes to mind), as well as "lexical decision tasks" (in which subjects are
timed as they decide whether or not various letter sequences represent words),
experiments with "priming" (after a word is mentioned, tests are done to see
whether that word "primes," or facilitates retrieval of related words) (24–25, 83).

110. These examples are cited in Hussey, *Literary Language of Shakespeare*,
22–23. Hussey particularly remarks Shakespeare's tendency to "double" native
and Latinate words.

111. Aitchison, *Words in the Mind*, notes that information about lexical storage can be obtained from "slips of the tongue" as well as from word-association
tests; such slips usually involve errors of meaning (*week* for *day*) or sound (malapropisms) or a combination of the two (see 19–21).

112. John Taylor (*Linguistic Categorization*, 83–84) contrasts a structuralist
approach, which argues that the meaning of a word like *toothbrush* is "delimited
by the meanings of other items in the linguistic system, such as *nailbrush* and
hairbrush," with a cognitive approach, which defines toothbrush in the context
of cultural knowledge about dental hygiene.

113. Ibid., 102.

114. Lewis, *Studies in Words*, 11.

115. Empson, *Structure of Complex Words*, 115.

116. Parker, *Shakespeare from the Margins*, 13.

117. Aitchison, *Words in the Mind*, 229.

118. Orgel, "What Is a Text?" For a similar idea, see Richard Helgerson,
Forms of Nationhood: The Elizabethan Writing of England (Chicago: University
of Chicago Press, 1992), 215: "Neither do I want to deny Shakespeare all agency.
As an actor-sharer-playwright in the most successful theatrical company England
had ever known, he occupied a unique position, a position that his plays did much
to create. He helped make the world that made him."

119. Masten, "Beaumont and/or Fletcher," 345.

120. Brothers, *Friday's Footprint*, 146.

121. See esp. Arthur Marotti, *Manuscript, Print, and the English Renaissance
Lyric* (Ithaca: Cornell University Press, 1995); Joseph Loewenstein, "The Script
in the Marketplace," in *Representing the English Renaissance*, ed. Stephen
Greenblatt (Berkeley and Los Angeles: University of California Press, 1988): 265–
78; and Mary Thomas Crane, *Framing Authority: Sayings, Self, and Society in
Sixteenth-Century England* (Princeton: Princeton University Press, 1993).

122. See Jean E. Howard, *The Stage and Social Struggle in Early Modern England* (New York: Routledge, 1994), 9; and Greenblatt, *Shakespearean Negotiations*, 5.

Chapter One
No Space Like Home: *The Comedy of Errors*

1. Anne Barton, introduction to *The Comedy of Errors* in *The Riverside Shakespeare*, ed. G. Blakemore Evans (Boston: Houghton Mifflin, 1974), 81. All quotations from Shakespeare's plays are from this edition.

2. See Katherine Eisaman Maus, *Inwardness and Theater in the English Renaissance* (Chicago: University of Chicago Press, 1995), 1–34, for an account and critique of the argument that inwardness was only beginning to be developed as a concept in this period.

3. Harold Brooks, "Themes and Structure in *The Comedy of Errors*," in *Early Shakespeare* (New York: St. Martin's, 1961), 70.

4. Barbara Freedman, *Staging the Gaze: Postmodernism, Psychoanalysis, and Shakespearean Comedy* (Ithaca: Cornell University Press, 1991), 110.

5. Jean Mandler, "How to Build a Baby II: Conceptual Primitives," *Psychological Review* 99 (1992): 592. Mandler does not necessarily agree with Lakoff's sense that image schemas emerge from a kinesthetic experience of embodiment since she argues that "perceptual analysis" of objects in the environment is adequate to build them. However, embodiment is clearly relevant to the version of the "containment" schema that I discuss here.

6. George Lakoff, "Sorry, I'm Not Myself Today: The Metaphor System for Conceptualizing the Self," in *Spaces, Worlds, and Grammar*, ed. Gilles Fauconnier and Eve Sweetser (Chicago: University of Chicago Press, 1996), 91–123, argues that in contemporary English-speaking culture the spatial metaphors used to conceptualize subjectivity are complex and inconsistent.

7. See Jacques Lacan, "The Mirror Stage," in *Ecrits: A Selection*, trans. Alan Sheridan (New York: Norton, 1977), 1–7. Frederic Jameson, "Imaginary and Symbolic in Lacan: Marxism, Psychoanalytic Criticism, and the Problem of the Subject," in *Literature and Psychoanalysis: The Question of Reading: Otherwise*, ed. Shoshana Felman (Baltimore: Johns Hopkins University Press, 1982), 351–58, provides a useful explication of the spatial implications of the mirror stage.

8. Antonio Damasio, *Descartes' Error: Emotion, Reason, and the Human Brain* (New York: Avon, 1994), 230.

9. However, Elizabeth Bradburn has argued that the Lacanian mirror stage shares with cognitive theory a sense of the subject as "the location for the registration of movement," ("The Poetics of Embodiment" [paper presented at the annual meeting of the Modern Language Association, San Francisco, December 1998], 6).

10. Lacan, "Mirror Stage," 2. Among Lacanian theorists, Charles Shepherdson offers a reading of Lacan that seems closest to cognitive theories of subject formation (see "The Role of Gender and the Imperative of Sex," in *Supposing the Subject*, ed. Joan Copjec [New York: Verso, 1994]). His account of the Lacanian triad of real, imaginary, and symbolic seems to resemble to some extent the cognitive theory of subsymbolic, image schematic, and linguistic modes of thought. Shepherdson emphasizes Lacan's distinction between *organism* and *body*, with *body* defined as the organism as it is "organ-ized . . . by the image and the word" (170). He further suggests that the imaginary and the symbolic should not be conflated or confused: "Where the image provides us with an illusion of

immediacy and presence, supposedly available in a 'physiological' perception, the symbolic confronts us with a play of presence and absence, a function of negativity by which the purportedly 'immediate' reality (the 'natural' world) is restructured" (168).

11. Bruce Fink, *The Lacanian Subject: Between Language and Jouissance* (Princeton: Princeton University Press, 1995), 6.

12. Joan Copjec, *Read My Desire: Lacan Against the Historicists* (Cambridge: MIT Press, 1995), 50.

13. Damasio, *Descartes' Error*, 95.

14. For a discussion of anosognosia, see ibid., 62–69.

15. Gaston Bachelard, *The Poetics of Space*, trans. Marie Jolas, rev. ed. (Boston: Beacon, 1994), xxxvi. His assumption that thought is deeply imagistic, as well as his sense of the centrality of spatial images to thought, seems very similar to cognitive theory.

16. Maus, *Inwardness and Theater*, traces religious and philosophical conditions for this sense of self in the period. Francis Barker, in *The Tremulous Private Body: Essays in Subjection* (London: Methuen, 1984), argues for a link between the location of the subject "as a private citizen in a domestic space, over against a public world" (11) with the formation of the bourgeois individual in the early modern period. Catherine Belsey, *The Subject of Tragedy: Identity and Difference in Renaissance Drama* (London: Methuen, 1985), similarly argues for the formation of a new kind of subject in this period and links it to a number of cultural changes, including "the transition to the liberal-humanist family, itself a mechanism of regulation more far-reaching but less visible than the repressive ecclesiastical courts" (145).

17. R.R., "The House-holders Helpe, for Domesticall Discipline: Or, a Familiar Conference of Household Instruction and Correction, Fit for the Godly Government of Christian Families" (London, 1615), quoted in Lena Cowen Orlin, *Elizabethan Households: An Anthology* (Washington, D.C.: Folger Shakespeare Library, 1995), 27.

18. Richard Bernard, "Joshua's Godly Resolution in Conference with Caleb, Touching Household Governement for Well Ordering a Familie" (London, 1612), quoted in ibid., 28.

19. Prayer from Richard Day, *A Book of Christian Praiers, Collected out of the Ancient Writers, and Best Learned in Our Time* (London, 1608), quoted in ibid., 29.

20. Damasio describes anosognosiacs as having lost "the substrate of the neural self" (*Descartes' Error*, 237).

21. Freedman, *Staging the Gaze*, 5, where Freedman discusses her practice of bringing "early modern and postmodern models of the mind into dialogue."

22. Lakoff, "Sorry, I'm Not Myself Today," suggests that contemporary metaphors used to imagine our subjectivity reflect a similar split.

23. Margreta de Grazia and Peter Stallybrass, "The Materiality of the Shakespearean Text," *Shakespeare Quarterly* 44 (1993): 267.

24. Harry F. Berger Jr., *Making Trifles of Terrors: Redistributing Complicities in Shakespeare* (Stanford: Stanford University Press, 1997), 213.

25. De Grazia and Stallybrass, "Materiality of the Shakespearean Text," 269.

26. Freedman, *Staging the Gaze*, 25.

27. Meredith Anne Skura, *Shakespeare the Actor and the Purposes of Playing* (Chicago: University of Chicago Press, 1993), esp. the afterword, "Circles and Centers."

28. *The Comedy of Errors* uses *house* 21 times and *home* 31 times, a much higher number in both cases than in most other Shakespearean comedies. Although *Merry Wives* uses *house* more frequently and *Coriolanus* has more references to *home*, neither of these plays has near the frequency of the other word— that is, there are hardly any references to *home* in *Merry Wives* or to *house* in *Coriolanus*. In addition, *Comedy of Errors* contains unusual cognate words and phrases, such as *housed, homeward, home return, homely*. My argument is not that the frequency of use is statistically significant but that these words are repeated and punned on in striking ways.

29. John Taylor, *Linguistic Categorization: Prototypes in Linguistic Theory*, 2nd ed. (Oxford: Clarendon, 1995), 102–3, argues that "the boundary between monosemy and polysemy is fuzzy" and suggests a case in which "a non-central member of a monosemous category increases in salience to the point where it constitutes a second conceptual centre of the category. . . . Before the full establishment of the secondary prototype within the category, there will be uncertainty as to whether the category is no longer monosemous or not yet polysemous."

30. Orlin, *Elizabethan Houses*, 3. Orlin here builds on the work of W. G. Hoskins, *Provincial England: Essays in Social and Economic History* (London: Macmillan, 1963). See also Don E. Wayne, *Penshurst: The Semiotics of Place and the Poetics of History* (Madison: University of Wisconsin Press, 1984), 81–123, for an account of the relationship between *house* and *home* some years later in the early seventeenth century.

31. See David W. Lloyd, *The Making of English Towns* (Hampshire: Gollancz, 1984), 48–51, on urban houses in the late medieval and early modern periods.

32. Jeremy Boulton, *Neighbourhood and Society: A London Suburb in the Seventeenth Century* (Cambridge: Cambridge University Press, 1987), stresses that "pre-industrial urban society can be seen as an aggregate of households" and that households were "the primary social unit" (102).

33. On this shift, see Valerie Pearl, "Change and Stability in Seventeenth-Century London," *London Journal* 5 (1979): 15.

34. Boulton, *Neighbourhood and Society*, 102.

35. Lawrence Stone, *The Family, Sex and Marriage in England, 1500–1800* (New York: Harper & Row, 1977). This argument is, of course, controversial. Joan Kelly-Gadol, "Did Women Have a Renaissance?" in *Becoming Visible: Women in European History*, ed. Renate Bridenthal and Claudia Koonz (Boston: Houghton Mifflin, 1977), 139–40, argues that women lost economic opportunities in the transition from feudalism to capitalism. Others, including Judith C. Brown, "A Woman's Place Was in the Home: Women's Work in Renaissance Tuscany," in *Rewriting the Renaissance: The Discourses of Sexual Difference in Early Modern Europe*, ed. Margaret W. Ferguson, Maureen Quilligan, and Nancy J. Vickers (Chicago: University of Chicago Press, 1986), 206–24, argue that in parts of Italy women did gain economic power during this period. For an excellent brief summary of this controversy, concluding that in England opportunities for women

probably did shrink, see Carol Leventen, "Patrimony and Patriarchy in *The Merchant of Venice*," in *The Matter of Difference: Materialist Feminist Criticism of Shakespeare*, ed. Valerie Wayne (Ithaca: Cornell University Press, 1991), 62–63, 76.

36. Ferguson, Quilligan, and Vickers, in their introduction to *Rewriting the Renaissance*, xviii–xix, provide a useful summary of historical information.

37. Alice T. Friedman, *House and Household in Elizabethan England: Wollaton Hall and the Willoughby Family* (Chicago: University of Chicago Press, 1989), 49.

38. Ibid., 68. In her study of the Willoughby family of Wollaton Hall, Friedman shows how most domestic duties were carried out by male servants under the direction of the husband. Women supervised the care of children but spent most of their time playing cards and doing needlework within limited areas of the house. Friedman argues that some lower female servants had more freedom of movement about the estate than their mistresses did.

39. *Oxford English Dictionary* (hereafter *OED*).

40. For this pattern of pejorative change, see Joseph M. Williams, *Origins of the English Language: A Social and Linguistic History* (New York: Macmillan, 1975), 196–98. Pejorative terms that applied to both sexes in the medieval period narrowed to include only women (*harlot, shrew*), while originally neutral class indicators (*villain, churl*) came to be applied as pejorative terms for men. The *OED* locates the change in *harlot* from masculine to feminine in the fifteenth century, although it could still be applied to men in the sixteenth (as it is in this play, at 5.1.205). *Minion* originally meant a male or female favorite, and the *OED* cites Shakespeare's *Two Gentlemen of Verona* as one of the first uses of the word as an insult.

41. Catherine Belsey, *Subject of Tragedy*, 145.

42. See, e.g., Boulton, *Neighbourhood and Society*, 275–76, for some "grounds for supposing the church was *not* a significant social force in St Saviour's [parish] in the early seventeenth-century." He goes on to offer some evidence that the church continued to play a role in cementing an urban community.

43. Mark Girouard, *Life in the English Country House: A Social and Architectural History* (New Haven: Yale University Press, 1978), 84–87, charts the causes and effects of this change and notes that by the early seventeenth century "the weight of tradition and the need to keep up local prestige maintained the old ceremonies, even if in reduced form; but court and city life had given the great a taste for a more private and intimate luxury, and for the conversational liveliness of meals uninhibited by ceremony" (85). He cites R.B.'s *Some Rules and Orders for the Government of the House of an Earle* (1605) as a contemporary work critical of such practices.

44. Douglas Bruster, "Local *Tempest*: Shakespeare and the Work of the Early Modern Playhouse," *Journal of Medieval and Renaissance Studies* 25 (1995): 33–53, of course, stresses the role of the theater as a market, but with emphasis on its consequent centrality (rather than marginality) in early modern culture. I am more interested in the interactions of house and market, especially within the theaters that incorporated aspects of both.

45. T. F. Reddaway, "The Livery Companies of Tudor London," *History* 51 (1966), 298, ties increasingly international trade to the weakening of the guild system: "For generations the leading men in the city had sought their fortunes in many trading ventures. Any freedman could engage as a wholesaler in any trade, but geography, well-entrenched rivals like the Hansards or the Italians, and the limitations of shipping had all combined to keep the Londoner mainly within the area bounded by the Atlantic coast of Spain, France, the Low Countries, and the North Sea. Now [in the late sixteenth century] the whole world was opening to him and to the improved varieties of English shipping," with the result that guild members had more incentive to leave the closely regulated practice of their trades.

46. Boulton, *Neighbourhood and Society*, concludes that in the London suburb of Boroughside, only "a substantial minority" of households "were involved in locally based kin networks" (260). Such "kin networks were loose," and "extensive kin networks were untypical," probably because of mobility, "turnover and population increase" (261).

47. Jean-Christophe Agnew, *Worlds Apart: The Market and the Theater in Anglo-American Thought, 1550–1750* (Cambridge: Cambridge University Press, 1986), 41–42.

48. Barbara Freedman, *Staging the Gaze*, makes a similar move in her chapter on this play, beginning with an identification of "the major reading styles offered by the major characters" (84), then going on to complicate this approach.

49. N. Katherine Hayles, "The Materiality of Informatics," *Configurations* 1 (1992), differentiates the discursively constructed "body" from the experience of "embodiment" in this way: "Embodiment is contextual, enwebbed within the specifics of place, time, physiology, and culture that together comprise enactment. . . . Whereas the body is an idealized form that gestures toward a Platonic reality, embodiment is the specific instantiation generated from the noise of difference" (154–55). Michel de Certeau's argument in *The Practice of Everyday Life*, trans. Steven Rendall (1984; reprint, Berkeley and Los Angeles: University of California Press, 1988), that subjects are able "tactically" to inhabit a space in ways that do not coincide with the "strategies" of power seems similar in attributing some possibility for agency to the moment-by-moment experiences of living, as a body, in space (34–39).

50. For an excellent discussion of the chain as a means of exploring new mechanisms of identity formation and social relationships, see Bruster, "Local *Tempest*," 73–77.

51. The speech prefixes in the folio text of this play (the earliest extant version) are among the most confused and irregular in the Shakespearean corpus. Both Egeon and the Duke are identified by name only in the text; speech prefixes stress their social roles (and orientation to home, Egeon as a traveling merchant and Solinus as the ruler of his native state). Additional confusion results from the identification of a character in act 1, scene 2, as "Mer." and "E. Mer" and still another in acts 3 and 4 as "Mar." in addition to "Bal.," "Baltz," and other abbreviations of his name. This does not seem to represent a failure to distinguish among these characters (as T. S. Dorsch notes in his introduction to the New Cambridge Shakespeare edition [Cambridge: Cambridge University Press, 1988],

"The merchants are not on the stage as perplexing as they could well have been to the compositor," 36) but instead the relative importance of this occupation as one determinant of social identity. For a discussion of the prefixes in the play, see ibid., 34–37.

52. Damasio describes a case of "transient anosognosia" or "asomatognosia," wherein the patient experienced "loss of the sense of her entire body frame and body boundary (both left and right sides) but was nonetheless well aware of visceral functions (breathing, heartbeat, digestion)" (*Descartes' Error*, 237).

53. Gerald Edelman, *Bright Air, Brilliant Fire: On the Matter of the Mind* (New York: Basic Books, 1992), 150.

54. On the declining role of kinship and extended family in St. Saviour's Parish, Southwark, in the early seventeenth century, see Boulton, *Neighbourhood and Society*, 247–61. For the role of companionate marriage in this play, see Thomas P. Hennings, "The Anglican Doctrine of the Affectionate Marriage in *The Comedy of Errors*," *Modern Language Quarterly* 47 (1986): 91–107, who argues that the play replaces the Saturnalian release of farce with a Christian "celebration of marriage and the family" (92–93).

55. Several new critical studies of the play stress these images; see Vincent F. Petronella, "Structure and Theme through Separation and Union in Shakespeare's *The Comedy of Errors*," *Modern Language Review* 69 (1974): 481–88; and Barbara Freedman, "Egeon's Debt: Self-Division and Self-Redemption in *The Comedy of Errors*," *English Literary Renaissance* 10 (1980): 360–83. Freedman partially repudiates this essay in *Staging the Gaze*. On the economic significance of the chain, see also Bruster, "Local *Tempest*," 73–77.

56. Bruster, "Local *Tempest*," 74, notes that "as in one of its source plays, Plautus' *Amphitruo*, identity in Shakespeare's play is connected with gold."

57. Members of the Boston College doctoral seminar in the fall of 1992 called to my attention the role of beating as a means of stabilizing identity in this play.

58. Freedman, *Staging the Gaze*, 92.

59. See Dorsch, introduction to New Cambridge Shakespeare, 8–10, for a discussion of these prefixes. If, however, "Sereptus" is meant to be "Surreptus," and "Erotes" is really "Errantes," as some have argued, these tags would reinforce what the play suggests about the relationship of each character to home. Antipholus Surreptus feels "snatched up," imprisoned and confined by his home, while Antipholus Errantes feels himself to be "wandering" and in search of a home. On an initial confusion about which parent ends up with which twin, see Patricia Parker, *Literary Fat Ladies: Rhetoric, Gender, Property* (London: Methuen, 1987), 78–81.

60. Jean Howard, "Scripts and/versus Playhouses: Ideological Production and the Renaissance Public Stage," in Wayne, *Matter of Difference*, 221–25, cites the concern of antitheatrical tracts in the period to keep women confined to home and out of the playhouses.

61. See, e.g., the note to 1.2.9 in the *Riverside Shakespeare*: "Not only inns but shops had such signs; see below, I.ii.75, where we learn that the house in which Antipholus of Ephesus lives and carries on his business is called the Phoenix."

62. Under feudalism, "there was a special form of land holding, called burgage tenure, through which the tenant was free, or partly free, from feudal obligations,

especially those requiring him to work on his lord's land." Such tenants owed "fixed annual rents" to the "overlord of the burough," and their plots could be neither bought nor sold (Lloyd, *Making of English Towns*, 38). Boulton, *Neighbourhood and Society*, notes that in late-sixteenth-century and early-seventeenth-century Boroughside neighborhoods "owner-occupation was extremely rare. In 1617 only two householders held the freehold to their dwelling house. . . . Most housing was held either by lease or 'at will' " (204).

63. Dayton Haskin reminded me, in comments following a talk based on this chapter at Boston College in November 1992, that the abbey would also have been known as a religious "house."

64. Brooks, "Themes and Structure in *The Comedy of Errors*," 68.

65. See Patricia Parker, *Shakespeare from the Margins: Language, Culture, Context* (Chicago: University of Chicago Press, 1996), 56–82, for a similar conclusion that the play offers a "disjunctive combination of old and new, commercial and biblical Ephesus, apocalyptic end with elements not so easily assimilable to it" (81).

66. Andrew Gurr, *The Shakespearean Stage, 1574–1642*, 3rd ed. (Cambridge: Cambridge University Press, 1992), 115.

67. See, e.g., the Arden edition of R. A. Foakes, rev. ed. (London: Methuen, 1969), xxxiv–xxxix. There does seem to be some disagreement about the arrangement of the "houses," with some editors accepting Chambers's belief that Antipholus's house was in the center, and others (e.g., G. Blakemore Evans in the *Riverside Shakespeare*) giving the central place to the Priory. Various scholars have argued that the houses in the play represent actual buildings in late-sixteenth-century London. Foakes notes that the Phoenix was a London tavern and a shop in Lombard Street (16, note to 1.2.75) and that the Porpentine was a Bankside inn (49, note to 3.1.116). T. W. Baldwin argued, not quite persuasively, that the abbey is meant to be "Holywell Priory, where, across the ditch from the Theater, two priests received the full rites of treason in the wake of the Spanish Armada in 1588." He claimed that Shakespeare "uses exactly the topography of Holywell Priory" in the play and that Egeon's threatened execution was inspired by that of the priests (see T. W. Baldwin, *On the Compositional Genetics of The Comedy of Errors* [Urbana: University of Illinois Press, 1965], 352–53).

68. Dorsch, New Cambridge Shakespeare, 22–24, concludes that staging in front of the screen was the most likely alternative. Foakes, Arden edition, xxxv, mentions the audience's awareness of "the conventionalized arcade settings with which Renaissance editors illustrated editions of Terence and Plautus, apparently in the belief that they were imitating the Roman stage."

69. Alan Nelson, *Early Cambridge Theatres: College, University and Town Stages, 1464–1720* (Cambridge: Cambridge University Press, 1994), 124.

70. Scholars are divided over whether the three *domi* constituted the only possible means of entrance and egress or there were also side entrances that could represent arrival from or departure to seaport or mart. Dorsch, New Cambridge Shakespeare, believes that the five doors of the Gray's Inn hall screen could provide both the three "houses" and two other means of entrance or exit (24).

71. The Cambridge play *Gammer Gurton's Needle* capitalizes for humorous effect on the inability of the audience to see inside the stagehouses.

72. Barton, introduction in the *Riverside Shakespeare*, 81.

73. Foakes, Arden edition, xxxvii.

74. The drawings are reproduced in Dorsch, New Cambridge Shakespeare, 25–27.

75. Controversy over the role of such freestanding "houses" in pre-Shakespearean private performance has been as heated as that over the public theater "inner stage" and indeed probably stems from similar ideas about the representation of domestic space. Richard Southern, *The Staging of Plays before Shakespeare* (London: Faber & Faber, 1973), 146–54, summarizes various arguments and concludes that no such "houses" existed. I tend to think he is right.

76. *The Comedy of Errors*, ed. J. Dover Wilson and Arthur Quiller-Couch (Cambridge: Cambridge University Press, 1922), 98.

77. Richard Southern, *The Open Stage and the Modern Theatre in Research and Practice* (London: Faber & Faber, 1953); John Cranford Adams, *The Globe Playhouse* (1942; reprint, New York: Barnes & Noble, 1961), 135–71, 275–85.

78. For refutations of the inner-stage theory, see C. Walter Hodges, *The Globe Restored* (London: Ernest Benn, 1953), 50–54; and Richard Hosley, "The Discovery-Space in Shakespeare's Globe," *Shakespeare Survey* 12 (1959): 35–46.

79. Adams, *Globe Playhouse*, 275. He believed that the entire tiring-house facade was based on "a short row of London houses" (135).

80. Robert Weimann, "Bifold Authority in Shakespeare's Theatre," *Shakespeare Quarterly* 39 (1988): 409.

81. Weimann associates the *platea* with madness, wordplay, impertinence, disguise, misrule, "topsy-turveydom," and subversion (ibid., 410). Emily Bartels, "Breaking the Illusion of Being: Shakespeare and the Performance of Self," *Theatre Journal* 46 (1994): 175–76, has argued that *platea* characters actually represent more clearly coherent and self-determined subjects than do *locus* characters.

82. Lawrence Stone, in *The Family, Sex and Marriage in England, 1500–1800*, abr. ed. (London: Penguin, 1979), 169–72, argues that "the most striking change in the life-style of the upper classes in the seventeenth and eighteenth centuries was the increasing stress laid upon personal privacy" (169). See also Girouard, *Life in the English Country House*, 1–118, for the architectural innovations that contributed to the development of domestic privacy.

83. Adams, *Globe Playhouse*, 284.

84. On the shocking nature of this scene and the importance of the location of the bed throughout the play, see Michael Neill, "Unproper Beds: Race, Adultery, and the Hideous in *Othello*," *Shakespeare Quarterly* 40 (1989): 383–412.

85. Hodges, *Globe Restored*, 54.

86. Their opinions are based on stage directions such as that preceding *Othello* 5.2, "Enter Othello and Desdemona in her bed."

87. Freedman, *Staging the Gaze*, 25.

88. Steven Mullaney, *The Place of the Stage: License, Play and Power in Renaissance England* (Chicago: University of Chicago Press, 1988), 54.

89. Catherine Belsey argues that "the impression of interiority" was largely produced by "the formal development of the soliloquy," another means of revealing what is inside to public view (*Subject of Tragedy*, 42).

90. Bruster, "Local *Tempest*," 1–28, describes some of the implications of the theater as market and of playhouses as "centers for the production and consumption of an aesthetic product" (3).

91. John Stockton, *A Sermon Preached at Paules Crosse*, 24 August 1678, quoted in E. K. Chambers, *The Elizabethan Stage*, 4 vols. (Oxford: Clarendon, 1903–23), 4:200. Bruster, "Local *Tempest*," 2, cites other similar passages.

92. Thomas White, *A Sermon preached at Pawles Crosse on Sunday the thirde of November 1577 in the times of the Plague*, in Chambers, *Elizabethan Stage*, 4:197.

93. Boulton, *Neighbourhood and Society*, 75–77, notes that "the restrictive marketing regulations enforced in the manorial courts were often broken and frequently evaded by many Boroughside residents. . . . The need to avoid irksome market regulations was increasingly driving individuals to trade in inn yards and private houses in London and the nation in the seventeenth century. This well-documented function of the urban inn ran contrary to the laws of London markets." Once again, confusion of market and private house is the occasion for anxieties about regulation. Agnew, *Worlds Apart*, 49–52, similarly notes the avoidance of sanctioned markets by "middlemen" who purchased commodities and resold them "at the inns and shops ringing the market squares" (49–50). Agnew also identifies the Liberties, site of many theaters, as a center of unregulated commercial transactions (50).

94. See Girouard, *Life in the English Country House*, 34–36, which details the ceremonial and hierarchical traditions associated with dining in the great hall.

95. Richard Hosley, "The Origins of the Shakespearean Playhouse," *Shakespeare Quarterly* 15 (1964): 29–40. However, Alan Nelson, "Hall Screens and Elizabethan Playhouses," in *The Development of Shakespeare's Theater*, ed. John H. Astington (New York: AMS Press, 1992), 57–76, has argued that since hall screens were not used as backgrounds for performances in halls, it is unlikely that they provided a model for the tiring-house facade in the public theater.

96. Jean Howard, *Stage and Social Struggle*, 221–23, notes anxiety about the social leveling that might occur when money, rather than social status, allowed one access to performances.

97. Nelson, "Hall Screens and Elizabethan Playhouses," 71.

98. Suzanne Westfall, *Patronage and Performance: Early Tudor Household Revels* (Oxford: Clarendon, 1990), 109–25, discusses the ambiguous place of players within noble households during the period before public theaters.

99. Antony Munday (?), *A Second and third blast of retrait from plaies and Theaters* (1580), in Chambers, *Elizabethan Stage,*, 4:210–12.

100. Stephen Gosson, *The Schoole of Abuse* (1579), in ibid., 204. For the exemption of players from sumptuary laws see Peter Stallybrass, "Worn Worlds: Clothes and Identity on the Renaissance Stage," in *Subject and Object in Renaissance Culture*, ed. Margreta de Grazia, Maureen Quilligan, and Peter Stallybrass (Cambridge: Cambridge University Press, 1996), 301–4.

101. Gosson, *Schoole of Abuse*, 218.

102. I.H., *This World's Folly* (1615), in Chambers, *Elizabethan Stage*, 4:254.

103. John Northbrooke, *A Treatise wherein Dicing, Dauncing, Vaine playes, or Enterluds, with other idle pastimes, &c., commonly used on the Sabboth day,*

are reproued by the Authoritie of the word of God and auntient writers (1577), in ibid., 198.

104. Munday (?), *A Second and third blast*, 209.

105. Ibid., 210; Gervase Babington, "A very Fruitful Exposition of the Commandements" (1583), in Chambers, *Elizabethan Stage*, 4:225.

106. Henry Crosse, *Vertues Common-wealth* (1603), in Chambers, *Elizabethan Stage*, 4:247; Phillip Stubbes, *The Anatomie of Abuses* (1583), ibid., 223–24.

107. As Stallybrass, "Worn Worlds," 292, has noted, their livery marked the location of "the London professional theater at the juncture of the court and the city guilds." Actors' livery "thus simultaneously related to the 'servitude' of household livery and to the 'freedom' of guild livery."

108. For the term *housekeeper*, see Chambers, *Elizabethan Stage*, 2:417. The term seems to have become current somewhat later than the period under discussion here, surfacing in seventeenth-century lawsuits among the heirs of original shareholders.

109. Sigmund Freud, "The 'Uncanny,' " in *The Standard Edition of the Complete Psychological Works*, trans. James Strachey, vol. 17 (London: Hogarth, 1953), 245.

110. Freedman, *Staging the Gaze*, 56.

Chapter Two
Theatrical Practice and the Ideologies of Status in *As You Like It*

1. On the workings of ideology to reproduce conditions of production see Louis Althusser, "Ideology and Ideological State Apparatuses," in *Lenin and Philosophy and Other Essays*, trans. Ben Brewster (New York: Monthly Review, 1971), 127–88.

2. See George Lakoff, *Women, Fire, and Dangerous Things: What Categories Reveal about the Mind* (Chicago: University of Chicago Press, 1987), 283 ff., for the idea that "hierarchical structure is understood in terms of PART-WHOLE schemas and UP-DOWN schemas."

3. E. K. Chambers, *The Elizabethan Stage*, 4 vols. (Oxford: Clarendon, 1923), 4:340–41.

4. Charles Read Baskervil, *The Elizabethan Jig and Related Song Drama* (Chicago: University of Chicago Press, 1929), 113–19. Contemporary references, cited at length by Baskervil, suggest that the jig centered around an itinerant garlic seller and included a prostitutes' dance.

5. On postperformance admission to jigs, see David Wiles, *Shakespeare's Clown* (Cambridge: Cambridge University Press, 1987), 46–47, who speculates, partly based on the passage cited above, that the "anarchy" attendant upon jig performances was in part caused by "the swelling of the audience by many who could not afford the entry fee for the main play," although "whether they paid, stampeded their way in, or entered freely is still unclear."

6. Baskervil, *Elizabethan Jig*, 55, 117, gives evidence for such baboon dances, including the passage cited above.

7. Wiles, *Shakespeare's Clown*, 14–16, describes the practice of Richard Tarlton, the first famous Elizabethan clown, who would reply to rhymes suggested by the audience.

8. Baskervil, *Elizabethan Jig*, 110–11, cites both quotations and several more. The satirist is Edward Guilpin, in his *Skialetheia*, satire 5.

9. Wiles, *Shakespeare's Clown*, 56.

10. On Kemp's Norwich undertaking, see Max W. Thomas, *"Kemps Nine Daies Wonder*: Dancing Carnival into Market," *PMLA* 107 (1992): 511–23. Thomas argues that Kemp's published account of his journey is part of "a larger cultural transition, which effectively replaced the liminal space offered by the carnivalesque with the fungible commodity of Renaissance theatrical representation" (521). I am arguing that Shakespeare in *As You Like It* uses the absence of Kemp to do something very similar.

11. See Peter Thomson, *Shakespeare's Theatre*, 2nd ed. (New York: Routledge, 1992), 12; Wiles, *Shakespeare's Clown*, 47; and Baskervil, *Elizabethan Jig*, 114, which suggests that "after 1600 the policy of private houses probably tended to discredit the jig and to throw it more definitely into the hands of companies that catered to the populace. The fact that by 1600 Kemp had left the Chamberlain's Men and by 1602 had joined Worcester's may reflect a shift in attitude on the part of his old company." Max Thomas, *"Kemps Nine Daies Wonder,"* similarly attributes Kemp's departure from the company to possible "resentment" over his tendency to improvise, his "derogatory jests and exaggerated gestures" (511).

12. Wiles, *Shakespeare's Clown*, 47.

13. Wiles suggests that the jigs highlight the "communal" nature of authorship in the Elizabethan theater (ibid.). I see the assimilation of the jig into the main play as a more difficult and problematic process, however. Richard Helgerson, *Forms of Nationhood: The Elizabethan Writing of England* (Chicago: University of Chicago Press, 1992), 199, sees the move away from Kemp and jigs as a step toward what he calls an "author's theater."

14. Margreta de Grazia and Peter Stallybrass, "The Materiality of the Shakespearean Text," *Shakespeare Quarterly* 44 (1993): 255–83, suggest some of the ways the problematic status of the text forces us to "reconceptualize the fundamental category of a *work* by Shakespeare" (255). A consideration of material conditions of performance is beyond the scope of their essay, but I believe that the presence of the jig similarly problematizes our conception of the Shakespearean play.

15. I would associate this position with most American New Historicist work done in the 1980s. Certainly Montrose makes such an assumption in both "Of Gentlemen and Shepherds: The Politics of Elizabethan Pastoral Form," *ELH* 50 (1983): 415–59 and " 'The Place of a Brother' in *As You Like It*: Social Process and Comic Form," *Shakespeare Quarterly* 32 (1988): 28–54. Stephen Greenblatt, *Shakespearean Negotiations* (Berkeley and Los Angeles: University of California Press, 1988), seems to make a similar assumption, despite his focus on a more complex circulation of "social energy" (6). Leonard Tennenhouse, *Power on Display: The Politics of Shakespeare's Genres* (London: Methuen, 1986), is another example. Richard Wilson, " 'Like the old Robin Hood': *As You Like It* and the Enclosure Riots," *Shakespeare Quarterly* 43 (1992): 1–19, argues that the play

includes elements of popular revolt only to "incorporate the energies of charivari in a reconstituted order" (14).

16. A recent example of this approach is Annabel Patterson, *Shakespeare and the Popular Voice* (Oxford: Blackwell, 1989), who ties some very persuasive evidence of interest in popular political goals to be found in Shakespeare's plays with insistence on a "common-sense" (87) view of agency and authorship arguing that Shakespeare was engaged in a "conscious analytic project" (65) in his plays.

17. Thus Helgerson sees the history plays as standing for "a particularly anachronistic state formation based at least symbolically on the monarch and an aristocratic governing class" (*Forms of Nationhood*, 244).

18. See A. L. Beier, *Masterless Men: The Vagrancy Problem in England, 1560–1640* (London: Methuen, 1985).

19. For one account of this familiar story of sheep enclosure, deracination, and increasing vagrancy, see Richard Halpern, *The Poetics of Primitive Accumulation: English Renaissance Culture and the Genealogy of Capital* (Ithaca: Cornell University Press, 1991), 71–73.

20. C. S. Lewis, *Studies in Words*, 2nd ed. (Cambridge: Cambridge University Press, 1967), 21.

21. For "depreciative specialization," see Gustaf Stern, *Meaning and Change of Meaning*, 3rd ed. (Bloomington: Indiana University Press, 1931), 411–14. He includes "specialization" under the class of semantic change called "adequation," whereby a referent is initially named "by a single characteristic which happens to strike us" but "may be of subordinate importance for the real status of the referent in our universe of action and discourse." The "most important" characteristic of the referent subsequently "becomes more closely associated with the name than any other," and "the meaning undergoes adequation to what is now considered by speakers as the main characteristic of the referent, and the basis of naming, now considered relatively unimportant, recedes, and eventually disappears" (380–81). For a list of gendered depreciations, see Joseph M. Williams, *Origins of the English Language: A Social and Linguistic History* (New York: Macmillan, 1975), 196–97. For an extended account of "the semantic legacy of the Middle Ages," including a section on the moralization of status terms, see Geoffrey Hughes, *Words in Time: A Social History of English Vocabulary* (Oxford: Blackwell, 1988), 32–66.

22. Geoffrey Hughes, for example, has suggested that this pattern of change has its roots in the Anglo-Saxon legal system and its "concept of *wergild*, an equation between a person's status and material value, and a strong correlation between status and implied moral quality" (*Words in Time*, 47).

23. Lee Patterson, *Chaucer and the Subject of History* (Madison: University of Wisconsin Press, 1991), 262. Patterson cites Rodney Hilton, *Class Conflict and the Crisis of Feudalism* (London: Hambledon Press, 1985), 138, for this "caste interpretation of peasant status."

24. Patterson, *Chaucer and the Subject of History*, cites, among others, Honorius of Autun, *De imagine mundi*, for peasants' descent from Ham.

25. For this proverb, see Albert B. Friedman, " 'When Adam Delved . . .': Contexts of an Historic Proverb," in *The Learned and the Lewd: Studies in Chaucer*

and Medieval Literature, ed. Larry D. Benson (Cambridge: Harvard University Press, 1974), 213–30.

26. Quotation from *The Boke of Seynt Albans* (St. Albans, 1486) in Patterson, *Chaucer and the Subject of History*, 268.

27. Halpern, *Poetics of Primitive Accumulation*, 88.

28. The etymology of *clown* is obscure. Wiles notes a spurious etymology deriving it from the Latin *colonus* (farmer) (*Shakespeare's Clown*, 61), but the OED suspects a derivation from Germanic terms for "clod, clot, lump."

29. Wiles, *Shakespeare's Clown*, 62.

30. Helgerson argues that "most of the status abuse—terms like *villain, clown, churl, hind, peasant, swain*—refers specifically to countrymen. Perhaps the city dwellers who populated the theaters thought themselves exempt. But if so, it was an uncomfortable and unstable exemption, for this conceptual universe allotted no terms, whether favorable or unfavorable, specifically to them" (*Forms of Nationhood*, 206). Comedy seems more directly *about* the new range of uses for such terms, within semantic fields of court, countryside, and pastoral. *As You Like It* in particular is concerned with the ways context can alter the meanings of words.

31. Wiles traces this shift in a chapter called " 'The Clown' in Playhouse Terminology" (*Shakespeare's Clown*, 61–72).

32. On the "cultural work" of pastoral in this regard, see Montrose, "Of Gentlemen and Shepherds," and for the negotiations of status and mobility in this play, see idem, "The Place of a Brother."

33. Wilson, " 'Like the old Robin Hood,' " 17, 16.

34. Annabel Patterson finds moments of social critique in sympathy with lower-class interests in *A Midsummer Night's Dream, Hamlet, King Lear, Coriolanus*, and *The Tempest*, arguing that earlier plays "could cross social boundaries without obscuring them, and by these crossings imagine the social body whole again." She argues that with *King Lear*, "Shakespeare was forced to admit that the popular voice had grievances that the popular theater could no longer express comedically" (*Shakespeare and the Popular Voice*, 69).

35. Wilson, " 'Like the old Robin Hood,' " similarly notes the ways in which the play "graft[s] the old rural games" onto classical mythology in order to "neutralize" their disruptive force (16–17). He does not see the irony and regret about this neutralization that I argue for here.

36. Thomson, *Shakespeare's Theatre*, 66–68, 94–96, discusses the roles of Kemp and Armin in the company and suggests that *As You Like It* alludes to the change. Wiles, *Shakespeare's Clown*, 146, makes a similar argument.

37. Althusser, "Ideology and Ideological State Apparatuses," 171–72.

38. Daniel Stern, *The Interpersonal World of the Infant: A View from Psychoanalysis and Developmental Psychology* (New York: Basic Books, 1985), 42.

39. Gerald Edelman, *Bright Air, Brilliant Fire: On the Matter of the Mind* (New York: Basic Books, 1992), 170.

40. Hughes has noted that this linguistic change involves movement from viewing fortune as "something which controlled one" to "something which can be 'made,' allowing one control over one's life" (*Words in Time*, 69).

41. Madeline Doran, "Yet am I inland bred," *Shakespeare Quarterly* 15 (1964): 105, suggests that Oliver here reflects "the belief, always present in Shake-

speare, that in spite of all, birth will tell, that the gently born, with or without nurture, are naturally gentle in behavior." Doran, I think, overestimates the extent to which such a view, usually held by "gentle" characters, can be attributed to Shakespeare himself.

42. Quoted from *An Acte for the punishment of Vacabondes and for Releif of the Poore and Impotent* (14 Eliz., c. 5), of 29 June 1572, as cited in Chambers, *Elizabethan Stage*, 4:269–70.

43. For the argument about the class affiliation and financial means of Shakespeare's audience, see Ann Jennalie Cook, *The Privileged Playgoers of Shakespeare's London, 1576–1642* (Princeton: Princeton University Press, 1981), who argues against an earlier view that the theaters brought together a socially heterogeneous audience; and Andrew Gurr, *Playgoing in Shakespeare's London* (Cambridge: Cambridge University Press, 1987), who argues that different theaters had different audiences.

44. Wilson, " 'Like the old Robin Hood,' " 6–7, suggests that Orlando, with his "combination of rebelliousness and conservatism," represents a "noble robber" or upper-class leader of a peasant revolt. In my view, Orlando, as upper-class "rebel," voices a more conservative view than the play as a whole seems to support.

45. Montrose has suggested the importance of a character named Adam in establishing "resonances" between the brotherly animosities in the play and the story of Cain and Abel in Genesis ("The Place of a Brother," 45–46).

46. Montrose, "Of Gentlemen and Shepherds," 432. Montrose argues that pastoral forms, "by reconstituting the leisured gentleman as the gentle shepherd, obfuscates a fundamental distinction in cultural logic: a contradiction between the secular claims of aristocratic prerogative and the religious claims of common origins" (432). See also Patterson, *Chaucer and the Subject of History*, 262.

47. Wilson, " 'Like the old Robin Hood,' " 8–9, notes that "the outlaw ballads of medieval England legitimated peasant protest, but *As You Like It* is one of a cluster of plays written in the late 1590s that exalt the rank of Robin Hood to make him a gentleman or even . . . an aristocrat" in order to dramatize "the divided loyalty of the propertied." Wilson cites a contemporary document describing the denizens of the woods as "people of very lewd lives and conversations, leaving their own and other counties and taking the place for a shelter as a cloak to their villainies" (9). *As You Like It*, however, represents the court as the source of "villainy."

48. Rodney Hilton, *Bond Men Made Free* (London: Methuen, 1977), 72.

49. Quoted from a proclamation "Prohibiting Encroachment in Waltham Forest," Westminster, 17 June 1548, 2 Edw. 6, in *Tudor Royal Proclamations*, ed. Paul L. Hughes and James F. Larkin, vol. 1, *The Early Tudors (1485–1553)* (New Haven: Yale University Press, 1964), 430. For the frequency of charges of stealing wood in manorial court records, see John West, *Village Records* (London: Macmillan, 1962), 35.

50. Hilton, *Bond Men Made Free*, 72. Lee Patterson connects this peasant desire for control over nature to a desire to return to the prelapsarian state of equality, "when Adam dalf, and Eve span" (*Chaucer and the Subject of History*, 265).

51. Helen Child Sargent and George Lyman Kittredge, eds., *English and Scottish Popular Ballads* (Boston: Houghton Mifflin, 1904), 274.

52. Anne Barton, "The King Disguised: Shakespeare's *Henry V* and the Comical History," in *The Triple Bond*, ed. Joseph G. Price (University Park: Pennsylvania State University Press, 1975), 97, alludes to this ballad as illustrating the motif of "the King-in-disguise," a "wish-dream of a peasantry harried and perplexed by a new class of officials" that they could have recourse to the king himself. Barton sees a critique of this motif in *Henry V*; however, Annabel Patterson, *Shakespeare and the Popular Voice*, 89–90, argues that Henry's appropriation of the motif is questioned by a lower-class voice.

53. See Helgerson, *Forms of Nationhood*, 231–32, which suggests that Shakespeare's *Henry V* alludes to the dream of "commonality . . . between the ruler and the ruled" found in the Robin Hood ballads but then "unequivocally denies it."

54. Wilson, " 'Like the old Robin Hood,' " 8.

55. On hunting and other leisure activities as manifestations of aristocratic privilege, see Mervyn James, *Society, Politics, and Culture: Studies in Early Modern England* (Cambridge: Cambridge University Press, 1986), 271–78; Frank Whigham, *Ambition and Privilege: The Social Tropes of Elizabethan Courtesy Theory* (Berkeley and Los Angeles: University of California Press, 1984), 88; and Mary Thomas Crane, *Framing Authority: Sayings, Self, and Society in Sixteenth-Century England* (Princeton: Princeton University Press, 1993), 101–2.

56. Orlando Patterson, *Freedom in the Making of Western Culture* (New York: Basic Books, 1991), 344–75, discusses the use of such terms as *nativus* and *villanus* initially to distinguish between slaves and serfs, but as these two categories fused during the medieval period, the words became synonyms.

57. Montrose, "Of Gentlemen and Shepherds," 452.

58. *Ceorl* was the Anglo-Saxon term for "serf"; it was replaced after 1066 by its French equivalent, *villein*. However, the term depreciated in a similar way.

59. Montrose, "Of Gentlemen and Shepherds," 429–33.

60. Wiles, *Shakespeare's Clown*, 20–23, 104.

61. Thomson, *Shakespeare's Theatre*, 9–12; Wiles, *Shakespeare's Clown*, 40–41. See also Thomas, "*Kemps Nine Daies Wonder*," for a treatment of one episode in Kemp's subsequent career.

62. See Wiles, *Shakespeare's Clown*, 136–63. M. C. Bradbrook, *Shakespeare the Craftsman* (London: Chatto & Windus, 1969), notes that Armin's fool often "underlines or calls attention to social gradations; although living outside the social order he enforces it" (57). See Helgerson, *Forms of Nationhood*, 199, for Kemp's replacement as part of the transition from a "player's theater" to an "author's theater."

63. Helen Gardner, "As You Like It," in *Modern Shakespearean Criticism: Essays on Style, Dramaturgy, and the Major Plays*, ed. Alvin B. Kernan (New York: Harcourt, 1970), 191.

64. Wiles, *Shakespeare's Clown*, 56–60, argues for an assimilation of jig elements into *Hamlet*, arguing that once "the possibility of perfect order disintegrates [in the tragedies and dark comedies], the celebration of anarchy ceases, necessarily, to be an admissible complement to the play" (60). I see the incorpora-

tion of jig elements into the play as perhaps a bit more problematic, both for the play and for the jig ethos, than Wiles does.

65. I use the text found in Baskervil, *Elizabethan Jig*, 389–92. This "jig" is one of a number of ballads with the subtitle "jig." Baskervil speculates that such ballads, especially those, like this one, in dialogue form, were performed on the stage and published as ballads (164). The date of this jig is, of course, uncertain. It was printed for Henry Gosson, which means that it was published between 1602 and 1649; a date of performance, it there is one, is impossible to determine. I do not mean to argue for direct influence of this jig on the play but rather to call attention to the similarities (and differences) between the ethos of the play and of the jig. Barbara J. Bono, "Mixed Gender, Mixed Genre in *As You Like It*," in *Renaissance Genres*, ed. Barbara K. Lewalski (Cambridge: Harvard University Press, 1986), 201–4, discusses Rosalind's use of misogynist discourse and Orlando's resulting skepticism "of fanciful love at first sight" (204).

66. Bono notes that Orlando has "painfully earned the 'real' love he is given" ("Mixed Gender, Mixed Genre," 204. He must seem to "earn" his new status as well.

67. Wiles argues that in this scene "the traditional simple-minded rustic clown is symbolically dismissed from the new Globe stage" (*Shakespeare's Clown*, 146).

68. Wiles notes that this line "reminds the audience that clowning is his—Armin's—livelihood" (ibid.) Wiles does not see irony in this admission, however.

69. Baskervil, *Elizabethan Jig*, 432.

70. Doran, "Yet am I inland bred," 106–11, traces the history of "viewing civilized man as sophisticated and in some sense morally declined from an earlier stage of innocence and honest simplicity" (106).

71. Wiles, *Shakespeare's Clown*, 52–56, where he notes that "the clown in *As You Like It* is allowed to complete his wooing" (55).

72. Ibid., 158–59.

73. The socioeconomic level of Shakespeare's audience has been much debated. Cook, *Privileged Playgoers of Shakespeare's London*, questioned Harbage's belief that the audience was heterogeneous and composed chiefly of artisans and craftsmen, positing instead a privileged audience even in the public theaters. Gurr, *Playgoing in Shakespeare's London*, argues that the Globe "stood midway between the familiar extreme of amphitheatre reputation and the hall playhouse snobbery which first began to show themselves in the year the Globe was built" (190). If this is true, then *As You Like It* and the exclusion of the jig probably represented an initial attempt to appeal to a more privileged audience.

74. See Chambers, *Elizabethan Stage*, 4:270.

75. See Helgerson, *Forms of Nationhood*, 199.

76. On the role of Shakespeare's contemporary Ben Jonson in formulating and promulgating the concept of the author's ownership of, and control over, his text, see, e.g., Joseph Loewenstein, "The Script in the Marketplace," in *Representing the English Renaissance*, ed. Stephen Greenblatt (Berkeley and Los Angeles: University of California Press, 1988), 265–78.

77. Antonio Damasio, *Descartes' Error: Emotion, Reason, and the Human Brain* (New York: Avon, 1994); Leslie Brothers, *Friday's Footprint: How Society Shapes the Human Mind* (New York: Oxford University Press, 1997).

78. See esp. C. L. Barber and Richard P. Wheeler, *The Whole Journey: Shakespeare's Power of Development* (Berkeley and Los Angeles: University of California Press, 1986); and Marianne Novy, "The Bonds of Brotherhood" in *Shakespeare's Personality*, ed. Norman N. Holland, Sidney Homan, and Bernard J. Paris (Berkeley and Los Angeles: University of California Press, 1989), 103–15.

Chapter Three
Twelfth Night: Suitable Suits and the Cognitive Space Between

1. Cristina Malcolmson, " 'What You Will': Social Mobility and Gender in *Twelfth Night*," in *The Matter of Difference: Materialist Feminist Criticism of Shakespeare*, ed. Valerie Wayne (Ithaca: Cornell University Press, 1991), 32, notes the universality of the perception of desire while extending its scope from desire for love and music to desire for social status.

2. John Hollander, "*Twelfth Night* and the Morality of Indulgence," in *Modern Shakespearean Criticism: Essays on Style, Dramaturgy, and the Major Plays*, ed. Alvin B. Kernan (New York: Harcourt, 1970), 228–41, argues in New Critical and humanist terms that the play enacts a "surfeiting" of appetite that results in the emergence of a self previously hidden "behind a mask of comic type" (230). Coppélia Kahn, "The Providential Tempest and the Shakespearean Family," in *Representing Shakespeare: New Psychoanalytic Essays*, ed. Murray Schwartz and Coppélia Kahn (Baltimore: Johns Hopkins University Press, 1980), argues that the play "traces the evolution of sexuality as related to identity, from the playful and unconscious toyings of youthful courtship, through a period of sexual confusion, to a final thriving in which . . . men and women truly know themselves through choosing and loving the right mate" (229).

3. See Malcolmson, "What You Will"; and Leonard Tennenhouse, *Power on Display: The Politics of Shakespeare's Genres* (London: Methuen, 1986), 62–68. An exception is Stephen Greenblatt, "Fiction and Friction," in *Shakespearean Negotiations* (Berkeley and Los Angeles: University of California Press, 1988), who argues that *Twelfth Night* represents "the emergence of identity through the experience of erotic heat," as the audience learns that "the threat to the social order and the threat to the sexual order were equally illusory" (88, 72). Jean Howard, "Power and Eros: Crossdressing in Dramatic Representation and Theatrical Practice," in *The Stage and Social Struggle in Early Modern England* (New York: Routledge, 1994), 114, argues that the play is concerned with the disciplining of Olivia, who is "a real threat to the hierarchical gender system in this text."

4. Barbara Freedman, *Staging the Gaze: Postmodernism, Psychoanalysis, and Shakespearean Comedy* (Ithaca: Cornell University Press, 1991), 192–236; Geoffrey Hartman, "Shakespeare's Poetical Character in *Twelfth Night*," in *Shakespeare and the Question of Theory*, ed. Patricia Parker and Geoffrey Hartman (London: Methuen, 1985), 45. Greenblatt, "Fiction and Friction," similarly offers a reading that disrupts the illusion that sexual difference is reaffirmed at the end of the play.

5. For "family resemblance," see John R. Taylor, *Linguistic Categorization: Prototypes in Linguistic Theory*, 2nd ed. (Oxford: Clarendon, 1995), 99–121. Taylor borrows the term from Wittgenstein's work on categorization (Ludwig

Wittgenstein, *Philosophical Investigations*, trans. G.E.M. Anscombe [Oxford: Blackwell, 1978], 31–33). However, as Taylor also suggests, the boundaries between homonymy and polysemy are fuzzy, and *suit* clearly falls somewhere along that boundary. Frantisek Lichtenberk, "Semantic Change and Heterosemy in Grammaticalization," *Language* 67 (1991): 475–509, has suggested that some words exhibit "heterosemy," a condition in which words are derived from a common etonym and still exhibit some signs of their historical origin without, however, being similar enough to belong to a single category.

6. Taylor, *Linguistic Categorization*, 119–20, entertains the idea "that a category, no matter how extended or rambling, cannot accommodate contraries." But he is able to find "many cases where different meanings of a polysemous word are characterized by incompatible attribute specifications."

7. George Lakoff, *Women, Fire, and Dangerous Things: What Categories Reveal about the Mind* (Chicago: University of Chicago Press, 1987).

8. Daniel Stern, *The Interpersonal World of the Infant: A View from Psychoanalysis and Developmental Psychology* (New York: Basic Books, 1985), 42.

9. Gerald Edelman, *Bright Air, Brilliant Fire: On the Matter of the Mind* (New York: Basic Books, 1992), 131–32.

10. F. Elizabeth Hart, "Matter, System, and Early Modern Studies: Outlines for a Materialist Linguistics," *Configurations* 6 (1998): 343.

11. Lakoff, *Women, Fire, and Dangerous Things*, 275.

12. Greenblatt, "Fiction and Friction," 68.

13. For the idea that "we have universal, perceptually determined possible options for spatializing time," see Eve Sweetser, *From Etymology to Pragmatics: Metaphorical and Cultural Aspects of Semantic Structure* (Cambridge: Cambridge University Press, 1990), 7.

14. For these schemas, see Lakoff, *Women, Fire, and Dangerous Things*, 271–78. See Lichtenberk, "Semantic Change and Heterosemy in Grammaticalization," 480, for the definition of *heterosemy* as a case where "the semantic (as well as the formal) properties of the elements are too different to form a single conceptual category. Rather, the category has an historical basis: what unites its members is their common ultimate source." Laura A. Michaelis, "Cross World Continuity and the Polysemy of Adverbial Still," in *Spaces, Worlds, and Grammar*, ed. Gilles Fauconnier and Eve Sweetser (Chicago: University of Chicago Press, 1996), 181, extends Lichtenberk's work to suggest that speakers are able to reconcile the sense of a heterosemic word by extracting "a set of accidental yet salient semantic commonalties from these senses," which is perhaps what Shakespeare does here with *suit*.

15. John West, *Village Records* (London: Macmillan, 1962), 30.

16. Ibid., 33. The original Latin reads: "Nich(ola)s de Monte fec(it) defalta(m) et negat secta(m) cur(iae). Et inq(ui)sitio dicit q(uod) debet secta(m). Et ideo distringat(ur) p(ro) defalta."

17. Ibid., 36.

18. C. E. Moreton, *The Townshends and Their World: Gentry, Law, and Land in Norfolk, c. 1450–1551* (Oxford: Clarendon, 1992), 82–114.

19. Ibid., 107–9.

20. Paul L. Hughes and James F. Larkin, eds., *Tudor Royal Proclamations*, vol. 3, *The Late Tudors (1588–1603)* (New Haven: Yale University Press, 1969), 121.

21. "Ordering Arrest of Vagabonds, Deportation of Irishmen," in ibid., 135–36.

22. See Michel Foucault, *Discipline and Punish: The Birth of the Prison*, trans. Alan Sheridan (New York: Vintage, 1979).

23. Peter Stallybrass, "Worn Worlds: Clothes and Identity on the Renaissance Stage," in *Subject and Object in Renaissance Culture*, ed. Margreta de Grazia, Maureen Quilligan, and Peter Stallybrass (Cambridge: Cambridge University Press, 1996), 289–90.

24. "Antik sutes" is a category of an inventory in the hand of Edward Alleyn; "The Enventary of the Clownes Sewtes and Hermetes Sewtes" lists costumes of the Lord Admiral's Men as of 10 March 1598; the specific costumes are taken from an "Enventorey of all the aparell of the Lord Admeralles men, taken the 13th Marche 1598," in Philip Henslowe, *Henslowe's Diary*, ed. R. A. Foakes and R. T. Rickert (Cambridge: Cambridge University Press, 1961), 292, 317, 321–23.

25. See Jean MacIntyre, *Costumes and Scripts in the Elizabethan Theatres* (Edmonton: University of Alberta Press, 1994), 187–88; and Henslowe, *Henslowe's Diary*, 205.

26. Malcolmson, "What You Will," 44.

27. I.M., *A Health to the Gentlemanly Profession of Serving-Men*, ed. A. V. Judges (Oxford: Oxford University Press, 1931), H2v.

28. *House* appears approximately 21 times in the play, *home* only 6 times, possibly reflecting the sense that *home* is associated with households of lower status.

29. Greenblatt, "Fiction and Friction," 68, makes this point. Howard, "Power and Eros," stresses that Olivia's "unruliness" in rejecting Orsino is "punished, comically but unmistakably" (114); however, she is not made to marry Orsino.

30. As Freedman puts it, it "is not simply that there is an absence in Olivia's house which all the hangers-on seek to fill, but that there is an absence in that object Olivia which nothing can close up" (*Staging the Gaze*, 218).

31. See Howard, "Power and Eros," 112–16.

32. Heather Dubrow, *Shakespeare and Domestic Loss: Forms of Deprivation, Mourning, and Recuperation* (Cambridge: Cambridge University Press, 1999), 45–61, provides a complex discussion of the early modern cultural analogy between a woman's body and her house in the context of Shakespeare's *Rape of Lucrece*.

33. Peter Thomson, *Shakespeare's Theatre*, 2nd ed. (New York: Routledge, 1992), 112.

34. Interestingly, the author of the *Health to the Gentlemanly Profession of Serving-Men* associates sober qualities such as those that make Malvolio "suitable" for Olivia with exactly the kind of preferment through marriage that he comes so unsuitably to desire: "Some of them [gentlemen servants] would cary themselues so soberly, discreetely, and wisely, as they came to great wealth, worth, and preferment by Mariage" (E4v).

35. Gail Kern Paster, *The Body Embarrassed: Drama and the Disciplines of Shame in Early Modern England* (Ithaca: Cornell University Press, 1993), 34.

36. Alice T. Friedman, *House and Household in Elizabethan England: Wollaton Hall and the Willoughby Family* (Chicago: University of Chicago Press, 1989, 185–86.

37. I.M., *A Health to the Gentlemanly Profession of Serving-Men*, G4v.

38. Susan Amussen, *An Ordered Society: Gender and Class in Early Modern England* (Oxford: Blackwell, 1988), 8, notes that "between 1500 and 1620 . . . prices multiplied sixfold."

39. I.M., *A Health to the Gentlemanly Profession of Serving-Men*, D2v.

40. Malcolmson, "What You Will," 37, notes that Viola rewards the captain "bounteously" as a sign that "she is no commoner." Viola thus twice rewards servants appropriately, whereas Olivia never does so.

41. L. G. Salingar, "The Design of *Twelfth Night*," in *Twelfth Night: Critical Essays*, ed. Stanley Wells (New York: Garland, 1986), 212, notes that Feste is "exceptionally given to scrounging for tips." I think the play emphasizes the comparative generosity (or lack of generosity) on the part of the wealthier characters in the play, as well as Feste's interest in remuneration.

42. Howard, "Power and Ethos," 115.

43. Karen Greif, "Plays and Playing in *Twelfth Night*," in Wells, *Twelfth Night: Critical Essays*, 263.

44. On the development of the antithesis between "grotesque" and "enclosed" bodies in relation to discourses of gender and class in this period, see Peter Stallybrass, "Patriarchal Territories: The Body Enclosed," in *Rewriting the Renaissance: The Discourses of Sexual Difference in Early Modern Europe*, ed. Margaret W. Ferguson, Maureen Quilligan, and Nancy J. Vickers (Chicago: University of Chicago Press, 1986), 123–44.

45. Malcolmson, "What You Will," 37.

46. See Jean Howard, "Crossdressing, the Theatre, and Gender Struggle in Early Modern England," *Shakespeare Quarterly* 39 (1988): 418–40; Lisa Jardine, " 'As Boys and Women are for the Most Part Cattle of This Colour': Female Roles and Elizabethan Eroticism," in *Still Harping on Daughters: Women and Drama in the Age of Shakespeare*, 2nd ed. (New York: Columbia University Press, 1989), 9–36; and Catherine Belsey, "Disrupting Sexual Difference: Meaning and Gender in the Comedies," in *Alternative Shakespeares*, ed. John Drakakis (New York: Routledge, 1985), 166–90.

47. Malcolmson, "What You Will," 38.

48. See G. K. Hunter, "Flat Caps and Blue Coats," *Essays and Studies*, n.s., 33 (1980): 27–28; and MacIntyre, *Costumes and Scripts in the Elizabethan Theatres*, 13.

49. Jardine, "As Boys and Women are for the Most Part Cattle of This Colour," 141.

50. MacIntyre, *Costumes and Scripts in the Elizabethan Theatres*, 13.

51. MacIntyre comments on the use of matching suits to designate twins in ibid., 188.

52. The size of the Duke's household is indicated by the presence of attendants and musicians in scenes where he appears, as well as by Maria's comment that Cesario is "a fair young man, and well attended" (1.5.102).

53. MacIntyre, *Costumes and Scripts in the Elizabethan Theatres*, 87, notes that such costumes for the gentry make up most of Henslowe's costume inventory, because "a gallant's doublet, hose, cloak, and hat . . . were subject to whimsical changes in the fashion and so would become stale if shown too often."

54. Stallybrass, "Worn Worlds," 294–301.

55. I.M., *A Health to the Gentlemanly Profession of Serving-Men*, B3r. Jane Ashelford, *A Visual History of Costume: The Sixteenth Century* (London: B. T. Batsford, 1983), notes that "the association that the colour blue had with servitude ensured that gentlemen never wore it" (14). MacIntyre notes "the inexpensive blue coats of servingmen, whose mention in *Henry VI Part 1*, *The Case is Altered*, *Every Man In His Humour*, *The Roaring Girl*, and many other plays belonging to every company shows they were common to all wardrobes" (*Costumes and Scripts in the Elizabethan Theatres*, 145).

56. See Ashelford, *Visual History of Costume*, 134, fig. 148, portrait of "The Browne brothers and their page," where "difference in social rank is indicated by dress. The brothers wear the latest fashion, whereas their page does not."

57. Jardine, "As Boys and Women are for the Most Part Cattle of This Colour," 29, argues that "these figures [cross-dressed female characters] are sexually enticing *qua* transvestied boys, and that the plays encourage the audience to view them as such."

58. Stephen Gosson, *The Schoole of Abuse* (1579), quoted in Chambers, *Elizabethan Stage*, 4:204.

59. See MacIntyre, *Costumes and Scripts in the Elizabethan Theatres*, 76.

60. Ibid., 83.

61. "Regulations for the Apparel of London Apprentices," quoted from John Nichols, *The Progresses of Queen Elizabeth*, 2.204–6, in Hunter, "Flat Caps and Blue Coats," 30. On the nature of theatrical apprenticeship in this period, see Gerald Eades Bentley, *The Profession of Player in Shakespeare's Time* (Princeton: Princeton University Press, 1984), 125–26.

62. Stern, *Interpersonal World of the Infant*, 162.

63. Jacques Lacan, "The Agency of the Letter in the Unconscious," in *Ecrits: A Selection*, trans. Alan Sheridan (New York: Norton, 1977), 154.

Chapter Four
Cognitive *Hamlet* and the Name of Action

1. Katherine Eisaman Maus, *Inwardness and Theater in the English Renaissance* (Chicago: University of Chicago Press, 1995), 1–5. As adherents of the view that such interiority did not yet exist in 1600 Maus cites Francis Barker, *The Tremulous Private Body: Essays in Subjection* (London: Methuen, 1984); Catherine Belsey, *The Subject of Tragedy: Identity and Difference in Renaissance Drama* (London: Methuen, 1985); Jean Howard, "The New Historicism of Renaissance Studies," *English Literary Renaissance* 16 (1986); Patricia Fumerton, *Cultural Aesthetics: Renaissance Literature and the Practice of Social Ornament* (Chicago: University of Chicago Press, 1991), and several others. Like Maus, Anne Ferry, *The "Inward" Language: Sonnets of Wyatt, Sidney, Shakespeare, Donne* (Chicago: University of Chicago Press, 1983), also argues that Hamlet's words repre-

sent a genuine, if newly developed, sense of inner life. For a different but fascinating approach to this issue, see Richard Halpern, "Hamletmachines," in *Shakespeare among the Moderns* (Ithaca: Cornell University Press, 1997), 227–88, which traces a persistent modernist interpretation of Hamlet as a machine.

2. Maus, *Inwardness and Theater*, 29–30.

3. Nigel Alexander, *Poison, Play, and Duel: A Study in Hamlet* (London: Routledge, 1971), 62–64, argues that Hamlet's seven soliloquies examine, in turn, the mental faculties of memory (the first two); understanding or reason (2.2.543–601, 3.1.56–88); will (3.2.378–89, 3.3.73–96); and all three together (4.4.32–66). Although I agree that the contemporary understanding of cognitive faculties shapes Hamlet's accounts of cognitive process, I find Alexander's division too schematic.

4. Maynard Mack, in "The World of Hamlet," *Yale Review* 41 (1952): 512–14, notes the centrality to the play of an "image pattern . . . evolved around three words, show, act, play" (512); and Alice Rayner, *To Act, to Do, to Perform: Drama and the Phenomenology of Action* (Ann Arbor: University of Michigan Press, 1994), devotes two chapters to a phenomenological approach to the nature of *action* and *acting* in *Hamlet*. J. Dover Wilson, *What Happens in Hamlet* (1935; reprint, Cambridge: Cambridge University Press, 1979), 309–20, presents evidence (largely verbal parallels) that Bright's treatise was a source for the play and also provides a list of previous scholars to make that case. He cites an early piece in *Notes and Queries* 8 (1853): 546 citing Bright as a source for the phrase *discourse of reason*, as well as William Blades, *Shakespeare and Typography* (1872), which argued that early in his life in London Shakespeare worked for Bright's publisher, Thomas Vautrolier, to whom his fellow Stratfordian (and later publisher of *Venus and Adonis*) Richard Field was apprenticed. Wilson also cites M. I. O'Sullivan, "*Hamlet* and Dr. Timothy Bright," *PMLA* 41 (1926): 667–79, whose list of verbal parallels resembles his own.

5. Ellen Spolsky, *Gaps in Nature: Literary Interpretation and the Modular Mind* (Albany: State University of New York Press, 1993), 61–72.

6. Barker, *Tremulous Private Body*, 35.

7. There have been too many psychoanalytic readings of *Hamlet* to cite even a representative sample. A few major examples include Ernest Jones, *Hamlet and Oedipus* (Garden City, N.Y.: Doubleday, 1954); Norman Holland, *Psychoanalysis and Shakespeare* (1966; reprint, New York: Octagon Books, 1979), 163–206; Janet Adelman, *Suffocating Mothers: Fantasies of Maternal Origin in Shakespeare's Plays, Hamlet to The Tempest* (New York: Routledge, 1992), 11–37.

8. Judith Butler, "Performative Acts and Gender Constitution: An Essay in Phenomenology and Feminist Theory," *Theatre Journal* 40 (1988): 523.

9. See, e.g., Belsey, *Subject of Tragedy*, 42–54, on the development of the soliloquy and the construction of the bourgeois individual.

10. Maus, *Inwardness and Theater*, 1–2, notes that for Hamlet, "the frank fakeries of the playhouse, its disguisings and impersonations, stand for the opacities that seem to characterize all relations of human beings to one another."

11. James L. Calderwood, *To Be and Not to Be: Negation and Metadrama in Hamlet* (New York: Columbia University Press, 1983), 32.

12. Here I follow Emily Bartels, who has made a similar argument, in "Breaking the Illusion of Being: Shakespeare and the Performance of Self," *Theatre Journal* 46 (1994): 173–75, suggesting that "Hamlet's problem (and our problem with him), then, is not that he plays by the book, but, paradoxically, that he does not" (174).

13. Belsey, *Subject of Tragedy*, 42, argues that the Hamlet of act 5, "who no longer struggles towards identity and agency," is "an inhabitant of a much older cosmos, no more than the consenting instrument of God, received into heaven at his death by flights of angels."

14. I do not wish to include an exhaustive list of verbal parallels, which, to my mind, are convincing although not overwhelming. Phrases that occur in both Bright and Shakespeare include *discourse of reason, custom of exercise,* and *expence of spirit.* Bright also offers close parallels for the ghost's "posset / And curd, like eager droppings into milk" (Bright: "the braine is tender as a posset curd") and Hamlet's concept of being "but mad north-north-west" (Bright: the best air for melancholics is "especially to the South, and Southeast"). A number of similar parallels are cited by Wilson, *What Happens in Hamlet;* and O'Sullivan, "*Hamlet* and Dr. Timothy Bright." Carol Thomas Neely, "Melancholy Distinctions and Subject Formation: Aristotle, Bright, Freud" (paper presented at the annual meeting of the Shakespeare Association of America, Cleveland Ohio, March 1998), has suggested that the parallels "need not reveal the influence of Bright on Shakespeare but perhaps manifest shared cultural images for representing human self-division which don't distinguish between material and spiritual causation."

15. Both Wilson, *What Happens in Hamlet,* and O'Sullivan, "*Hamlet* and Dr. Timothy Bright," argue that Hamlet shows some but not all of the clinical signs of melancholy.

16. My account of Bright's purposes, as well as all quotations from the text, are taken from *A Treatise of Melancholie by Timothy Bright,* ed. Hardin Craig (New York: Facsimile Text Society, 1940); hereafter, all page references appear in the text.

17. See Antonio Damasio, *Descartes' Error: Emotion, Reason, and the Human Brain* (New York: Avon, 1994), 247–52, for a discussion of ways in which modern cognitive neuroscience approaches the mind-body problem. Damasio identifies with Descartes the erroneous "separation of the most refined operations of mind from the structure and operation of a biological organism" (250). Before Descartes, Galenic medicine offered the possibility of a material theory of mind; Bright, in his concern to separate soul and body, anticipates the Cartesian split.

18. Katherine Rowe, " 'God's handy worke': Divine Complicity and the Anatomist's Touch," in *The Body in Parts: Fantasies of Corporeality in Early Modern England,* ed. David Hillman and Carla Mazzio (New York: Routledge, 1997), traces how anatomy texts in the period focused on the hands in their representation of "a *mechanics* of agency relations" (287), which seems very similar to Bright.

19. Contemporary cognitive science is still interested in the nature of emotion and the relationship between the bodily manifestation of emotion and human "feeling" of it. Research by Paul Ekman on the relationship between facial expression and feeling has suggested that people who are asked to imitate the expression

associated with a give emotion will display some of the bodily signs of actually experiencing it (see Paul Ekman, "Facial Expressions of Emotion: New Findings, New Questions," *Psychological Science* 3 [1992]: 34–38). However, as Antonio Damasio explains in *Descartes' Error*, 140–43, research has also shown that different parts of the brain seem to control the expression of "genuine" emotion and "false" emotion. Damasio notes that the difficulty of falsifying the signs of emotion "has long been recognized by professional actors, and has led to different acting techniques," a traditional kind, which relies on "skillfully creating, under volitional control, a set of movements that credibly suggest emotion," and "method acting," which "relies on having actors generate an emotion, create the real thing rather than simulate it" (142).

20. Michael Goldman, "Hamlet and Our Problems," from *Shakespeare and the Energies of Drama* (Princeton: Princeton University Press, 1972), reprinted in *Critical Essays on Shakespeare's Hamlet*, ed. David Scott Kastan (New York: G. K. Hall, 1995), 44.

21. While not quite making this connection, Barker, *Tremulous Private Body*, 31, argues that in the world of *Hamlet* "the body of the king is . . . the body that encompasses all mundane bodies within its build" and "is the deep structural form of all being in the secular realm." John Hunt, "A Thing of Nothing: The Catastrophic Body in *Hamlet*," *Shakespeare Quarterly* 39 (1988), traces how "isolated parts of the body function as metonymic or synecdochal equivalents for actions and states of being."

22. See Jonathan Gil Harris, *Foreign Bodies and the Body Politic: Discourses of Social Pathology in Early Modern England* (Cambridge: Cambridge University Press, 1998), for a recent reassessment of the role of this organic metaphor in early modern England.

23. Margaret W. Ferguson, "*Hamlet*: Letters and Spirits," in *Shakespeare and the Question of Theory*, ed. Patricia Parker and Geoffrey Hartman (London: Methuen, 1985), 295.

24. Stephen Booth, "On the Value of *Hamlet*," in Kastan, *Critical Essays on Shakespeare's Hamlet*, 20–23.

25. In Adelman's psychoanalytic reading, Hamlet's imagery here reflects "the deep fantasy" that Gertrude is "the missing Eve: her body is the garden in which her husband dies, her sexuality the poisonous weeds that kill him, and poison the world" (*Suffocating Mothers*, 30). I want to emphasize not the psychological resonance of these images but their relation to an interest in cognitive process and particularly in the extent to which excrescences (such as tears or vegetative growth) accurately reveal the matter from which they are produced.

26. According to Alexander, Claudius repeatedly "uses the great cannon of the castle to emphasize his own power and position" (*Poison, Play, and Duel*, 185). I want to emphasize his tendency to use them to display his emotions outwardly, using the castle itself as an extension of his own body.

27. Bright, as noted above, allows some scope for the influence of occupational custom on the perceptions of the senses but does not admit that such customary action can alter the mind or soul.

28. See Ferguson, "*Hamlet*: Letters and Spirits," 295.

29. David Scott Kastan, " 'His semblable is his mirror': *Hamlet* and the Imitation of Revenge," in Kastan, *Critical Essays on Shakespeare's Hamlet*, 200.

30. Booth, "On the Value of *Hamlet*," 34, has argued that Hamlet is sometimes mad.

31. Patricia Parker, *Shakespeare from the Margins: Language, Culture, Context* (Chicago: University of Chicago Press, 1996), 260. Parker cites, among others, Alison Plowden, *The Elizabethan Secret Service* (New York: St. Martin's, 1991).

32. For a fascinating account of the cognitive bases of emotion in theatrical performance, see Richard Schechner, "Magnitudes of Performance," in *The Anthropology of Experience*, ed. Victor W. Turner and Edward M. Bruner (Champaign: University of Illinois Press, 1986), 344–72. Schechner applies research by Paul Ekman on facial expression and emotion to argue that "method" acting, in which the actor relies on thoughts of past experience to conjure up "real" emotion, and acting that relies on mimicry of facial expressions that convey emotion register similarly in the nervous system: in other words, "real" emotion and "acted" emotion are experienced by the brain in similar ways and are not really fundamentally different.

33. Patricia Parker suggestively links issues of showing and telling in this play with a contemporary "crisis of representation . . . a problem shared by the law-courts and other contestatory sites of epistemological or evidentiary certainty, of what might be reliably substituted for what could not be directly witnessed" (*Shakespeare from the Margins*, 259).

34. The "problem of the dumb-show" and question why the poisoning scene is performed twice and why Claudius does not react to it the first time are long-standing issues. Wilson, *What Happens in Hamlet*, 138–63, clearly outlines the problems and provides various unsatisfactory answers.

35. However, see Adelman, *Suffocating Mothers*, 11–37, for a psychoanalytic reading of Hamlet's obsession with imagining women's inner spaces.

36. Maus, *Inwardness and Theater*, 191.

37. Adelman, *Suffocating Mothers*, 34, suggests that Gertrude here "seems to accept [Hamlet's] version of her soiled inner body" but nevertheless remains "relatively opaque, more a screen for Hamlet's fantasies about her than a fully developed character in her own right." Her opacity, as well as Hamlet's fantasies, might also be read as part of the play's general preoccupation with essentially unknowable inner processes.

38. Elaine Showalter, "Representing Ophelia: Women, Madness, and the Responsibilities of Feminist Criticism," in Parker and Hartman, *Shakespeare and the Question of Theory*, 80.

39. R. D. Laing, *The Divided Self: An Existential Study in Sanity and Madness* (London, 1960), 95, quoted in David Leverenz, "The Woman in Hamlet: An Interpersonal View," in *New Casebooks: Hamlet*, ed. Martin Coyle (New York: St. Martin's, 1992), 134.

40. Calderwood, *To Be and Not to Be*, 15–17.

41. Calderwood suggests that one reason for Laertes' easy acceptance of instrumentality in this instance is that "Claudius is a symbolic stand-in for Polonius. . . . incorporating the Polonius principle of paternal domination" (ibid., 16–17).

42. See David Hillman, "Visceral Knowledge: Shakespeare, Skepticism, and the Interior of the Early Modern Body," in Hillman and Mazzio, *Body in Parts*, 81–106, for the argument that in *Hamlet*, as in other Shakespearean plays, "the problem of knowledge of or access to the viscera is intimately tied . . . to the skeptical problem of other minds" (81). Hillman is right to emphasize that "self-hood and materiality . . . were ineluctably linked in the pre-Cartesian belief systems of the period" (83), but he may overemphasize the role of skepticism (and underemphasize the role of the cognitive) in Shakespeare's fascination with bodily inner spaces.

43. See Bartels, "Breaking the Illusion of Being," 173–74, for the theatricality of this and other moments in the play.

44. Ferguson, "*Hamlet*: Letters and Spirits," 292, traces "a disturbing kind of materializing that occurs, with increasing frequency, in the later part of the drama," which "highlights the thin but significant line that separates" deeds and words and "almost always results in a literal death." Her "materializing" effect is related to, but slightly different from, the process of externalization I trace here.

45. Terence Hawkes, "*Telmah*," in Parker and Hartman, *Shakespeare and the Question of Theory*, 312. His name for this recursive play is *Telmah*, or *Hamlet* backwards.

46. Jennifer Low, "The Art of Fence and the Sense of Masculine Space," in *Manhood and the Duel: Constructing Masculinity in Early Modern Drama* (forthcoming), describes some of the ways in which fencing with a rapier involved an extension of "the fencer's sense of personal space as far as his outstretched hand or even to the point on the sword where it can parry most effectively."

47. Goldman, "Hamlet and Our Problems," 52.

48. Harris, *Foreign Bodies and the Body Politic*, 52.

49. Ferguson, "*Hamlet*: Letters and Spirits," 304, makes this connection.

50. So Terence Hawkes, who notes that "it is Horatio who gets it wrong. We know, from what we have seen, that the story he proposes to recount to the 'yet unknowing world' . . . is not really the way it was. It was not as simple, as like an 'ordinary' revenge play, as that" (Hawkes, "*Telmah*," 310–11).

51. But see Lars Engle, "Dramatic Pragmatism in Hamlet," in *Shakespearean Pragmatism: Market of His Time* (Chicago: University of Chicago Press, 1993), 63, for the argument that *Hamlet* is "a meditation on the balance between the power of circumambient discourses and the capacity of an exemplary (and, in this case, privileged) human subject to find his way therapeutically among them toward a pragmatic kind of agency."

52. This sense of impressionability is a common Shakespearean image for character, playing on the literal sense of character as "inscription." *Measure for Measure* and *Twelfth Night* both use images of a seal in wax or a stamp in metal to figure human subjectivity and its vulnerability or imperviousness to change. For a Derridean reading of these passage from Hamlet as revealing "the body as locus of inscription, to be read rather than heard," see Jonathan Goldberg, "Hamlet's Hand," *Shakespeare Quarterly* 39 (1988): 313.

53. J. L. Austin, *How to Do Things with Words* (Cambridge: Harvard University Press, 1962).

54. Maus, *Inwardness and Theater*, 21. Austin, of course, distinguishes between the validity of a performative and what he calls its "felicity," which may, in fact, depend upon "having certain thoughts or feelings" (Austin, *How to Do Things with Words*, 15).

55. Maus, *Inwardness and Theater*, 20–23, citing Henry Garnet, *A Treatise of Equivocation*, ed. David Jardine (London: Longman, Brown, 1851), 9–12.

56. See Judith Anderson, "Translating Investments: The Metaphoricity of Language, 2 *Henry IV*, and *Hamlet*," *Texas Studies in Literature and Language* 40 (1998): 250–53.

57. Austin distinguishes locutionary acts, "roughly equivalent to uttering a certain sentence with a certain sense and reference"; illocutionary acts, "such as informing, ordering, warning, undertaking, etc., i.e. utterances which have a certain (conventional) force"; and perlocutionary acts, "what we bring about or achieve *by* saying something" (Austin, *How to Do with Words*, 108).

58. Ellen Spolsky, *Satisfying Skepticism: The Evolved Mind in the Early Modern World* (forthcoming), argues persuasively that our flawed cognitive apparatus leads to a skepticism that is not necessarily tragic, though it may be culturally interpreted as such.

Chapter Five
Male Pregnancy and Cognitive Permeability in *Measure for Measure*

1. See Leonard Tennenhouse, "Representing Power: *Measure for Measure* in Its Time," *Genre* 15 (1982): 139–58; Steven Mullaney, "Apprehending Subjects," chap. 6 in *The Place of the Stage: License, Play and Power in Renaissance England* (Chicago: University of Chicago Press, 1988); Jonathan Dollimore, "Transgression and Surveillance in *Measure for Measure*," in *Political Shakespeare: New Essays in Cultural Materialism*, ed. Jonathan Dollimore and Alan Sinfield (Ithaca: Cornell University Press, 1985), who argues that the play "is about both kinds of discipline, the enforced and the internalised" (75); Jonathan Goldberg, *James I and the Politics of Literature* (Baltimore: Johns Hopkins University Press, 1983), 230–39; and Steven Greenblatt, "Martial Law in the Land of Cockaigne," in *Shakespearean Negotiations* (Berkeley and Los Angeles: University of California Press, 1988), 129–64.

2. Dollimore, "Transgression and Surveillance," 74.

3. Thus, Harry F. Berger argues in *Making Trifles of Terrors: Redistributing Complicities in Shakespeare* (Stanford: Stanford University Press, 1997) that in *Measure for Measure* "speech and discourse are not about sexuality, but rather sexuality and the sins associated with it are about discourses" (415).

4. Janet Adelman, *Suffocating Mothers: Fantasies of Maternal Origin in Shakespeare's Plays, Hamlet to The Tempest* (New York: Routledge, 1992), 88. Feminist readings of the play generally have focused on the extent to which unruliness is gendered and women in the play (and in criticism of the play) function as scapegoats for male power. In addition to Adelman's feminist-psychoanalytic reading, see Jacqueline Rose, "Sexuality in the Reading of Shakespeare: *Hamlet* and *Measure for Measure*," in *Alternative Shakespeares*, ed. John Drakakis (New York: Routledge, 1985), 95–118; and Laura Lunger Knoppers, "(En)gendering Shame:

Measure for Measure and the Spectacles of Power," *English Literary Renaissance* 23 (1993): 450–71, for a materialist feminist approach.

5. Mullaney, "Apprehending Subjects," 113.

6. Berger, *Making Trifles of Terrors*, similarly argues that the play focuses not so much on "the generic ideological and political practices of patriarchal rulers" as on "the particular discursive and ethical practices of Duke Vincentio" (365). Berger is mostly interested in the Duke's "ethical self-representation" (365) and sees him as maintaining more control over his various discursive strategies than I believe he does.

7. See Gail Kern Paster, *The Body Embarrassed: Drama and the Disciplines of Shame in Early Modern England* (Ithaca: Cornell University Press, 1993); Jonathan Sawday, *The Body Emblazoned: Dissection and the Human Body in Renaissance Culture* (New York: Routledge, 1995); and David Hillman and Carla Mazzio, eds., *The Body in Parts: Fantasies of Corporeality in Early Modern Europe* (New York: Routledge, 1997).

8. Paster, *Body Embarrassed*, 19.

9. Gail Kern Paster, "Nervous Tension," in Hillman and Mazzio, *Body in Parts*, 122.

10. Mario Di Gangi, "Pleasure and Danger: Measuring Female Sexuality in *Measure for Measure*," *ELH* 60 (1993): 589–609, also focuses on images of pregnancy and, he argues, abortion in *Measure for Measure*. He reads these images as offering space for an oppositional reading of the play: "To unravel male-constructed meanings for erotic pleasure, pregnancy, and abortion is to discover a fear of the dangers thought to ensue from a woman's control over her own body" (590). I emphasize instead the extension of these metaphors to male bodies in order to suggest that no one in the play can control his or her own body.

11. In this respect, a cognitive reading differs from Foucault's argument in *Power/Knowledge*, ed. Colin Gordon (New York: Pantheon, 1986), 186, that disciplinary techniques are capable of "materially penetrating the body in depth without depending even on the mediation of the subject's own representations. If power takes hold on the body, this isn't through it's having to be interiorized in people's consciousness." Cognitive theory, as well as this play, suggests that such penetration is completely dependent not on conscious representations but on the internal mediating structures of thought itself.

12. To date, cognitive theory has been less interested in gender differences than other critical theories, largely because the processes described above seem to work very similarly in both men and women. Although there is some evidence of physiological differences in brain structure that can be correlated with gender, the nature and effect of these differences is not clear. This essay accords with cognitive practice in focusing on processes that seem to work across categories of sexual difference (without, however, denying that such categories exist on various levels).

13. See John R. Taylor, *Linguistic Categorization: Prototypes in Linguistic Theory*, 2nd ed. (Oxford: Clarendon, 1995), 99–141, for an account of how a polysemous category is structured as a gradient radiating out from a prototypical example.

14. See N. Katherine Hayles, "The Materiality of Informatics," *Configurations* 1 (1992): 147–70. Hayles's distinction between "the body" and "embodiment"

(148) is useful for understanding Paster's work in relation to cognitive theory. Hayles argues that whereas the body "is always normative relative to some set of criteria" (and her example of this is "how the body is constructed within Renaissance medical discourse"), embodiment is "contextual, enwebbed within the specifics of place, time, physiology and culture that together comprise enactment." Thus, "whereas the body is an idealized form that gestures toward a Platonic reality, embodiment is the specific instantiation generated from the noise of difference" (154–55).

15. Paster, *Body Embarrassed*, 4.

16. Ibid., 19.

17. Nancy Siraisi, *Medieval and Early Renaissance Medicine: An Introduction to Knowledge and Practice* (Chicago: University of Chicago Press, 1990), 108.

18. Thomas Laquer, *Making Sex: Body and Gender from the Greeks to Freud* (Cambridge: Harvard University Press, 1990), 42. Laquer cites writers as diverse as Aristotle and William Harvey as holding this belief. Laquer's book makes clear that many aspects of the theory of human reproduction were controversial, for example, where semen was manufactured and whether both parents contributed "seed" to conception. But all versions of humoral theory posited a basic fungibility of bodily fluids and permeability of the body.

19. See Jay L. Halio, "The Metaphor of Conception and Elizabethan Theories of the Imagination," *Neophilologus* 50 (1966): 454–61, who sees the metaphor as "live," though not literal, in the sixteenth century; Katherine Eisaman Maus, *Inwardness and Theater in the English Renaissance* (Chicago: University of Chicago Press, 1995), 196, notes that when male writers describe their own creative processes in terms of conception and birth, it can be difficult to determine "when we are dealing with metaphor and when with a bare statement of fact." I believe, however, that in this play the literal force of the analogy is almost always relevant.

20. George Lakoff, *Women, Fire, and Dangerous Things: What Categories Reveal about the Mind* (Chicago: University of Chicago Press, 1987) 272–73, identifies our sense of the body as a container with an interior, an exterior, and variously permeable boundaries as grounding one of the most basic "kinesthetic image schemas" that structure thought.

21. Siraisi, *Medieval and Early Renaissance Medicine*, 128–30.

22. For these theories, see Winfried Schleiner, "Infection and Cure through Women: Renaissance Constructions of Syphilis," *Journal of Medieval and Renaissance Studies* 24 (1994): 502–5.

23. Adelman, *Suffocating Mothers*, 102, notes that "the persistence of Juliet reminds us [that] maternal origin cannot simply be wished away."

24. On exotic fruits as aphrodisiacs, see Paster, *Body Embarrassed*, 132, who specifically comments on Mrs. Elbow's craving. Di Gangi, "Pleasure and Danger," 602–3, provocatively reads Mrs. Elbow's prunes and visit to the stew as abortifacients.

25. See Paster, *Body Embarrassed*, 268–69, on the conflation of pregnancy, eating, and fish in *The Winter's Tale* as suggesting "the oral component of male jealousy." Di Gangi, "Pleasure and Danger," 594–95, reads this series of male interpretations of Juliet's pregnant body as "stressing her body's compliance with male instrumentality."

26. Greenblatt, "Martial Law in the Land of Cockaigne," 140–41. I do not agree with Greenblatt's conclusion that Shakespeare here uses this fictional representation of anxiety primarily "to offer the spectators pleasure in the spectacle" and that "his ironic reflections on salutary anxiety do not at all diminish his commitment to it as a powerful theatrical technique" (142). The play, I believe, is equally ambivalent about the theatrical technique.

27. Hayles, "Materiality of Informatics," 156.

28. Berger, *Making Trifles of Terrors*, 361.

29. Graham Bradshaw, *Shakespeare's Skepticism* (New York: St. Martin's, 1987), 216–18, briefly notes the connection between images of "forging and pregnancy."

30. Knoppers, "(En)gendering Shame," rightly emphasizes the extent to which Isabella's "excessive chastity" (465) is threatening to men in the play. However, I would add that the Duke's (and Angelo's) similar self-enclosing gestures are equally problematic.

31. Adelman, *Suffocating Mothers*, 287 n. 25. Adelman relates this image to "a perfectly orthodox rendering of the Aristotelian position on generation," namely, that the mother is simply a passive vessel for the father's seed.

32. Humanist educational theorists often depicted education as "fortifying" the mind against dangerous and seductive ideas (see Mary Thomas Crane, *Framing Authority: Sayings, Self, and Society in Sixteenth-Century England* [Princeton: Princeton University Press, 1993], 72–76).

33. Ibid., 72–75.

34. That both *pregnant* and *prone* begin with *pr* might also reflect cognitive structures, since, as Jean Aitchison notes, "words which have similar beginnings, similar endings, and similar rhythm are likely to be tightly bonded" within the mental lexicon. Further, "words seem to be grouped in clumps rather than in a list, suggesting that, once again, we are dealing with a network" (see Jean Aitchison, *Words in the Mind: An Introduction to the Mental Lexicon*, 2nd ed. [Oxford: Blackwell, 1994], 142).

35. Berger, *Making Trifles of Terrors*, 411. Berger cites Robert N. Watson, "False Immortality in *Measure for Measure*: Comic Means, Tragic Ends," *Shakespeare Quarterly* 41 (1990): 418–19, as emphasizing the misogynist implications of parthenogenetic fantasies.

36. Antonio Damasio, *Descartes' Error,: Emotion, Reason, and the Human Brain* (New York: Avon, 1994), xii, xiii.

37. Hamlet, interestingly, uses *unpregnant* seemingly to convey rationality that is insufficiently influenced by emotion. In his soliloquy in response to the player's emotional speech about Hecuba, Hamlet berates himself for being "a dull, and muddy-mettled rascal . . . unpregnant of my cause" (2.2.567–68).

38. Damasio, *Descartes' Error*, xiv.

39. Isabella here seems to reiterate gynecological treatises from the period, which, as Paster has noted, use "physiology. . . to reinforce a conventional construction of the female body as dangerously open and the female imagination as dangerously impressionable" (*Body Embarrassed*, 181). However, this play to some extent seems to depict men as subject to a similar openness and impressionability.

40. Di Gangi, "Pleasure and Danger," 597, notes the buried image of pregnancy here, which he sees as a sign of the Duke's influence over Isabella.

41. For the Duke as agent of surveillance and the gaze, see Dollimore, "Transgression and Surveillance," 80–86; and Mullaney, "Apprehending Subjects," 110–11. Berger, *Making Trifles of Terrors*, similarly describes the Duke as a voyeur who repeatedly encourages scenes of "sensuality he himself doesn't participate in or condone so that as he watches others fall he can enjoy not only his own probity and tolerance but also his disapproval of the sins of others" (360–61).

42. F. David Hoeniger, *Medicine and Shakespeare in the English Renaissance* (Newark: University of Delaware Press, 1992), 94–97. See also Siraisi, *Medieval and Early Renaissance Medicine*, 108.

43. Vision also sometimes involved a version of pregnancy called "looking babies." Donne's poem "The Ecstasy" reflects this common belief that penetration by eyebeams could cause a kind of pregnancy when the image of the gazer was reflected in miniature in the beloved's eye: "And pictures in our eyes to get / Was all our propagation." For a cognitive reading of the problems with vision as a source of knowledge, see Ellen Spolsky, *Satisfying Skepticism: The Evolved Mind in the Early Modern World* (forthcoming), ch. 2.

44. Richard Wheeler, *Shakespeare's Development and the Problem Comedies* (Berkeley and Los Angeles: University of California Press, 1981), 124–39.

45. Daniel Stern, *The Interpersonal World of the Infant: A View from Psychoanalysis and Developmental Psychology* (New York: Basic Books, 1985).

46. See Gerald Edelman, *Bright Air, Brilliant Fire: On the Matter of the Mind* (New York: Basic Books, 1992), 129–30.

47. Wheeler, *Shakespeare's Development and the Problem Comedies*, 133–34, argues that Lucio's "irrational tenacity in attacking the Duke suggests the dramatic emptiness of Vincentio's characterization, as if through Lucio Shakespeare is obliquely trying to fill a void he has created at the heart of the play."

48. Ibid., 134.

49. Meredith Anne Skura, *Shakespeare the Actor and the Purposes of Playing* (Chicago: University of Chicago Press, 1993), 87.

50. Skura argues that Vincentio is vulnerable because he is "too closely identified with the actor Angelo, too much in love with the actress Isabella" (ibid., 143).

51. Mullaney, "Apprehending Subjects," 115.

52. Knoppers, "(En)gendering Shame," 460.

53. Berger, *Making Trifles of Terrors*, 426.

54. Di Gangi, "Pleasure and Danger," 597.

55. Watson, "False Immortality in *Measure for Measure*," 419.

56. Katherine Maus, *Inwardness and Theater*, 178, argues that the Duke represents "Shakespeare's rather desperate contrivance to mediate between the characters' secret, subjective worlds and the external domain of publicly administered law." She emphasizes the extent to which the "Duke's powers . . . are still conceived as 'external' to the subjects he coerces," and she concludes that the play seems, in its final scene, "deliberately to puncture the illusion of complete revelation, reasserting the problem of unknowable inward truth just at the moment when it might be supposed to disappear" (181, 178, 180).

57. Psychoanalytic readings of the play, such as Adelman's *Suffocating Mothers*, generally adduce personal reasons for Shakespeare's dark view of sexuality in this play. For more extensive speculation on this topic, see Wheeler, *Shakespeare's Development and the Problem Comedies*; and Norman N. Holland, Sidney Homan, and Bernard J. Paris, eds., *Shakespeare's Personality* (Berkeley and Los Angeles: University of California Press, 1989).

58. See Berger, *Making Trifles of Terrors*, for a recent relatively positive reading of the Duke. For a famously negative reading, see William Empson, *The Structure of Complex Words* (London: Chatto & Windus, 1951), 283.

Chapter Six
Sound and Space in *The Tempest*

1. It would be impossible to list all such readings. Important examples include Stephen Greenblatt, "Learning to Curse: Aspects of Linguistic Colonialism in the Sixteenth Century," in *First Images of America*, ed. Fred Chiappelli, 2 vols. (Berkeley and Los Angeles: University of California Press, 1976), 2:561–80; Francis Barker and Peter Hulme, "Nymphs and Reapers Heavily Vanish: The Discursive Con-Texts of *The Tempest*," in *Alternative Shakespeares*, ed. John Drakakis (New York: Routledge, 1985), 191–205; Terence Hawkes, "Swisser-Swatter: Making a Man of English Letters," in ibid., 26–46; and Paul Brown, " 'This Thing of Darkness I Acknowledge Mine': *The Tempest* and the Discourse of Colonialism," in *Political Shakespeare: New Essays in Cultural Materialism*, ed. Jonathan Dollimore and Alan Sinfield (Ithaca: Cornell University Press, 1985), 48–71. See also Curt Breight, " 'Treason doth never prosper': *The Tempest* and the Discourse of Treason," *Shakespeare Quarterly* 41 (1990): 1–28. For a psychoanalytic reading of the possible issues behind Prospero's control over himself, see Meredith Skura, "Discourse and the Individual: The Case of Colonialism in *The Tempest*," ibid. 40 (1989): 42–69.

2. A cursory search of the online *MLA International Bibliography*, covering the years 1963–99, revealed at least ten essays on *The Tempest* whose titles contained either *discourse* or *discursive*, compared with one on *Measure for Measure* and only three or four on *Othello*, both plays that have also received a great deal of attention from New Historicist and cultural materialist critics.

3. Michel Foucault, *The Archaeology of Knowledge and the Discourse on Language*, trans. A. M. Sheridan Smith (New York: Pantheon, 1972), 107.

4. Brown, "This Thing of Darkness I Acknowledge Mine," 69.

5. Skura, "Discourse and the Individual," 47, has similarly observed that "what is missing from the recent articles is the connection between the new insights about cultural phenomena like 'power' and 'fields of discourse' and the traditional insights about the text, its immediate sources, its individual author—and his individual psychology." Where Skura uses psychoanalysis to forge this connection, I will use cognitive theory in order to connect the individual, the material, and the discursive in different ways.

6. Bruce Smith, *The Acoustic World of Early Modern England: Attending to the O-Factor* (Chicago: University of Chicago Press, 1999), 22.

7. Denise Albanese, *New Science, New World* (Durham, N.C.: Duke University Press, 1996), 70.

8. Jean Aitchison, *Words in the Mind: An Introduction to the Mental Lexicon*, 2nd ed. (Oxford: Blackwell, 1994), 142, My account of sounds is based on chapter 12 of her book.

9. See David Fay and Anne Cutler, "Malapropisms and the Structure of the Mental Lexicon," *Linguistic Inquiry* 8 (1977): 506–8, on the difficulty of making this distinction.

10. Russ McDonald, "Reading *The Tempest*," in *Critical Essays on Shakespeare's The Tempest*, ed. Virginia Mason Vaughan and Alden T. Vaughan (London: Hall, 1998), 218, 222, 229.

11. Keith Sturgess, " A Quaint Device': *The Tempest* at The Blackfriars," in ibid., 116; see also Caroline Spurgeon, *Shakespeare's Imagery and What It Tells Us* (1935; reprint, Cambridge: Cambridge University Press, 1971), 300.

12. Albert S. Bregman, *Auditory Scene Analysis* (Cambridge: MIT Press, 1990), 36–37.

13. Edward A. Armstrong, *Shakespeare's Imagination*, rev. ed. (1963; reprint, Lincoln: University of Nebraska Press, 1982).

14. Spurgeon, *Shakespeare's Imagery*, 197.

15. Armstrong, *Shakespeare's Imagination*, 42–49.

16. Meredith Skura, *Shakespeare the Actor and the Purposes of Playing* (Chicago: University of Chicago Press, 1993), 136–37, 205.

17. Breight, "Treason doth never prosper," 1.

18. Elaine Scarry, *The Body in Pain: The Making and Unmaking of the World* (Oxford: Oxford University Press, 1985), 15.

19. Ibid., 4.

20. Barbara A. Mowat, "Prospero, Agrippa, and Hocus Pocus," *English Literary Renaissance* 11 (1981): 281–303, outlines a number of occult traditions that seem to lie behind Prospero's magic, arguing that he combines elements of the magus, the enchanter, the wizard, and the carnival trickster. She does not specifically mention fairies.

21. John Aubrey (1633), in W. J. Thoms, *Three Notelets on Shakespeare* (London, 1865), quoted in Katharine Briggs, *The Vanishing People: Fairy Lore and Legends* (New York: Pantheon, 1978), 165. Briggs notes that this story is "strongly characteristic of English fairy beliefs of that period."

22. Lewis Spence, *British Fairy Origins* (London: Watts, 1946), 96.

23. Keith Sturgess, *Jacobean Private Theatres* (London: Routledge, 1987), 85.

24. Brown, "This Thing of Darkness I Acknowledge Mine," 55, similarly notes that Stephano and Trinculo's "subsequent punishment, being hunted with dogs, draws full attention to their bestiality."

25. Ibid., 60.

26. Sir Thomas Gates, Sir George Somers, and Captayne Newport, *A Discovery of the Barmudas, Otherwise called the Ile of Divels* (1610), reprinted in *A Discovery of the Bermudas*, ed. Silvester Jourdain (New York: Scholar's Facsimiles and Reprints, 1940), 9.

27. See Michel de Certeau, *The Practice of Everyday Life*, trans. Steven Rendall (1984; reprint, Berkeley and Los Angeles: University of California Press, 1988). De Certeau distinguishes "place," which is "the order (of whatever kind) in accord with which elements are distributed in relationships of existence," from "space," which is "composed of intersections of mobile elements" and thus "in contradistinction to the place" has "none of the univocity or stability of a 'proper' " (117).

28. Lawrence Buell, *The Environmental Imagination: Thoreau, Nature Writing, and the Formation of American Culture* (Cambridge: Belknap, 1995), 6.

29. Albanese, *New Science, New World*, 70. Albanese notes that "Prospero needs operants in the phenomenal world, extensions of himself beyond his reading and signifying mind."

30. An environmental critic would note that even Caliban's detailed description does not seem to describe the flora and fauna of Bermuda (as described in the pamphlets) but instead describes a composite of English and exotic creatures.

31. Greenblatt, "Learning to Curse," cites this passage as an example of "the independence and integrity of Caliban's constructions of reality" (31).

32. Brown, "This Thing of Darkness I Acknowledge Mine," 59, 66. Greenblatt, "Learning to Curse," argues that the play represents the "relationship between a European whose entire source of power is his library and a savage who had no speech at all before the European's arrival" (23).

33. Albanese, *New Science, New World*, 68.

34. Scarry, *Body in Pain*, 54, notes that physical pain has the "ability to destroy language, the power of verbal objectification, a major source of our self-extension, a vehicle through which pain could be lifted out into the world and eliminated."

35. Skura, "Discourse and the Individual," 64–65.

36. Douglas Bruster, "Local *Tempest*: Shakespeare and the Work of the Early Modern Playhouse," *Journal of Medieval and Renaissance Studies* 25 (1995): 33–53.

37. For a summary of evidence and current thinking on the Chamberlain's Men and their use of Blackfriars, see Peter Thomson, *Shakespeare's Theatre*, 2nd. ed. (New York: Routledge, 1992), 167–74. Thomson notes that the plays Shakespeare wrote "with an eye to performance at Blackfriars may not have been written as they were *because* they would be performed there, but it would be strange if they were utterly unaffected" (173).

38. For the history of the second Blackfriars, see Sturgess, *Jacobean Private Theatres*, ch. 3. On *The Tempest*, see chapter 5, "*The Tempest* at the Blackfriars," 97.

39. See ibid., 37–44, for these figures.

40. For example, John Marston, *Jack Drum's Entertainment*, act 5, scene 1, reads: "I like the Audience that frequenteth there / With much applause: A man shall not be choakte / With the stench of Garlicke" (quoted in Andrew Gurr, *The Shakespearean Stage, 1574–1642*, 3rd ed. [Cambridge: Cambridge University Press, 1992], 199, in a discussion of "social divisions in the playhouses").

41. Bruster, "Local *Tempest*," 39.

42. Sturgess, *Jacobean Private Theatres*, 82.

43. Smith, *Acoustic World of Early Modern England*, 214, 222.

44. This connection is much noted by critics. For a recent example, see Greenblatt, "Learning to Curse," who draws the connection but also notes that "there are many aspects of the play itself that make colonialism a problematic model for the theatrical imagination" (24).

45. Sturgess, *Jacobean Private Theatres*, 81.

46. Roger Warren, "Rough Magic and Heavenly Music: *The Tempest*," in Vaughan and Vaughan, *Critical Essays on Shakespeare's The Tempest*, 152.

47. Sturgess, *Jacobean Private Theatres*, 114.

48. Bruster, "Local *Tempest*," 39.

49. Bregman, *Auditory Scene Analysis*, 37.

50. Scarry, *Body in Pain*, 49.

51. Sturgess, *Jacobean Private Theatres*, 115.

52. Julie Robin Soloman, "Going Places: Absolutism and Movement in Shakespeare's *The Tempest*," *Renaissance Drama* 22 (1991): 30, notes the parallel between Alonso's and Prospero's "plummet," suggesting that "both rulers envision the essence of their powers, both sovereign book and body, as beyond the measuring capacity of the 'plummet,' " which she associates with nascent empiricism.

53. See Terence Deacon, *The Symbolic Species: The Co-evolution of Language and the Brain* (New York: Norton, 1997), 225–36.

54. Breight, "Treason doth never prosper," 28.

55. Deacon, *Symbolic Species*, 454.

56. Greenblatt, "Learning to Curse," 31.

Index

Abelson, R. P., 216n.51

act, action, and *actor,* and cognitive reading of *Hamlet,* 116–55, 246n.32

Adams, John Cranford, 58–59, 229nn.77, 79, 83

Adelman, Janet, 156, 166, 211n.3, 243n.7, 245n.25, 246nn.35, 37, 248n.4, 250n.23, 251n.31, 253n.57

agency: and *As You Like It,* 67–93; and authorship, 35, 213n.13, 221n.118; and *Hamlet,* 120, 154–55; and humoral theory, 123, 124; and polysemy, 32; and subject, 19–22

Agnew, Jean-Christophe, 45, 226n.47, 230n.93

Aitchison, Jean, 27, 28, 181, 217n.64, 219n.93, 221nn.109, 117, 251n.34, 254n.8

Albanese, Denise, 179, 192, 196, 254n.7, 255nn.29, 33

Alexander, Nigel, 243n.3, 245n.26

Alleyn, Edward, 111

Altarriba, Jeanette, 219n.94

Althusser, Louis, 6, 7, 20, 231n.1, 234n.37

Amussen, Susan, 241n.38

Anderson, Judith, 14, 151–52, 216nn.56, 57, 221n.108, 248n.56

Armin, Robert, 31, 69, 71, 74, 75, 84, 91, 234n.36, 237n.68

Armstrong, Edward A., 183, 220n.105, 254n.15

Ashelford, Jane, 242nn.55, 56

As You Like It: cognitive reading of, 25, 29, 31, 67–93, 234n.30; and early modern subject, 158; and *The Tempest,* 189; and *Twelfth Night,* 96

Aubrey, John, 186–87, 254n.21

Austin, J. L., 150, 247n.53, 248n.54, 57

author and authorship: and agency, 35, 213n.13, 221n.118; and *As You Like It,* 67–93; and cognitive interpretations of Shakespeare's plays, 3–35; and *Hamlet,* 213n.10; jigs and communal nature of in Elizabethan theater, 232nn.13, 14; and *Measure for Measure,* 173–74

Babington, Gervase, 231n.105

Bachelard, Gaston, 39–40, 223n.15

Baldwin, T. W., 228n.67

Barber, C. L., 211n.3, 238n.78

Barker, Francis, 6, 117, 196, 213n.14, 223n.16, 242n.1, 243n.6, 245n.21, 253n.1

Bartels, Emily, 229n.81, 244n.12, 247n.43

Barton, Anne, 36, 222n.1, 229n.72, 236n.52

Baskervil, Charles Read, 68, 231nn.4, 6, 232nn.8, 11, 237nn.65, 67

Beeson, Christopher, 111

Beier, A. L., 233n.18

Belsey, Catherine, 44, 223n.16, 225n.41, 229n.89, 241n.46, 242n.1, 243n.9, 244n.13

Bentley, Gerald Eades, 242n.61

Benzon, William, 212n.5

Berger, Harry F., Jr., 41, 60, 165, 170, 171, 223n.24, 248n.3, 249n.6, 251nn.28, 35, 252nn.41, 53, 253n.57

Berlin, Brent, 12, 215n.45

Bernard, Richard, 40, 223n.18

Bickerton, Derek, 219n.91

Blackfriars Theatre, 70, 202–203, 204, 205, 255n.37

Blades, William, 243n.4

Bodmer, Walter, 23

body: changing depictions of in Shakespeare's plays, 26–27; and embodiment, 226n.49, 249n.14; and *Hamlet,* 124, 245nn.21, 26; and materialist theory, 4–5, 6–8; and *Measure for Measure,* 156–77, 249nn.10, 12, 250n.20; and production of image schemas, 220n.99, 222nn.5, 10; and *The Tempest,* 199, 200, 208. *See also* mind-body problem

Bono, Barbara J., 237nn.65, 66

Booth, Stephen, 125, 245n.24, 246n.30

Boulton, Jeremy, 224nn.32, 34, 225n.42, 226n.46, 227n.54, 228n.62, 230n.93

Bradbrook, M. C., 236n.62

Bradburn, Elizabeth, 222n.9

Bradshaw, Graham, 251n.29

LaVergne, TN USA
18 February 2010

173457LV00002B/28/P